COMPLETE GUIDE
TO BOATING
AND SEAMANSHIP

COMPLETE GUIDE
TO BOATING
AND SEAMANSHIP

Vin T. Sparano

UNIVERSE

Published by Universe Publishing
A Division of Rizzoli International Publications, Inc.
300 Park Avenue South
New York, NY 10010
www.rizzoliusa.com

Disclaimer: While all of the information in this book—both in text and illustrations—has been fact checked and field tested, the publisher and author make no warranty, express or implied, that the information is appropriate for every individual, situation, or purpose, and assume no responsibility for errors or omissions. All information in this book is presented for entertainment value only, and for an adult audience. Before attempting any new activity, make sure that you are aware of your own limitations and all applicable risks. This book is not intended to replace sound judgment or professional advice from an experienced instructor or outdoor guide.

Always follow any and all manufacturer's instructions when using any equipment featured in this book. If the manufacturer of your equipment does not recommend the use of the equipment in the manner herein described or depicted, you should comply with the manufacturer's recommendations. You assume all risk and full responsibility for all of your actions, and the publisher and author will not be held responsible for any loss, damage, or injury of any sort, whether consequential, incidental, special, or otherwise, that may result from the information presented in this book.

In addition, masculine pronouns were used throughout the text in this book. This was done for the sake of simplicity only, and was not intended to exclude female outdoors enthusiasts.

Project Editor: Candice Fehrman
Book Design: Lori S. Malkin
Text: Vin T. Sparano

2017 2018 2019 2020 / 10 9 8 7 6 5 4 3 2 1

Printed in China

ISBN-13: 978-0-7893-3287-5

Library of Congress Catalog Control Number: 2016952447

*To my wife, Betty,
my lifelong friend and
partner in all that I do*

Contents

Preface

There's something special about being on the water. Water constantly changes and it doesn't make any difference whether it's fresh or salt water. It can be still or raging. It can be 12 inches or a mile deep. Water can also change colors from green to deep blue to muddy. It can be your friend or your worst nightmare. But something magical happens when you take the wheel and pull away from a dock with your boat. You suddenly become the captain of your ship. For a boater, nothing can match such an energizing experience.

I've owned boats all my life, from canoes to a 54-foot Hatteras sportfisherman. I'm very comfortable on the water—whether a farm pond or offshore—but I also have a healthy respect for it. It can turn on you in a matter of minutes, thrusting you and your crew into danger. I also learned a long time ago that a sloppy boat is a dangerous boat. But, like most boaters, I do not let these potential threats deter me from my love of boating. Over the years, I have learned to equip my boats for nearly anything the water could throw at me.

If you are thinking of getting your first boat, I say go for it. You will experience nothing like it. I don't care where you live—a coastal state or the lake country of the Midwest—there's a special boat for you and your budget. This book will offer experienced recommendations for boats built for fishing and cruising on lakes, ponds, and rivers. The big news is that there are now special boats and outboard engines designed and built for inshore and offshore waters. I have also included a special section on water sports, including step-by-step how-to photographs on water skiing, wakeboarding, and tubing.

But there's more to boating than buying a special boat and engine. Most important is to make your boat safe. I have included a detailed section on U.S. Coast Guard regulations and required safety equipment. The safety of you and your crew may depend on how well your boat is equipped with Coast Guard–approved gear. Due to major improvements over the years, boating has never been safer. Boats are more seaworthy, four-stroke outboard engines are amazingly reliable, and GPS chartplotters will get you to your destination and back. If you break down, EPIRBs will tell your rescuers your exact location.

I learned a long time ago never to totally rely on electronics and batteries, though, so I asked my friend Tom Beard, a retired U.S. Coast Guard commander and rescue pilot, to simply explain the basics of plotting a course with a compass and nautical charts. Tom and his wife live aboard their boat and cruise extensively on both coasts. Tom taught navigation for both the U.S. Power Squadron and the U.S. Coast Guard Auxiliary. His illustrated section in this book simplifies compass deviation, dead reckoning, and other areas of navigation that you might find confusing.

My goal with this new book was to not only introduce new people to boating, but also bring experienced boaters up to date on all the amazing advances in electronics and accessories that can make boating more fun. Just a few years ago, who would have thought that we would see outboard engines of 627 horsepower or center consoles of 53 feet? Or the amazing boom in fishing kayaks and paddleboards?

I've always been a fisherman and all my boats have been rigged for serious fishing, but not all boaters are so dedicated. For those boaters who may need a push toward fishing, I've included a special section on hook and line sport. This section is more than just a primer; it will guide you from your first fishing rod to baits, rigs, lures, and all the fish species you can catch. I have even included how-to photos for cleaning and filleting fish.

The biggest challenge in compiling a book that encompasses the boating world and its constantly changing array of gear is dealing with such a volume of material, photos, and illustrations. As with my other books in this series for Rizzoli/Universe, I relied on the instinctive advice of Jim Muschett, my publisher. Jim is a good friend and instrumental in the development of this series. The heavy load eventually landed on the desks of Candice Fehrman, my editor, and Lori Malkin, who designed this book page by page. Without the talent and patience of these two ladies, this book would never have found its way between covers.

There are many more people to thank for their help in creating this new book. Many industry people also played an important role, including Mac McKeever at L.L. Bean, Katie Mitchell and Tanza Smith at Bass

Pro Shops, Isaiah James at Windsor Nature Discovery, and many others who answered my requests for photos and information. A special thanks has to go to Scott Atkinson, director of communications at USA Water Ski, who patiently answered all of my requests for photos.

Now you are holding *Complete Guide to Boating and Seamanship*, a massive effort to bring you the most valuable guide to boating and seamanship ever published. For those who may be buying a boat for the first time, this volume will teach you everything you need to know to safely begin a lifetime as a boater. For the old salts, it will keep you up to date on the latest innovations in boating. I hope I have succeeded in bringing you a comprehensive guide to boating, one that will keep you safe whenever you leave the dock.

—Vin T. Sparano
Editor Emeritus/Senior Field Editor
Outdoor Life

BOATING
DESIGN AND
CONSTRUCTION

BOATING DESIGN AND CONSTRUCTION

HULL DESIGN

The shape of a boat's hull is the biggest factor in how it will do its job for you. Hull design has always been the most intriguing subject among people who know boats and keep up with new developments, for changes in hull lines—skillfully conceived—have brought about some dramatic developments in how boats perform.

There are really just two types—displacement and planing hulls—but boat hulls in common use today are far from simple. In some, characteristics of the two types have been combined in order to get the best of both. Also, a variety of specific shapes have been designed to do certain things well that another shape cannot do. And there remain several traditional hull shapes that have changed little in the midst of a marine-design revolution, continuing to do a modest job well, and often at minimum cost.

■ Displacement Hulls

Displacement hulls push through the water rather than planing on top of it, and therefore speed is limited. A round-bottomed, full-keeled displacement hull rides comfortably down in the water where wave and wind action have relatively little effect. The Indian canoe, the Viking ship, and the Great Banks fishing dory (a flat-bottomed boat) were all displacement-type hulls. They were narrow beamed and pointed at both ends—for excellent reasons. They could be moved through the water more easily with only oars or a sail for power; they could be maneuvered in either direction; following seas

had much less effect on them than on a flat stern; and a pointed trailing end dissipated suction created by the water displacement. Today, there are squared-off sterns to provide useful space for the motors and deck, but the displacement hull is probably tapered back from a wide point amidships.

The sea-kindliness of a displacement hull is due principally to its low center of gravity. It rises with the swells, and a surface chop has little effect. A full-displacement hull with round quarters is less affected by beam seas (waves rolling in from one side or the other), while its full keel gives a good bite in the water, helping you hold a course through winds and current. Because weight in a displacement hull is much less critical than in a planing hull, it can be sturdily, even

The 38-foot Sabre Salon Express is a classic example of a sea-worthy displacement hull. With a 13-foot beam, it is powered by a Volvo Penta pod propulsion drivetrain.

heavily, built to take the worst punishment. Good examples of displacement hulls are present-day trawlers.

Small displacement hulls are excellent for passing rocky river rapids and surviving the worst chop on a lake. In large boats, cabin space is lower in the water, where it is more comfortable and feels more secure, especially on long cruises. On big water, you might be annoyed at first by the constant roll, but the roll period is slower than the chop-chop surface banging of a planing hull on the same water and never as sharp. What's more, the displacement hull will keep you dry in wave action that would soak you continually in a planing hull.

Just how limited is a displacement hull's speed? There is an actual formula. The square root of the waterline length times 1.5 equals possible speed. For example, an 11-foot lake fishing boat might measure 9 feet at the waterline. Thus, the square root of 9 is 3, which is then multiplied by 1.5, and then you get 4.5. That boat's probable maximum speed is 4.5 miles per hour. Load it deeper so the waterline is extended and you increase the possible top speed slightly. But there's no point in loading it down with more power, for you won't increase the speed significantly above the formula figure. How narrow is the hull width? Designers work on ratios from 3.5:1 up to 5:1, length to width. To some, this describes a "tippy" boat, tender when you step in or lean over.

While a small displacement hull, such as a canoe, can dump you and then skitter away high and dry on top of the water while you try to grab it, a bigger displacement hull, say from 18 feet up, is as safe, even for novices, as anything in the water. And since speed is inherently limited, a small motor is in order. This makes for a safe, economical way to cruise or fish all day. You just move along at a modest, steady rate, dry and comfortable in big water (though not as comfortable in a small displacement-type boat on calm water, where tippiness is tiresome). You conserve your resources and enjoy the boat's natural action, and the boat is always under control. That's the portrait of boating with a displacement hull.

Modified displacement hulls and semi-planing hulls are made so that the after-third or more of the bottom is flattened. A flat bottom toward the stern rides higher as speed is applied, instead of digging in and pushing the bow up, as will happen in a full-displacement hull. The flat section aft also reduces the tendency to roll. These boats have wider transoms, and can use bigger motors and run faster. You'll find modified round-bottomed hulls in small aluminum fishing boats, as well as in offshore fishing boats, with a wide range of variations in design.

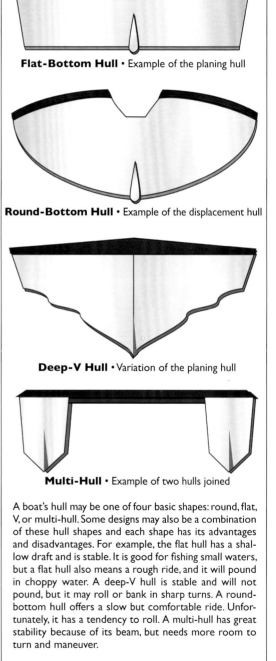

Boat Hulls

Flat-Bottom Hull · Example of the planing hull

Round-Bottom Hull · Example of the displacement hull

Deep-V Hull · Variation of the planing hull

Multi-Hull · Example of two hulls joined

A boat's hull may be one of four basic shapes: round, flat, V, or multi-hull. Some designs may also be a combination of these hull shapes and each shape has its advantages and disadvantages. For example, the flat hull has a shallow draft and is stable. It is good for fishing small waters, but a flat hull also means a rough ride, and it will pound in choppy water. A deep-V hull is stable and will not pound, but it may roll or bank in sharp turns. A round-bottom hull offers a slow but comfortable ride. Unfortunately, it has a tendency to roll. A multi-hull has great stability because of its beam, but needs more room to turn and maneuver.

Cruisers

Cruisers are generally more seaworthy and comfortable than runabouts. Size can range from 20 to more than 100 feet. Cruisers usually have overnight accommodations.

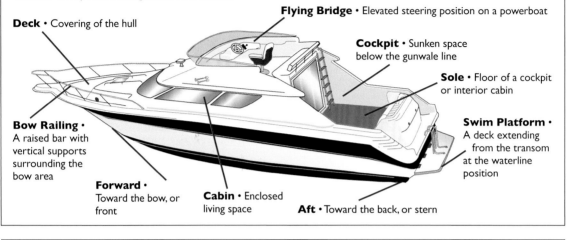

Flying Bridge • Elevated steering position on a powerboat

Deck • Covering of the hull

Cockpit • Sunken space below the gunwale line

Sole • Floor of a cockpit or interior cabin

Bow Railing • A raised bar with vertical supports surrounding the bow area

Swim Platform • A deck extending from the transom at the waterline position

Forward • Toward the bow, or front

Cabin • Enclosed living space

Aft • Toward the back, or stern

Runabouts

Most runabouts range in size from 16 to 25 feet and can be either outboard or inboard powered.

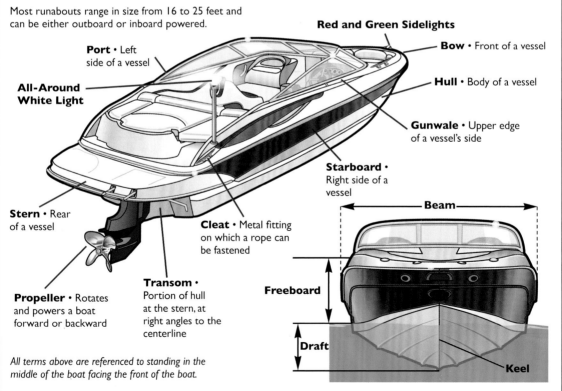

Red and Green Sidelights

Port • Left side of a vessel

Bow • Front of a vessel

All-Around White Light

Hull • Body of a vessel

Gunwale • Upper edge of a vessel's side

Starboard • Right side of a vessel

Stern • Rear of a vessel

Cleat • Metal fitting on which a rope can be fastened

Beam

Freeboard

Propeller • Rotates and powers a boat forward or backward

Transom • Portion of hull at the stern, at right angles to the centerline

Draft

Keel

All terms above are referenced to standing in the middle of the boat facing the front of the boat.

ROUND-BOTTOMED CARTOPPERS: Small aluminum fishing boats and fiberglass dinghies are often modified hulls that have round-bottom characteristics, yet they can move at high speed. You need a displacement hull for sitting on a choppy lake all day; nothing else will do. Using a motor of up to 25 horsepower, put the boat in the water and give it full speed. If the bow goes up and the stern digs in until you are depressed in a bowl the prop action makes in the water, reduce speed; it's a displacement hull, and your power is beyond the safe hull speed.

These boats have a rather full bow entry in relation to the beam, and there is a small keel. The middle and aft sections will be distinctly rounded, in contrast to the V-shaped cartop hull. If the sides taper toward the stern, you will find it better for rowing.

PUNT, PRAM, JOHNBOAT: Anyone can build and care for a flat-bottomed boat. This is the least complicated and least costly hull shape, and the amateur can build a large craft on simple lines at low cost. Flat-bottomed hulls pound more than others, but while newcomers dislike their clumsy appearance and strictly functional design, serious boaters continue to choose them for hunting and fishing on quiet waters, for they make an excellent platform.

The punt, pram, and johnboat are often indistinguishable except in name. What might be called a pram Down East and a punt on England's Thames River could be called a johnboat in Missouri. These square-ended, flat-bottomed hulls are the most stable and best load carriers of all little boats. They are rather heavy handling, and are designed for use in quiet water, where their low sides and flat bottoms come into their own.

The true punt is made to be poled. The sides are straight, and both ends are identical, rising flat at about 45 degrees. The bottom slopes up slightly toward the ends. The pram has bowed sides, tapering forward, and the bottom rises toward the bow. The bow end rises at a rather shallow angle, and the stern end is broader. The pram is usually rowed or sailed, but may be powered with a small outboard or electric motor.

The johnboat, the most popular with sportsmen, is made by a number of aluminum and fiberglass boat manufacturers. The hull figure has nearly as many variations within the basic plan as the number of regions in which it has been built and used. For instance, in marshy country, a coffin-shaped johnboat was built with a stern wide enough only for one person; it tapered toward a slight flare forward, then in again toward a narrow bow.

Sometimes the bow was decked over to cover gear. The bottom sloped up from the flare both fore and aft, easing the push through vegetation and making it easy to maneuver in open water. This version continues to be a useful fishing boat in marshland and bayous.

Modern aluminum johnboats have riveted or welded hulls and range from 12 to 20 feet long. The bottom slopes up a bit forward from a low point directly in the midsection, and is rockered aft. The sides may be bowed somewhat forward and slope in toward the bottom. Three or four seats, with a wide bow seat, provide reinforcement in a broad-beamed hull that can carry a big load. Johnboats are rowed, poled, or powered.

Fiberglass johnboats are a better choice for saltwater fishermen. Saltwater corrosion will eventually take its toll on riveted aluminum hulls. Fiberglass johnboats can be molded in a variety of designs and are virtually maintenance free. Some manufacturers, such as Carolina Skiff, will custom design the interior, starting with the basic hull. These skiffs are also unsinkable and can be left in the water indefinitely with the scuppers open.

FLAT-BOTTOMED SKIFF: Put a pointed bow on a flat-bottomed shape and you have a hull that gives sharper entry to oncoming waves and reduces the tendency to pound that is characteristic of the square-ended johnboat or pram. It does, however, reduce stability.

For good rowing qualities, a skiff is built with a relatively narrow stern; the sides curve upward both fore and aft so that the tip of the bow and stern both clear the water slightly. The "active" bottom is the broad midsection. Such a boat is relatively easy to control and safe. For outboard power, the stern is built wider and lower. Flat-bottomed skiffs 12 to 16 feet long are common in all parts of the country. In shorter lengths, this hull is unstable, for the bow is too light.

THE DORY: This hull is fun to handle and is also very competent. You can take it through the surf or into fast, shallow rivers, for its two pointed ends and narrow bottom make it easy to row and control. Flaring, tall sides keep it dry inside, but this shape is somewhat tender, especially in small sizes. For use with an outboard, the design is modified by squaring off the stern. This presents a V-shaped transom, far from ideal for handling an outboard. Modern dory hulls have wider and lower sterns to improve handling with a motor. Mounting a small inboard engine amidships is the solution to powering the traditional double-end dory.

▇ Planing Hulls

Planing hulls are built for speed. Given enough acceleration (called planing speed), the hull rises to the water's surface, levels off, and planes along the top. Design efficiency and possible power impose the only limits on its speed. The objective is to reduce wetted surface (friction) and the weight of the bow wave that a nonplaning hull pushes before it. To achieve this, a lightweight hull is important, but weight is related to power. A planing hull can have a wider beam, with length-to-width ratios ranging from 2.5:1 to 3.5:1. A wider beam, especially in the aft section, makes more space for the power plant. In relation to power carried, the hull is lightweight.

On plane, this hull is more nimble in handling, since a substantial part of it is airborne and steering action is quicker. The wider beam and hard chines (where the bottom and sides meet) make for a more stable boat in calm water, though less so in a big roll.

But advantages in speed and handling bring penalties. A planing hull is more subject to wind and wave action—a surface chop can sometimes feel like a rock-strewn road at high speed. The lack of a useful keel on some planing hulls makes it hard to hold a course in heavy going. Aggravating these effects is the tendency of the bow to lift as more power is applied; the "active" hull on plane is aft, where the greatest weight is located in the broad beam and power plant. Power trimming the outboard engine may adjust the planing angle to level. Or, trim tabs may be added at the stern. These are metal power-operated tabs installed at the bottom of the hull at the transom that adjust the stern and bow up and down at planing speeds. Trim tabs are also used to adjust the boat's ride to compensate for passengers and gear that may be off-center or when running in a rough sea to avoid spray and a wet ride. When a planing boat holds a horizontal angle at plane, it is easier to steer, gives a drier ride, and rides better.

But it goes without saying that much boating is on quiet water, where the planing hull has few if any serious problems. In any case, not many planing hulls now made are the pure type—flat bottoms or simple Vs. Manufacturers have adapted planing advantages to practical conditions, and come up with combinations that are safe, fast, comfortable, and still easy to handle. Some newer hull designs include stepped hulls, which have multiple, smaller planing surfaces. The advantages of a stepped hull are that you can get on plane faster and make tighter turns.

CABIN DORY: This is one flat-bottomed boat that is still being made in sizes of 20 feet or more. The explanation is that the dory hull's sloping sides and narrow bottom give it some of the features of a deep-V hull in handling rough water. On the Gulf and the northwestern and northeastern coasts, you will see cabin boats with dory hulls made locally that have high bows running back to a flat, low stern, which is also wider than the stern of a displacement dory hull. The wide, flat section of the bottom aft makes this a planing hull. But even at low speed, it draws less water than a V-shaped hull and can be run in rough surf and shoal water where no other boats of this size would be safe.

V-BOTTOMED SKIFF: The first design aimed to combine planing ability with the kinder qualities of the displacement hull was the simple V bottom, with flat planes rising from the keel to hard chines. V-bottomed skiffs under 20 feet have slightly rounded chines to improve turning and reduce the slap of beam waves; the bottom aft is flattened; and the bow is deeper, with a sharp forefoot section. This makes a hull that is comfortable for all-day use on big lakes and bays, and can still plane off for a fast trip there and back. The bow deck line often has a wide flare overhanging the fine pointed bow. As the bow cuts the waves, the flare casts the spray aside, keeping passengers dry in moderate waves.

Stepped Hull

A stepped hull has multiple planing surfaces, which allows a boat to trim at one angle at various speeds.

V-BOTTOMED CARTOPPER: Most cartop boats have planing hulls. To be light enough to qualify as a cartop boat, construction must be so light that you can lift it to a rack on top of a car. A planing hull is the logical type. Cartoppers that plane are usually modified-V hulls, though they may look round bottomed at a glance. The bow is sharp, molding to a flat aft bottom with rounded chines and a broad stern. If the shape tapers back to a narrower stern for easy rowing, you'll pay for it in reduced planing ability. Depending on the physical strength of the fisherman, 100 pounds seems to be the upper limit for a manageable cartop boat. There are racks designed for one-man loading and unloading.

DEEP-V BOTTOM AND CENTER CONSOLES: From a performance standpoint—when big demands are put on a hull—the best combination of displacement- and planing-hull traits is the deep V. Invented by designer Ray Hunt, the deep-V bottom extends from a slightly rounded forefoot all the way to the stern. The V shape at the stern works well with single or multiple outboards.

In a well-designed deep-V hull, the rounded, deep forefoot and full keel enable it to perform well in big waters, rising with the seas and rounding off a chop even at high speed. But how does such a hull rise on plane? With the help of longitudinal strakes, or steps in the bottom. As power is poured on, the strakes help the hull step up onto plane, while the V shape and flared bow part the wave tops and keep passengers reasonably dry. World ocean-racing records have been broken again and again with deep-V hulls.

Tough seagoing center-console boats ranging up to 53 feet with multiple outboard motors have created a brand-new category of offshore boats. It is not unusual to see these tough offshore boats with three and even four 300-horsepower outboard engines totaling up to 1,200 horsepower mounted on their transoms. In some respects, this breed of boat is safer than the big inboard-powered sportfisherman. It can run faster with less horsepower to offshore grounds on less fuel and get back to port more quickly in case of bad weather. It is exceptionally seaworthy in all but extremely rough and dangerous waters. These center consoles are also excellent fishing machines, giving fishermen 360 degrees of space to fight big fish. Smaller center consoles, say up to 26 feet, are trailerable with 8-foot beams. Bigger models, up to 53 feet, feature beams of nearly 13 feet, creating huge cockpit space for fishermen, tackle, and gear. Added advantages are that the engines can be replaced and there are no smelly and oily bilges to worry about. If

an outboard-powered boat runs aground or hits underwater debris, it is less likely to incur serious damage, whereas an inboard risks damaging rudders and shafts.

HydraSports Custom features its 53-foot Sueños center console. With its 1,000-gallon fuel tank, the Sueños has no maximum horsepower rating and is powered by four 350-horsepower outboard motors. This center-console HydraSports weighs more than 28,000 pounds and has a 13-foot beam.

FLATS AND BAY BOATS: There was a time when flats boats were made by a handful of local builders. The boats weren't big and the hulls weren't very user-friendly in rough water. Those early boats just didn't perform well north of the bonefish flats. A lot has happened since those early years, and constantly evolving flats-boat designs have now migrated north and west of the Florida flats.

What is a flats boat? Essentially, it's a boat designed for shallow-water fishing, usually for bonefish, permit, and tarpon. It also has low freeboard, which means the wind won't blow it around and the low profile won't spook fish. A flats boat has a wide beam, which makes it exceptionally stable for two standing fishermen. The casting decks are flat fore and aft. The decks are also uncluttered, as gear is stored out of sight in hatches. Boat cleats and hardware are minimal to avoid line snagging. A poling platform is usually mounted over the outboard engine. Before the time of poling platforms at the stern, guides poled their boats from the bow, which proved a tiring task.

Flats boats are also fast. Some 18-footers are rated for outboards up to 150 horsepower. Flats boats can run at speeds of 50 miles per hour or more and maneuver like sport cars. Typical sizes range from 16 to 18 feet.

Take a close look at a flats boat and its special features, and you'll suddenly realize that it could also make an acceptable bass boat. But a flats boat is perfectly designed for saltwater anglers stalking tidal flats, rivers, and barrier islands for striped bass, bluefish, weakfish, bonefish, and tarpon.

Bay boats are designed for fishermen who prefer to fish inshore waters, including bays, rivers, and sounds. Most bay boats are built to handle bigger waters than a flats boat. Bay boats are also bigger, ranging up to 25 feet with 8½-foot beams, and are powered with outboards up to 300 horsepower. Even the bigger models will have a draft of only 11 inches. On good weather days, some bay boats can also handle inshore waters. Typical bay boats are center consoles, though dual-console designs are becoming more popular and practical as family boats.

Planing-Hull Designs

▲ The MAKO Pro Skiff is a 17-footer with an inverted-V hull. Rated for outboards up to 60 horsepower and with a weight capacity of 1,400 pounds, this is an ideal utility craft for sportsmen.

▲ The G3 Eagle 166 SE is a 16½-foot rigged johnboat with a welded hull. Rated for a maximum of 60 horsepower, this model is ideal for most freshwater fishing. It comes with a 19-gallon livewell.

▲ The G3 Bay 20 DLX Tunnel is a 20-foot aluminum-welded center console rated for a 150-horsepower outboard motor. Designed for fishing, this model includes a 14-gallon livewell for baitfish and a 31-gallon divided livewell with an insulated lid.

▲ The tunnel hull design on the G3 Bay 20 DLX Tunnel allows it to run in shallow water when trying to reach remote areas.

▲ Maverick's Mirage 18 HPX-V is a typical well-equipped flats boat. This 18-footer has a 150-horsepower rating, draws only 9 inches, and has both a poling tower and a bow casting platform.

▲ The Tahoe 450 TS, powered with a Mercury 90-horsepower four-stroke, is a bowrider runabout ideal for water skiing and tubing.

▲ The Viking 92 Enclosed Bridge Convertible is the ultimate offshore sportfisherman. With a beam of 24 feet and a fuel tank capacity of 4,015 gallons, this 92-footer can go anywhere. This Viking has power options up to 2,635 horsepower.

▲ The Yellowfin 42, a 42-footer, is a good example of progress made in center consoles built to get offshore quickly with four 300-horsepower outboards totaling 1,200 horsepower.

SEA SKIFF: This boat is often described as round bottomed, but in fact it is usually a combination of a V-hull and displacement-hull design. Forward, a rounded bilge helps it rise with waves and pound less in a chop. The bottom, with rounded chines, slants to a shallow V to form a keel, and flattens aft. The Jersey sea skiff, a remarkably practical and able hull for fishing in bigger waters, will taper to a narrower stern than many planing hulls. This raises the planing speed, but makes it a safer boat for getting home and running inlets when following seas may present the most trouble. Sea skiffs are usually planked with lapstrake. The strakes help lift the hull to reach plane when power is applied, and reduce roll in big water. But this also increases the total wetted surface or drag on the hull. Wood lapstrake hulls have great pliability and shock resistance, which admirably suits fishing the coasts. Today, nearly all wood skiffs of this design are custom built.

■ Multiple Hulls

You've heard them called tri-hulls, cathedral, trihedral, gullwing, and more. The basic principle is the catamaran, adding stability to a hull by means of a secondary hull. In the catamaran, the secondary hull is called an outrigger. A trimaran has two outriggers—one on each side of the load-bearing hull.

This idea, applied to modern fiberglass and aluminum boat design, has just about taken over boat manufacturing in the 15- to 40-foot class. First, it has brought unbelievable stability to small boats, even in rough water. Second, it has made the entire deck usable; you can fight a big fish standing on the gunwale or bow of such a boat without rocking it dangerously. The deck area is actually increased up to 100 percent since a much wider beam in the same length is possible, with a bowline topside that is more square than pointed. This makes a boat that is useful all over. For families and fishermen who tend to concentrate on matters other than boat handling when the fun and action warms up, it has great value.

You can see why the multiple-hull design has brought about a revolution in small boats. Naturally, the hulls are unified—built in a single structure—while the Polynesian and East Indian catamaran and trimaran boats had hulls joined with wood poles bound at each hull. Between keel points are sculptured hollow spaces, where air is trapped when the boat is on plane, making a cushion against the chop and providing a lifting effect. In a tri-hull design, the middle hull is deepest (often with a deep-V bow and forefoot line), and the

Multiple-Hull Designs

▲ The SunCatcher Elite 326 SS is a 26.5-foot pontoon boat that is rated for a 250-horsepower outboard motor, probably powerful enough to pull water skiers and wakeboarders. It's equipped with three lounge couches and a changing room.

▲ The Boston Whaler 19-foot Montauk is a good example of a multiple-hull design. This popular unsinkable Montauk design is also available in 15-, 17-, and 21-foot models. With a 96-inch beam and a 115-horsepower outboard, this Montauk is a good choice for lakes, bays, and inshore waters.

▲ The World Cat 330TE is a 34-foot center-console catamaran built for offshore waters. A 10½-foot beam makes it a stable fishing platform. This World Cat is rated for twin 300-horsepower outboards. The twin-hull design affords stability and handles rough water very well.

Is This Boat Captain Nuts?

We have all heard some wild fishing tales from boat captains. Some stories stretch the imagination. In the immortal words of Ed Zern, writer and outdoor philosopher, "Fishermen are born honest—but they get over it."

I've also been guilty of stretching the truth, but not this time. I want to tell you about a true mind-boggling fishing adventure.

The bizarre tale starts with Scott Stancyzk, a Florida Keys charter captain. Scott has been guiding fishermen on the *Catch 22*, a 54-footer, for about 30 years. He was trolling for billfish about 20 miles from Alligator Light, which marks the Keys Reef. He had four doctors aboard and his mates, Travis and Roman Butters. They were out only a short time when the boat blew a blower shaft, which meant Scott would be running his boat on a single engine all day. Would this be Scott's lucky or unlucky day? You be the judge.

From the bridge, Scott suddenly saw five or six blue marlin all over his ballyhoo baits. He quickly hooked up two blues and put a doctor on each rod. When Scott saw another marlin still hanging around the boat, he put out another bait and the marlin slammed it as soon as it hit the water. Scott and his crew were now fighting a tripleheader on blue marlin.

"I've never had a doubleheader on blue marlin, much less a triple," said Scott. "I wasn't about to lose these fish." At one point, according to Scott, all three blue marlin, weighing more than 100 pounds each, were jumping at the same time.

Luckily, the first blue marlin was landed, tagged, and released without mishap. But the remaining two marlin were not cooperating. Both fish ran in opposite directions, making it impossible to fight both at the same time. Scott chose one fish and told Travis that when the other marlin ran off all the line on the reel, he was to hook another rod to the reel harness lug and toss the first rod overboard, hoping that the marlin wouldn't run all the line off the second rod. You guessed it! That's exactly what the marlin did.

"Hook on another rod!" shouted Scott. Travis followed orders and now there were two trolling outfits trailing behind the marlin. This may be hard to believe, but that marlin also peeled off all the line on that third rod. But Scott was still determined to land all the fish.

"Put on another rod!" he again shouted. Does a mate argue with his skipper? Not a chance! By this time, Scott had become possessed by the challenge and he was going to land all three marlin at all costs. Travis hooked a fourth rod to the marlin that was already trailing three trolling outfits in its wake.

What happened next would test the determination of Ahab. The marlin did what marlin do best: fight with all their strength. The fish ran all the line off the fourth rod. There was no stopping the fish and Scott had no choice. The crew and fishermen had tagged and released one marlin, were fighting a second marlin, and the third marlin was dragging three trolling outfits through the ocean.

Did Scott call it quits? Not a chance. "Hook up a fifth rod!" he shouted to Travis, who obediently hooked up a fifth rod and tossed the fourth rod into the sea. By this time, the doctors probably questioned the sanity, as well as the wealth, of their skipper.

All was going well—the doctor eventually landed that second blue marlin and it was tagged and released. But then the fight with the third marlin ended tragically.

Now trailing a total of four 30-pound-class Hurricane trolling rods, four Shimano TLD20 reels, and more than 1,600 yards of monofilament in its wake, the marlin broke the line. Scott lost all his tackle, valued at nearly $2,000, but what he and his crew really lamented was the loss of that third blue marlin.

Would Scott do it again? Would he risk all that expensive tackle just to catch a fish that he planned to tag and release? "Of course," he said. "A tripleheader on blue marlin may happen once in a lifetime, if you're very lucky. You can always buy more tackle."

This story may be tough to swallow. If you doubt it, just ask Captain Scott Stancyzk yourself. You can find him at Bud N Mary's Marina in Islamorada, Florida. Just look for the *Catch 22*.

side hulls are minor points interrupting the rise of the V toward the waterline, sometimes acting as deep chines.

This hull is slower to plane than the other V hulls, as the multiple points tend to push a bow wave ahead of the boat until planing speed is reached. Also, the wetted area is greater, holding the hull off plane until considerable power pushes it up. It's also a heavy hull compared to others of the same length. Obviously, it takes more gas to operate. You have to reckon the greatly increased useful deck area and stability against these drawbacks.

A second revolution that has become as big as the multiple-hull takeover is the continuous boom in bass boats with multiple-hull characteristics. These bass boats, made of fiberglass, aluminum, or Kevlar, are mostly 14- to 25-foot boats with two- or three-point molded hulls. The difference is that the beam is narrow, requiring less power and making them practical in weedy waters and in the brush-filled shorelines of reservoir lakes. This hull is potentially very fast, but that's hardly the purpose in a bass boat.

BOAT CONSTRUCTION

The material of which a boat is made and the way that material is used in building a boat has a direct effect on its cost, strength, weight, buoyancy, and durability. Commercial builders have turned mostly to fiberglass and aluminum hulls because they are easier to mass-produce. And people are buying them because the man-made materials require less upkeep than wood. But there are still wood-boat builders in business today, and some of the woodworking techniques are worth noting.

■ Wood

It's hard to appreciate the work and time needed to keep a wood boat in good shape until you have stripped a hull down to clean, bare board, repaired rot and loose fastenings, filled and sanded it all smooth, and then fiberglassed, repainted, and refinished it inside and out.

Wood is a natural material. It feels good, absorbs sound and shock, and can be worked and repaired by anyone. An important advantage over fiberglass and aluminum is that wood is naturally buoyant. Wood burns, but it's less flammable—especially the hardwoods—than most people think.

Generally, round-bottomed, wood displacement hulls are built on temporary molds with ribbands connecting to delineate the shape. Structural members are bent to the molds. Planking is lined up and secured by the structure. V-bottomed, planing hulls are generally built on sawn frames (sawn lumber firmly jointed at angles where the contour changes). Here, the frames make permanent molds to which the planks or plywood are attached. But wood boats take their characteristics from the way the hull is covered as well as from the hull shape. Structural features, weight, strength, and, to an extent, water characteristics go hand in hand with the planking method. Some of the methods have been almost abandoned in favor of simpler and cheaper ones, but they are described here because valuable older hulls made with great skill are still available.

PLYWOOD: The advantages of building with marine-grade plywood are economy, simplicity, and availability of the material. Most amateur boat builders, especially those who build from kit plans, use plywood. There are fewer fastenings, and the tricky work of fitting plank lines into a pleasing boat shape is largely avoided. Of course, plywood works best in boats with a rather simple design, since it won't take compound bends. The dory, with a flat bottom and flat-curved sides, is a good example. In bigger boats, plywood is used with hard chines and flat bottoms for flat-V designs.

One big-boat builder starts with a frame of white oak ribs, over which sheets of plywood are laid from sheer to sheer as a tough and tight inner hull. Over the inner hull, another of solid mahogany planks is built in carvel fashion.

Don't be alarmed when you see fist-size patches in marine plywood: voids in the core have been filled. When used in exterior hull covering, the seams, which expose the laminations, must be thoroughly treated and sealed, and the surface must be fiberglassed to protect the end-grain exposed in all plywood. Repair is simpler than in any other wood boat. Maintenance is relatively easy, but must be regular. Delamination of the wood plies can result from spray collecting in the bilges, as well as from

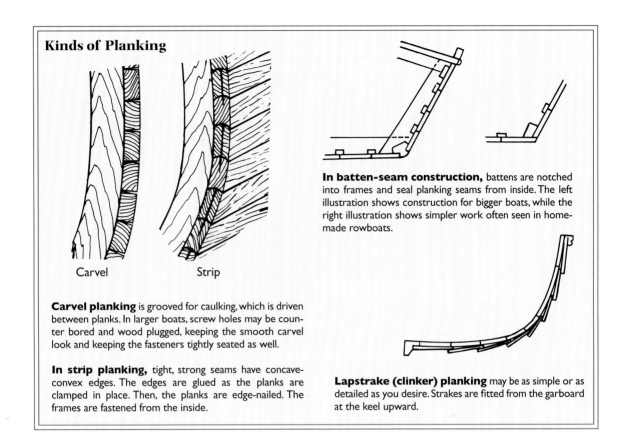

Kinds of Planking

Carvel   Strip

Carvel planking is grooved for caulking, which is driven between planks. In larger boats, screw holes may be counter bored and wood plugged, keeping the smooth carvel look and keeping the fasteners tightly seated as well.

In strip planking, tight, strong seams have concave-convex edges. The edges are glued as the planks are clamped in place. Then, the planks are edge-nailed. The frames are fastened from the inside.

In batten-seam construction, battens are notched into frames and seal planking seams from inside. The left illustration shows construction for bigger boats, while the right illustration shows simpler work often seen in home-made rowboats.

Lapstrake (clinker) planking may be as simple or as detailed as you desire. Strakes are fitted from the garboard at the keel upward.

outside the hull, so many plywood boats are fiberglassed both inside and out.

Plywood is also used in sawn strips for other planking methods.

CARVEL: This is a tighter and stronger form of carvel planking, originated thousands of years ago. Planks are laid edge to edge to form a smooth hull. Simple carvel planking is fastened only to ribs or frames, which must be closely spaced and therefore make a boat heavier. Caulking is put between planks, the exterior edges of which are grooved slightly to hold the caulk. In water, planks swell into the caulk for tightness; out of water (and this goes for planks above the waterline as well), drying tends to open seams. A simple carvel-built boat is not a very dry one, and requires seasonal work to keep shipshape.

BATTEN-SEAM: This is another tighter and stronger form of carvel planking. Staunch battens are notched into the frames, and planks are laid so that the seams fall at the centers of the battens. This closes the seams from behind, and planks are shaped so that the seams are tight when laid, without caulking on the exterior. Pliable batten compound is spread on the battens and plank edges, and planks are screwed along the edges through the battens into the frames.

LAPSTRAKE: A favorite method for building boats that are very light and strong, lapstrake is also referred to as clinker-built or clinch, referring to clinched nails traditionally used in fastening. Planks are overlapped, resembling clapboard on a house. The effect looks "boaty." Relatively thin, wider planks can be used, and are fastened to each other along the overlap and also through frames where they occur. Frames can be wider spaced than in most other construction. Seam compound is applied to the overlap before fastening.

Lapstrake building is an expert's job; planking must be painstakingly lined up with the boat's shape, without stealers (which are cut to fit awkward places in carvel construction, where their use in the flat skin does not destroy the appearance). Repairing damage to lapstrake is also an expert's job.

STRIP PLANKING: This is a popular and successful way for amateurs to build wood boats, but it requires too many fastenings to be the choice of professional builders. Narrow strips (about 1¼ inches for a 20-foot boat) are used in planking. Another variation of carvel, it combines light weight with great strength, long life, and minimum maintenance compared to ordinary carvel planking. The narrow planks will not often warp or lift, which happens even with professionally built carvel boats when planking that is too wide and thin has been used.

Tight, strong seams are achieved by shaping the edges, one side concave, and the other convex. The edges are covered with marine glue as a plank is laid, and then the plank is clamped tight in place and edge-nailed through the width of two planks and into a third. Only each third or fourth plank is fastened through frames. Fewer and lighter frames reduce weight and save interior space, as in lapstrake planking. All the fastenings in strip planking make it hard to repair; the job should be turned over to a skilled worker.

DIAGONAL PLANKING: Strong, true, and trim boats are produced this way. An amateur can handle it successfully in its simpler forms. For instance, a single layer of ¼-inch diagonal strips can be applied to plywood transverse frames for very small and light boats, such as a shallow duckboat. Strips are laid at 45-degree angles to the centerline, glued and fastened to each frame at the crossing point. The edge of each strip is glued before the next is laid, and clamped in place for fastening to the frames. In this lightweight construction, fiberglassing the hull both inside and out is imperative for watertightness and strength.

In larger and heavier boats, planks are laid tight in two layers and overlapped. This is an easy way for an amateur to build a dinghy-shaped boat. The keel, sheer, and longitudinal frames make the bones in this construction without transverse framing, except in offshore boats. Double-planking compound, available in marine stores, is laid between the layers of planks. An unusually strong, lightweight hull results.

Professionals build double-diagonal hulls. One method is to plank in two layers laid at opposite 45-degree angles. Another is to lay the first layer at the angle, and the second straight fore and aft as in strip planking. The first layer is fiberglassed. You will find older boats with a first layer that has been covered with construction canvas and glued before laying the second layer of planking.

■ Aluminum

Light weight, low cost, and low maintenance make aluminum a popular and useful material, especially in small boats such as cartoppers. Another important quality often overlooked: it won't burn. These boats can be noisy, and poorly made aluminum hulls will "pong" as panels flex under pressure and temperature change. Some makers use sound-deadening rubber-based paints and other coatings on the inside. In larger hulls, a layer of flotation is sandwiched between two aluminum skins, providing safety and quiet operation, too. It may surprise you, but an unpainted and uninsulated aluminum boat is not hot, but cool. Sun rays are radiated through the metal into the water.

Aluminum boats are tough and easier to maintain than fiberglass boats. They are a good choice for fishermen and hunters, who frequently take their boats in shallow or timbered shoreline waters.

Aluminum boat building came of age with the development of the 5000 and 6000 series of marine aluminum, which contain no copper. The 5000 is alloyed with magnesium and manganese, the 6000 with magnesium and silicon. Corrosion is not a problem, even in salt water, if the boat is built with marine aluminum. A reputable maker will declare this in a label on the boat.

Electrolysis presents a real danger to aluminum hulls in salt water, however. Copper, steel, nickel, or chromium, for instance, will cause electrolytic decay in aluminum in the presence of an electrical current in salt water. Motor ignitions and electronic gear and lighting systems must be properly grounded by a qualified technician to avoid this danger. For this reason, aluminum boats sell better in freshwater areas.

Aluminum hulls may be welded or riveted, and frequently both fastening methods are used. Stretch-forming presses make almost any hull form possible. Smooth, structurally sound extrusions provide strength needed in keels, stringers and ribbing, transoms, and gunwales. You will dent an aluminum hull more often than you will crack and rip it open, but even at the worst, it is surprisingly easy to repair.

◼ Fiberglass

Seamless and impervious to marine parasites, rot, or electrolysis, fiberglass is popular because it needs little maintenance or caution in use in either fresh or salt water. Laminated fiberglass has great strength and versatility. Because it can be molded in any shape, it has aided development of hull shapes that are more useful and popular, such as cathedral hulls. If made with a good gel coat, the slick surface is faster in the water.

A well-made fiberglass boat will be totally free of leaks, but it's a common misconception that fiberglass can't leak and that therefore any fiberglass boat will be securely dry. In careless production, pinhole leaks will occur because resin has been unevenly applied to the glass cloth and mat, resulting in dry patches in the glass where water can enter. These patches are also weak.

Fiberglass boats are production boats now; the cost and complexity of molds, skills, and technology have made custom- or amateur-built boats rather rare. Building methods are by contact or hand layup or matched-die molding.

CONTACT OR HAND LAYUP: Improvements and techniques in fiberglass boat construction continue to produce better boats. Typically, quality construction of larger and more valuable boats is by the hand-layup method. A male mold is carefully made of wood, the details complete. On this, a female mold is formed of plastic materials. Laminations are laid, outside in. First, the gel coat: this is the outside surface of the boat and is an epoxy or polyester resin in which desired color is mixed, but without the fiberglass body. Next comes a layer of fiberglass mat made of random fibers woven together, very porous but a suitable base for the finish just laid. Into this is laid polyester resin with a mohair or nylon roller, binding the fibers and creating a bond to the gel coat. Depending on required strength and weight of the hull, additional layers of fiberglass cloth and woven rovings (cord-twisted fiberglass for strength) are laid, and then the reverse order—cloth, mat, and inside gel coat. All layers are rolled or painted with resin to bond them together and to the next layer. The exact composition and number of laminations may vary to suit design requirements. When layup is complete, the laminate is cured at atmospheric temperature. When the resin hardens, it permanently bonds the fiberglass in a tough sheet.

The roller or brush work with resin is most important. Too much laid on will result in weakness in any lamination because a bulk of resin will be unstructured—without fiberglass. Too little anywhere will result in a dry patch that may become porous, delaminate, and leak, as noted above.

Foam planks, balsa wood, or plywood can be laid at the core to add strength and built-in flotation, and these cores also help to reduce noise and vibration. In bigger boats, the core is laid with resin I-beams joining laminations on either side at intervals to give structure to the sandwich construction. Some builders avoid any wood in the construction to dispel fear of rot and parasites. Others swear by the shock resistance and flex of wood in the core.

The big advantage of contact or hand layup is that the whole hull or deck is visible at one time. Defects such as air bubbles or dry patches can be seen and remedied before proceeding. Sometimes a hull mold is made in halves to aid this; a large wheel is often built into the mold platform to roll the lamination into accessible positions as it proceeds.

Extra layers of lamination needed at the chines, keel, stem, and transom are applied according to design needs. Stringers and stiffening of fiberglass or plywood may be bonded in place as the schedule proceeds, and bulkheads and motor mounts in larger craft laid after the glass hull is complete. Even hardware may be fastened and bedded in during glassing.

History of Cement Boats

Considering the amazing technology of boat building today, it's hard to imagine a boat built with cement. But it happened back in the 1970s, when this method of boat building stimulated considerable interest in the industry. This technique was never developed, and little if any activity in ferro-cement boats exists today, but it's an interesting footnote in the history of boat construction.

Why build a boat of cement? The cost at that time ran from half to three-quarters the cost of other materials. And ferro-cement boats seemed like they would last forever. They were practically maintenance free—without seams and impervious to rot and insects—and of course were fireproof. Their resistance to shock and abrasion was said to be excellent. Penetration of a ferro-cement hull by severe impact was practically unknown. Collision and grounding could cause local damage with limited cracks, but leakage was easy to control and repair was made by hammering out a bulge and sealing cracks with epoxy or patching cement.

It sounds heavy? Not necessarily so. At that time, ferro-cement, wood, fiberglass, and steel boats of 35 to 45 feet all weighed about the same. Longer than 45 feet, ferro-cement boats were usually lighter than boats of other materials; shorter than 35 feet, they were usually heavier. Under 20 feet, using conventional methods, the weight per foot was prohibitive.

Here's how these cement boats were built: A ferro-cement boat could be built of any shape that steel reinforcing could be formed to. Vertical frames of steel pipe or bar were shaped on plans or plywood forms, and then stringers were welded to space and hold the frames rigidly and vertical bars of smaller size were added. Six to eight layers of chicken wire, half on each side of the rod structure, were stapled on to hold firmly when loaded with mortar. Galvanized chicken wire was used conventionally, but good results with square welded mesh were also reported. Two layers were used on each side, with stringers of only a quarter inch. This reduced structural bulk, and the finished hull thickness did not exceed half an inch and weighed only 8 or 9 pounds per square foot. Using this method, boats shorter than 20 feet could be entirely practical in ferro-cement.

Type I Portland cement, the common building material, proved suitable for use in fresh water. In salt water, Type II was needed to withstand sulphate action. Air-entrained mortar produced the best results. This was mortar made with countless tiny air bubbles from a chemical agent in the mix. It flowed on smoother and, when hardened, was a safety factor in freezing temperatures. Only sand—no gravel—was used in the mix.

Plastering the hull required two workers. One on the inside pushed the mortar through the structure while one on the outside smoothed the surface. The quality of the work depended on leaving no voids while filling the mesh, and working rapidly without dry joints (wet on dry concrete). A cement hull could have been epoxied to reduce surface drag. Bulkheads and cabins were usually ferro-cement as well. Engine mounts were plates welded into the hull structure.

About 50 years ago, cement boats seemed like a good idea, but modern boat-building techniques have killed the concept. Most of the boats made with ferro-cement in the United States were sailboats. Before the technique could be applied to powerboats, however, the ferro-cement concept faded out.

MATCHED-DIE MOLDING: This method is used in large-volume production of fiberglass hulls under 20 feet. A fiberglass preform is made on a shaped vacuum screen placed over a metal male mold. The female mold is pressed onto it, heat is applied, and the hull (including any core and ribs) is quickly fused into a unit. Voids and flaws cannot be seen during fabrication, but techniques of reputable builders are advanced and there are few rejects.

In some production lines, fiberglass fibers and catalyzed resin are shot with a chopper gun into a female mold and cured at atmospheric temperature.

■ Fabric

WOOD-CANVAS: Making a wood-canvas canoe is started by shaping white cedar ribs around a canoe form. Red cedar planking is clinch-nailed to these, and then mahogany gunwales are attached. Seamless canvas, Dacron, or a reinforced plastic is used for the outside skin. Seats are framed with ash; seat bottoms are cane. Thwarts are separate, not embodied in the seats. A small keel may extend the entire bottom length for directional stability, or may be omitted on white-water canoes. Coats of waterproof varnish are laid on exposed wood surfaces, and the entire exterior is brushed with a high-gloss enamel to reduce water friction. Such a canvas canoe will stand many years of hard use.

Duckboats, kayaks, and portable canvas-covered rowboats are made by similar methods.

INFLATABLES: Serviceable inflatables are made by laminating nylon on both sides with neoprene or Hypalon, which toughens the fabric, resists aging, and withstands petroleum and sun, as well as abrasion. Thick patches reinforce wear and chafing points. The neoprene-nylon ply is tremendously strong for its weight, and a boat made of it can take collision and grounding on rocks better than any other hull.

The secret to the serviceability of a quality inflatable is its low air pressure—only 2 or 3 pounds. It inflates quickly, but leaks, if any, are slow—usually very small breaks that are easy to repair. A good inflatable is made with at least three buoyancy chambers, any of which will keep the boat afloat.

In the bigger sizes, longer than 20 feet, these inflatables are extremely tough and rigid. Some models, rigged with twin outboard motors, are used for rescue work by the Coast Guard in coastal offshore waters.

Serviceability, almost no maintenance, and portability are the main reasons for the popularity of most of these inflatables.

The Sea Eagle 14 SR is a good example of a rugged inflatable capable of handling lakes, bays, or oceans. This 14-footer has a fiberglass-reinforced transom and plastic floorboards. With a capacity of 2,000 pounds, this model weighs 187 pounds. Sea Eagle sport/runabouts are also available in 10.6- and 12.6-foot models.

BOATS
FOR OUTDOOR
RECREATION

Section Two
BOATS FOR OUTDOOR RECREATION

• BOATS FOR FISHING, HUNTING, AND CAMPING •
• KAYAKS AND CANOES • PADDLEBOARDS •
• WATER SPORTS •

BOATS FOR FISHING

You'll catch more fish and enjoy it more if you suit your boat and motor combination to the type of fishing you do. A good rule is small boats for sheltered waters and big, beamy boats for big waters. But that is only the beginning. Most people want a boat that will handle more than one type of fishing, so they look for the best combination of qualities. If you analyze your needs and preferences and decide what is really important, you'll be able to select a boat-motor combination with confidence.

■ Boats for Sheltered Waters

Trout ponds, little bass lakes, and such are not called quiet waters because nothing happens there. They are truly quiet, and the noise you make there will be the loudest heard all day unless it's moose country. Therefore, it is sensible to use the quietest boat you can find. If you stay within the 12- to 14-foot range, the size of your shadow will be reduced, and boat action will be in scale with the surroundings. Inflatables, canoes, kayaks, and 12-foot cartop boats fit quiet waters perfectly. The new paddleboards rigged for fishing are also worth a look. You can launch these boats into the water soundlessly, with little more than a ripple. If you want to catch fish and keep the fishing good, make your outfit as simple as possible. Leave the outboard at home, bring only a paddle or pole, and be proud of your inexpensive rig. You've matched nature, and that is the sportsman's art.

For small rivers and streams, canoes, kayaks, lightweight johnboats, or cartop boats are time-honored choices and cannot be beat. They move easily against the current. Add a small outboard and you're in clover. The johnboat is probably more comfortable for two fishermen and gear when casting and moving for long hours, but a canoe or kayak will win you over with its easy movement, light weight, and silence. A length of 15 feet or more offers enough space for two fishermen.

When you fish lakes only a few miles across, many types of boats will do the job. First, observe the wave

Small aluminum boats in the 12- to 14-foot range are ideal for ponds, lakes, and rivers. In the 12-foot length, they can be cartoppers.

Bass Boats

The Nitro Z-8 is typical of the modern bass boat. This model is a 20-footer with a maximum horsepower rating of 250. In addition to electronics and a bow-mounted electric motor, it also has two 20-gallon livewells.

The Ranger RT188C is an 18-foot crappie/bass boat rated for 115 horsepower. Built with a 92-inch beam, this aluminum model has an all-fiberglass console and comes with a custom-fitted trailer. This model is also available in camo for waterfowl hunters.

The G3 Eagle Talon 17 PFX is an 18-foot bass boat with a 92-inch beam and a maximum 90-horsepower rating. The hull is welded aluminum. The boat features an extra-large 33-gallon livewell and a bow 10-gallon livewell for bait.

The Action Craft 19 ACE Flatsmaster is a classic flats boat designed for shallow-water fishing. It's a 19-footer and draws only 9 to 11 inches. This model is rated for a maximum of 200 horsepower. Ideal for flats and backcountry fishing, this Action Craft could double as a freshwater bass boat.

action, wind, and depth; then, take a good look at the boats commonly used there. They probably suit those conditions remarkably well.

If the surface is usually quiet, consider a boat that will give you platform space with shallow draft, such as the johnboat or pontoon boat. If your sport is fishing for bass and crappies in brush and weeds, look for a boat that is easy to push and pry loose; the canoe, kayak, or johnboat works well.

The most popular boat in America today may well be the bass boat. The phenomenal boom in this new breed is

well deserved because it fits the sport so well. The hull, developed on southern lakes, is a cross between the johnboat and tri-hull. Forrest L. Wood, founder of Ranger Boats, is credited with the creation of the first bass boat. It is very stable yet rises quickly to the top of the water and moves fast when you want to cross the lake. With its shallow draft, you can get in almost anywhere there is water that holds fish. The seats are designed for all-day fishing, rod holders are located where you want them—it's all thought out. The typical bass boat today is built of fiberglass or Kevlar or a combination of both materials.

These boats can range from 15 to 23 feet and can handle outboard motors up to 300 horsepower. The hulls are designed to handle almost any kind of water and speed. There are only two drawbacks: weight and price. Both are big. You'll also need a trailer for these rigs.

The favorite all-arounder, however, is the aluminum fishing boat. Successful makes are designed to adapt to the widest variety of conditions. With flotation built in, they are good in fairly rough water, are lightweight and easy to handle, can be stored anywhere, and certainly cost little for the service they give. You see them on all inland waters, whatever the area and fishing sport. They come in sizes from 12 feet up; probably the most serviceable length is 14 feet. A 10-horsepower outboard is the common power match, but they will take huskier motors if that's what you need.

For remote waters where the approach is on foot, check out inflatables. You can backpack in, and then inflate at the water's edge with a CO_2 cartridge or foot pump. Inflatables handle rather badly, but they are very stable, surprisingly tough, and a lot of fun. They can also handle small outboard motors and electrics. Other candidates for backwaters are canoes and kayaks, but most of those take two persons to tote.

■ Float-Trip Boats

Several schools of thought about boats for float trips are all cogent and tend to follow regional custom—not for custom's sake, but because water conditions vary considerably. A broad, fairly slow river without rapids will usually see shallow-draft boats that maneuver slowly but offer comfort and convenience in their broad-

Open boats are good equipment carriers for extended float trips. Some can even be rigged to carry a couple of kayaks for exploring backwaters.

beamed stability. Johnboats, large inflatables, pontoon boats, and river-style houseboats fit these conditions. Such boats have broad front ends that are inefficient in meeting waves or cutting much speed, but those aren't the needs. All you need is enough power to push a heavy bow wave upstream when you return. Knowing your stream, the weight and size of the boat will help you determine how much power you need.

For fast rivers with rapids and white water, the needs are more demanding. First, you need a hull that will withstand a lot of punishment; it must be built strong to survive bumping hard into rocks, logs, and gravel bottoms without damage. Flotation must be positive—sufficient to support the craft, occupants, and load if swamped. Maneuverability is very important, as is a bow design that will lift and throw off white water. Light weight is necessary so that portages will be easy. The choice is usually a canoe or kayak for rivers where narrow bends and fast water between rocks make maneuverability essential. Expert white-water canoeists and kayakers prefer craft under 15 feet, with round bottoms and no keel for quicker handling. However, since canoes and kayaks won't hold much, the choice for float trips is usually a bigger canoe with high ends. Kayaks are always an excellent choice when you will encounter some white water. Kayaks in the 12- to 14-foot range designed for fishing are more than adequate for float trips.

Inflatables are usually chosen for big, fast rivers. A big inflatable has great stability and is forgiving when you bounce it off banks and obstructions, and it's roomy enough to let you relax when the going is straight. But maneuvering a big inflatable is a real problem. Some experienced float men add a broad, shallow tiller for steering. On some rivers, this is essential. Don't plan on powering your boat on fast streams, but arrange for transport at the lower end of your float trip.

■ Offshore Outboard-Powered Boats

Perhaps the most versatile boats available are the center-console, deep-V boats. A deep bow permits them to handle the seas, but this slopes into a moderately flat mid and stern bottom that permits them to plane easily. This design is also very stable for its seaworthiness. These boats are best described as inshore-offshore boats, great for fishing coastal bays and reefs, for running the inlets, and for going offshore—weather permitting—into really big-water country.

It is increasingly common to see these boats, some of them powered with up to three and four outboard

▼ The Boston Whaler 345 Conquest is designed for offshore waters. The length is 34 feet with a beam of nearly 12 feet. The Conquest has a maximum horsepower rating of 900. The fuel capacity is 391 gallons. A big, comfortable cabin makes this a good choice when fishing in unpredictable ocean waters.

engines, running to far offshore canyon waters. Typical rigs are in the 28- to 42-foot range and are usually powered by twin 300- to 350-horsepower four-stroke outboard engines. Some boats, however, can range up to 45 feet with four 300-horsepower outboard engines for power. Some of these boats have beams exceeding 12 feet, weigh 24,000 pounds, and can carry about 500 gallons of fuel. Digital technology makes synchronizing revolutions per minute and trimming multiple outboard engines easy. With the right preparations, these boats are canyon ready.

▼ The World Cat 330, a catamaran-hulled offshore boat, will handle twin outboards totaling 600 horsepower. A 34-footer with a beam of nearly 11 feet, the hull is designed to cushion impact when running in a rough ocean. The fuel capacity is 300 gallons.

▼ The Ocean Master 27-foot Ocean Skiff is designed for offshore waters. The hull is built with a flaring-V form that softens aft for faster planing and is combined with high gunnels and a transom for a drier ride.

▲ The HydraSports 53 Sueños is a 53-foot center console with a 13-foot beam. The Sueños has no maximum horsepower rating and easily handles four 350-horsepower Yamaha motors. The tanks will hold 1,000 gallons of fuel and 100 gallons of fresh water. Built for offshore fishing in nearly all weather conditions, the Sueños has two 60-gallon livewells.

■ Boats for Open Waters

On big lakes, river estuaries, coastal bays, inlets, and inshore waters, size and seaworthiness are absolutely essential. The bigger the water, the greater the potential dangers—and the need for a capable hull that will bring you safely back through all weather yet serve you comfortably in routine use and help you catch more fish. Open waters are not the places for a flat-bottomed, 12-foot skiff. Look at what is being used. You will see deep-V bow points, rounded chines on smaller boats, probably with flat planing surface aft, and enough freeboard to keep dry when the wind comes up. If your waters commonly have a sharp chop, as in many Great Lakes locations, you will need more freeboard, and the hull shape should ride comfortably in those conditions. Too much freeboard can be a curse, however, making fish handling difficult and presenting a big profile to the wind, causing eternal drifting.

Fishermen who run out to the reefs on the Great Lakes to anchor and drop a line for perch want a boat that gives a comfortable seat for hours on end, riding the waves without slapping and shipping water. The sportsman who trolls for lake trout or coho salmon prefers a competent running boat that also provides a good platform for fighting and landing the fish, with a bow shape that will handle the waves when they rise, and that can move off fast to change locations and make the run home.

Calm days on open waters—and many big lakes a fraction of the size of the Great Lakes fit the case—are deceptive. The water looks calm when you start out in the morning. By noon, you are occupied with sunburn and poor fishing, so that when the wind and big waves come up at 3:00 p.m., you're taken by surprise. Getting back to shore can be dangerous if you are out in a 12- or 14-footer with a 10-horsepower motor. Think in terms of 16 feet or more in length, with plenty of beam in relation to length. For big inland lakes and coastal bays, you will need a motor of 25 horsepower and up. For trolling along inshore ocean beaches with these smaller boats, 16- to 21-footers, motors of 90 horsepower and up are necessary. If you plan to troll, choose a boat with a broad, clear stern for handling the lines. For casting, you should consider a boat that also provides a good casting platform both fore and aft.

■ The Sportfisherman

The sportfisherman is a well-designed fishing machine with all the comforts of home that can sail in nearly

The open cockpit and flying bridge on this Viking 92 sport-fisherman are designed for maximum fishing comfort and efficiency. At 92 feet, this Viking is capable of big-game fishing nearly anywhere in the world.

all kinds of weather and offshore seas. It is, indeed, a breed apart from all other fishing boats. Until you have handled a boat on the ocean, following fish on really big water, it's hard to imagine what is required of a boat in these conditions. Not only are these boats bigger (typically 35 to 90 feet), with deeper hulls and more beam, but they are built to take tremendous force. Big power is needed, as well as great reliability and fuel economy, and a frequent choice is twin diesels. For example, an 82-foot sportfisherman has a 22-foot beam and a fuel capacity of 3,000 gallons. Cockpit space measures a huge 255 square feet. This boat would likely be powered by twin diesel engines putting out more than 2,000 horsepower each.

Fortunately, there are more economical choices if a fisherman is interested in a sportfisherman. Much more common and affordable to serious bluewater fishermen are sportfisherman boats in the 38- to 54-foot range. Regardless of size, in any sportfisherman, layout and cockpit space is critical. Captains, mates, and fishermen must be able to handle the boat efficiently when baiting and hooking a big fish, so that it is not broken off or lost due to a slack line or pulled hook. With an inadequate boat or inept skipper, it can take hours to boat a good billfish. In that time, tackle and equipment break down, people have accidents brought about by fatigue, and the boat itself can be endangered.

The steering station, whether it is from the bridge or tuna tower, should give the captain a clear view of the cockpit and stern as well as forward. The cockpit should be clear of all equipment except the fighting chair and tackle with a clean and unobstructed transom. The sportfisherman should be built with engine hatches under the cabin floor for easy access. Several staterooms, a galley, air-conditioned salon, extensive electronics, a generator, bait wells, and refrigerated fish boxes are typical features on most sportfisherman models.

BOATS FOR HUNTING

Any boat is potentially a hunting boat. If you have a fishing boat, it will probably serve your hunting needs well. Every boat discussed in the previous section has been used successfully in hunting, even the big sportfisherman.

If hunting is your sole game, you may want a specialized boat, such as a duckboat. There are good reasons, however, for having a boat that will do several things well. If you must travel far on water to reach your hunting ground, you need outboard speed to save time. If you usually hunt in protected waters, you may still want to go to the big lakes or the shore to hunt. You may want to spend the night in your boat on some trips. You may like more than one kind of boat hunting—float hunting for deer, for small game, or waterfowling.

If you already own a good-size fishing boat and trailer, a good solution for the all-around hunter is to get an additional, specialized hunting boat. On the water, you can use the big boat to cover distance, then use it as your "lodge," where you make your meals, keep supplies, and bed down overnight. Towing the small hunting boat behind, you can hop in when you're ready to hunt and have a small, maneuverable boat that is quiet, easy to handle, and able to get in close and keep a low profile.

■ Float Hunting

Any of the flat-bottomed, low-sided boats, such as the johnboat, make practical float hunters. These boats have tremendous load-carrying capacities for their size, so that two hunters and their gear, including camping equipment and a tent, are no problem at all to fit. And I have seen two deer laid across the gunwales of a johnboat in addition to everything else, and there was still enough freeboard to run slowly back upstream to the car.

The stability and broad beams of these boats is another reason for their popularity with float hunters. You can stand to shoot with confidence, take a wide stance, and move around easily. Besides, bird dogs and

Tough aluminum johnboats with a shallow draft are ideal for waterfowl hunting. Johnboats can be camouflage painted, built into duck blinds, and can safely be dragged up on sandbars and gravel beaches. Most johnboats are also extremely stable.

retrievers like them, while they dislike tippy and confining boats.

The flat bottom is ideal for setting up the frame of a blind, and you can pop up a small aluminum-framed tent there for overnight shelter if you're in marshland. Waiting hour after hour in cold, cramped quarters is not the experience of hunters in a johnboat. There's plenty of room for sleeping bags and a heater to keep you warm.

Big inflatables are also popular with float hunters. They are comfortable to lounge around in while floating or waiting it out. But the flexible construction means that you should kneel or sit to shoot. A big plus is the light weight of an inflatable, making portages easy, and you can turn it over on shore for a blind, propping up one side for gunning while you stay in the shadow.

An outboard of 10 to 20 horsepower is suitable for either of these types. You have to be guided by the boat's size, the load you carry, the distance you have to motor upstream and the strength of the current, and, of course, the maximum-horsepower rating of the boat.

Important: Check out your state's hunting laws before you shoot from a boat. Some states require that you have the outboard tilted up and not operating when you shoot. Others will not permit shooting from a boat equipped with a motor.

■ Duckboats

Duckboats suit any hunting for shy game, especially in small hunting grounds such as tidal marshes, where you need something stealthy to succeed. Double-enders are the most popular: a small duckboat, canoe, or kayak. If you can, leave the motor at home and use paddles or oars; work around your base, and move your base often. If you need a motor to cover distance and reach fallen game before the current takes it, think of a really small outboard. An electric trolling motor is preferred by some hunters because it's quiet.

The decked-over double-ender will keep you dry and snug, but the limitation is tight space. There is room for only one hunter and little else. A classic example of this type of hunting boat is the Barnegat sneakbox, which was designed by Captain Hazelton Seaman in 1836 in West Creek, New Jersey. The sneakbox was designed for hunting waterfowl and marsh birds. Originally built with white cedar, it will float in 4 to 6 inches of water and can be sailed, rowed, poled, or sculled. There are a limited number of builders in the Barnegat area of New Jersey still building the sneakbox.

Canoes afford more space. If you use a canoe, treat yourself to detachable buoyant pontoons. This makes shooting more secure and the whole platform more relaxed. A well-made aluminum canoe is great for beaching in a marsh, and also for breaking through the thin sheet of ice in late fall. You would wreck a wooden or canvas canoe doing this unless you cover the ends with aluminum.

Take the trouble to paint your aluminum canoe before you go hunting. There's nothing more alarming to waterfowl than sun rays reflected from the mirrored finish of unpainted aluminum. Camouflage paint colors should be chosen to suit the seasonal color of your hunting grounds.

BOATS FOR CAMPING

Boat camping is a natural way to extend your enjoyment of fishing, hunting, and life in the outdoors. Instead of having to backtrack to your starting point toward the end of the day, just when things are going well, you can put ashore at the first suitable site if you are prepared for camping. If your boat is big enough, you can anchor and camp aboard. Still another version of boat camping is to trailer or cartop a boat to your base camp and extend your range from there by means of the boat.

For those whose primary pleasure is camping, a boat gets you away from crowded, metropolis-like campgrounds. Going camping by boat gives you a private preserve in the outdoors, brings you closer to unspoiled nature, and increases your alternatives for camping locations tenfold.

The Sun Tracker Fishin' Barge 20 DLX, a 20-foot pontoon boat, is a good choice for overnight fishing and camping on big lakes and bays. With an economical 40-horsepower four-stroke outboard, this pontoon boat can easily hold anglers and camping gear.

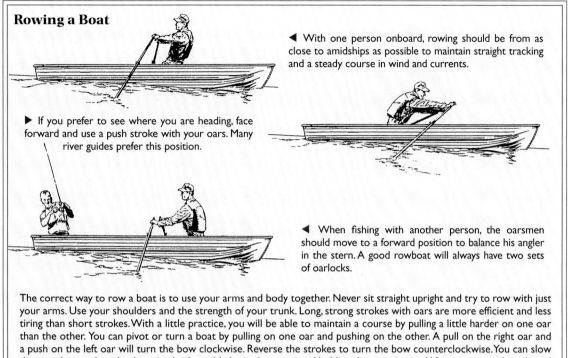

Rowing a Boat

◀ With one person onboard, rowing should be from as close to amidships as possible to maintain straight tracking and a steady course in wind and currents.

▶ If you prefer to see where you are heading, face forward and use a push stroke with your oars. Many river guides prefer this position.

◀ When fishing with another person, the oarsmen should move to a forward position to balance his angler in the stern. A good rowboat will always have two sets of oarlocks.

The correct way to row a boat is to use your arms and body together. Never sit straight upright and try to row with just your arms. Use your shoulders and the strength of your trunk. Long, strong strokes with oars are more efficient and less tiring than short strokes. With a little practice, you will be able to maintain a course by pulling a little harder on one oar than the other. You can pivot or turn a boat by pulling on one oar and pushing on the other. A pull on the right oar and a push on the left oar will turn the bow clockwise. Reverse the strokes to turn the bow counterclockwise. You can slow down and stop a boat by dropping both oar blades in the water and holding them stationary. When rowing with outboard power, tilt the engine up and keep the weight forward to reduce transom drag.

■ Camping with Small Boats

When you camp with a canoe, kayak, cartopper, inflatable, johnboat, or other really small boat, you can pack your supplies and tent or sleeping bags in the boat, travel through the wilderness on water, and then make your camp ashore. This style suits many lake chains and small rivers. With careful packing, there is room for your supplies and gear, two adults, or a couple and a small child in this size of boat.

When you plan your trip, make a list based on roughing it, with the minimum of equipment, only one change of clothing, backpack-style tents, concentrated and freeze-dried foods, and a streamlined fishing or hunting outfit. There is a distinct pleasure in traveling light, and as the experience progresses, you'll be glad to have discovered a simple way to camp. Portages will be light, and if you get a dunking the damage will not be irreparable.

A canoe for camping should be from 16 to 18 feet long. If you are going to camp on a lake, use a canoe with a keel. This will help you hold your course easily in a wind. With canoe ends slightly rockered, you can adjust course fairly easily even with a heavy load. For canoe camping on a river, avoid a canoe with much of a keel, and stick to the camping length. Loaded with gear, a canoe with a keel will catch rocks and snags too often for comfort. The camping length, as opposed to shorter white-water canoes, will keep handling easy. There is a lot in favor of using a small motor on a canoe for camping. In that case, choose a canoe with full rather than fine ends so the motor will not cause the ends to dig in.

Kayaks also make excellent boats for camping. Select a touring or expedition model with a sit-in cockpit. This design will allow you to store gear where it will be safe and dry. A 14-foot kayak might be adequate, but a 16- or 17-footer will give you more space for gear.

A cartop boat will increase your load capacity, and by using an outboard you will extend your range considerably compared to paddling or drifting. Don't forget that you will have to carry enough gas to make it between refueling points. Determine gas-pump locations in advance, and make sure you can get to them from the water's edge. Cartop fishing boats are ideal for light camping.

Inflatable boats are excellent for drift camping on a large river. Four passengers can camp with a 16-foot inflatable. An inflatable of this size can carry big loads, and the relatively wide beam makes it easy to load and stay aboard for long hours without getting cramped. At night, you can use an inflatable as a lean-to over your sleeping bags and avoid carrying a large tent.

A full-size johnboat of 16 feet or so is too big and heavy to cartop, but it's a good candidate for trailering or loading in the back of a truck with your gear already packed in the boat. The johnboat design is excellent for boat camping, as it can carry great loads for its size. Depending on the number of campers, you may prefer a smaller johnboat that can be cartopped. It's always easier to drive with your boat on top of your car than trailering it behind the vehicle.

Another option for on-water camping is a pontoon boat, which can be beached or anchored near shorelines. For a bigger group, a pontoon boat makes sense. Depending on the size, a tent can even be pitched on the deck and, with safety precautions, food can be cooked on a grill.

Family Runabouts

When a family with a new runabout gets over its novelty and has learned to water ski, going camping with the boat is an interesting next stage. This is an imaginative and ambitious way to use the family's recreational resources.

Since runabouts have more beam and weight capacity than a fishing boat or canoe of the same length, you are not quite so limited in the amount of gear and supplies aboard. Often there is enough space to do simple cooking and bed down. Runabouts from 16 to 19 feet suit camping best. You can use the runabout to go greater distances at faster speeds with its greater horsepower capacity. If the boat is not big enough to eat and sleep aboard, use its range to reach choice campsites with more variety.

A family boat of 18 or 19 feet is generally big enough for four passengers, if they are good organizers. Boats of this size have several advantages. You can travel on large, open waters such as the Great Lakes, large river estuaries, and the Inland Waterway, moving in close along shore on bad-weather days or to camp for the night, and also pass through fairly shallow places when

necessary. Many families enjoy camping vacations in the Florida Keys aboard large runabouts. These boats are a size that can be trailered at fair highway speeds, so that reaching a distant vacation area is not a big problem.

Many makers offer camper tops as options for family runabouts. These vary considerably in quality of materials, workmanship, and design. Shop with your eyes open when buying a runabout if you think you will use it for camping. A good camper top is made of high-grade nylon with double seams, double zippers, tough plastic windows, and nylon-mesh screening. Designs that have at least one large area with stand-up height are the most useful. A tight closure all around is usually achieved with a plastic rubber channel that presses together, and strong grommets and double-reinforced eyelets anchor the camper top to the boat. If you cannot get a camper top to suit you with the boat you want to buy, shop around for a good tent maker who will make the top to your specifications.

Optional camper built-ins are a good investment if they are efficiently designed and well made. Choose your gear and boat options carefully, such as a fold-up alcohol stove or a portable propane stove that stows out of the way in a side storage space under the gunwales. Deluxe double lounge seats with comfortable padding and vinyl covering are made to fold down to make a bed for one person. Removable seats can be lifted out to make more space on deck for sleeping bags.

Houseboats and Cruisers

Whether this should be called camping depends on your own point of view and how you go about it. If you want to camp, you'll do so, and some families are inveterate campers even in a 50-foot houseboat with automatic laundry and an electric stove. The lure of building a campfire ashore, and tenting along the way, is very attractive when you have a boat with shallow draft that can be beached. With a small houseboat or pontoon boat, camping is still a natural extension of what you can do with such a boat. Planning is more relaxed because you can keep more aboard. People who like camping in a travel trailer or motor home will find houseboats to their taste.

Houseboats and small cruisers are used extensively on big rivers, along the shores of the Great Lakes, and on other open waters where you can keep in touch with shore and duck in if the weather blows up. These hulls usually have fairly shallow drafts, so you have many options in where you go.

One pleasure with a houseboat or small cruiser is to nose up to a riverbank or anchor near shore, and then have a barbecue ashore, follow deer tracks, explore islands, or walk the beaches. You can tow a small dinghy or stow it on the cabin roof for fishing and going ashore. Some houseboats and cruisers carry a bicycle to run into towns along the way for groceries, laundry, and mail.

KAYAKS AND CANOES

A camper or a fisherman who has never used a canoe or kayak to reach backwater havens is missing a rare wilderness experience. These silent boats can take you deep into remote areas that are hardly ever reached by most people.

Most canoes in the 16- to 17-foot range will work fine. Aluminum canoes are noisy, but they are also tough. Some space-age canoes made of Kevlar or Royalex ABS material are so tough that they can take as much abuse as aluminum.

For most canoe camping and fishing, pick out a 17-footer. It will weigh 60 to 80 pounds and hold roughly 1,000 pounds of gear and people. Don't plan on putting more than two passengers in a canoe this size.

If you're new to canoeing, pick a model with a keel, which will make it easier to paddle in a straight line for long distances. White-water models that have no keel (or a very shallow keel) are designed for fast maneuverability and not suitable for cruising. A good cruising canoe

Tough Canoes

If your choice is a traditional canoe design and you expect to encounter rocky rivers and shorelines, an aluminum canoe might be a good choice. The most common damage to an aluminum canoe is a dent, but it's also the easiest to repair. If it's a large dent with no crease lines, there's a fair chance you can pop it back into shape by striking the center of the dent with your hand. Small dents may require a rubber mallet. Hold a block of wood against the hollow part of the dent, and then pound it out with the mallet.

should have a beam of at least 36 inches and a center depth of 12 to 14 inches. The beam should be carried well into the bow and stern, so it can carry the maximum amount of gear and food.

The Ocean Kayak Hands-Free model is motorized with a Minn Kota 36-pound thrust electric motor. It measures 14 feet and weighs 86 pounds with the motor.

Wood canoe paddles may look pretty, but you're better off with tough resilient fiberglass paddles. If you insist on wood, always carry a spare. For both the bow and stern paddler, pick a paddle that reaches between your chin and eyes.

The kayak is a direct descendant of the seagoing kayaks of the Eskimos of the Far North. The basic kayak is a slender, closed-decked craft with a body-fitting cockpit and a waterproof skirt that seals the hatch around the paddler, who feels that he is "wearing the boat."

A two-bladed paddle propels the boat and a small rudder at the stern assists in steering, making the kayak track straight, or holding the craft in position. The kayak is light, fast, and easy to handle in nearly all types of water.

Various models are designed for touring, fishing, white-water, and sea kayaking. White-water kayaks are nearly always single-cockpit crafts designed for high maneuverability and minimal effort in paddling upriver or downriver. White-water models are usually 13 to 15 feet long with beams of 23 inches or so. Skilled paddlers can run white water forward, backward, or even broadside in a kayak.

Touring kayaks, sometimes called expedition kayaks, are designed to carry one or two paddlers and range from 16 to 18 feet. Sea kayaks are bigger crafts with exceptional load capacities, as much as 900 pounds, and range from 18 to 22 feet in length with 30-inch beams. Some sea kayaks can accommodate three paddlers, and several manufacturers build collapsible and inflatable

Canoes and Kayaks

▲ The Freedom Hawk Pathfinder Kayak has multi-position 50-inch outriggers for fishermen who prefer to stand in their kayaks. The outriggers also provide greater stability in rough waters. This 14-footer weighs 79 pounds. It is a good choice for fly fishermen.

▲ The Ocean Kayak Tetra model is good for beginners. It's 10 feet, 8 inches long, and weighs 51 pounds. The polyethylene hull will hold a maximum load of 275 pounds.

▲ The Point 65 is a modular three-piece sit-in kayak design. The sections snap apart for easy storage or transportation. The sections snap together to form a 13½-foot kayak. Two-piece and four-piece models are also available. It is a good choice where storage space is a problem.

▲ L.L. Bean's Manatee Deluxe, a 10-foot sit-in kayak, weighs only 40 pounds and has a capacity of 275 pounds. The cockpit is oversized and roomy enough for paddlers to comfortably move around. It is ideal for ponds, lakes, and calm waters.

▶ The Old Town 169 is a durable family canoe from L.L. Bean. With a length of 16 feet, 9 inches, it's roomy enough for an overnight canoe trip. It will hold 1,400 pounds. Construction is three layers of polyethylene, and the weight is 85 pounds.

The Old Town Pedal-Driven Predator PDL offers hands-free kayak control with a through-hull pedal system and propeller. For fishermen, this means you have forward and reverse capability, which is essential for boat control and positioning in wind and current and over bottom structures.

kayaks for ease of storage for traveling kayakers. Some inflatables feature multi-chambered bodies and aluminum-frame reinforcements. One touring model for two paddlers measures 12 feet with a beam of 34 inches. It weighs only 37 pounds and has a capacity of 350 pounds. It will store into a package that measures 35 by 19 by 7 inches.

■ Paddling a Kayak

If you have paddled a canoe, paddling a kayak may come easier to you. The first mistake beginning kayakers make is that they spread their hands either too far apart or too close together. Either hand position will tire you out quickly. Gripping the double-paddled paddle, your hands should be no wider than your shoulders. Never grip the paddle tightly. Keep your hands a bit loose and your fingers slightly separated. Your knuckles should be pointing upward.

Basically, there are only four strokes that you will have to learn: forward stroke, sweep stroke to turn, draw stroke to move the kayak sideways, and reverse stroke to stop or move the kayak backward.

The forward stroke is simple. Put your paddle in the water to one side of the kayak and draw it past you, and then repeat the stroke on the other side of the kayak. The sweep stroke will turn your kayak. Put the paddle near your feet and sweep the blade in a wide arc toward the stern, turning the kayak. The draw stroke will move the kayak sideways. Place the paddle about 2 or 3 feet

from you, depending on your reach, and draw it toward you, moving your kayak sideways. The reverse stroke simply means you paddle backward, which will slow down or stop your kayak. These basic strokes sound simple, but it will take practice to do them all comfortably.

■ Fishing Kayaks

Almost any kayak can be used for fishing, but beginning around 2010, kayaks designed specifically for fishing literally stormed the outdoor market. Today, kayaks are used to fish all waters, from farm ponds to offshore waters for billfish. Kayaks can now take anglers into remote backwaters of fresh and salt water that were previously inaccessible.

There are at least a dozen kayak manufacturers producing models suitable for fishermen. First, a fisherman must decide whether he wants a sit-in or a sit-on model. Sit-in kayaks have a cockpit in which you sit, which is the traditional kayak design. Sit-on models have no cockpit, but are molded with exposed seat arrangements on top of the kayak, a design most fishermen seem to prefer. The sit-in models may be drier and warmer in some waters and allow you to keep more gear covered and dry, but the sit-on kayaks are easier to get on and off, an important factor for fishermen who also like to wade.

There are additional advantages to sit-on models. Some newcomers to kayaking harbor a fear of capsizing and getting trapped upside down underwater. If you capsize with a sit-on kayak, you simply roll the kayak over

Ins and Outs of Canoes

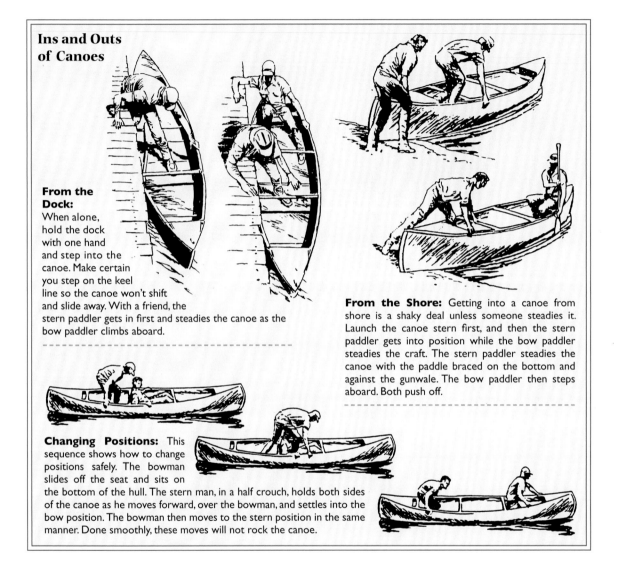

From the Dock: When alone, hold the dock with one hand and step into the canoe. Make certain you step on the keel line so the canoe won't shift and slide away. With a friend, the stern paddler gets in first and steadies the canoe as the bow paddler climbs aboard.

From the Shore: Getting into a canoe from shore is a shaky deal unless someone steadies it. Launch the canoe stern first, and then the stern paddler gets into position while the bow paddler steadies the craft. The stern paddler steadies the canoe with the paddle braced on the bottom and against the gunwale. The bow paddler then steps aboard. Both push off.

Changing Positions: This sequence shows how to change positions safely. The bowman slides off the seat and sits on the bottom of the hull. The stern man, in a half crouch, holds both sides of the canoe as he moves forward, over the bowman, and settles into the bow position. The bowman then moves to the stern position in the same manner. Done smoothly, these moves will not rock the canoe.

and climb back on. Sit-on kayaks are also more comfortable if you are big with long legs. Most sit-on models have watertight hatches, which make them a good choice for divers and photographers. Sit-on kayaks also tend to be more stable than the traditional sit-in models.

Good fishing kayaks should measure 12 to 14 feet with a beam of about 30 inches and weigh 60 to 80 pounds. Stability in a fishing kayak is a key factor. Those long, slender kayaks may be faster, but short, beamier models will be more stable and a better choice for fishing. For extra stability, some models offer removable outrig-

gers. The Old Town Loon series is a typical sit-in kayak designed for fishing. The Loon 106 is 12½ feet with a beam of 31 inches and weighs only 58 pounds. Multiple fishing features include a USB port for charging cell phones and GPS devices.

■ Ins and Outs of Canoes

The cardinal rule for sportsmen who use canoes is don't stand! Learn to cast, fight fish, and haul an anchor from a sitting position. Standing is one of the most common

Unswamping a Canoe

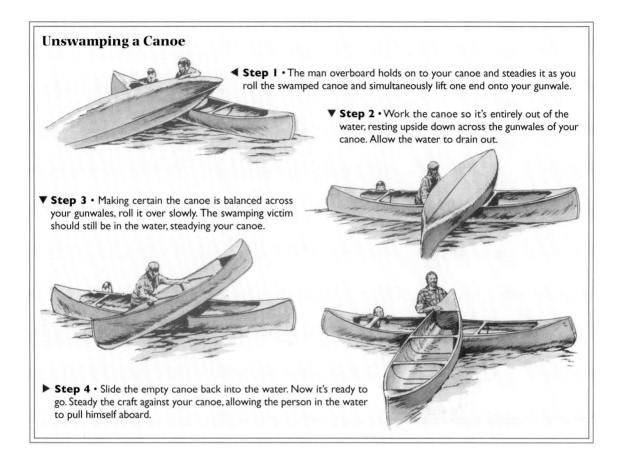

◄ **Step 1** • The man overboard holds on to your canoe and steadies it as you roll the swamped canoe and simultaneously lift one end onto your gunwale.

▼ **Step 2** • Work the canoe so it's entirely out of the water, resting upside down across the gunwales of your canoe. Allow the water to drain out.

▼ **Step 3** • Making certain the canoe is balanced across your gunwales, roll it over slowly. The swamping victim should still be in the water, steadying your canoe.

► **Step 4** • Slide the empty canoe back into the water. Now it's ready to go. Steady the craft against your canoe, allowing the person in the water to pull himself aboard.

causes of people falling out of, or capsizing, canoes. The second rule is never swim away from your canoe if you get dumped. Most canoes have enough flotation to keep afloat until help arrives. Never be afraid of your canoe. I did some testing several years ago and I was amazed at how difficult it was to intentionally capsize or tip a canoe over from a sitting position. Getting in and out of a canoe, however, can be tricky unless you follow some basic procedures (see illustrations opposite).

◼ Unswamping a Canoe

As mentioned, the most important rule in canoeing is don't stand! Standing is the most common cause of people falling out of canoes, but the rule is often violated by sportsmen who are casting, fighting fish, or hauling an anchor. Equally important if your canoe swamps is to never leave it to try to swim toward shore. Most modern canoes will keep you afloat, even when full of water.

In fact, you can sometimes paddle a swamped canoe to shore with only your hands.

If another canoe swamps, you can use your canoe as a rescue craft to get the swamped canoe back into service without having to beach it (see illustrations above).

What Size Canoe Paddle?

Here's the general rule on choosing a canoe paddle. The bow paddler needs a shorter paddle and typically uses more strokes. The bow paddler, standing, should select a paddle that reaches from the ground to the middle of his chest. The stern paddler, who is usually responsible for steering the canoe, needs a longer paddle and should choose one that reaches from the ground to his chin.

Sailboats

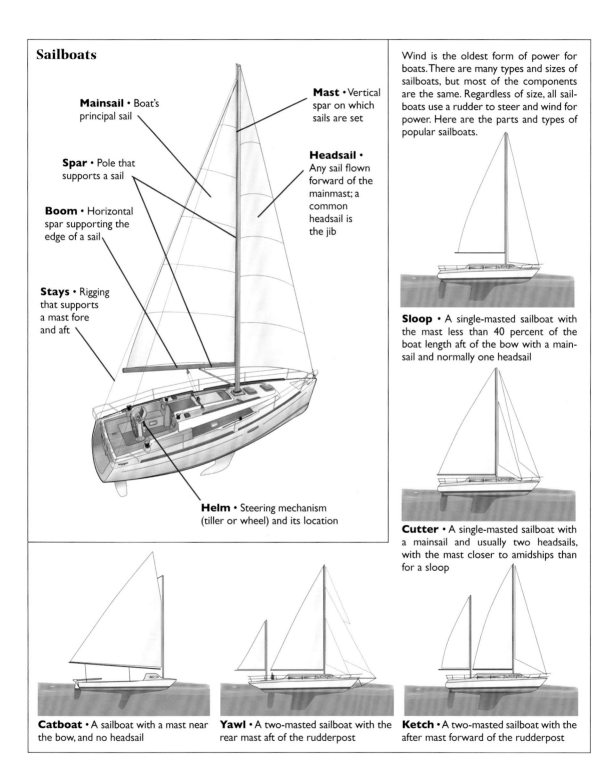

Mainsail • Boat's principal sail

Spar • Pole that supports a sail

Boom • Horizontal spar supporting the edge of a sail

Stays • Rigging that supports a mast fore and aft

Mast • Vertical spar on which sails are set

Headsail • Any sail flown forward of the mainmast; a common headsail is the jib

Helm • Steering mechanism (tiller or wheel) and its location

Wind is the oldest form of power for boats. There are many types and sizes of sailboats, but most of the components are the same. Regardless of size, all sailboats use a rudder to steer and wind for power. Here are the parts and types of popular sailboats.

Sloop • A single-masted sailboat with the mast less than 40 percent of the boat length aft of the bow with a mainsail and normally one headsail

Cutter • A single-masted sailboat with a mainsail and usually two headsails, with the mast closer to amidships than for a sloop

Catboat • A sailboat with a mast near the bow, and no headsail

Yawl • A two-masted sailboat with the rear mast aft of the rudderpost

Ketch • A two-masted sailboat with the after mast forward of the rudderpost

PADDLEBOARDS

Fishermen and campers who are interested in kayaks and canoes are also likely to be interested in paddleboarding, and this is especially true for shallow-water anglers. Paddleboarding is a water sport dating back to 1926, when some boards were made of redwood. The big comeback of paddleboarding started around 1996 and this water sport is still growing. Paddleboarders can lie down or kneel on a paddleboard, but standing has become the new norm. Most manufacturers recommend paddleboards that are 10 to 12 feet long with a fixed rudder and a weight capacity of about 250 pounds. The boards, which look like surfboards, are usually constructed of a polyethylene outer shell over a watertight polyurethane inner core. Paddles should be 8 to 10 inches taller than the paddler. Some paddles have an angle built in for better efficiency.

Most paddleboards are designed for use in calm or light surf conditions. As a beginner, you should start out by kneeling on the paddleboard first. When you feel comfortable with the balance and stability, place your hands on the sides of the paddleboard and try to stand up, placing your feet where your knees were. Falling is part of the learning process. If you fall, aim for the water on either side of the paddleboard. Never fall on the board, which could cause injury.

It didn't take long for fishermen, especially shallow-water anglers, to recognize the potential of paddleboards. With a paddleboard, anglers can reach waters that even kayaks and canoes have trouble navigating. Or maybe it's the simplicity of fishing from a paddleboard that attracts anglers. Several paddleboard manufacturers have also recognized the potential of a fishing paddleboard. BOTE offers the Ahab Classic, which is specially designed for fishermen. The Ahab is a 14-footer with a 34-inch beam. The construction is of EPS foam core with a fiberglass skin. Weighing 45 pounds, it has a maximum weight capacity of 500

BOTE's 14-foot Ahab is a paddleboard rigged for fishing with rod holders, a cooler, and two holes for push-pole anchoring. The Ahab has a load capacity of 500 pounds.

The Pelican Surge Stand-Up Paddleboard is 10 feet, 4 inches long, and weighs 33 pounds. It's made of a polyethylene outer shell over a polyurethane inner core. The EVA deck is skidproof. A removable fiberglass fin helps tracking.

pounds. This fishing paddleboard has a large, flat deck and is fitted with rod holders, a cooler, and two through holes for stakeout push poles.

The designers of the Ahab have obviously focused on shallow-water fishermen, particularly anglers who fish backcountry flats for bonefish, permit, trout, and similar species that inhabit the shallow waters of the southern states. During spring and summer in the

The BIC ACE-TEC Stand-Up Paddleboard is 11 feet, 6 inches long, and will support paddlers up to 260 pounds. The construction is multiple layers of styrene polymer and fiberglass with a foam core. It's designed for ponds, lakes, bays, and calm ocean waters.

northern states, fishermen may find paddleboarding an exciting way to fish back-bay waters and tidal flats for striped bass, flounder, weakfish, bluefish, and similar species. For freshwater anglers, a light and easily transported paddleboard allows easy access to small ponds and lakes for bass, trout, crappies, and panfish. Paddleboards even exceed the expectations of kayakers for the ability to reach those inaccessible waters. Paddleboards also average about 40 pounds in weight, which makes portaging to backwaters easy.

Backcountry anglers will find paddleboards can reach some waters that might be inaccessible to all other boats, including kayaks. Paddleboards also have the added advantage of allowing anglers to stand to cast, which may be difficult in some kayaks.

PERSONAL WATERCRAFT (JET SKIS)

All personal watercraft are officially considered powerboats by the U.S. Coast Guard. No matter how simple they are to ride, under the law, they have the same requirements for registration and regulation, and come under the same laws as other powerboats. Technically, personal watercraft are termed "Class A Inboard Boats" (boats less than 16 feet in length) by the U.S. Coast Guard.

What makes personal watercraft different from other boats on the water? The main difference is the innovative jet-drive propulsion system. With this drive system, a personal watercraft does not have an exposed propeller like most powerboats on the water today. Personal watercraft are smaller boats powered by an inboard engine and a jet-pump mechanism—but they are still boats. Their capabilities and limitations are a little bit different from other boats on the water. They can operate in shallower water and are quickly and easily maneuvered. They can accelerate quickly, but they may be more affected by waves, turbulence, and obstructions than larger craft.

There are several types of personal watercraft on the market. They vary in performance, stability, and the amount of skill necessary to operate them. Some are ridden in a sitting position, while others are ridden while kneeling or standing. Some have the capacity for one person, while others can carry up to three persons. One thing all personal watercraft have in common is that they are designed to allow the operator to fall safely overboard and reboard the boat with little risk if safety guidelines are followed. This reduced risk is because the jet-propulsion system in personal watercraft replaces the rudder and propeller on the outside of the hull.

The jet drive used in a personal watercraft is somewhat similar to the jet drive on modern aircraft. The unit is pushed through the water by the action of a jet pump driven by the engine. To give you an idea of how the jet drive in your personal watercraft works, think about a balloon. Just as the air exiting a released balloon pushes the balloon in the opposite direction around

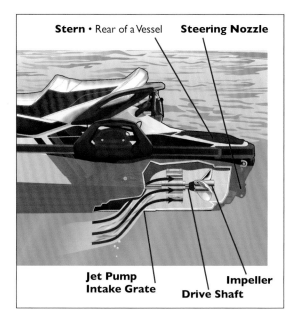

Stern · Rear of a Vessel   **Steering Nozzle**

Jet Pump Intake Grate   **Impeller**   **Drive Shaft**

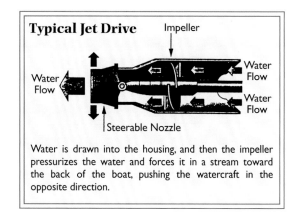

Typical Jet Drive   Impeller

Water Flow

Water Flow

Water Flow

Steerable Nozzle

Water is drawn into the housing, and then the impeller pressurizes the water and forces it in a stream toward the back of the boat, pushing the watercraft in the opposite direction.

the room, the water leaving the jet pump pushes the personal watercraft through the water.

The pump works by drawing water into the housing ahead of the impeller. The impeller (a type of precision propeller contained within the housing) pressurizes the water and forces it in a stream toward the back of the personal watercraft. The force of the exiting water pushes the boat in the opposite direction.

Although you will not have to worry about hurting yourself from an exposed propeller, there are some

precautions you should take with the jet pump on your personal watercraft:

- Keep your hands and feet, as well as hair and clothing, away from the pump intake.

- When checking the pump intake for possible obstructions, make sure the engine is off.

- Don't operate your boat in shallow water (less than 24 inches deep).

- Anything stirred up from the bottom, such as sand or vegetation, can be sucked into the jet pump and damage your personal watercraft, as well as possibly injuring someone if particles are expelled out of the pump.

Most personal watercraft have a steerable nozzle at the rear of the pump housing that is controlled by the

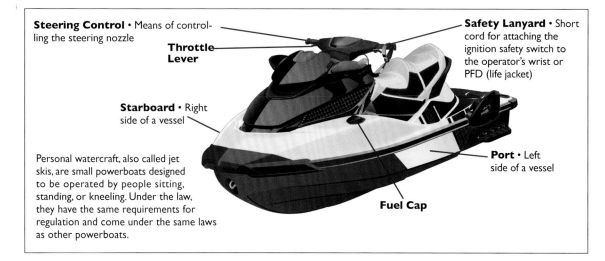

Steering Control · Means of controlling the steering nozzle

Throttle Lever

Safety Lanyard · Short cord for attaching the ignition safety switch to the operator's wrist or PFD (life jacket)

Starboard · Right side of a vessel

Port · Left side of a vessel

Fuel Cap

Personal watercraft, also called jet skis, are small powerboats designed to be operated by people sitting, standing, or kneeling. Under the law, they have the same requirements for regulation and come under the same laws as other powerboats.

When the steering control is turned right, the jet stream also turns to the right, pushing the back of the boat to the left, causing the craft to turn right.

handlebars. The steering control directs the stream of water to the left or right. When the steering control is turned to the right, the steerable nozzle also turns to the right. As throttle is applied, the force of the water stream, pointed right, then pushes the back of the boat to the left, which causes the craft to turn to the right.

For safety purposes, the most important thing to remember about steering is that you must have power to the pump in order to maintain steering control. If you allow the engine to return to idle or shut off during a turn, the craft will continue in the same direction as it was moving at the point the power was cut, regardless of the steering input from the operator. Reverse is available on some types of personal watercraft. This is accomplished by a clamshell-type device that moves over the directional nozzle and reverses the water flow, allowing the personal watercraft to "back up." This mechanism is not a brake and should not be regarded as such.

If you take a spill, most personal watercraft have one of the following options:

- The engine will run at idle speed while the boat circles slowly so that the operator can board as it circles past. It is important that the idling speed be properly set.

- An engine-stop lanyard is attached to the operator's wrist or personal flotation device and shuts off the engine when the operator falls off. For this reason, it is essential that the lanyard is always properly attached to the watercraft and the operator.

Swim to your personal watercraft, reboard carefully, reattach the lanyard (if applicable), restart your engine, and continue your ride. If the watercraft has turned upside down, follow the instructions in your owner's manual and turn the watercraft upright. If your personal watercraft has stalled or will not restart, do not attempt to swim to shore. Stay with your vessel and continue to wear your personal flotation device.

The Yamaha WaveRunner VX Deluxe will seat one to three persons. This WaveRunner weighs 681 pounds, has a fuel capacity of 18½ gallons, and is powered by a four-cylinder, four-stroke Yamaha engine. It is a good choice for a multiuse personal watercraft.

All personal watercraft (PWCs) are inboard-powered boats and fall under the same Coast Guard rules and regulations as other powerboats. In addition to recreational use, PWCs have proven effective in rescue operations.

WATER SPORTS

The world of water sports has come a long way since the days of old wood skis. Today's recreational equipment designed for water enthusiasts is far superior to what it was even a decade ago and it continues to improve every year. There seem to be no limits to innovative activities on the water. Today it is unusual to

The Triton 206 Allure is typical of newly designed multiuse boats for water sports and fishing. It's 20 feet, 6 inches, and handles outboard motors for 175 to 250 horsepower, plenty of power to pull water skiers and fast enough to get to fishing grounds.

spend a day on the water without seeing water skiers, wakeboarders, paddleboarders, tubers, jet skiers, windsurfers, and maybe even parasailers.

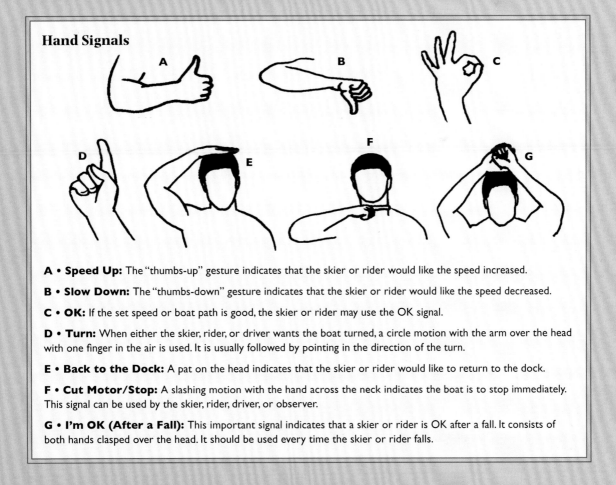

Hand Signals

A · Speed Up: The "thumbs-up" gesture indicates that the skier or rider would like the speed increased.

B · Slow Down: The "thumbs-down" gesture indicates that the skier or rider would like the speed decreased.

C · OK: If the set speed or boat path is good, the skier or rider may use the OK signal.

D · Turn: When either the skier, rider, or driver wants the boat turned, a circle motion with the arm over the head with one finger in the air is used. It is usually followed by pointing in the direction of the turn.

E · Back to the Dock: A pat on the head indicates that the skier or rider would like to return to the dock.

F · Cut Motor/Stop: A slashing motion with the hand across the neck indicates the boat is to stop immediately. This signal can be used by the skier, rider, driver, or observer.

G · I'm OK (After a Fall): This important signal indicates that a skier or rider is OK after a fall. It consists of both hands clasped over the head. It should be used every time the skier or rider falls.

Safety Codes for Water Skiing and Wakeboarding

Rule 1: Always wear flotation. A properly fitted personal flotation device (PFD) is designed to fit snugly so that it won't slip up on the body during a fall. The recommended type is a jacket or vest that covers the chest, abdomen, and back.

Rule 2: Always be sure your equipment is in good condition. Your personal safety and enjoyment depend on the equipment you use. Check your equipment regularly. Be sure that your skis or board do not have sharp or protruding surfaces that could cut or scrape the skier or rider. Check towropes for frayed areas or broken bridles and handles. Repair or replace damaged or unsafe articles.

Rule 3: Don't give the starting signal until ready. Make sure you are ready, the slack has been taken out of the rope, and you are clear of any dangerous obstacles around you. Keep your ski tips up.

Rule 4: Do not ski or ride near docks, pilings, other boats, or swimmers. Always look ahead and be sure you are aware of your surroundings and where you are going at all times. Many water ski and wakeboard injuries result from collisions with docks or other solid objects.

Rule 5: Never put any part of your body through the handle or wrap the line around yourself in any way.

Rule 6: Never ski or ride in shallow water or an area where there may be obstructions above or just beneath the surface.

Rule 7: When a fall is inevitable, try to fall backward or to either side. A forward fall increases the chances of contact with the ski or board.

Rule 8: Know and use the skier and rider hand signals. It is particularly important to use the "I'm OK" signal after a fall if you are all right.

Rule 9: If you fall in an area where there is other boat traffic, lift one ski or your board halfway out of the water. This will signal to other boats that there is a skier or rider in the water.

Rule 10: Never ski or ride to the point of excessive fatigue.

Rule 11: Always ski or ride during daylight, from sunrise to a half hour after sunset.

Rule 12: Never ski or ride directly in front of another boat.

Rule 13: Always use equal length ropes when skiing or riding double.

Rule 14: Always ensure that the motor is "off" when a skier or rider is entering and exiting the towboat.

Rule 15: Always have an observer in the towboat.

Improvements in boats have played a big role in these water sports. Outboard motors of 300 horsepower or more and specially designed multiple-use boats now have plenty of power to pull skiers and wakeboarders. Most of these sports, however, require a learning curve if they are to be done correctly and safely. It is with this water-sport growth in mind that we have, with the cooperation of USA Water Ski, the national governing body of organized water skiing and wakeboarding in the United States (www.usawaterski.org), produced this special section with clear and illustrated instructions on how to get started in water skiing, wakeboarding, and tubing.

Water Skiing

■ LEVEL ONE: GETTING STARTED

On land, demonstrate the seven skier hand signals (see previous page), placing feet in and adjusting bindings, holding the handle properly, proper body position for starting, and proper body position while skiing, and explain five of the 15 skier safety codes.

■ Placing and Adjusting Feet in Bindings

Make sure your feet are secured properly in the ski bindings and the proper adjustments are made (see above). Your feet should fit firmly in the bindings.

■ Proper Body Position for Starting

Demonstrate proper cannonball body position on land before entering the water to get the proper feel. Hold the handle and have a partner pull on the rope slightly to help pull you up. This will give you the feeling of being pulled up by the boat. While practicing this task, make sure your knees are together at all times, and stay in the cannonball position as shown. Let the boat do the work for you rather than trying to do the work yourself. ▼

■ Proper Body Position While Skiing

Initially remain in the chair position. This will ensure proper posture. You should have your arms straight, shoulders up, and knees flexible. Once comfortable, bring your hips underneath your shoulders. ▼

■ How to Properly Hold the Handle

For two skis, uses the knuckles grip; for one ski, use the baseball grip (with either hand up).

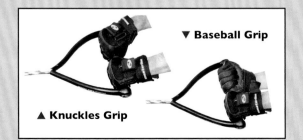

▼ Baseball Grip

▲ Knuckles Grip

■ LEVEL TWO: TWO-SKI STARTS ▲

Complete a deep-water start and maintain the proper two-ski body position for three seconds (above, right). To do so, place the rope and handle between your skis. When ready, signal the driver to begin accelerating. Let the boat slowly pull you up. Do NOT try to pull yourself out of the water by pulling in with your arms. When you feel the boat begin to pull you up, slowly rise to a sitting position using your legs. Once up, maintain the proper body position of arms straight, knees bent and flexible, and keep your head up, looking toward the boat. Practicing on land will speed the learning process (above, left).

■ LEVEL THREE: TWO-SKI BALANCE

Maintain proper two-ski body position for 20 seconds: head up, arms straight, and knees bent, and put some downward pressure on the handle. ▼

Suggested Towboat Speeds

Speeds are listed as a guide for the boat driver and will vary depending on the skier's experience and comfort level.

Approximate Weight of Skier	Less than 50 Pounds	50 to 100 Pounds	100 to 150 Pounds	150 to 180 Pounds	180 Pounds or More
Two-Ski Speeds	13 mph	16 mph	18 mph	21 mph	24 mph
One-Ski Speeds	16 mph	20 mph	24 mph	27 mph	32 mph

LEVEL FOUR: TWO-SKI STEERING

Steer back and forth in control inside the wakes. Initiate each turn by putting more pressure on the inside edge of the ski opposite to the direction you want to go. For example, to turn right, lean slightly to your right and away from the boat and apply more pressure on your left ski. Releasing pressure on one foot while placing pressure on the other foot will allow you to go in the direction you want to go. ▼

LEVEL FIVE: TWO-SKI WAKE CROSSING

Cross over to the outside of the boat wakes on one side only and return to the center of the wakes. Cross the wakes by turning both skis at a sharp angle to the wakes and bend your knees to absorb the shock. Crossing one ski at a time with not enough angle will result in a fall. Try to cross the wake at an angle. Turn toward the wake and keep pressure

on the ski closest to the boat (farthest away from the wake) until you are well over the wake. Trying to go over the wake slowly will also result in a fall. ▼

LEVEL SIX: TWO-SKI WAKE CROSSING

Leave the center of the boat wakes on one side and cross the wakes one time. The most common mistake for a skier is to pull on the handle while crossing the wakes. Keep your arms straight, and knees bent and together. Continue to maintain the proper body position.

LEVEL SEVEN: TWO-SKI WAKE CROSSING

Complete seven wake crossings in 60 seconds or less. Continue to emphasize proper body position.

LEVEL EIGHT: TWO-SKI, ONE-FOOT BALANCE

Inside the boat wakes, lift one ski clear of the water, and hold it in the air for five seconds. Shift all your

weight to one foot, then lift the opposite foot. Lift your knee to keep the tip of the ski from dragging in the water. Which foot are you most comfortable standing on? This will become your dominant foot that you'll put on the front of the slalom ski. If necessary, stand on both feet and have a partner give you a slight push from behind. Whichever foot you step with first is generally your dominant foot. ◄

■ LEVEL NINE: THE TRANSITION, TWO SKIS TO ONE

Inside the boat wakes, drop one ski and ride on the other for five seconds. Shift your weight to one foot and lift the heel of your other foot from the binding. Slowly move the ski back with your toes pointed down. The water will pull the ski away. When the ski is off, bring the free foot to the calf of your standing leg and move it down slowly until it is resting on the ski right behind your standing foot. Make sure you have an adjustable binding on the drop ski. Adjust this binding so you can lift the heel out easily. Place this ski on the less dominant foot. This will be the ski you kick off. Once you kick off the ski, continue to drag your toe in the water for a few seconds, and slowly slide your foot into the back binding. ▼

LEVEL TEN: ONE-SKI STEERING ▲

Steer back and forth in control inside the boat wakes. Initiate the turn by leaning slightly to the side and bringing the handle toward your hips to move in the direction you want to go. Before you attempt this maneuver, be sure to demonstrate the proper pulling position on land. You want your arms straight and hips to the handle. You should always lean with your shoulders to the side rather than back or forward. To initiate each turn, bring your hips to the handle while pointing the tip of the ski toward the wakes. Continue to maintain proper body position.

LEVEL ELEVEN: ONE-SKI, DEEP-WATER START ▼ ▶

Complete a one-ski, deep-water start. Bend the knee of your ski leg until it is touching your chest. Place the rope on the inside of the ski. Bend the knee of your free leg and use it as a stabilizer. As the boat begins pulling you, your shoulders should slowly move up and slightly back to keep your weight over the center of

the ski. To maintain your balance, drag your free leg and keep the tip of the ski in line with the boat. As you begin to rise, do NOT push the ski out from under your body. Let the water push the ski to you. Maintain the basic start position as the ski lifts you out of the water and stay low with your weight over the ski. Use your free foot as a stabilizer. Right-foot-forward skiers should have the rope on the left side of the ski and vice versa for left-foot-forward skiers. Some skiers have more control putting their back foot in the binding as well. This is based on comfort and control for the skier. Be sure to let the boat do the work of pulling you up.

■ LEVEL TWELVE: ONE-SKI WAKE CROSSING PART I

Cross over to the outside of the boat wakes on one side only and return to the center. Maintain proper body position. You should be well balanced and leaning to the side rather then back or forward. Make sure your shoulders are up with your hips close to the handle, and when you cross the wakes, use your knees to absorb the wakes. To initiate the turn, in order to prevent slack, turn the tip of the ski toward the wakes and slowly bring your hips toward the handle. ▼

■ LEVEL THIRTEEN: ONE-SKI WAKE CROSSING PART 2

Leave the center of the boat wakes on one side and cross both wakes and return to the center one time. Continue to emphasize proper body position and lean away from the boat. Make sure you're using (bending) your knees and not pulling on the rope (keeping your arms straight).

■ LEVEL FOURTEEN: ONE-SKI WAKE CROSSING PART 3

Leave the center of the boat wakes on one side and complete seven crossings of both boat wakes in 60 seconds or less.

■ LEVEL FIFTEEN: ONE-SKI WAKE CROSSING PART 4

Cross both boat wakes seven times in 45 seconds or less.

Wakeboarding

■ LEVEL ONE: GETTING STARTED

On land, demonstrate the seven rider hand signals and explain five of the 15 rider safety codes. (See boxes at the beginning of this section.)

■ Wakeboard Driving Tips

Driving for a beginner is a very important part of the wakeboarder's experience. The driver should begin with a slow, gentle pull and ease the rider out of the water. If the rider is having problems reaching a planing position, gradually accelerate the speed on the start.

Wakeboard Terms

- **Toeside:** Rider is edging in toward the wake with her weight on her toes.

- **Heelside:** Rider is edging in toward the wake with her weight on her heels.

- **Front and Backside:** On frontside spins, the rider rotates her front (or chest) toward the boat. On backside spins, the rider rotates her back toward the boat. Learn frontside spins first since they are easier. ▼

Toeside ▲
Heelside ▼

- **Switch Stance/Fakie/Revert:** These terms all mean the same thing (riding the board with the rider's opposite foot forward).

Once the rider is planing on the water surface, it is important to gradually back off on the throttle so that the boat does not obtain too much speed. Ease up to the desired speed once the rider is under control.

The most common mistake in pulling is accelerating too fast, which can result in the board sliding out from under the rider. When driving a beginner, slow the boat speed down slightly when the rider is learning to do surface turns. The slower boat speed will enable the wakeboard to slide easier on the surface of the water. Once the rider has mastered the surface turn, there is no need to adjust the boat speed.

If the rider appears to be out of control, cut back on the throttle to save him from a hard fall. For example, you may see a rider coming down from a jump over the wake and notice that his elbows are straight and the handle is far from his hips. Pull the throttle

back to the "in gear" position while he is still in the air. This will relieve some of the line tension in the rope and almost always save him from taking a hard fall.

■ Handle Position

A golden rule in wakeboarding is to keep the handle close to your hips whenever you are doing a trick. If the rider is just going along behind the boat, it is fine to have his elbows straight and the handle out, but whenever the rider wants to get air off the wake, it's important to teach him to bring the handle in toward his hips. When the rider starts his cut toward the wake, instruct him to bring the handle in slightly, and as he gets air off the wake, he should pull the handle in a little more toward his hips while he is in the air. That way if the rider lands a little off balance he can give some of the line tension back to the boat without getting pulled out in front of the board. Having the handle out and away from the hips on landings will always lead to hard falls.

■ Body Position

The key to wakeboarding is mastering the proper wakeboarding body position. It is a good idea to demonstrate this body position on dry land with your rider before entering the water. The proper wakeboarding body position is feet in a sideways stance to the boat; upper body twisted slightly toward the boat through the hips and shoulders; weight centered over the feet with slightly more weight on the rear foot; handle down and arms straight; and knees slightly bent with head up.

■ Suggested Towboat Speeds

Most riders will ride between 16 and 20 miles per hour, depending on the rider's size and weight. For beginners, a speed of 12 miles per hour for children and 18 miles per hour for adults is recommended.

■ LEVEL TWO: DEEP-WATER START

Complete a deep-water start and maintain the proper wakeboard position for three seconds.

■ Adjusting the Bindings ▼

Before getting on the water, remember that it is important to adjust the positioning of the binding. If you are right-foot forward, the term for this is goofy-foot. If you are left-foot forward, this is called regular stance. The location of the bindings should be shoulder width apart. The angle of the binding is also important. To

start, your feet should be at a slightly ducked angle and should always be symmetrical. A good rule of thumb if your board has measuring degrees on it would be 12 degrees for both feet. Be sure to check your screws before each set. Don't worry about which foot forward you are going to be; as you get up, the board is going to turn in the most natural position.

■ Getting up on a Wakeboard ▲

Try to relax in the water. Sit upright and the board will float out in front of you. You have three main points to remember: keep your arms straight, keep your knees bent, and let the boat do the work of pulling you out of the water (see above).

When the rope gets tight and the boat slowly accelerates, really focus on keeping your knees as bent

Avoid Fishing Boats

In addition to being a matter of courtesy, water skiers should avoid other boats, especially fishermen who may be trolling lines with lures. All fishing lures have hooks and a potential danger exists. The same applies to docks, pilings, buoys, and swimmers. Steer clear of these obstacles at all costs. Most ski accidents are the result of collisions with these objects.

as possible. You want to roll your heels down under your bottom while keeping your knees at your chest. This means that your board will go underwater a bit, but that is good as long as you stay balled up like a cannonball. Don't worry about turning your board sideways—that will happen later. Keep your feet, knees, and shoulders facing the boat. Look straight ahead (not at your feet) and remember the boat will pull you out of the water. Stay in the crouched position until the board rises completely out of the water.

Two common mistakes when learning to get up is trying to stand up too quickly or keeping the board in front of you and it plows too much water. If you bring your heels down and stay balled up (for longer than you think you need to), there should be very little resistance coming out of the water. Once you are on top of the water, stand up slowly, as if you are rising from a squat. Let the board rotate so one foot is ahead of the other. Your dominant foot usually will be the

rear foot. You will still keep your knees bent and your arms straight/relaxed.

■ LEVEL THREE: MAINTAIN PROPER WAKEBOARD POSITION FOR 20 SECONDS

Start with the board touching the water, raise the board off the water (minimum of 6 inches), and then lower the board to the water. Complete five controlled board lifts. Continue to maintain proper body position.

■ LEVEL FOUR: STEER BACK AND FORTH IN CONTROL INSIDE THE WAKES ▼

You obtain edge control of the wakeboard by rolling or applying pressure from edge to edge, placing weight on the heels or toes (see below). To edge the board, first slowly roll (pressure) the weight onto your heels. This will cause the board to angle in the water. By releasing the weight on the heels, the board will flatten out and ride straight. This motion is done slowly and slightly. Cutting toeside is generally harder. Face the direction you are trying to go and push your hips over your toes to move in that direction. Keep your handle still and low and don't pull in on the handle.

■ LEVEL FIVE: CROSS OVER TO THE OUTSIDE OF THE BOAT WAKES (HEELSIDE ONLY) AND RETURN TO THE CENTER OF THE WAKES

Roll your weight to your heels and turn your hips and shoulders toward the wakes. Keep your knees bent and the rope tight; carve a smooth, slow, easy

turn through the wake with the edge of the board. Make sure that you continue edging all the way across the wakes with your knees soft. Do not cut hard and then let up. This will cause slack in the rope and make the board ride flat, causing you to lose edge control (left). ◀

■ LEVEL SIX: LEAVE THE CENTER OF THE BOAT WAKES (TOESIDE ONLY) AND RETURN TO THE CENTER OF THE WAKES

Once you are outside the wake from your heelside carve, you are going to come back into the wake going toeside. As you approach the wake toeside, make sure that you put pressure on your toes while keeping your knees bent, arms straight, and handle down. Slowly and smoothly carve the board toward the wake. Make sure you keep your direction.

■ LEVEL SEVEN: COMPLETE SEVEN WAKE CROSSINGS ▼

Cross over the wakes seven times and remember to keep your knees bent and rope tight and low and stay in control of the board (see below).

■ LEVEL EIGHT: LEAVE THE CENTER OF THE BOAT WAKES ON TOESIDE, JUMP ONE WAKE HEELSIDE WITH THE BOARD CLEARING THE WATER, AND LAND IN THE CENTER OF THE WAKES

To jump the wakes, you must first start with the proper setup into the wake. Carve to the outside of the wake for a heelside jump, keeping the towrope tight and applying constant pressure on the edge or rail of the wakeboard. This is done by leaning against the tow-rope and boat with the whole body. Wait for the boat to start pulling back toward the center of the wakes. Start to angle the wakeboard toward the wakes and cut progressively, picking up speed as you approach the wake. This setup is called loading the line. Start with a smooth approach from only a few feet away from the wake. Keep the board pointed in the direction of travel.

With arms low and legs resisting, the wake will spring you up in the air. When landing the wake jump, you should keep your knees bent slightly and absorb the shock of landing with your knees. As you start to drop for the landing, take your back hand off the handle. This means if you are left-foot forward you will hang on with your left hand and let go with your right hand, and vice versa.

■ LEVEL NINE: FROM THE OPPOSITE SIDE (TOESIDE), JUMP ONE WAKE WITH THE BOARD CLEARING THE WATER AND LAND IN THE CENTER OF THE WAKES

Toeside will feel awkward at first and jumping this way is more difficult (left). It is not as natural as heelside. Put weight on the toeside of the board and use the same approach and landing as you did in the heelside wake jump. Make sure your whole body is facing the direction you are going. Lead with your front hip. This is the most important time to land with only one hand on the handle. Make sure that you really absorb the shock of the landing with your knees. ◄

■ LEVEL TEN: PERFORM A SURFACE 180

Slow the boat down to 10 to 15 miles per hour. This will allow the board to slide easier on the water. The easiest place to learn this trick is in between the wakes, right behind the boat. To initiate the surface

180, pull the handle and your rear hip together. This will slowly spin the board into the switch stance position. The turning of the wakeboard is a smooth and continuous motion (see above). Make sure you keep your knees bent and head up! ▲

■ LEVEL ELEVEN: PERFORM A SURFACE 180 FROM FAKIE TO FRONT

You are going to follow the same steps as in level ten. Bring your handle and back hip together. This should be done in a slow, controlled movement. Make sure you keep your knees bent and head up.

■ LEVEL TWELVE: PERFORM A ONE-WAKE HEELSIDE 180 ROTATION

Slow the boat down to 15 to 16 miles per hour when teaching this trick. Start 5 to 10 feet outside the wake and set a nice easy edge toward the wake. When you've reached the peak of your height, you will start to rotate the board 180 degrees, as you did in the surface 180, keeping the handle into your body and towrope tight. In the beginning, you only want to get approximately 6 inches of air. When landing in the fakie position, you want to keep your knees bent to act as shock absorbers and the handle at your hip. One of the most common errors is to start spinning too soon. Make sure you wait until you are off the wake completely to start turning the board (left). ◀

■ LEVEL THIRTEEN: PERFORM A ONE-WAKE FAKIE 180 (HALF CAB) ROTATION

Start 5 to 10 feet outside the wake and set a nice easy edge toward the wake. When you've reached the peak of your height, you will start to rotate the board 180 degrees, as you did in the surface 180, keeping the handle and your body and towrope tight. In the beginning, you only want to get approximately 6 inches of air. When landing in the regular position, you want to keep your knees bent to act as shock absorbers and the handle at your hip. To "jump" the wake, you need to push down on the board by extending your legs just before you hit the crest of the wake. This downward push will propel you into the air off the top of the wake. Remember to bend your knees again for the landing.

■ LEVEL FOURTEEN: LEAVE THE CENTER OF THE BOAT WAKES ON TOESIDE, JUMP BOTH WAKES HEELSIDE WITH THE BOARD CLEARING THE WATER, AND LAND ON THE OUTSIDE OF THE OPPOSITE WAKE

Start from the center of the wakes edging out toeside across the wakes (see below). This will put you in the position to cross both wakes heelside. Carve outside of the wake, allowing you to get a few feet from the wake. Start to angle the wakeboard toward the wakes and cut progressively, picking up speed as you approach the wake. Each time you attempt this, try to get farther and farther out to allow more momentum to cross boat wakes. Keep the board pointed in the direction of

travel. Remember to make sure you keep your knees bent and use them as shock absorbers. You may also want to shorten the rope at the beginning. As your jump gets stronger, you can lengthen the rope. ▼

■ LEVEL FIFTEEN: FROM THE OPPOSITE SIDE (TOESIDE), JUMP BOTH WAKES WITH THE BOARD CLEARING THE WATER, AND LAND ON THE OUTSIDE OF THE OPPOSITE WAKE

Put your weight on the toeside of the board and use the same approach and landing as you did in the heelside wake jump. The intensity of the cut must stay the same or get stronger the closer you get to the wake. Do NOT let up off your edge. Really absorb the shock of the landing with your knees. Make sure you land with only your front hand on the handle. You should take your back hand off as you start to drop from the peak of your jump.

Ski Aids for the Young Beginner

The EZ Ski trainer makes it easy and fun for young children to learn to water ski—it is easy to board, builds confidence, and there is no fighting with ropes or skis in the water. The EZ Ski trainer teaches basic skiing fundamentals: proper stance, balance, weight shift for turning, and handle position.

Steady the EZ Ski when the child climbs aboard. It is easy to board from the swim platform, when alongside the boat, or from the water. Pull the child across the water by hand to get him or her used to the

PFD Fit Is Critical

When you are putting a personal flotation device (PFD) on a child, make sure it is the right size and fits properly. If the PFD is too big and the fit is too loose, there is a risk of the child slipping through the PFD or the device sliding up on the body in the water. The PFD should always be secure before any ski lesson begins. In addition, children may not yet have developed the techniques to steer clear of obstacles. It is up to the ski boat driver and observer to avoid docks, buoys, and other obstacles that could present a danger of collision.

feeling of motion. Hold the rope in your hand—do NOT fasten it to the boat. Release the line in case of a fall. The child can sit or stand on the EZ Ski, whichever feels more comfortable. Slowly increase the speed up to 10 miles per hour (the maximum speed for the trainer). Slow down when crossing wakes and avoid sharp turns (left and below). ◀ ▼

Tubing

Riding in a tube can be a very positive experience for a young child and non-athletic older children, including teenagers. To ensure that the tube rider has a positive initial tubing experience, certain safety precautions must be observed. Drive a gently curving boat pattern at a speed of 10 to 15 miles per hour for young beginners. Do NOT use excessive speed or drive in an erratic pattern in an effort to throw the child off the tube. Excess speed is likely to scare a first-time rider and may cause injuries.

OUTFITTING YOUR BOAT

Section Three
OUTFITTING YOUR BOAT

• MARINE MOTORS • BOATING ELECTRONICS •
• ANCHORS, MOORINGS, AND ROPES • BOAT TRAILERS •
• PREPARING FOR WINTER STORAGE
AND SPRING LAUNCHING •

MARINE MOTORS

Naturally, your choice of power should be matched to the boat you select. Don't feel limited, however, to what you see already mounted. The great variety of motor designs and horsepower ratings available, and the versatility of these motors, give you options that boaters have never had before. You can customize your boat-motor rig precisely to your own preferences—if you inform yourself before you buy.

An offshore fishing boat up to 40 feet and longer, for instance, doesn't have to be powered by inboard engines. It's common now to see unusually seaworthy deep-V hulls in the 25- to 53-foot range heading offshore with two, three, or four outboard engines totaling up to 1,400 horsepower.

Similarly, a 14-foot bass boat doesn't necessarily "take" a 10-horsepower trolling motor; depending on the boat's power rating, you can mount a much bigger outboard for covering distance, plus a small electric trolling motor. And for that matter, you don't have to paddle your own canoe; a 2.5-horsepower gas or electric motor will do it for you handsomely.

The motor to buy is the one that you particularly want and that is safe and sensible for your use. Power your boat adequately, but take care not to overpower it. Check the Boating Industry Association (BIA) plate and the maker's specs for the recommended and maximum power rating for that boat.

■ Outboard

The outboard is a self-contained power unit that, happily, does not require through-hull fittings. It is lightweight in relation to the horsepower produced and it can be installed or removed quickly and inexpensively.

Mounted outside the boat, its fuel and vapor can be kept safely out of bilges and the cabin; deck space is clear of engine boxes or hatches. You have positive steering with outboard power—the whole motor turns, and the propeller thrust is in the direction that will help turn the boat, instead of at an angle to a rudder. The outboard tilts up for shallow running, beaching, or trailering. There are no underhull fittings that have to be protected at all costs.

A large outboard presents something of an obstacle to fishing lines, and the propeller, out from the hull, can be a hazard to divers and skiers. Mounted on the transom, the outboard is an unbalanced weight that is trimmed by adjusting the position of its thrust relative to the plane on which the boat is moving—but it can be trimmed, whereas an inboard-powered boat must have its load trimmed instead.

Trim is easy to understand if boaters remember that at normal running speeds the outboard propeller

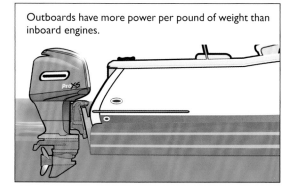

Outboards have more power per pound of weight than inboard engines.

Trimming In (Down)
- Lowers the bow
- Results in quicker planing, especially with a heavy load
- Improves the ride in choppy water
- Increases steering torque or pull to the right

Neutral Trimming
- Levels the bow
- Normally results in greater efficiency

Note that the propeller shaft, which connects the propeller to the drive shaft, is parallel to the surface of the water.

Trimming Out
- Lifts the bow
- Increases top speed
- Increases clearance in shallow waters
- Increases steering torque or pull to the left
- In excess, causes the boat to bounce

How Outboard Trim Affects Planing

Bow too low:
Trim outboard out

Bow too high:
Trim outboard in

Boat and outboard
properly trimmed

Porpoising

(Boat bottom at 3-degree angle to water)

Trim is easy to understand if you remember that at normal running speeds the outboard propeller shaft should be parallel to the surface. Some boats, however, obtain optimum planing attitude with the motor trimmed out slightly past this point. When trimmed out too far, the boat will not operate efficiently.

shaft should be parallel to the surface. Some boats, however, obtain optimum planing attitude with the motor trimmed out slightly past this point. When trimmed out too far, the boat will not operate efficiently. The bow may plane too high or too low.

Boaters should have their outboards "tucked" under (trimmed in) when starting. This forces the bow down and the stern up, and the boat pops up on plane much quicker. As the engine is trimmed out, the bow rises and more of the boat clears the surface. With reduced drag (less friction between the boat and water),

the boat gains speed. Once on plane at wide-open throttle, the outboard should be running in the middle of the recommended revolutions-per-minute range.

On bigger outboards, the power trim control button is on the end of the throttle control. With one finger, the boater can trim the engine for the best performance. The operator can easily adjust the engine for optimum boat attitude as boat load or water conditions change. Power trim improves acceleration and helps get a boat on plane quicker. It also means top-end speed advantages.

Outboard Motors

▶ The Lehr 2.5-horsepower outboard is fueled by a propane cylinder. Lehr also builds 5-, 9.9-, and 25-horsepower propane-powered outboards.

▶ The Mercury 2.5 horsepower is an economical four-stroke outboard and an ideal choice as a portable motor for dinghies, small boats, and inflatables.

▼ The Mercury Verado 250 horsepower is a six-cylinder, four-stroke outboard engine. Mercury's Verado series ranges from 175 to 350 horsepower. The 225- to 350-horsepower engines have six cylinders; the 175- to 200-horsepower engines have four cylinders.

▼ The Evinrude E-TEC G2 models range from 150 to 300 horsepower. No break-in period is required and the E-TEC G2 features push-button winterization. The engines also feature a variety of hood covers, including Mossy Oak camouflage and Ice Blue, which allow boaters to customize their vessels.

▶ This cutaway view of the Yamaha F350 four-stroke shows the internal compactness of a 350-horsepower outboard. The engine, a V8 with a 325.3-cubic-inch displacement, produces 350 horsepower at 5,500 revolutions per minute. The engine weight with a 30-inch shaft is 780 pounds.

▶ The Suzuki 9.9 horse-power is a two-cylinder, four-stroke outboard with an electric starting system. The weight is 95 pounds with a short shaft and 100 pounds with a long shaft. It is a good portable outboard for waters with horsepower limitations.

The Seven Marine 557-horse-power outboard V8 engine (right) has a 376-cubic-inch displace-ment, develops 5,400 revolutions per minute, and weighs 1,094 pounds. Seven Marine also makes a 627-horsepower outboard. These powerful outboards were designed to replace multiple outboard installations.

Outboard manufacturers now produce four-stroke engines up to 400 horsepower. One manufacturer, Seven Marine, has gone a step further and introduced 557- and 627-horsepower eight-cylinder outboards for boaters who would rather have one or two outboard engines on their boats rather than four. Surprisingly enough, some of these big outboards with V6 engines are more fuel efficient per horsepower than smaller motors. A 250-horsepower outboard, for example, burns less gas at cruising speed than twin 150s. Some manufacturers used to produce special outboard engines for saltwater use. Today, however, nearly all outboard motor manu-facturers build engines up to 350 horsepower that han-dle salt water and its corrosion problems.

■ Electrics

The small, silent electric trolling motor purred along unnoticed by all but the most devoted fishermen and hunters until a decade ago, when it took off. Why? Better

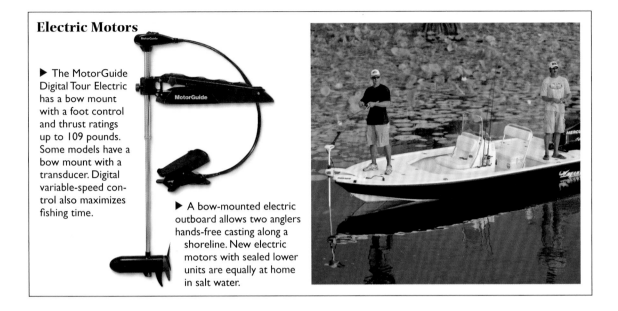

Electric Motors

▶ The MotorGuide Digital Tour Electric has a bow mount with a foot control and thrust ratings up to 109 pounds. Some models have a bow mount with a transducer. Digital variable-speed control also maximizes fishing time.

▶ A bow-mounted electric outboard allows two anglers hands-free casting along a shoreline. New electric motors with sealed lower units are equally at home in salt water.

designs have made electric motors more versatile, there are more models to match boats that people buy, and the new motors are more efficient—that is, they run longer on a battery charge. These motors are also slimmer, more powerful, saltwaterproof, and they pass through water and weeds with less resistance.

Because models and characteristics are changing rapidly, partly due to the developing popularity, a detailed discussion about how they work and what features are important is included here. All electrics are easy to start and operate. Endearing traits include low cost, light weight, and near-silent running. Electric is the ideal power for quiet waters, where silence and small movement are important to the careful fisherman and hunter.

Electric motors are powered with one of three systems. Motors listed as 12-volt models are powered with one 12-volt battery; 24-volt motors require two batteries; and 36-volt motors require three batteries. It's also best to use deep-cycle marine batteries. Obviously, the bigger electrics will provide more power (thrust) and will allow you to stay out on the water longer. Always use a model with a built-in battery gauge.

Nearly all electric motors are rated in pounds of thrust ranging from 8 to 109 pounds. If you have a 14-foot aluminum boat, motors with 30 to 40 pounds of thrust will be adequate. Bigger and heavier bass boats

and flats boats, however, might need 75 to 100 pounds of thrust to handle the weight and bigger waters.

The penalty of electric motors? Slow speed (about 3.5 miles per hour with a canoe and one man and gear, 2.5 miles per hour with a cartop boat), and the storage battery, which gives you about four hours of continuous trolling time on one charge. But it's unlikely that you'll ever run an electric continuously for that long. In the careful sport it suits, your electric will be turned off frequently, and with experience, you'll learn how to conserve a battery charge. If you are casting or staked out with decoys, it's not hard to get a full day's use from one battery with a full charge. Trolling is another matter; then, a second battery and your own battery charger are good investments.

How much current a motor draws, of course, determines how many hours of running time you can get on a battery charge. Several things affect this. First, always use a deep-cycle marine battery; some are specially designed for electric motors. Speed is also a big factor in current draw—electrics are most efficient at low speed settings. If your motor draws six amps to move your boat at 1.5 miles per hour, it might draw 16 to 18 amps to go 2.5 miles per hour. Also, some motors are designed with a higher speed range than others and will take more from your battery throughout the range. Most models house the motor in a pod underwater, connected to the propeller by direct drive. A sturdy control shaft from 20 to 50 inches long mounts to the boat's transom or bow, and the controls are located at the top. This motor position eliminates transmission gears, gives quieter operation, and leaves only the control head at the top to get in the way of action. Waterproof shaft seals and tough motor housings take care of the once-important problem of a wet motor resulting from hitting rocks and logs.

For regular use in water that is filled with weeds and obstructions, some boaters prefer electrics that have the motor on top of the shaft, with the tiller and controls attached to the motor housing.

The ultimate convenience is a remote foot-pedal control that's available with many top-of-the-line models. All remotes give you no-hands steering and an on-off motor. Depress the pedal and the motor goes. Roll the ball of your foot over the pedal and three switches can activate a servomotor on the shaft that will give you right, middle, or left "rudder." A variable-speed control, which comes with remote-controlled models, is realized to full advantage only if you can control it from a remote box placed on the seat beside you.

Remote controls radically change the weight and cost features of electrics, however. Weight is increased by two or three times; price is increased drastically. Plug-in remotes, which let you detach the controls from the mounted motor unit, keep it a manageable package to tote to the car. Remote digital controls are also available for some models, as well as GPS control systems.

Most electrics can be mounted on the transom, on either side of the boat, or at the bow. Canoes give you an even choice, but most boats handle best with the electric attached to the transom. It's hard to hold a true course when it's attached on a midship gunwale, and at the bow—unless you have a remote control—you have to sit in the most uncomfortable place in the boat in order to run it. Many experienced hands prefer bow mounting because they can see the direction of steering while looking ahead, and because this gives them more exact steering since the motor leads the boat. With a foot control, it also leaves both hands free for casting.

Other things to look for on electrics: Make sure the shaft length fits the freeboard of your boat, especially at the bow. The prop should be 6 inches down in the water for its best bite. Brackets and tilt-control hardware must be well designed, so that the unit does not wobble or shift. Also, it should permit you to swing or bring the motor inside the boat readily for moving out fast with your regular outboard power.

■ Inboard (Gasoline)

The typical inboard engine's similarity to an auto engine brought it to popularity and keeps it there. Inboard engine blocks are manufactured by car or truck engine makers, and then are converted to marine use. It is always possible to make repairs locally because it's the most common type of engine available.

The four-cycle inboard is heavier than a comparable outboard, requires permanent installation, and keeps fuel and vapor inside the boat. It also occupies a lot of space. But it's lighter on gas and oil, the lubricating oil system puts out less smog and takes less maintenance, and muffling and insulation can control its noise.

A major advantage is the inboard motor's location amidships, where the hull is capacious and weight is best handled. With a fixed, through-hull propeller shaft and separate rudder, however, an inboard installation presents rather delicate bottom gear that must always be protected. Since the shaft runs at a downward angle to clear the prop action, its thrust is less efficient, pushing at an upward angle.

The V drive helps to beat these drawbacks. It may also permit a lower engine location right against the stern, an advantage on some smaller inboard boats. Penn Yan boats, no longer in production, had improved this design with its tunnel drive section in the hull to protect the propeller. The Shamrock boat company features models with a pocket drive system in its hull. Another solution is the popular stern drive or inboard/outboard.

The first and last word about inboards is to the skipper: keep critical attention on good ventilation and fuel fixtures, and on the quality and condition of fuel lines.

■ Diesel

You'll see diesels now in many sport-fishing boats under 50 feet that could not have accommodated this heavy machinery years ago. Compact designs and lighter metals in the high-compression cylinder walls have put them in hearty competition with gasoline engines in some categories.

While the diesel burns only half as much fuel as its gasoline counterpart, the diesel doing the same job weighs a third more, and the initial cost is twice as much. But with a diesel, you can increase your cruising range with the same gallons, or reduce the fuel carried to save weight. Because this fuel is less volatile, you have a safer boat. On a still day, however, diesel exhaust odor

Diesel Engine

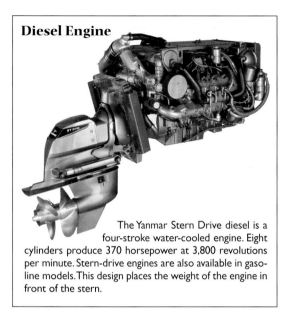

The Yanmar Stern Drive diesel is a four-stroke water-cooled engine. Eight cylinders produce 370 horsepower at 3,800 revolutions per minute. Stern-drive engines are also available in gasoline models. This design places the weight of the engine in front of the stern.

Stern-Drive Engine

The Mercury MerCruiser 4.3L stern-drive package shows typical stern-drive construction. These engines are typically water cooled.

will not be pleasant. This engine makes sense if you use your boat hundreds of hours each year for extended cruising, chartering, and chasing game fish.

■ Stern Drive

The stern drive, or inboard/outboard, as you might know it, is an inboard four-cycle engine mounted at the stern with an outboard drive. The propeller of a stern drive drives parallel with the boat, and the lower unit of the outdrive turns, giving positive prop steering as with an outboard motor. There is no separate rudder. A power lift is much favored, as is an automatic kickup release that may save the lower unit when it hits an obstacle.

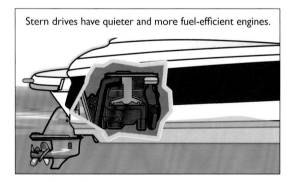

Stern drives have quieter and more fuel-efficient engines.

A stern drive is popular on smaller cruisers and open boats, for it is a compact inboard power arrangement that is feasible even where there is insufficient space for underdeck installation. The stern drive is a heavy machine to be located at the transom on small boats. It is a successful match with fast, deep-V hulls, for the point of the V helps to protect the propeller, and prop steering combines with the keel action of the V bottom to reduce sideslip in turns and maneuvers. It is more expensive than a straight inboard engine, but obviously more versatile. It is also the choice power for most racing boats.

■ Jet Drive

The jet drive is another exciting design that is a practical buy for some boaters. Water-jet propulsion is most efficient at high speeds, and it's an attractive choice for water skiers and personal watercraft (PWCs), also called jet skis.

Any inboard engine can be used with a jet pump. The engine is linked by direct drive to a high-speed impeller, and a water jet is forced out a nozzle to propel the boat. With the nozzle gate raised, the jet pushes the boat forward. With the gate down, the jet is deflected downward and forward to reverse the boat.

Jet boats used to spin out at high speeds. To improve directional stability, manufacturers have put a small

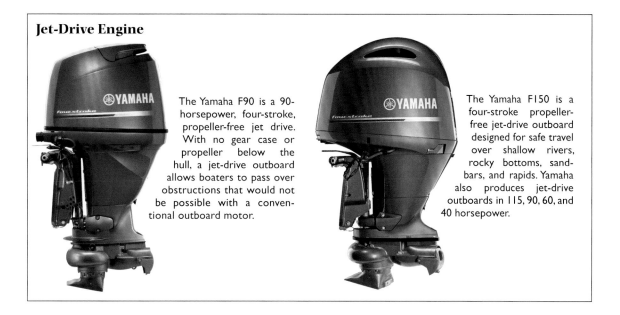

Jet-Drive Engine

The Yamaha F90 is a 90-horsepower, four-stroke, propeller-free jet drive. With no gear case or propeller below the hull, a jet-drive outboard allows boaters to pass over obstructions that would not be possible with a conventional outboard motor.

The Yamaha F150 is a four-stroke propeller-free jet-drive outboard designed for safe travel over shallow rivers, rocky bottoms, sandbars, and rapids. Yamaha also produces jet-drive outboards in 115, 90, 60, and 40 horsepower.

rudder under the jet nozzle and keels 1 inch deep on either side of the impeller screen on the boat's bottom.

Any jet intake can be clogged eventually by thick weeds, but the impeller shrugs off sand, and passes small gravel without harm. One innovation incorporates water-jet drives into conventional outboard fishing motors to permit operation in water too shallow for a prop. Initially, a jet-conversion unit had to be purchased, but now it's a standard propulsion system in most models. A crankshaft-driven impeller draws water through an intake grill, and the water is jetted rearward at high pressure, like the compressed air in a jet aircraft engine. When the motor is put in reverse, a cup swings over the jet stream, channeling it in the opposite direction. The throttle, shift, and, of course, steering are conventional.

There was a time when jet-drive outboard motors were limited in horsepower, but that has changed dramatically. Today some companies build outboard jet-drive engines ranging from 40 to 150 horsepower. These engines, particularly in Alaska, have revolutionized river and shallow-water fishing.

BOATING ELECTRONICS

Once you have selected your boat, you will need to rig it. And this means learning the basics of marine electronics. Basic electronic gear ensures the safety of your boat and passengers. A radio will summon help in case of an accident, and a depthsounder will help keep you out of trouble in unfamiliar waters. Once you've met the basic safety requirements, however, you'll quickly discover that electronics can be interesting and useful—whether cruising or fishing.

It's easy to pick out rod holders and similar accessories, but electronic equipment is a different story. If you make the wrong choice there, you could be out hundreds of dollars and stuck with something that doesn't perform as needed. Let's look at some of the electronics to consider.

■ Depthsounders

How does a sounder work? The word sonar is an acronym for SOund, NAvigation, and Ranging. It was developed during World War II as a means of tracking enemy submarines. With sonar, an electrical impulse is converted to a sound wave and transmitted into the

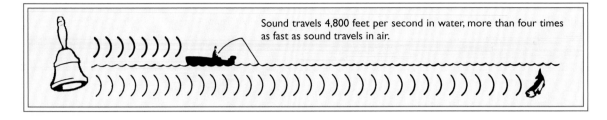

Sound travels 4,800 feet per second in water, more than four times as fast as sound travels in air.

water. When this sound wave strikes an obstacle, it rebounds. Sound transmitted through water travels at approximately 4,800 feet per second, compared with 1,100 feet per second through air. And since the speed of sound in water is a known constant, the time lapse between the transmitted signal and the received echo can be measured and the distance to the obstacle determined. An electronic sonar unit can both send and receive sound waves, as well as time, measure, and record them.

A depthsounder's transducer sends a high-frequency sound wave through the water. This sound wave is inaudible to fish as well as humans. When the echo returns, the transducer picks it up and reconverts it to electrical energy. The unit times the interval and puts a signal on the screen of your depthsounder. The signal identifies the distance between the transducer and the obstacle that returned the echo.

Some of the early depthsounders, rarely in use today, were called flashers and used a dial with a high-intensity neon bulb whiling at a constant speed. The biggest disadvantage of these early flashers was that they had no recording features. If a fisherman did not constantly monitor his flasher, he could pass over fish and not see them.

TYPES OF DEPTHSOUNDERS: There are three main types of depthsounders: paper chart recorder, liquid-crystal recorder, and video sonar.

- **The Paper Chart Recorder Depthsounder:** There are not many paper chart recorders in use today with recreational boaters. Sophisticated and affordable GPS chartplotters/depthsounders have pretty much taken over the recorder market. When a paper chart recorder is operating, an electronically regulated motor drives a lightweight belt at the edge of the recording paper. A stylus is attached to this belt. When the stylus is at the top of the paper, a small mark is burned onto the paper. This is called the zero mark, and represents the water surface. The stylus continues to move down the edge of the paper while the second pulse is traveling through the water. When an echo is detected, the stylus burns another mark

Depthsounders

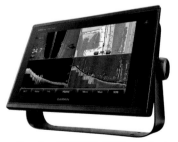

The Humminbird Helix 10 SI GPS combines a depthsounder that features side imaging with GPS capability on a 10.1-inch screen.

The Garmin GPSMAP 7600xsv Series is available with a 7-, 8-, 10-, or 12-inch screen. The unit features CHIRP sonar with down view and side view. It will read to depths of 1,000 feet and is preloaded with U.S. Coastal BlueChart maps.

The Lowrance HDS-12 Fishfinder/Chartplotter combines a multitouch 12-inch screen with CHIRP sonar, StructureScan HD, and wireless Bluetooth connectivity. The unit is 8.85 inches high and 13 inches wide.

on the paper. The depth of the object that reflected the echo can be read in feet by comparing its location on the paper to the depth scale printed on the paper.

The paper speed is controlled by a variable-speed motor. During one revolution of the stylus belt, a very narrow mark will be made by the flexible stylus, but the paper will move a small amount before the next revolution. Each mark will blend into the one before so that a composite "picture" of the target will be made, one tiny mark at a time.

- **The Liquid Crystal Recorder Depthsounder:** In principle, the liquid-crystal recorder, or graph, works like a paper recorder, except that these "paperless recorders" use liquid-crystal squares, called pixels, on a display screen. When an impulse or electronic signal is sent to the screen, it hits the liquid and turns it so the tiny square shows black on the screen. A continuing series of signals will literally draw a picture of the bottom or any object or fish between the bottom and the boat. Some of the latest liquid-crystal recorders, or graphs, have features that border on the amazing. Some have memories with playback. Others have a split screen that shows two segments of the water. Many units have down and side imaging features and optional fish alarms and water-temperature readouts.

  Some units, such as Humminbird's Helix Sonar/ GPS/Chartplotter series, are multifunctional, combining GPS depthsounding with down and side imaging capabilities. The unit is also available with 7-, 9-, 10-, and 12-inch screens. The bigger units, such as the Helix 12, let you see into the depths with CHIRP (Compressed High Impact Radar Pulse) technology. Simply put, CHIRP replaces time with frequencies. Garmin also has chartplotter/sonar units with the CHIRP features. Garmin's echoMAP CHIRP SV Series with 7- and 9-inch displays also features down and side imaging.

- **The Video-Sonar Depthsounder:** Instead of using chart paper or liquid-crystal squares, an underwater video sonar produces a sharp, clear black-and-white or color picture on a cathode ray tube (CRT) screen. The imaging principle is the same as that of a television picture. With color video sonar, the screen shows signal intensity by color difference, making it easier to distinguish individual fish from structures and the bottom. With black-and-white video sonar, the unit provides a constant view of the bottom, underwater structures, drop-offs, schools of fish, and even single fish in distinct, easy-to-identify shades of gray.

USES FOR DEPTHSOUNDERS: Though most fishermen believe the primary use for a depthsounder is to find fish, there are many other uses. Since a depthsounder tells depth accurately, it can be used for making contour maps of lakes, bays, saltwater areas, or large streams. It is useful in navigation because it warns you when you are approaching shallow water. It will find the deep holes in rivers. It is useful in salvage operations because it will accurately show a sunken boat on the bottom. It even tells what kind of bottom your boat is passing over. Divers use it to study the depths before descending.

It tells the depth of the water accurately, but since everything it reports is shown by signals on a screen, the amount it can tell is limited by your ability to interpret the signals. The more skillful you become at reading the signals, the more your depthsounder will tell you about the mysterious world beneath the surface.

■ Marine Radios

In times of serious boating emergencies, the ability to summon help quickly can make the difference between life and death. If you don't already own one, consider purchasing a Very High Frequency (VHF) marine radio. VHF radios have channels that are reserved for distress calls and are continuously monitored by the U.S. Coast Guard. You may legally use your VHF radio for distress, safety, operational, and public correspondence communications. Distress and safety communications include calls relating to danger to life and property, safety bulletins, weather warnings, and talking with other boats to avoid a collision.

If you have a life-threatening emergency, issue a MAYDAY signal on Channel 16 (the calling and distress channel). This is a call to ask for assistance if there is immediate danger to life or property. A MAYDAY call has priority over all other radio calls. Use a MAYDAY call only for life-threatening medical emergencies or if your boat is sinking or on fire.

If you hear a MAYDAY call, remain silent, listen, and write down the information being given by the boat in distress. If the U.S. Coast Guard or other rescue authority does not respond, try to reach the Coast Guard while traveling toward the boat. If you cannot reach the Coast Guard, try to assist the other boat to the best of your ability while not placing yourself or your passengers in danger.

Channel 16 is a calling and distress channel only. It is not to be used for conversation or radio checks. Penalties exist for misuse of a radio; hoax MAYDAY calls are felonies.

Marine Radios

◀ The Standard Horizon GX1300 Class D Radio is a VHF radio with DSC calling. It features GPS position display capacity and handles all U.S., international, and Canadian marine channels.

▶ The Uniden Atlantis 250 Handheld VHF radio will handle U.S., Canadian, and international channels, including 10 NOAA weather channels. This compact unit has a 10-hour battery life on a rechargeable NiMH battery pack. VHF handheld units are a must-have investment for all boaters.

▲ The Cobra MR F77W GPS Radio has a 30- by 56-millimeter LCD display with a GPS receiver with checker and alarm.

▶ The Standard Horizon HX300 Floating VHF has a power output of 1 or 5 watts and is submersible to 1.5 meters for 30 minutes. It also has an emergency strobe and is powered with a rechargeable lithium-ion battery. It's a good choice for small-boat owners.

Be aware that the distance of sending and receiving messages is limited by the height of the antenna and the power of the radio.

■ Global Positioning System (GPS)

The Global Positioning System (GPS) is a constellation of satellites that orbit the earth twice a day, transmitting precise time and position (latitude, longitude, and altitude) information. With a GPS receiver, users can determine their location anywhere on earth. Position and navigation information is vital to a broad range of professional and personal activities, including boating, fishing, surveying, aviation, vehicle tracking and navigation, and more.

The complete system consists of 24 satellites orbiting about 12,000 miles above the earth, and five ground stations to monitor and manage the satellite constellation. These satellites provide 24-hour-a-day coverage for both two- and three-dimensional positioning anywhere on earth.

Development of the GPS satellite navigation system began in the 1970s by the U.S. Department of Defense, which continues to manage the system to provide continuous, worldwide positioning and navigation data to U.S. military forces around the globe. However, GPS now has an even broader civilian and commercial application. The GPS signals are available to an unlimited number of users simultaneously.

HOW GPS WORKS: The basis of GPS technology is precise time and position information. Using atomic clocks (accurate to within one second every 70,000 years) and location data, each satellite continuously broadcasts the time and its position. A GPS receiver receives these signals to determine the user's position on earth.

By measuring the time interval between the transmission and the reception of a satellite signal, the GPS receiver calculates the distance between the user and each satellite. Using the distance measurements of at least three satellites in an algorithm computation, the GPS receiver arrives at an accurate position fix.

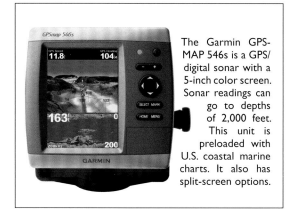

The Garmin GPS-MAP 546s is a GPS/digital sonar with a 5-inch color screen. Sonar readings can go to depths of 2,000 feet. This unit is preloaded with U.S. coastal marine charts. It also has split-screen options.

The position information in a GPS receiver may be displayed as longitude and latitude, military grid, or other system coordinates. Information must be received from three satellites in order to obtain two-dimensional (latitude and longitude) fixes, and from four satellites for three-dimensional (latitude, longitude, and altitude) positioning.

Newer GPS units are now also equipped with either Differential Global Positioning System (DGPS) or Wide Area Augmentation System (WAAS) capabilities, which simply means a fisherman can return to a fishing hot spot with 3-meter accuracy.

GPS receivers provide positioning, velocity, and navigation information for a variety of purposes. Anyone who needs to know the precise time or the exact location of people or objects will benefit from a GPS. In turn, this information can be used in charting and mapping, plotting a course, navigating from point to point, tracking vehicle movement, locating previously identified sites, or any number of similar functions.

GPS/PLOTTER/SOUNDER: GPS/plotters/sounders are the ultimate in boating electronics for recreational boaters and fishermen. These combination split-screen units allow you to chart courses, mark waypoints, and record fishing hot spots while giving you a detailed picture of the depth, bottom structures, and the fish under your boat. Newer models include both down and side imaging. With a GPS/plotter/sounder, you can return to a wreck or reef with an accuracy of 3 meters. These sophisticated units can cost several thousand dollars, depending on the features. They will help you find and catch fish, but bear in mind that GPS/plotter/sounders will also keep you and your boat safe in unfamiliar waters.

■ Radar

RADAR means RAdio Detection And Ranging. Basically, it's an electronic device that provides ranges and bearings as well as visual pictures of boats, planes, land, and so on. Radar is extremely valuable to boaters on the water in times of low visibility, such as fog and night.

Radar operates much the way a depthsounder does, except that the transmission is through air rather than water. A radar unit transmits pulses of super-high-frequency radio waves that are reflected by objects in the distance. The time it takes for the radio wave to go out and the echo to return is the measure of the distance to the object.

There are four components to a radar set:

1. The transmitter, which transmits radio waves in brief impulses.

2. The antenna, which radiates the impulses and collects the returning echoes.

3. The receiver, which picks up the returning echoes.

4. The screen, which produces a visual display of the objects in the path of the radar signals.

Makers of modern radar units for small boats have managed to combine these four components into two units: the transmitter and antenna in one unit, and the receiver and screen in another.

As with other marine electronics, stiff competition has driven down the price of radar. Radar, at one time, was found only on big private yachts or commercial vessels. Today, it is not uncommon to see radar on small

The Furuno Far-1518 is a radar unit with a range of 96 nautical miles with a 12-kilowatt output. Features include automatic clutter elimination and fast target tracking. After selecting a target, it takes only seconds for a speed and course vector to be displayed. With accurate tracking information, estimation of other vessels' course and speed is made easier. The screen size is 15 inches.

Avoiding a Collision

Whether you are cruising at sea or trolling on a bay or lake, when you see an approaching boat that remains constant in relation and bearing to your vessel but increases in size as it gets closer to you, you are on a dangerous collision course. You must either slow down or increase the speed of your boat to safely change course.

fishing boats in the 25-foot range. There's no doubt that radar can give you a much greater edge of safety.

■ EPIRB

EPIRBs (Emergency Position Indicating Radio Beacons) are electronic devices that transmit signals that can guide rescuers to your disabled boat. If you regularly go far offshore, especially beyond 20 miles or so, where you will be stretching the range of your Very High Frequency (VHF) radio, it's wise to carry an EPIRB. In an emergency, this device will transmit a continuous international distress signal on 406 megahertz (MHz). High-flying aircraft can pick up these signals as far away as 200 miles. More important, Coast Guard planes are equipped with automatic direction finders for EPIRB frequencies. EPIRBs are classified as Category 1 or Category 2. Category 1 EPIRBs are automatically activated when the unit hits the water and the signal can be detected anywhere in the world. Category 2 EPIRBs are similar to Category 1, except some models have to be manually activated. EPIRBs use a special lithium battery for long-term low consumption. EPIRBs must also be properly registered with the Federal Communications Commission (FCC) and Coast Guard.

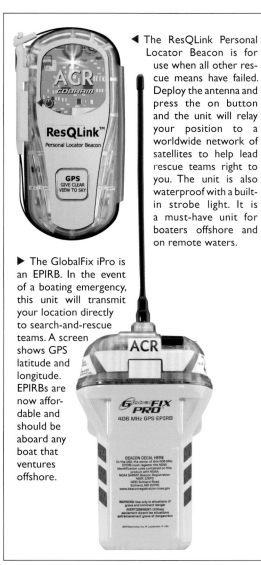

◄ The ResQLink Personal Locator Beacon is for use when all other rescue means have failed. Deploy the antenna and press the on button and the unit will relay your position to a worldwide network of satellites to help lead rescue teams right to you. The unit is also waterproof with a built-in strobe light. It is a must-have unit for boaters offshore and on remote waters.

► The GlobalFix iPro is an EPIRB. In the event of a boating emergency, this unit will transmit your location directly to search-and-rescue teams. A screen shows GPS latitude and longitude. EPIRBs are now affordable and should be aboard any boat that ventures offshore.

ANCHORS, MOORINGS, AND ROPES

An anchor is essential to safe boat operation, yet some boat liveries where small fishing boats are rented put their boats out without either an anchor or lines. When you know the importance of having an anchor, you will insist on having an effective one aboard even on a normally calm lake, and enough anchor line to give safe scope. In addition to safety, an anchor is necessary to hold position in a breeze or current when fishing and hunting. For a boater, a boat is half useless without a good anchor.

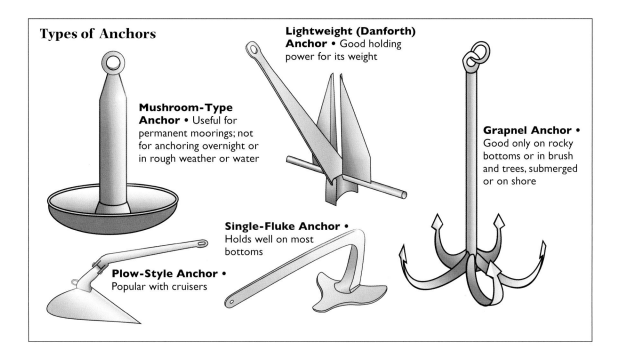

Types of Anchors

Mushroom-Type Anchor • Useful for permanent moorings; not for anchoring overnight or in rough weather or water

Lightweight (Danforth) Anchor • Good holding power for its weight

Grapnel Anchor • Good only on rocky bottoms or in brush and trees, submerged or on shore

Single-Fluke Anchor • Holds well on most bottoms

Plow-Style Anchor • Popular with cruisers

The major misconception about anchors is that the heavier the anchor, the more it will hold. This is not the case. The key is the meaning of hold. An anchor does not function by weighing down, but by holding on to the bottom effectively. A concrete block weighing 20 pounds may roll on a sloping bottom and slide on a hard bottom as the wind tugs at the boat. In the same situation, a Danforth anchor weighing only 3 pounds will probably hold the boat fast after kedging only several feet until its sharp flukes find a grip on the bottom.

Many small boats are equipped with mushroom-type anchors. These have a solid, weighty feel—even the small ones. Regardless of the direction in which they are

▶ If you fish in shallow water, you may never have to touch a rope or a muddy anchor again if you have a shallow-water anchoring system. These anchor systems, mounted on a boat's transom, can anchor your boat in waters up to 10 feet deep. Minn Kota's Talon Shallow Water Anchor is typical of these anchoring systems. Powered by a boat's battery, an anchoring spike is slightly driven into the bottom. These anchors can be lowered by a dash or foot switch. Protected from saltwater corrosion, these shallow-water anchors are ideal for flats boats and freshwater lakes and ponds where deep water is rarely encountered.

Mushroom Anchor Weights

Length of Boat (feet)	Power (pounds)	Sail: Racing (pounds)	Sail: Cruising (pounds)
25	225	125	175
35	300	200	250
45	400	325	400
55	500	450	550

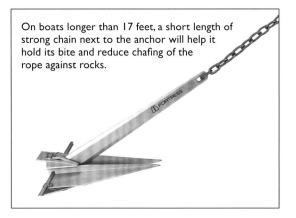

On boats longer than 17 feet, a short length of strong chain next to the anchor will help it hold its bite and reduce chafing of the rope against rocks.

pulled, the lip of the cup will drag in contact with the bottom and possibly hold. But when they hook a bottom snag or settle in mud, the weight of the cast-iron mushroom plus the weight of the bottom becomes a formidable load to haul up through the water.

A mushroom anchor may be adequate on a protected lake with a firm bottom, but on a fast-moving stream this anchor will be ineffective. On big open water, a concrete block or any other simple, heavy anchor can be a hazard. When the wind blows, the anchor will roll until the boat is in water deeper than the length of the anchor rope. The anchor then becomes a load on the bow, dipping deeper in the trough of waves than it should.

A number of anchor designs for pleasure boats have been developed that are effective by application rather than weight. One of the best is the Danforth. This anchor will hold on a hard bottom and can be retrieved on a rock-filled bottom. Most have trip features for releasing the anchor when it gets caught on the bottom.

Since anchor weight and size suitable for a boat of a given size vary widely according to the anchor design and to local conditions, no guidelines can be given that apply to all anchor types in common use. (Remember that concrete blocks and cans filled with concrete are among the most common small-boat anchors.) However, guidelines for mushroom-type and Danforth anchors are provided in the accompanying charts.

The length of the anchor line is an important factor in effective anchoring. In calm waters, twice the depth of the water is enough line. This assumes you are in the boat and can bring it easily to shore if a sudden storm comes up or your motor gives out. In open waters, your anchor line should be three to five times the depth of the water. For riding overnight or when the boat is unattended, you need seven times the depth. Obviously the reason is holding power. If the length of the line plus

Suggested Danforth Anchor Sizes

Length of Boat (feet)	Beam		Standard Sizes		Hi-Tensile Sizes		
	Sail	Power	Working	Storm	Lunch	Working	Storm
10	4	4	2½	4	Hook	5	5
20	6	6	8	13	—	5	12
25	6½	7	8	13	5	12	12
30	7	9	13	22	5	12	18
35	8	10	22	22	5	18	18
40	9	11	22	40	5	18	28
50	11	13	40	65	12	28	60
60	12	14	65	85	12	60	90

the anchor design permit the pull to be applied horizontally against the anchor's purchase on the bottom, it will help it to hold. On boats 17 feet and longer, a short length of strong chain next to the anchor will help it hold its bite and reduce chafing of the rope against rocks and the anchor itself.

The best way to free most anchors that are stuck in the bottom is by pulling straight up. If you find you cannot do this, try snubbing the line until it runs vertically down to the snagged anchor. Take a bit around the cleat to hold the line tight, and then rock the boat fore and aft, or let the wave action do this until the anchor is worked free. The force of the boat's motion is greater than the force you can apply by hand.

When anchoring on large or windy waters, check the direction of the wind and wave action before setting anchor. If you have a choice of anchoring on a lee or windward shore, choose the lee. Then your boat won't be blown or washed onto the rocks by morning. In a popular mooring place, set your anchor so that you have several boat lengths between you and any other craft. Then, if a storm arises, even the worst fury won't cause damage.

Some fishermen like to drag or tow their anchor when drift fishing in windy, deep waters. This is a hazard to the anchor and line, and the anchor must be fully hauled to start the motor again to regain the best position. You might prefer instead to store a sea anchor or two for this purpose. This is a canvas bucket that acts as a drag. It is attached with a halter to a light nylon line that can be hauled in easily.

▪ How to Set a Mooring

An anchored mooring is cheaper than a dock, and in many crowded public facilities it is the only choice. The authorities may stipulate the minimum mooring that is acceptable. You may want to improve on this, particularly if you have a valuable boat. In any case, remember that your boat might do damage if it drags its mooring or breaks loose—and the responsibility is yours.

On soft bottoms, heavy iron mushroom-type moorings are often used successfully. A chain is attached from the mooring anchor to a floating buoy, where the boat is tied, usually with a snap hook on a short line from the bow. Even a big mushroom mooring can be pulled through the mud if a really hard storm or hurricane blows, however, and it is for this occasional danger that you must prepare when setting a permanent mooring. A single mooring anchor assumes adequate scope on the

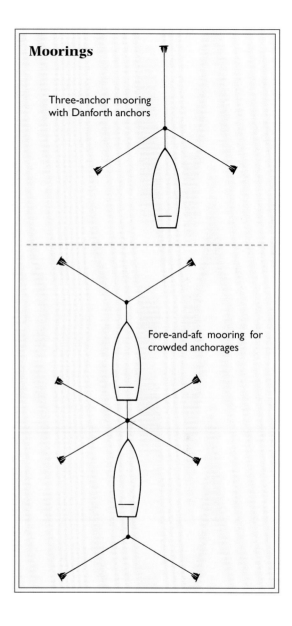

Moorings

Three-anchor mooring with Danforth anchors

Fore-and-aft mooring for crowded anchorages

line to hold in a blow, but scope of this length is impossible in crowded anchorages. Therefore, three anchors are sometimes used, set in an equilateral triangle with only one boat length of extra scope to the buoy (see accompanying illustrations). An alternative in the most crowded locations is fore-and-aft anchoring, with two anchors to each buoy, and each boat tied to the buoy both fore and aft of it.

BOAT KNOTS

Part of the fun of owning a boat is in learning and using boat knots. Many of the knots commonly used in boating are illustrated in Section Five: Fishing Basics for Boaters. Here are ways to make knots and splices needed for anchoring and mooring your boat.

■ SHORT SPLICE

This is the strongest of splices for joining ends of two pieces of rope, but it cannot be used to run through a pulley due to the bulk of the splice. This procedure also applies to splicing nylon and other synthetic ropes, but one additional full tuck should be used.

1 • Lash rope about 12 diameters from each end (A). Unlay the strands up to the lashings. Whip the strands to prevent untwisting and then put together as in illustration, alternating the strands from each end. Pull it up taut.

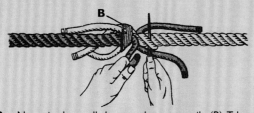

2 • Now, tie down all the strands temporarily (B). Take off the lashing from one side of the rope and raise one strand on this side, using a fid. Take the middle strand of the opposite side, and tuck it over one strand and under the raised strand. Pull it up taut.

3 • Tuck against the twist or "lay" of the rope. What happens is that the tuck goes over one strand, under the second, and out between the second and third.

4 • Roll the rope toward you. Pick up the second strand, and repeat the same operation. Then, do it again with the third strand. You have now made one full tuck.

5 • Take both lashings (which were applied in Steps 1 and 2) off the other side of the rope. Repeat the previous operations.

6 • To finish, cut off the ends of the strands, leaving about 1 or 2 inches protruding.

Note • To taper the splice, first make one more tuck just like the first one. Then, make the third tuck the same way, but first cut off one-third of the yarn from the strands. For the fourth tuck, cut off half of the remaining yarn. For the untapered short splice, you do not cut the strands. You just make three more tucks, exactly like the first one.

■ LONG SPLICE

This knot is slightly weaker than the short splice, but it allows the rope to run freely through a properly sized pulley and causes less wear at the point of splicing.

1 • Unlay the end of each rope about 15 turns and place the ropes together, alternating strands from each end as shown.

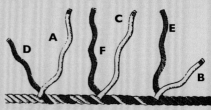

2 • Start with any opposite pair, unlay one strand, and replace it with a strand from the other part. Repeat the operation with another pair of strands in the opposite direction as shown.

3 • Now, tie each pair of opposing strands (see B and E) with an overhand knot, tuck each strand twice, as in the short splice, and then twice more. Or, halve each strand (see A and D) and tie with an overhand knot before tucking. With this latter method, a smaller splice results—but at a considerable sacrifice of strength.

4 • Roll and pound well before cutting the strands off close to the rope.

■ EYE OR SIDE SPLICE

The side splice is also called the eye splice because it is used to form an eye or loop in the end of a rope by splicing the end back into its own side.

▶ **1** • Start by seizing the working end of the rope. Unlay the three strands—A, B, and C—to the seizing and whip the end of each strand. Then, twist the rope slightly to open up strands D, E, and F of the standing part of the rope as shown.

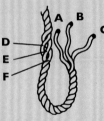

◀ **2** • The first tuck is shown. The middle strand is always tucked first, so strand B is tucked under strand E, the middle strand of the standing part.

▶ **3** • The second tuck is now made as shown. The left strand A of the working end is tucked under strand D, then passing over strand E.

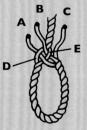

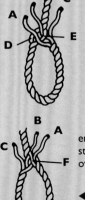

◀ **4** • This illustration shows how the third tuck is made. In order to make strand F easy to grab,

---

the rope is turned over. Strand C now appears on the left side.

▶ **5** • Strand C is then passed to the right of and tucked under strand F as shown. This completes the first round of tucks.

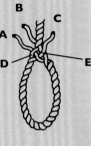

◀ **6** • This illustration shows the second round of tucks started, with the rope reversed again for ease in handling. Strand B is passed over strand D and tucked under the next strand to the left. Continue with strands A and C, tucking over one strand and then under one to the left. To complete the splice, tuck each strand in once more.

▶ **7** • The finished eye splice is shown. Remove the temporary seizing and cut off the strand ends, leaving at least ½ inch on each end. Roll the splice back and forth under your foot to even up and smooth out the strands.

■ FIGURE-EIGHT KNOT

This knot can be tied simply and quickly. Used in the end of a rope to temporarily prevent the strands from unlaying, it does not jam as easily as the overhand knot and is therefore useful in preventing the end of a rope from slipping through a block or an eye.

■ BOWLINE

The bowline is often used for temporary anchor knots. It never jams or slips if properly tied.

DOUBLE BOWLINE

Make an overhand loop with the end held toward you, exactly as in the ordinary bowline. The difference is that you pass the end through the loop twice—making two lower loops, A and B. The end is then passed behind the standing part and down through the first loop again as in the ordinary bowline. Pull tight. Used as a seat sling, the outside loop B goes under the person's arms, and the inside loop A forms the seat.

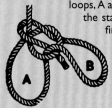

BOWLINE IN BIGHT

Here's a useful knot to know when you want to attach tackle to, say, the middle of a line when both ends of it are made fast. Grasp the rope where you want the new knot, shape it into a loop in one hand, and strike this against the two lines leading to the loop held in the other hand. Next, complete the first bight used in tying a regular bowline. Then, open up the loop after it has passed through the bight and bring the whole knot through it. Pull the loop tight over the standing part.

RUNNING BOWLINE

Tie the regular bowline around a loop of its own standing part. This makes an excellent slipknot, commonly used to retrieve spars, rigging, etc. And with lighter rope or twine, it's good for tightening to begin package tying.

SURGEON'S KNOT

This knot is usually tied with twine. It is a modified form of the reef knot, and the extra turn taken in the first tie prevents slipping before the knot is completed.

FISHERMAN'S BEND

An important knot because of its strength and simplicity, it is used for making the end of a rope fast to a ring, spar, or anchor, or for a line to a bucket. It is more secure when the end is tied as shown.

REEF KNOT

Probably the most useful and popular of all knots, this is also known as the square knot. Used to join two ropes or lines of the same size, it holds firmly and is easily untied.

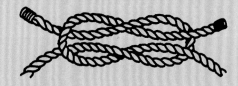

TIMBER HITCH

This knot is very useful for hoisting spars, boards, or logs. It is also handy for making a towline fast to a wet spar or timber. It holds without slipping and does not jam.

SHEET BEND

Used aboard a boat for joining small or medium-sized ropes, this knot is sometimes used for attaching the end of a rope to an eye splice.

FISHERMAN'S KNOT

This is probably the strongest known method of joining fine lines such as fishing lines. It is simple to tie and untie.

CLOVE HITCH

This is the most effective and quick way to tie a boat line to a mooring post. It can be tied in the middle or end of a rope, but it is apt to slip if tied at the end. To prevent slipping, make a half hitch in the end to the standing part.

TYING LINE TO A CLEAT

This is the correct method for tying line to a cleat. The half hitch that completes the fastening is taken with the free part of the line. The line can then be freed without taking up slack in the standing part.

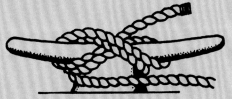

KNOTS FOR POLYPROPYLENE CORD

These are the knots to use for polypropylene cord.

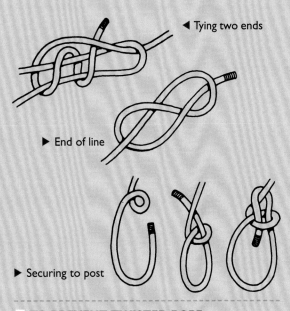

◀ Tying two ends

▶ End of line

▶ Securing to post

TO PREVENT TWISTED ROPE FROM UNRAVELING WHEN CUT

For nylon, polyester, and polypropylene, tape the rope around the circumference as shown. Cut in the middle, leaving tape intact on either side. When cutting these synthetic fibers with a pocketknife or scissors, fuse the cut ends by match flame to prevent untwisting. Tape is unnecessary if a "hot knife" is used. Heat will melt and fuse the cut ends.

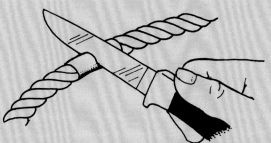

For manila and sisal, tape the rope as shown. Cut in the middle so that each end remains permanently taped. Natural fibers do not fuse with heat.

■ Anchor Lines and Strength

Synthetic fibers have produced ropes that are a blessing to boatmen. The new ropes are somewhat more expensive than manila, but they are stronger for their size, lighter, and more comfortable to handle. They also won't rot or mildew, and are easy to work with. One drawback is that they resist bite in tying; therefore, knots must be positive. Granny knots and loose knots are out.

Elasticity is always a factor to be considered when using any line for anchoring or tying a boat at a dock. Nylon rope is more than four times as elastic as manila

when loaded repeatedly; Dacron is about 50 percent more elastic than manila, but it is more sensitive than nylon to abrasion.

Nylon dock lines may be a blessing, but let them pile up and become kinked on a dock and they can be dangerous. Coiled dock lines not only look good, but your guests are also less apt to trip on them. After a fishing trip, I wet down my loose dock lines, which makes them easier to coil next to deck cleats. Once the lines dry out, they will stay in place neatly until your next trip.

Ropes: Minimum Tensile Strength (pounds)*

Circumference (inches)	Diameter (inches)	Ship Brand Manila	Yacht Manila	Linen Yacht	Nylon and Gold Line	Dacron	Poly-ethylene	Poly-propylene
9/16	3/16	450	525	600	1,100	1,050	690	1,050
3/4	1/4	600	688	1,020	1,850	1,750	1,150	1,700
1	5/16	1,000	1,190	1,520	2,850	2,650	1,730	2,450
1 1/8	3/8	1,350	1,590	2,090	4,000	3,600	2,400	3,400
1 1/4	7/16	1,750	1,930	2,700	5,500	4,800	3,260	4,300
1 1/2	1/2	2,650	2,920	3,500	7,100	6,100	4,050	5,300
1 3/4	9/16	3,450	3,800	4,350	8,350	7,400	5,000	6,400
2	5/8	4,400	4,840	5,150	10,500	9,000	6,050	7,600
2 1/4	3/4	5,400	5,940	7,100	14,200	12,500	9,000	10,000
2 3/4	7/8	7,700	8,450	9,400	19,000	16,000	12,000	13,000
3	1	9,000	9,900	12,000	24,600	20,000	15,000	16,500
3 1/2	1 1/8	12,000	13,200	—	34,000	21,500	18,500	19,500
3 3/4	1 1/4	13,500	14,850	—	38,000	24,500	21,000	22,000
4 1/2	1 1/2	18,500	—	—	55,000	36,000	29,000	31,500

*For the approximate average tensile strength, add 20 percent for Ship Brand, Yacht Manila, and Linen Yacht ropes.

Recommended Anchor Lines for Power Craft

	Anchor	Overall Length of Boat					
		Under 20 Feet	20–25 Feet	25–30 Feet	30–40 Feet	40–50 Feet	50–65 Feet
Length of anchor lines	Light	100 feet	100 feet	100 feet	125 feet	150 feet	180 feet
	Heavy		150 feet	180 feet	200 feet	250 feet	300 feet
Diameter if nylon	Light	3/8 inch	3/8 inch	1/2 inch	9/16 inch	3/4 inch	7/8 inch
	Heavy		1/2 inch	9/16 inch	3/4 inch	1 inch	1 1/8 inches
Diameter if first-class manila	Light	1/2 inch	1/2 inch	5/8 inch	3/4 inch	1 inch	1 1/4 inches
	Heavy		5/8 inch	3/4 inch	1 inch	1 3/8 inches	1 1/2 inches
Diameter if Plymouth bolt manila	Light	7/16 inch	7/16 inch	9/16 inch	5/8 inch	7/8 inch	1 inch
	Heavy		9/16 inch	5/8 inch	7/8 inch	1 1/8 inches	1 1/4 inches

Easy Anchor Retrieval

This simple and easy method of pulling up your anchor is a boon to bad backs and big boats. Learn this technique and the hard work is done by an inflated net ball, the kind usually found on commercial fishing boats. The only equipment you will need is a stainless-steel anchor ring, heavy-duty stainless snap, 5 or 6 feet of nylon, and the net ball. The accompanying illustration shows all of the elements of an anchor-retrieval system properly rigged. This anchor-retrieval rig is available at all marina stores. The accompanying chart shows the suggested ball sizes.

Ball	Anchor/Chain
NB-40	40 pounds
NB-50	75 pounds
NB-60	130 pounds
NB-75	240 pounds

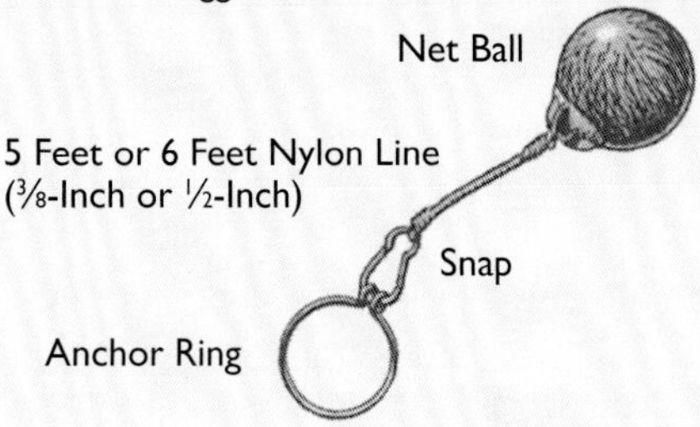

Net Ball

5 Feet or 6 Feet Nylon Line
(3/8-Inch or 1/2-Inch)

Snap

Anchor Ring

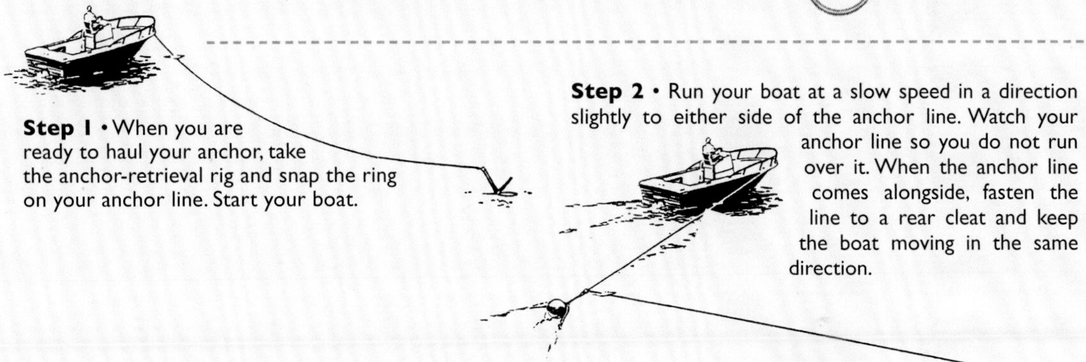

Step 1 • When you are ready to haul your anchor, take the anchor-retrieval rig and snap the ring on your anchor line. Start your boat.

Step 2 • Run your boat at a slow speed in a direction slightly to either side of the anchor line. Watch your anchor line so you do not run over it. When the anchor line comes alongside, fasten the line to a rear cleat and keep the boat moving in the same direction.

Step 3 • The net ball will slide down the anchor line and disappear. When it pops back up with the anchor, keep going to make sure the anchor ring rides all the way down the anchor chain to the blades. When you stop the boat, the net ball, anchor, and anchor line will be floating on the surface for an easy pickup.

BOAT TRAILERS

What size boat is trailerable? That is really a conundrum. The answer depends on how much you are willing to put into trailering. Each year's new-boat announcements include a large cabin cruiser with the claim ". . . and it can be trailered!" The fact is that it actually can be trailered, but it may be a professional transport job. You will need a heavy-duty, custom-built trailer, and should have a heavy-duty truck to make it go. And then it might do the boat no good. It's not a consumer proposition.

Common boat sizes for regular trailering are 14 to 26 feet. It is true that some 12-footers weigh more than 120 or 130 pounds, more weight than can be lifted to the top of a car by two persons. On the other end of the range, boats longer than 20 feet commonly have a deep bow, broad beam, and big weight that cause all sorts of problems in trailering. For a start, most state and all federal highways have a width limit of 8 feet; beyond that, you'll need a special permit and arrangements to travel.

If you are going to buy a boat in the prime size range for trailering, should you get a trailer at the same time? You will probably get a better fit for your boat if you do. The maker can supply information about trailer specifications for current-model hulls, and the dealer will probably carry trailers that suit.

But if you live near the water, why have a trailer? First, you save on mooring fees and winter storage. Second, your boat will be a much bigger asset if you can take it along on vacations, trailering it to another water when you want to fish and hunt or camp away from home. Keeping a boat on its trailer in your yard, you can keep bottom fouling cleaned off instead of facing a big job once or twice a year. Make it part of your routine when washing and waxing the car, and you will have a hull that is always in good shape. Keep a tarp over the boat and motor when it's idle on the trailer. When it sits in your own yard, there's no worry about vandalism at a mooring or a marina dock.

■ Choosing a Trailer

The best advice is to get a trailer one size bigger than your present boat requires. This will accommodate the occasional extra-heavy load you will pack in it. If you get a trailer larger than that, your boat will not be properly supported and the trailer will be awkward to tow, bouncing around because the boat is not heavy enough to hold it on the road.

Proper hull support is essential in a trailer. This is where the boat maker's advice is important. Three critical points are: full support at the transom, at the bottom forefoot, and at the construction center, either where the greatest weight is built in amidships or under the engine stringers in an inboard boat. You must avoid a trailer mismatch that will, over a period of time, cause the hull to hook or rocker. A well-engineered trailer for a boat of 500 pounds or more will have pairs of strong, securely set rollers on good bearings at frequent intervals for the entire bottom length.

Regardless of size, the trailer must enable you to back down to the water and launch your boat efficiently without getting the trailer-wheel hubs in the water. Winch quality is important for heavier boats. A wobbly or ill-fitting crank, wheel, and ratchet won't do. For a

boat of 1,500 pounds or more, you might consider adding an electric winch. It saves a lot of knuckle busting.

Trailer suspension, wheel mounts, and general construction should be spelled out by the trailer maker. Study these and get full information from the dealer about use and maintenance. Leaf springs are good on a heavy trailer; a soft ride is not important, while good support is. If you trailer 3,500 pounds or more, tandem wheels are needed.

You will have to look up state laws on trailers for your region, and then equip your trailer and the tow vehicle according to those laws. The laws specify over what weights trailer brakes are required, but you may decide you want brakes even if your trailer is below the limit. In that case, look into brakes that operate in tandem with your car's foot pedal. Quality trailer brakes are practically foolproof, make driving safer and easier, and they reduce wear on the tow vehicle's rear suspension and tires.

Insist on a frame-mounted hitch, even though the salesman may try to give you a shallow hitch bolted to the body pan when you buy that new wagon. As for bumper-mounted hitches, they are dangerous. With a frame-mounted hitch, you will be able to step up in weight over a big range without additional expense, and you'll be able to trailer your present boat without worry. You will need an umbilical electric hookup to your car's electrical system for trailer lights and brakes and other accessories. The cable, clamps, and plugs come in a package at a reasonable price. On your car you'll need western-type rearview mirrors—big, rectangular ones mounted on arms on each side that let you see around the trailer. For a trailer load of 3,000 pounds or more, you should have an equalizing hitch that compensates for a big load in normal travel and substantially reduces danger in a crash stop.

■ Loading Your Boat and Trailer

Most makers recommend loading with 5 to 7 percent more weight ahead of the trailer axle. This prevents fish-tailing and gives you good load control. If you are going on an extended trip with camping gear loaded inside the boat, watch the weight distribution. Weigh big items as they are loaded, and don't under any circumstances exceed the maker's maximum weight limit. Your trailer will be designed to haul your boat and motor with the correct load in front of the axle. Additional weight inside the boat should maintain this distribution, or the position of the boat on the trailer bed should be adjusted accordingly. A well-made trailer will let you do this.

The best advice is to get a trailer one size bigger than your boat requires. This will allow for the extra weight of the gear you pack in the boat.

■ Trailer Maintenance

Wheel bearings are the critical point. When traveling, stop every few hours to feel for excessive heat at the hubs. If the hubs are hot, let them cool off, and then drive slowly to the nearest service station and have them repack the wheel bearings. Have the bearings inspected before each trip, and have them repacked at the start of each season.

Keep the hitch and mount free of rust, repaint each season with metal paint on clean metal, and grease moving joints on an equalizing hitch only as the maker specifies. You'll find that a well-made boat trailer will last at least as long as the boat if it's well maintained. And you will be delighted when you learn how much extra gear you can take along in the boat.

■ On the Road and Launching

The U.S. Coast Guard makes the following recommendations for trailering a boat. Heeding their advice will ensure your safety on the road and also at the launch ramp.

UNDERWAY: Once underway, never forget that you have a boat behind you. This sounds foolish, but when you're wheeling along at highway speeds it is all too easy to lose a feel for the tow—until you have to pass, turn, or brake. Always start slowly, in low gear, and take the car up through the gears gently. Think twice about passing other vehicles—but if you decide to pass, don't delay. Be alert for signs restricting trailers. Remain sensitive to unusual sounds or handling factors, and if there's anything that seems at all strange, pull over immediately and check. In fact, you should pull over and check the entire rig every hour or so—check for high temperatures in the wheel bearings and slackening tie-downs,

and make sure the lights, tire pressure, and car-engine temperature are OK. Here are some other safety tips to keep in mind when towing a trailer:

- Never let anyone ride in the trailer while moving. It is dangerous, and illegal in many states.

Pre-Departure Checks

Make a complete check of the trailer and towing vehicle. Inspect tires for tread wear, inflation, and condition. Examine the hitch and associated safety devices, and check brakes on both vehicles.

- Check the tightness of the wheel lugs. Repeat this periodically during the trip.
- Equip the towing vehicle with large rearview mirrors on both sides. Check the inside rearview mirror. The boat and the load should be low enough so that it does not obstruct the view.
- Check shocks and springs on both vehicles.
- Load tools, emergency equipment, and foul-weather gear in a readily accessible location in the towing vehicle.
- Check the load on the trailer. It must be loaded correctly from front to rear, and from side to side for the best balance.
- Couple the trailer to the tow vehicle and observe the attitude of it. Check the trailer lights.
- Check the wheel bearings on the trailer.
- Check all tie-down straps.

- Observe speed limits. In many states, the speed limit for a car towing a trailer is lower than for a car traveling by itself.

- Maintain a greater following distance between your vehicle and the one in front of you. With the trailer, you need much more room to stop.

- When traveling over bumpy roads or crossing railroad tracks, slow down. Going too fast may cause the tow vehicle to bottom out and the hitch to scrape, causing damage to both the car and the trailer.

- Large trucks and buses create considerable turbulence, which may cause the trailer to fishtail. Keep a firm grip on the steering wheel and tension on the hitch ball. If there is a manual lever that will operate the trailer brakes separately from those on the car, a quick application of the trailer brakes may slow the trailer sufficiently to eliminate sway.

LAUNCHING: Launching will be the critical part of your trailer-boating expedition. It's embarrassing, as well as expensive, to safely travel many highway miles just to do something dumb at the moment of truth. Before going to the ramp, check with the marina operator or others to determine if there are any unusual hazards, such as a drop-off at the end of the ramp. You should prepare your boat for launching away from the ramp so that you don't hold up other boaters. This is known as "ramp courtesy." Preparations for launching should include raising the lower unit to avoid scraping, installing the drain plug, releasing the tie-downs, and disconnecting or removing the trailer's stop and directional lights.

When launching or recovering, never turn the car's engine off, and keep the parking brake set while you work the boat off the trailer. Only the driver should be in the towing vehicle during launching and recovering. One or two observers can help the driver watch the trailer and traffic. Keep everyone else away from the launching ramp. It is also prudent to use a tire stop to avoid an unexpected dunking of trailer and car.

Many trailer-boat owners' worst moments have occurred at busy launching ramps because they have not practiced backing their rig. Before you attempt a launching, you should put in a couple of hours in a deserted parking lot learning how to back your rig through a maze of cardboard boxes. A helpful hint when backing is to place your hand on the bottom of the steering wheel and move the wheel in the direction you want the trailer to go. Do **not** oversteer.

If you have an unwieldy trailer, you may want to get an auxiliary front bumper hitch, which will make close-quarters maneuvering much simpler, as well as keep the drive wheels of the towing vehicle on higher, drier ground.

Make sure you **never, ever** cast off all the lines from the boat before launching. Someone on shore must have a line that is made fast to the boat. The line makes it easy to shove the boat off the trailer and then pull the boat to a dock or boarding platform or back to the trailer at a wide, busy launching ramp. Above all, take the time necessary to launch safely, but as soon as the boat is afloat, move the vehicle and the trailer to the parking lot and the boat to the dock for loading. Don't loiter.

Always try to avoid getting the trailer hubs in the water. If you cannot avoid dunking them, at least let

When launching or recovering, never turn off the car's engine, and keep the parking brake set while you work the boat off the trailer.

them cool first. If you don't, the sudden cooling may crack or chip the bearings or suck them full of water. One way to pass the time, if you are a sailor, is to step the mast in the parking lot while waiting to launch. However, make sure that there are no low power lines or other overhead obstructions between you and the launching ramp. Unfortunately, a few boaters are electrocuted every year because their rigging comes in contact with overhead electrical wires.

BACKING A TRAILER: Backing a boat trailer down a tight, slick launch ramp can be tricky, and a busy ramp

Backing a Trailer

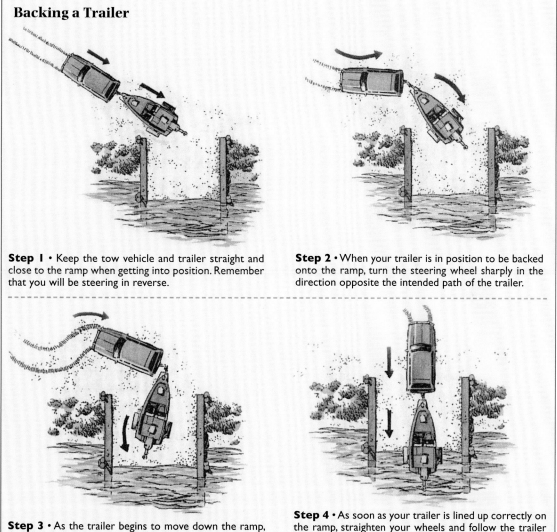

Step 1 • Keep the tow vehicle and trailer straight and close to the ramp when getting into position. Remember that you will be steering in reverse.

Step 2 • When your trailer is in position to be backed onto the ramp, turn the steering wheel sharply in the direction opposite the intended path of the trailer.

Step 3 • As the trailer begins to move down the ramp, start to turn your steering wheel to the left (as shown), which will push your trailer to the right. If possible, have a second person outside to assist you with hand signals.

Step 4 • As soon as your trailer is lined up correctly on the ramp, straighten your wheels and follow the trailer as you back it down the ramp for your launch. While waiting your turn on the ramp, watch other launchings to gauge the effects of wind and current.

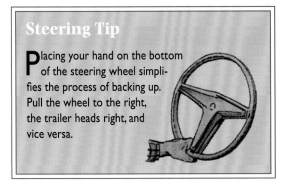

Steering Tip

Placing your hand on the bottom of the steering wheel simplifies the process of backing up. Pull the wheel to the right, the trailer heads right, and vice versa.

is not the place to learn. Practice in an empty parking lot on a Sunday morning. You'll be able to go at your own pace without an impatient audience.

When backing the trailer, keep in mind that you're pushing it, not pulling it. No big deal when you back straight up—you just have to keep the wheels of the tow vehicle perfectly straight. But when it's time to turn, everything is reversed: turning the steering wheel to the right will turn the rear end of the tow vehicle to the right, causing the trailer to turn left, and vice versa.

RETRIEVAL: Retrieving your boat is similar to launching and should be done with the same courtesy by reversing the procedures. Unload your boat at the dock and keep it there until the trailer is ready to move down the ramp. Move the boat to the trailer and raise the lower unit. Winch the boat on to the trailer and secure it. Finally, move the towing vehicle and trailer with the boat to the parking area for loading, housekeeping, and other general maintenance chores.

STORAGE: To prevent water from accumulating in the boat, remove the drain plug and tilt the trailer and the boat enough to allow drainage. This should be done for even short-term storage.

When storing the boat on its trailer for any length of time, get the weight off the wheels. Cinder blocks under the tongue and four corners of the frame of the trailer should be adequate support, shimmed up if necessary by boards. Once the trailer frame is jacked up, you should check to be sure that the boat itself is evenly supported. Be forewarned: the frame itself can easily be bent out of its normal shape by excessive jacking at a corner.

PREPARING FOR WINTER STORAGE

This work is necessary to keep your boat serviceable and to protect your investment in it. If you live where you can enjoy year-round boating, there are important semi-annual maintenance jobs that you will recognize. If you can store your boat at home, the job will be greatly simplified, but if you store it in a boatyard, you may have to work within the yard's schedule. In deciding whether to store your boat outside or in a heated garage, for instance, there are two dangers that must be avoided: formation of ice on the boat and continual dry heat. Small aluminum boats are affected less than wood, fiberglass, or fabric ones. Hard freezing and ice can pop fastenings, open seams, split and check the surface, and cause permanent warp in straight lines. If you still own a wood boat, dry heat for long periods can destroy the resins in woods (including wood stringers and fittings in all boats) and dry out caulking and seam compounds. If you store your boat outdoors in natural humidity conditions, keep it covered so that water cannot collect and form ice. Indoors or out, free ventilation is essential so that condensation

can evaporate. Here are the steps to preparing your boat for winter storage:

1. First, make sure your boat is properly cradled for storage. If you have a trailer that fits your boat, you have no problem. Level the trailer on chocks, wheels off the ground. If you own a small aluminum boat, it will store well turned facedown, resting on the strongly built gunwales. If you must build a cradle for a larger boat, make accurate templates and cut cradle supports for the transom, engine bed, construction center, and stem at least.

2. Clean the bottom and outside hull entirely of algae, fungi, and barnacles. This must be done immediately, before they harden and dry fast. At this time, you'll get a good look at the condition and know what repairs have to be made before spring launching.

3. Scrub down the entire boat inside, starting at the top. Flush and clean out bilges with bilge cleaner. Flush out freshwater tanks, fish and bait boxes, and fresh-

water lines with disinfectant solution and let them dry. Remove all traces of salt water, polish, clean, and spray with preservative.

4. Wash canvas tops, curtains, and rope lines with mild soap and rinse with fresh water. Spray with preservative before storing in a dry place. Whenever possible, have your boat entirely shrink wrapped for maximum protection. Make certain that several vent openings are in the shrink wrap to allow plenty of ventilation.

5. Treat serious rust at once. Clean down to the bare metal or remove and replace. Re-putty the fastenings, and spray fixed and moving hardware with light machine oil or WD-40.

6. Make sure every corner of the boat, every fitting and joint, is dry, clean, and free of fungi. Put desiccants wherever needed. Air the boat by opening all the hatches on a dry, bright day.

Follow motor-storage procedures in the owner's manual. Cover these points particularly:

I. Flush the cooling system with fresh water and a rust inhibitor, and then drain the system well.

2. Disconnect fuel lines and run idle until out of fuel.

3. Disconnect the battery, wipe the connectors and terminals clean, and then follow the maker's battery-storage procedures.

4. Clean the carburetor bowl with automotive carburetor cleaner or lacquer thinner. Slosh the cleaner fluid around in a portable gas tank and pour out through the fuel lines and drain it well. This removes the gummy substance left by fuel.

5. Remove the spark plugs with a spark-plug wrench, squirt lubricating oil into each cylinder, and then turn the crankshaft by hand to distribute the oil. Replace the spark plugs.

6. Leave the motor head and lower unit clean of heavy dirt, rust, and grease deposits. Wipe the head and lower unit with an oily cloth.

7. Make sure the lower unit grease reservoir is left full.

PREPARING FOR SPRING LAUNCHING

Most owners start too late, missing a month or two of good boating before they are ready to launch. Use the post-holiday season to do inside work you want to accomplish: build cabinets, a fish box, circulating baitwell, or do other basement or garage jobs. Keep your eye on the boat throughout the winter if it's stored outside. If the boat is stored at a marina, check the boat often head to foot. Make an estimate of jobs, tools, and materials you'll need. First, do the outside hull—everything it needs to give you a safe and trouble-free season. If you have a wood boat, the hull should be sanded down to clean, bare wood, whether you are restoring a few spots where needed or refinishing the complete hull. Peeling and cracking on top indicates trouble underneath. Down to bare wood, you may discover the source. Sand the wood smooth, fill in cracks and holes and over fastenings, replace damaged boards, and dust clean before starting to paint.

Proceed carefully until you know what to do. Get paint maker's recommendations and specifications for your hull. Polyester paints will give you an amazingly tough coat when properly applied, but you will probably do better with an epoxy-based paint over fiberglass. Talk to your dealer and other owners. If you want to paint an originally unpainted aluminum boat, get the boat maker's specifications; certain paints can't be used.

Before you paint a bare fiberglass hull or cabin, think twice. You will not be able to sand and strip as you would with a wood hull. To repaint, you have to leave the first coat of paint on or risk damaging the gel coat. Most owners for this reason try to bleach out discolorations and stains. Spots can be scoured and buffed. Ask for recommended materials at a marine store. Damaged spots can be patched with fiberglass. The best overall treatment is to wax well with a marine-grade wax and sail on. If you must paint, use steel wool, which will give tooth for the paint, and use paints recommended by the manufacturers. Any surface must be absolutely clean before repainting.

On cabin woods, spar varnish is usually used; it's tough and looks good. Whatever your choice, on high-wear areas that scuff and go bare quickly, use a good grade of marine spar varnish, preferably every season.

If you find mildew or water inside, note how they got in and repair the damage. Next fall, use more

The Unforgiving Ocean

I live in New Jersey, a state with multiple inlets and easy access to the ocean and offshore waters. We can fish bays and rivers with relative peace of mind. If your boat breaks down, you can simply drop anchor and wait for a tow or a friendly boater.

But all this changes the instant you clear an inlet. Then you are in the ocean and the rules change. A few years ago, we heard the terrible news that two 14-year-old boys were lost off the coast of Florida. They went offshore in a 19-footer, which was found capsized. The forecast was for stormy weather, which should have been enough for the boys not to venture offshore. When the Coast Guard discovered the boat, the outboard motor cover was missing. Did the boys capsize while trying to fix the engine? Did they have life jackets easily accessible? Was there a radio or an EPIRB onboard? We will never know.

The ocean is no place to prove you have more guts than brains. Spring is the time to make sure your boat is ready for all emergencies. PFDs should be clean and accessible. Before you leave the dock, always make your passengers try them on. It's difficult putting on and adjusting a PFD in the water. Non-swimmers and children should wear PFDs at all times. Make sure you have a good VHF radio, plenty of aerial flares, and orange smoke signals. A GPS is a must-have, and EPIRBs are now affordable and an essential piece of lifesaving equipment. A fully charged cell phone is fine inshore, but range is limited. Don't depend on it.

---

desiccants in some corners, buy a better tarp, or add weather stripping to your windows. Neutralize foul odors before you launch. It's easy; try the supermarket.

Flush out all freshwater systems again with disinfectant, fill the tanks, and turn on the pressure. A drip is a leak. Fix it before you sail and you'll have a drier, safer boat. Check all through-hull fittings. If you find any signs of leaking or rot, restore the watertight fit and get the best advice you can to make it permanent.

Here, from service experts, are some important steps to follow to get your outboard motor ready to go after winter storage:

1. Check the level of lubricant in the lower unit and make sure it's filled to the proper level. If it appears oil has been leaking, have a service expert check it out since it could indicate the lower seals and gaskets need replacing. And if you didn't do this before off-season storage, drain the gear case and refill it with the manufacturer's recommended lubricant.

2. If your motor has a power trim or power tilt unit, check the level of fluid in the system's reservoir, and refill it with the recommended fluid as needed.

3. Check your spark plugs. Your outboard can't start quickly and run efficiently if the plugs aren't sparking. Remove them, clean them, and make sure they are gapped to specification. Also make sure the spark-

plug terminal connections and wiring are clean, unfrayed, and snug-fitting.

4. Check the boat's battery. Make sure it's fully charged. Clean the terminal posts and connectors so they are free of corrosion.

5. If there was unused fuel left in the tank and engine over the winter, it should have been treated with a fuel conditioner before storage. If the fuel was conditioned, all you need to do in the spring is make sure the fuel-system clamps and fittings are tight and not leaking. Also check for cracked, worn, or aged fuel lines and replace as necessary. However, if no fuel conditioner was added before storage, clean the fuel-pump filter before adding fresh fuel. Although they vary from brand to brand, most outboard fuel filters are designed for easy cleaning. Check your owner's manual for instructions. Of course, all the old, untreated fuel should be drained from the tank and disposed of properly before new, fresh fuel is added. If you have an outboard with an oil-injection system, check to make sure the oil tank is filled. Also, check your owner's manual for any special maintenance the oil-injection system might require.

6. Many boaters use a fuel conditioner for winter storage, but then neglect its in-season use. Used in much smaller quantities during the boating season, out-

board fuel conditioners help keep the carburetor clean, reduce plug fouling, and reduce moisture in the fuel system. A note of caution: use only fuel conditioners designed for marine use in your boat, not automotive additives or conditioners, which can do your motor more harm than good.

7. Check your propeller. A little ding in the prop can make a big dent in your boat's performance. If the propeller is nicked, gouged, or bent, take it to your dealer or a prop shop for repair. If the prop is too far gone, invest in a new one. Stainless propellers offer much greater durability than most aluminum props. Here's a safety tip: before removing your propeller, always shift your motor to neutral and remove the key from the ignition switch to prevent the motor from accidentally starting. If you have trouble loosening the propeller nut, try wedging a piece of two-by-four between the prop blade and the antiventilation plate to keep the prop from turning. Before replacing the propeller, lube the prop shaft with grease as specified in your owner's manual. Also, check around the base of the prop shaft for monofilament fishing line that may have become wrapped around the shaft. Look closely—old monofilament might look like a plastic washer. Be sure to check your owner's manual for any special instructions and torque specifications before installing the propeller.

8. While you're checking the prop, also check the bottom of the boat. For clean, efficient running, the hull must be clean and efficient, too. Now's the time to remove any leftover barnacles or dried-up marine algae or weeds.

9. Spring is also a good time to touch up any scrapes or scratches in your motor's paint job. Most manufacturers offer factory-matched colors in easy-to-use spray-paint cans. If you're touching up the lower unit, be careful not to clog the water intake screen with paint. This could lead to the motor overheating. Also, don't make the mistake of painting over the sacrificial zinc anodes on your motor. They won't work if they're covered with paint. While you're inspecting the motor, check the anodes. If they are more than 50 percent destroyed, replace them with new ones. If you boat in salt water or brackish water, the anodes are supposed to dissipate as they protect your motor.

10. After the mechanical work is done, give your motor (and boat) a good cleaning. Remove all the dirt

The Elusive Green Flash

Consider yourself very lucky if you witness the green flash. Not many boaters are so fortunate and some don't even believe it actually happens. The green flash is an amazing sunset phenomenon. Watch the red ball of the sun descend at sunset when you're on the water, especially if you're offshore in the southern half of the country. When the sun touches the horizon, it will turn orange, and then yellow. When the sun drops out of sight, you may instantly see a brilliant green flash. The color change is caused by the refraction of the sun's rays passing through layers of atmosphere. Your best chance of seeing the green flash is on a calm ocean with a clear view of the horizon. Look for this phenomenon when conditions are right. If you see the green flash, you are one of the lucky ones to witness this amazing end-of-day display.

As sunset approaches, these Florida Keys anglers might see the green flash.

and grime collected over the winter. Use an engine degreaser to clean up your outboard's power head. As a final touch, give the motor a coat of automotive wax or polish. This will help it sparkle and protect the finish from the sun and water.

11. After the motor's all cleaned up, consult the lubrication section of your owner's manual. Most motors require a shot of lubricant on the throttle linkage or other moving parts on the engine. On motors with remote steering, the steering cable ram should be greased before the start of each season and periodically thereafter. Once again, check the owner's manual for detailed instructions.

BOATING
SAFETY AND
TIPS

Section Four
BOATING
SAFETY AND TIPS

SAFE BOATING

Many boaters don't have a clean record when it comes to accidents afloat. Boaters, especially fishermen and hunters, who have not schooled themselves in basic boating safety and safe habits will forget about them in an emergency. Here's your chance to start right.

◼ Basic Tool Kit

Every boat must be equipped to get home on its own. The exact selection of tools, spare parts, and supplies necessary must be suited to your boat and motor and to problems you are most likely to encounter. Here are the items that should be in a basic tool kit:

- Ordinary pliers
- Vise-grip pliers
- Diagonal-cutting pliers
- Long-nose electrician's pliers
- Screwdrivers
- Spark-plug wrench to fit
- Combination open-end and box wrenches in sizes ⅜ to ¾ inch
- Sharp knife
- Duct tape

◼ Spare Parts

Keep these spare parts on hand:

- Spark plugs of correct specifications
- Distributor cap, rotor, condenser, and point set
- Fuel pump and filter
- Oil filter

Outboard Motor Troubleshooting Checklist

Follow these steps to check the condition of your outboard motor:

- Check gas supply and tank pressure; squeeze the bulb several times.
- Check to be sure the propeller is not wrapped in weeds, line, or net. If line is wrapped around the prop, try to slow reverse to loosen it. Then, cut off pieces until you can pull the rest free.
- Look for loose wires and clamps at battery terminals.
- Remove ignition wire from any spark plug and crank the motor. A spark should jump from the wire end to the engine head; if there is no spark, check back to the ignition switch.
- If you have a hot spark, look into the fuel feed, pull the gas feed line off from the side of the outboard, and blow through the line until you hear bubbles in the tank.
- Clean the carburetor bowl and fuel filter.

- Hose clamps
- Water-pump impeller
- V-belts to match each size used
- Spare fuel lines, cocks, and fittings
- Gaskets and hoses
- Bailing-pump diaphragm
- Fuses and bulbs to double for each used

All-Purpose Kit

For an all-purpose kit, include the following:

- 50-foot chalk line
- Nails, screws, bolts and nuts, and washers
- Hose clamps
- Electrical tape
- Insulated wire
- Cotter pins
- Elastic plastic bandage material and duct tape
- Machine oil

Safe Boating Procedures

First, it is important to know your boat. Get familiar with its equipment and discover its limitations. If it's a livery rental, check it over completely before you push off.

Make a habit of checking off safety equipment aboard. First, locate the safety items required by law. Then, compare your optional equipment with the Coast Guard's list of recommended equipment. Count the life preservers, and make sure that each passenger has one that will keep him afloat in the water.

Carry a proper chart, GPS, compass, VHF, and a fully charged cell phone.

Put tackle, guns, decoys, nets, and other gear where they are secure and won't clutter walkways and footing.

Check the fuel supply, and the condition of the tank and feed line. Make sure the spark is strong and regular. Take along at least 1½ times as much fuel as you estimate you will need. If you run into heavy waves, your boat will take more fuel to go the same distance.

Gasoline vapors are explosive and will settle in the low areas of a boat. During fueling, keep doors, hatches, ports, and chests closed, stoves and pilot lights off, electrical circuits off, and absolutely no smoking! Keep the fill nozzle in firm contact with the fill neck to prevent static spark. Don't spill, for you'll have to dry it up before starting the engine. Do not use gasoline appliances aboard—they're lethal risks. Use alcohol and other less volatile fuels.

After fueling, ventilate thoroughly before pressing the starter. One minute is the minimum safe ventilation time. Big boats should be ventilated longer, with effective blowers operating and all ports opened. Keep your fuel lines in perfect condition and the boat's bilges clean.

Electrical equipment, switches, and wiring are some prime sources of boat fires and explosions. Keep batteries clean and ventilated.

Quartering a Following Sea

Quartering may be the only solution to crossing a following sea. Your speed, however, must be faster than the waves running at your stern. You'll have to make corrections with each wave you meet. As you cross the crest, wave action tries to turn a quartering boat broadside by pushing its stern into the trough between it and the next wave crest. You must power your boat into the direction of the trough to properly point your bow toward the next crest. (Note the direction of the outboard and prop in illustration.) Never allow wave action to push your boat parallel to the trough.

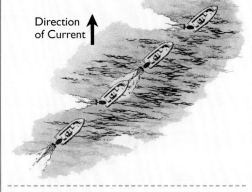

Direction of Current

Mouth of River or Inlet

Wherever a current enters a body of water—this is true for river mouths as well as ocean inlets—you can expect to find relatively calm water at the edge of the intruding flow. Usually this calm transition zone is marked by surface wave action. When running any inlet, always ride the back of the wave in front of you. Never power over its crest, or drift far enough back to be picked up by the crest of the following wave.

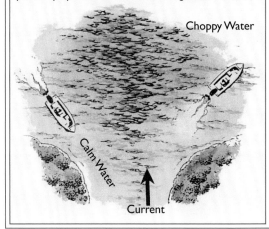

Choppy Water

Calm Water

Current

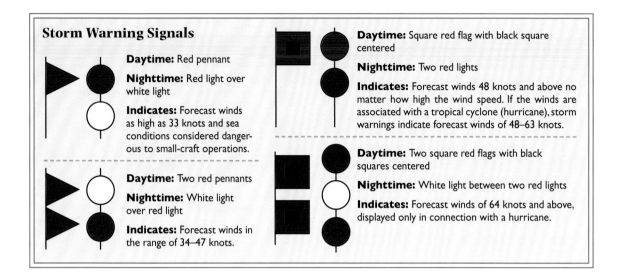

Storm Warning Signals

Daytime: Red pennant

Nighttime: Red light over white light

Indicates: Forecast winds as high as 33 knots and sea conditions considered dangerous to small-craft operations.

Daytime: Two red pennants

Nighttime: White light over red light

Indicates: Forecast winds in the range of 34–47 knots.

Daytime: Square red flag with black square centered

Nighttime: Two red lights

Indicates: Forecast winds 48 knots and above no matter how high the wind speed. If the winds are associated with a tropical cyclone (hurricane), storm warnings indicate forecast winds of 48–63 knots.

Daytime: Two square red flags with black squares centered

Nighttime: White light between two red lights

Indicates: Forecast winds of 64 knots and above, displayed only in connection with a hurricane.

Do not overload your boat. Make sure you have safely adequate freeboard before casting off. Look ahead to water conditions and weather changes you may encounter.

Keep an alert lookout. If you have a boat longer than 20 feet, name your mate and agree that he'll keep lookout any time you can't. You have more to watch out for than other boats and shallow water. Watch for obstructions such as rocks and floating logs.

Swimmers are hard to see in the water. Running through swimmers or a swimming area is the most sensitive violation a boat can make. If in doubt, give beaches and rafts a wide swing.

Your wake is potent. You can swamp small craft such as canoes or rowboats, damage shorelines and shore property, disturb sleepers, and ruin fish and wildlife sport for hours by running fast through small passages and shallows. You are always responsible for any damage caused by your wake.

Learn the Coast Guard navigation rules and obey them at all times. Copies are available to download free on the Coast Guard website. Most collisions are caused by one-time violations.

Make sure at least one other person aboard knows how to operate the boat and motor in case you are disabled or fall overboard. Know a plan of action you will take in emergencies such as a man overboard, bad leak, motor that won't run, collision, bad storm, or troublesome passenger.

Storm signals and danger signs are often informal. Learn to read the weather, and keep alert to what passing boats are trying to tell you.

Wear your life preserver and make all your passengers, especially children, wear life preservers at all times. In a capsizing, remember that you are safer if you stay with the boat, where you can be seen. It will also help you stay afloat until help arrives.

Under Coast Guard legislation, it is illegal for anyone to build, sell, or use a craft that does not conform to safety regulations. Check with your dealer, and check yourself to make sure your boat measures up.

■ Small Boat, Big Water

The best way to stay out of trouble on open water is to learn how to read the wind and weather. The National Oceanic and Atmospheric Administration (NOAA) issues marine weather forecasts every hour with details of winds and seas. If you have a VHF-FM radio, the NOAA broadcasts weather and warnings continuously on these frequencies: 162.400 MHz, 162.425 MHz, 162.450 MHz, 162.475 MHz, 162.500 MHz, 162.525 MHz, and 162.550 MHz. Matching the wind forecast with the accompanying chart will give you a good idea of the seas you can expect to encounter.

But such forecasts are regional, and local conditions can be radically different—thunderstorms, for instance. You can determine the distance in miles of an approaching thunderstorm by counting the interval between seeing a lightning flash and hearing its accompanying thunder in seconds, and then dividing by five. For example, if it takes 10 seconds to hear the thunder,

Wind/Sea Relationships

	Velocity (knots)	Conditions
Calm Conditions	0–3	Sea like a mirror
	4–6	Ripples, less than 1 foot
	7–10	Smooth wavelets, 1 to 2 feet
	11–16	Small waves, 2 to 4 feet
Small Craft Warning	17–21	Moderate waves, 4 to 8 feet, whitecaps
	22–27	Large waves, 8 to 13 feet, spray
	28–33	High waves, 13 to 20 feet, heaped seas, foam from breaking waves
Gale Warning	34–40	High waves, 13 to 20 feet, foam blown in well-marked streaks
	41–47	Seas rolling, reduced visibility from spray, waves 13 to 20 feet
Storm Warning	48–55	White seas, very high waves, 20 to 30 feet, overhanging crests
	56–63	Exceptionally high waves, 30 to 45 feet
Hurricane Warning	More than 63	Air filled with foam, sea white, waves over 45 feet

the storm is 2 miles away. There are also several apps you can download on your cell phone that will give you real-time radar readings for your area. You can actually time when a storm will hit your location.

But that knowledge won't help much if you don't have time to get to safety. Odds are you're going to get caught on the water eventually. Knowing how to handle difficult seas in a small boat is insurance all sportsmen should have.

■ Coast Guard–Approved Equipment

For safe boating under most conditions, you are required by federal law to carry Coast Guard–approved equipment aboard your craft. Coast Guard–approved equipment simply means that it has been approved by the Commandant of the U.S. Coast Guard and has been determined to be in compliance with U.S. Coast Guard specifications and regulations relating to materials, construction, and performance.

Here are the Coast Guard recommendations for the most essential lifesaving equipment you must have onboard under federal law.

FIRE EXTINGUISHERS: Each approved fire extinguisher is classified by a letter and a Roman numeral according to the type of fire it is designed to extinguish and its size. The letter indicates the type of fire:

A: Fires of ordinary combustible materials

B: Gasoline, oil, and grease fires

C: Electrical fires

Fire extinguishers must be carried on **all** motorboats that meet one or more of the following conditions:

- Inboard engines

- Closed compartments under thwarts and seats where portable fuel tanks may be stored

- Double bottoms not sealed to the hull or not completely filled with flotation materials

- Closed living spaces

- Closed stowage compartments in which combustible or flammable materials are stored

- Permanently installed fuel tanks

There is no gallon capacity to determine if a fuel tank is portable. However, if the fuel tank is secured so it cannot be moved in case of a fire or other emergency, or if the weight of the fuel tank is such that people onboard cannot move it in case of a fire or other emergency, then the Coast Guard considers the tank permanently installed.

Dry chemical fire extinguishers without gauges or indicating devices must be inspected every six months. If the gross weight of a carbon dioxide (CO_2) fire extinguisher is reduced by more than 10 percent of the net weight, the extinguisher is not acceptable and must be recharged. Check extinguishers regularly to be sure that the gauges are free and nozzles clear.

Fire-extinguisher requirements are classified by the size of the vessel:

Fire Extinguishers

Extinguishers approved for motorboats are hand portable, of either B-I or B-II classification or their UL equivalents, and have the following characteristics:

Coast Guard Classes	UL Listing	Foam (gallons)	CO_2 (pounds)	Dry Chemical (pounds)	Halon (pounds)
B–I	5B	1¼	4	2	2½
B–II	—	2½	15	10	10
—	10B	—	10	2½	5

1. Boats less than 26 feet in length with **no** fixed fire-extinguishing system installed in machinery spaces must have at least one approved Type B-I hand-portable fire extinguisher. When an approved fixed fire-extinguishing system is installed in machinery spaces, no Type B-I extinguisher is required. If the construction of the boat does not permit the entrapment of explosive or flammable gases or vapors, no fire extinguisher is required.

2. Boats 26 feet to less than 40 feet in length must have at least two approved Type B-I or at least one Type B-II hand-portable fire extinguishers. When an approved fixed fire-extinguishing system is installed, only one Type B-I extinguisher is required.

3. Boats 40 feet to not more than 65 feet in length must have at least three approved Type B-I or at least one Type B-I and one Type B-II hand-portable fire extinguisher. When an approved fixed fire-extinguishing system is installed, one fewer Type B-I or one Type B-II extinguisher is required.

Note: Coast Guard–approved extinguishers carry the following label: Marine Type USCG Approved, Size —, Type —, 162.208/, etc. UL-listed extinguishers not displaying this marking are also acceptable, provided they are of the above sizes and types and carry a minimum UL rating of 5-B:C.

PERSONAL FLOTATION DEVICES (PFDS): All boats must be equipped with U.S. Coast Guard–approved life jackets called personal flotation devices, or PFDs. The quantity and type depends on the length of the boat and the number of people onboard or being towed. Each PFD must be in good condition, the proper size for the intended wearer, and, very important, must be readily accessible.

■ **Type I: Offshore Life Jacket**
These PFDs provide the most buoyancy. They are effective for all waters, especially open, rough, or remote waters where rescue may be delayed. They are designed to turn most unconscious wearers to a face-up position.

■ **Type II: Near-Shore Vest**
These vests are intended for calm, inland waters or where there is a good chance of quick rescue. This type will turn some unconscious wearers to a face-up position, but will not turn as many people to a face-up position as a Type I.

■ **Type III: Flotation Aid**
These vests are good for calm, inland waters, or where there is a good chance of quick rescue. They are designed so wearers can place themselves in a face-up position. The wearer may have to tilt his head back to avoid turning facedown in the water. It is generally the most comfortable type for continuous wear.

■ **Type IV: Throwable Device**
These cushions or ring buoys are intended for calm, inland waters where help is always present. They are not designed to be worn, but to be thrown to a person in the water and held by the victim until they are rescued.

■ **Type V: Special-Use Device**
These PFDs are intended for specific activities and may be carried instead of another PFD only if used according to the label. Some Type V devices provide significant hypothermia protection. Type V PFDs must be used in accordance with their labels to be acceptable.

Note: U.S. Coast Guard–approved inflatable life jackets are authorized for use by people over 16 years of age. They must have a full cylinder and all status indicators on the inflator must be green or the device does not meet the legal requirements. Inflatable life jackets are more comfortable, which encourages regular wear.

VISUAL DISTRESS SIGNALS: All recreational boats, when used on coastal waters, the Great Lakes, territorial seas, and those waters connected directly to the Great Lakes and territorial seas, up to a point where a body of water is less than 2 miles wide, must be equipped with visual distress signals. Boats owned in the United States operating on the high seas must also be equipped with visual distress

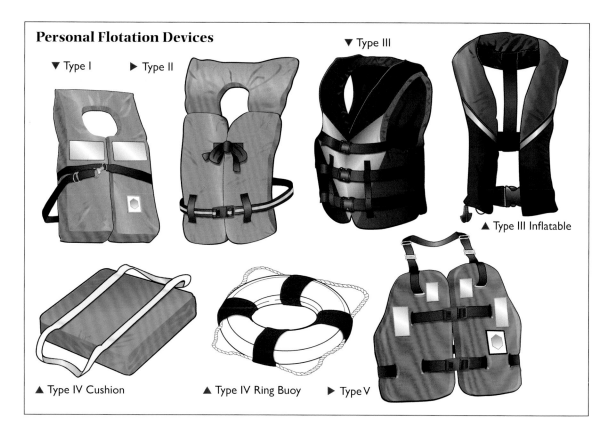

Personal Flotation Devices

▼ Type I   ▶ Type II   ▼ Type III

▲ Type III Inflatable

▲ Type IV Cushion   ▲ Type IV Ring Buoy   ▶ Type V

signals. The following are exempted from the requirements for day signals and only need to carry night signals:

- Recreational boats less than 16 feet in length
- Boats participating in organized events, such as races, regattas, or marine parades
- Open sailboats less than 26 feet in length not equipped with propulsion machinery
- Manually propelled boats

Pyrotechnic visual distress signals must be Coast Guard–approved, in serviceable condition, and stowed to be readily accessible. They are marked with a date showing the serviceable life, and this date must not have passed.

Coast Guard–approved pyrotechnic visual distress signals and associated devices include:

- Pyrotechnic red flares, handheld or aerial
- Pyrotechnic orange smoke, handheld or floating
- Launchers for aerial red meteors or parachute flares

Non-pyrotechnic visual distress signaling devices must carry the manufacturer's certification that they meet Coast Guard requirements. They must be in serviceable condition and stowed to be readily accessible. This group includes:

- Orange distress flags
- Electric distress flags

No single signaling device is ideal under all conditions and for all purposes. Consideration should therefore be given to carrying several types. For example, an aerial flare can be seen over a long distance on a clear night, but for closer work, a handheld flare may be more useful.

HANDLING AND STORAGE OF PYROTECHNIC DEVICES:
Pyrotechnic devices should be stored in a cool, dry location and must be readily accessible in case of an emergency. Care should be taken to prevent puncturing or otherwise damaging their coverings. A watertight container, such as a surplus ammunition box, painted red

Buoys

Buoys are traffic signals that guide boaters safely along waterways. They can also identify dangerous areas, as well as give directions and information. The colors and numbers on buoys mean the same thing regardless of what kind of buoy on which they appear.

Red colors, red lights, and even numbers • These indicate the right side of the channel as a boater enters from the open sea or heads upstream. Numbers usually increase consecutively as you return from the open sea or head upstream.

Green colors, green lights, and odd numbers • These indicate the left side of the channel as a boater enters from the open sea and heads upstream. Numbers will usually increase consecutively as you return from the open sea or head upstream.

Red and green horizontal stripes • These are placed at the junction of two channels to indicate the preferred (primary) channel when a channel splits. If green is on top,

the preferred channel is to the right. If red is on top, the preferred channel is to the left. The light color matches the top stripe. These are also sometimes referred to as junction buoys.

Nun buoys • These cone-shaped buoys are always marked with red markings and even numbers. They mark the right side of the channel as a boater enters from the open sea or heads upstream.

Can buoys • These cylindrical-shaped buoys are always marked with green markings and odd numbers. They mark the left side of the channel as a boater enters from the open sea or heads upstream.

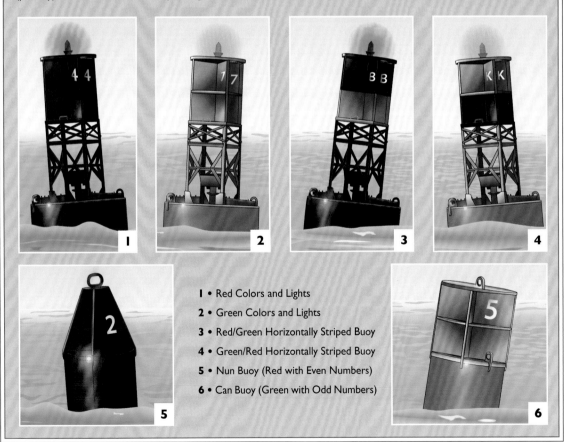

1 • Red Colors and Lights

2 • Green Colors and Lights

3 • Red/Green Horizontally Striped Buoy

4 • Green/Red Horizontally Striped Buoy

5 • Nun Buoy (Red with Even Numbers)

6 • Can Buoy (Green with Odd Numbers)

or orange and prominently marked "distress signals" is recommended.

If young children are frequently aboard your boat, careful selection and proper stowage of visual distress signals becomes especially important. If you elect to carry pyrotechnic devices, select devices that are in tough packaging and that would be difficult to ignite accidentally.

Coast Guard–approved pyrotechnic devices carry an expiration date. This date cannot exceed 42 months from the date of manufacture and at such time the device can no longer be counted toward the minimum requirements.

A wide variety of signaling devices, both pyrotechnic and nonpyrotechnic, can be carried to meet the requirements of the regulation.

Boats less than 16 feet long operating in coastal waters, and certain other exempted boats listed in the previous section, need only carry signaling devices when operating at night. All other recreational boats must carry both night and day signaling devices.

The following is an example of the variety and combinations of devices that can be carried in order to meet the requirements:

- Three handheld red flares (day and night)

- One electric distress light (night)

- One handheld red flare and two parachute flares (day and night)

- One handheld orange smoke signal, two floating orange smoke signals, and one electric distress light (day and night)

All distress-signaling devices have both advantages and disadvantages. The most popular, because of cost,

are probably the smaller pyrotechnic devices. Pyrotechnics make excellent distress signals, universally recognized as such, but they have the drawback that they can be used only once. Additionally, there is the potential for both injury and property damage if pyrotechnics are not properly handled. Pyrotechnic devices have a very hot flame and the ash and slag can cause burns and ignite materials that burn easily. Projected devices, such as pistol-launched and handheld parachute flares and meteors, have many of the same characteristics of a firearm and must be handled with the same caution and respect.

Under the Inland Navigational Rules, a high-intensity white light flashing at regular intervals from 50 to 70 times per minute is considered a distress signal. Therefore, a strobe light used in inland waters should only be used as a distress signal.

The handheld and the floating orange smoke signaling devices are good day signals, especially on clear days. Both signals are most effective with light to moderate winds because higher winds tend to keep the smoke close to the water and disperse it, which makes it hard to see.

The distress flag must be at least 3 by 3 feet with a black square and ball on an orange background. It is accepted as a day signal only and is especially effective in bright sunlight. The flag is most distinctive when waved on a paddle or flown from a mast.

The electric distress light is accepted for night use only and must automatically flash the international SOS distress signal (• • • – – – • • •). Flashed four to six times each minute, this is an unmistakable distress signal, well known to most boaters. The device can be checked anytime for serviceability if shielded from view.

Red handheld flares can be used by day, but are most effective at night or in restricted visibility, such as fog or haze. When selecting such flares, look for the Coast Guard approval number and date of manufacture. Make sure that the device does not carry the marking, "Not approved for use on recreational boats."

■ Navigation Lights

REQUIRED ON BOATS BETWEEN SUNSET AND SUNRISE: Recreational boats operating at night are required to display navigation lights between sunset and sunrise. Although most recreational boats in the United States operate in waters governed by the Inland Navigational Rules, changes to the rules have made the general lighting requirements for both the Inland and International rules basically the same. The differences between them are primarily in the options available.

Sound-Signaling Devices for Vessels Less than 20 Meters (65.6 Feet) in Length

1 • Vessels 12 meters (39.4 feet) or more in length, but less than 20 meters (65.6 feet), must carry onboard a power whistle or power horn and a bell.

2 • Vessels less than 12 meters (39.4 feet) need not carry a whistle, horn, or bell. However, the navigation rules require signals to be made under certain circumstances, and you should carry some means for making an efficient signal when necessary.

Range and Arc of Visibility of Lights

For Vessels Less than 20 Meters (65.6 Feet) in Length

Light	Visible Range in Miles		Arc in Degrees
	Less than 12 Meters	12 Meters or More	
Masthead light	2	3	225
All-around light	2	2	360
Side lights	1	2	112.5
Stern light	2	2	135

1. A power-driven vessel less than 20 meters (65.6 feet) in length shall exhibit navigation lights as shown in Figure 1. If the vessel is less than 12 meters (39.4 feet) in length, it may show the lights as shown in either Figure 1 or Figure 2.

2. On a vessel less than 12 meters (39.4 feet) in length, the masthead light must be 1 meter (3.3 feet) higher than the sidelights. If the vessel is 12 meters or more in length but less than 20 meters (65.6 feet), the masthead light must not be less than 2.5 meters (8.2 feet) above the gunwale.

3. A power-driven vessel less than 50 meters in length may also, but is not obligated to, carry a second masthead light abaft of and higher than the forward one.

4. A power-driven vessel less than 7 meters (23 feet) in length and whose maximum speed cannot exceed 7 knots may, in international waters **only**, in lieu of the lights prescribed above, exhibit an all-around white light, and shall, if practicable, also exhibit sidelights.

SAILING VESSELS AND VESSELS UNDER OARS:

1. A sailing vessel less than 20 meters (65.6 feet) in length shall exhibit navigation lights as shown in either Figure 3 or Figure 4. The lights may be combined in a single lantern carried at the top of the mast as shown in Figure 5.

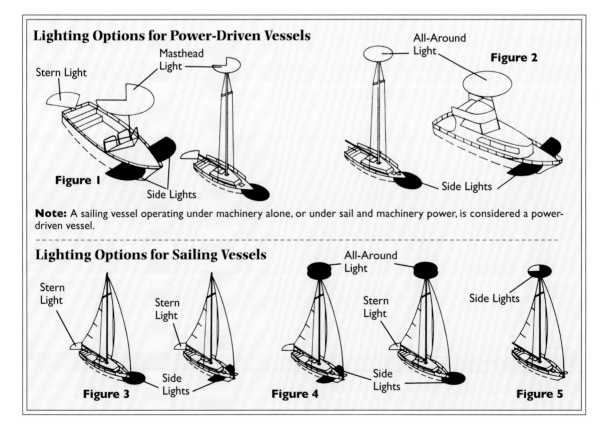

Lighting Options for Power-Driven Vessels

Stern Light

Masthead Light

Figure 1

Side Lights

All-Around Light

Figure 2

Side Lights

Note: A sailing vessel operating under machinery alone, or under sail and machinery power, is considered a power-driven vessel.

Lighting Options for Sailing Vessels

Stern Light

Stern Light

Figure 3

Side Lights

All-Around Light

Stern Light

Side Lights

Figure 4

All-Around Light

Side Lights

Figure 5

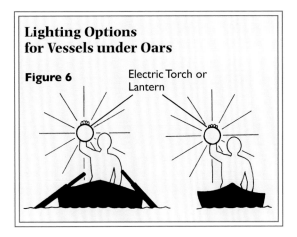

Lighting Options for Vessels under Oars

Figure 6

Electric Torch or Lantern

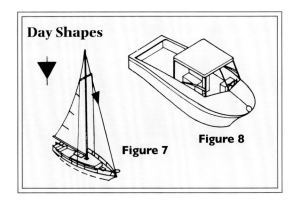

Day Shapes

Figure 7

Figure 8

2. A sailing vessel less than 7 meters (23 feet) in length shall, if practicable, exhibit those lights prescribed for sailing vessels less than 20 meters in length, but if it does not, it shall have ready at hand an electric torch or lighted lantern showing a white light that shall be exhibited in sufficient time to prevent collision (see Figure 6).

3. A vessel under oars may display those lights prescribed for sailing vessels, but if it does not, it shall have ready at hand an electric torch or lighted lantern showing a white light that shall be exhibited in sufficient time to prevent collision (see Figure 6).

LIGHTS USED WHEN ANCHORED: Power-driven vessels and sailing vessels at anchor must display anchor lights. However, vessels less than 7 meters (23 feet) in length are not required to display anchor lights unless anchored in or near a narrow channel, fairway, or anchorage, or where other vessels normally navigate.

An anchor light for a vessel less than 20 meters (65.6 feet) in length is an all-around white light visible for 2 miles exhibited where it can best be seen. A vessel less than 20 meters in length in inland waters, when at anchor in a special anchorage area designated by the Secretary of Transportation, does not require an anchor light.

DAY SHAPES: A vessel proceeding under sail when also being propelled by machinery shall exhibit forward, where it can best be seen, a conical shape, apex downward (see Figure 7), except that for Inland Rules, a vessel less than 12 meters in length is not required to exhibit the day shape (see Figure 8).

■ Loading Your Boat

There are several things to remember when loading a boat: distribute the load evenly, keep the load low, don't overload, don't stand up in a small boat, and consult the U.S. Coast Guard maximum capacities plate. On boats with no capacity plate, use the accompanying formula to determine the maximum number of people your boat can safely carry in calm weather.

The length of your vessel is measured in a straight line from the foremost part of the vessel to the aftermost part of the vessel, parallel to the centerline, exclusive of sheer. Bowsprits, bumpkins, rudders, outboard motors, brackets, and similar fittings are not included in the measurement.

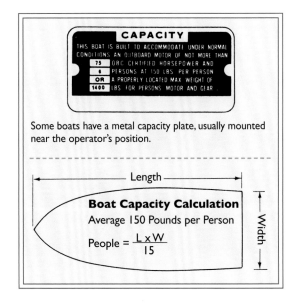

CAPACITY

THIS BOAT IS BUILT TO ACCOMMODATE UNDER NORMAL CONDITIONS AN OUTBOARD MOTOR OF NOT MORE THAN **75** OBC CERTIFIED HORSEPOWER AND **6** PERSONS AT 150 LBS. PER PERSON **OR** A PROPERLY LOCATED MAX WEIGHT OF **1400** LBS. FOR PERSONS, MOTOR AND GEAR.

Some boats have a metal capacity plate, usually mounted near the operator's position.

Length

Width

Boat Capacity Calculation
Average 150 Pounds per Person

$$\text{People} = \frac{L \times W}{15}$$

SMALL-BOAT NAVIGATION

Global Positioning Systems, Latitude, and Longitude

With global positioning systems (GPS), anyone can be an instant navigator. A GPS receiver scanning through at least 24 U.S. navigation satellites might receive signals from at least four anytime and anywhere on the globe. Each GPS satellite's signal creates a circular *line of position*. A GPS receiver in your hand sees itself somewhere on this line transmitted from a single satellite—like the edge of a light beam from a flashlight. Overlapping (circular) lines from at least three satellites intersect only at a single spot and define exactly where your receiver is on the earth's surface. This *position* is usually within about 3.5 meters (11.5 feet).

GPS information you see on a display screen is a *fix*, presented in most instances as figures showing *latitude* and *longitude*.

Latitude lines, measured in degrees, are horizontal slices of the earth beginning at the equator—numbered zero—and ending at the poles—numbered +90° for the North Pole and -90° for the South Pole. Latitude lines are like layers on a domed cake, each shorter in circumference as they progress toward the poles.

Longitude lines, sliced like an apple from top to bottom, are all of equal length and begin their numbering from zero on an arbitrary line passing through Greenwich, England, which is noted as 0° longitude. Lines are numbered in degrees progressing west with a plus number and east with a minus number. Longitude lines meet at the 180th meridian, which passes through the Pacific Ocean. The 180th and Greenwich meridians are neither positive nor negative.

A *nautical mile* is the distance between lines of latitude measured along the vertical longitude lines. One minute of one-degree latitude (or one-sixtieth of a degree) equals one nautical mile. One nautical mile is equal to about 6,080 feet, or about 1.2 statute miles, and because of its source in latitude and longitude measurements, it is used for marine and aviation navigation measurements.

A GPS receiver's ability to record repeated fixes rapidly creates *track lines* across the earth's surface. Time laps between fixes along this track determine *speed*. Distance divided by time equals speed.

But you, the modern mariner, finding yourself without a GPS or experiencing a rare security scrambling of satellites, can still navigate the original way—with a compass, timepiece, and chart (with tools).

Most compasses sold for marine use will work adequately, but two corrections are necessary before a *true magnetic heading* is available for your use; this is the ability for the compass on your boat to show you the correct heading in relation to true, or geographic, north.

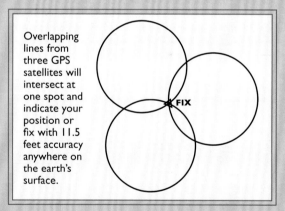

Overlapping lines from three GPS satellites will intersect at one spot and indicate your position or fix with 11.5 feet accuracy anywhere on the earth's surface.

Compass Deviation

Deviation is the first error for you to correct for a valid compass reading. Small errors in compass readings are induced by magnetic influences within the vessel. These errors also vary on each boat's heading. You need to eliminate this error by "swinging the compass" (usually done by professionals), where magnetic headings throughout 360 degrees are checked by rotating the boat on a mapped magnetic range. Differences or errors between the known headings and boat's compass are "adjusted" out by moving adjustable magnets on or near the compass. Any uncorrectable errors after swinging are noted in *deviation tables*, and you add or subtract these numbers to the compass readings. This card or table is kept near the compass for ready reference. Errors are noted in degrees "east" (minus) or "west" (plus).

Magnetic North

A magnetic compass points to the *magnetic North Pole*. This magnetic source is not colocated with the *geographic North Pole*, which is used for navigation. *Magnetic variation* (also referred to as *declination*) is the second value you must add or subtract to your compass reading to give you a magnetic reference to the geographic North Pole. Variation angles vary widely around the globe and their values are shown on charts—you can find them printed as *compass roses*. You will find variation errors exceeding 30 degrees at certain locations on earth, while other spots may register zero. This happens in instances where both poles are aligned.

For you to steer a desired heading from your compass, you have to subtract east variation or add west variation. For example, if you wish to steer 090° true magnetic heading from your compass reading where the chart notes a 15° east variation at your position, you must subtract 15° from 090° and steer a compass reading of 075°. (This is of course after correcting for compass deviation errors on this heading.) Concurrently, if you plan again on a 090° true magnetic heading with a 22° west variation reading from your chart, then you must add the west variation, giving a magnetic heading to steer of 102° for a resulting 090° true course.

The east/west corrections apply for both deviation and variation. Please note both an east and west deviation and variation error can apply to one heading. You might, for example, have a deviation error of 03° west (uncorrectable compass error) on a particular heading and a variation error of 12° east because of your location on the earth. The resulting correction for a compass reading on that heading would be a -09°.

When you start from one *fix* (known position), and arrive at the next, your boat will describe a *track*. This can be visualized as a line drawn on the earth's surface over which the boat traveled. This line may

not follow the compass heading or be your intended course between fixes, and could be quite squiggly or meandering as currents push the boat off course. The boat, in open waters, is floating in a moving fluid. Actual tracks and speeds over the ground are influenced by currents and winds.

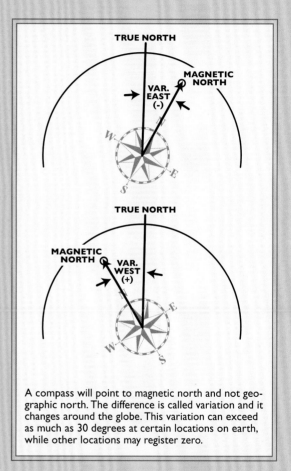

A compass will point to magnetic north and not geographic north. The difference is called variation and it changes around the globe. This variation can exceed as much as 30 degrees at certain locations on earth, while other locations may register zero.

Dead Reckoning

A *dead reckoning (DR)* fix is a location arrived at based on compass heading and speed, or time and possible current inputs calculated from the previous leg or other established values, such as current directions and velocities noted on charts and tidal current tables. The DR position does not take into account existing forces deflecting the boat from your intended path. This is not a true fix of your actual location, but an approximate

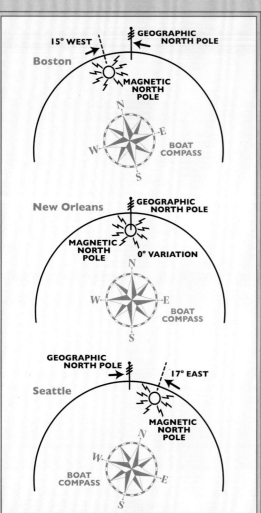

A • In Boston, a boat's magnet compass points to the magnetic North Pole, which is approximately 15 degrees west of the true North Pole. For a mariner to correct compass heading to get the desired course, he must add 15 degrees to the boat's compass reading.

B • In New Orleans, a boat's magnet compass points directly at both the magnetic North Pole and the true North Pole. The two poles coincide. There are no corrections for this variation.

C • In Seattle, a boat's magnet compass points to the magnetic North Pole, which is 17 degrees east of the true North Pole. For a mariner to correct compass heading to get the desired course, he must subtract 17 degrees from the boat's compass reading.

position based on the best knowledge, which possibly might be adjusted for known or perceived external forces acting on the boat. Dead reckoning navigation is based on a series of DRs recorded along a continuous track at intervals and also plotted at every change in direction and speed. Dead reckoning is used between available fixes or where no navigation aids are available.

Fixes

You, as a navigator, obtain *fixes* by determining *lines of position* from navigation aids and then drawing these lines on the chart. Aids providing you reference lines, for example, come from compass bearings or measured angles (with a protractor device) to known fixed objects, radio direction bearings, sea-bottom contours, or sun or celestial observations (with a sextant). In drawing these lines on the chart, you need to advance (or retard) them the distance the boat moved in the time elapsed between observations for each line.

Others' experiences prove that the lines you draw might not cross tightly, but frequently form a triangle or "top hat" symbol. You can mark the center of this triangle, if small, as your DR position unless the crossings show a large top hat and thus a less reliable location—one you might question in the fog along a rocky shore.

Prudent Navigator

If you plan to venture to sea any distance beyond recognizable landmarks, or at night or in fog, you should prepare yourself by taking navigation courses given by the U.S. Coast Guard Auxiliary or U.S. Power Squadron. This overview only briefly introduces the topic, but in their courses, you will learn all the navigation tools and their uses through practical exercises.

You as a prudent skipper may at any time unexpectedly—and seemingly always at the worst moment—not have your reliable single navigational aid. This will be the time when you must be prepared and resort to the basic navigation fundamentals outlined here—to keep rocks away from your keel. A prudent navigator never relies on a single source, even GPS, for safe navigation.

This brief overview was written by Lieutenant Commander Tom Beard, USCG (Retired), who split his military flying career between a Vietnam tour as a Navy carrier pilot and work as a Coast Guard rescue pilot.

HANDLING WIND, WEATHER, AND WATER

I recall a terrible boating tragedy years ago that could have been avoided. Eight men in a 28-foot pleasure craft got caught in 20-foot seas and 70-mile-per-hour winds about 30 miles off the East Coast of the United States. In a miraculous Coast Guard rescue, seven men were saved, but one man was never found.

The wife of a survivor told reporters, "I don't understand why the captain took the boat out. The captain didn't want to go. He said it was too windy."

I'll venture a guess why the captain took the boat out. It was probably a long-planned fishing trip, no one wanted to be disappointed, and the weather didn't look bad at the dock.

I remember that day and I also remember a weather forecast that would have kept me at the dock. I don't care how many friends showed up to go fishing, I would have treated them to breakfast at a local diner and sent them home. They would be disappointed, but alive. The open water is no place to prove that you have more guts than brains.

Never forget that if you own and run a boat, you are also the captain, and you are totally responsible for the safety of your passengers. If someone gets hurt on your boat, you have to take the blame.

I get scared when I see a boat pass me with young children sitting on the bow with their feet hanging over the side. One bumpy wake and a child could easily be killed by the prop. I get angry when I see a boater pulling a water skier in a channel with heavy boat traffic. I wonder what is going through the minds of small-boat operators who disappear in ground swells as they head offshore when a small-craft advisory flag is flying in plain view. I say a prayer when I see a family overload a rental boat and head out for a day of fishing with 2 inches of freeboard.

High winds and rough water can turn a pleasant day into a life-threatening nightmare. The best way to stay out of trouble is to learn how to read the weather, wind, and water. And it's equally important to know when to cancel a trip and stay home. This advice is even more important to fishermen who tend to use smaller boats and go out in marginal weather.

Rule No. 1: Check the weather. The National Weather Service issues marine forecasts every six hours with details of winds, seas, weather, and visibility. Heavy static on your AM radio may also indicate nearby storms. The National Weather Service also posts visible warnings at prominent locations along the shore, including Coast Guard stations, lighthouses, yacht clubs, and marinas.

One of the problems with weather forecasts is that they are not always right. Sometimes you may have to make judgment calls on your own. Learn to read simple weather signs. Watch for dark, threatening clouds, which nearly always indicate a thunderstorm or squall. Any steady increase in wind or sea is another sign of bad weather.

If you're on the water, don't wait too long to make a decision. Calm winds and water can turn into a gusty electrical storm in as little as 30 minutes. If you've taken all precautions and you still get caught in a storm, pinpoint your location or note your GPS location on a chart before heavy rain reduces your visibility. Watch for other boats, secure hatches, lower antennas and outriggers, stow all loose gear, and, most important, make sure everyone is wearing a life jacket.

Once the storm hits, try to take the first and heaviest gusts of wind on the bow of the boat. Approach waves at a 45-degree angle to keep the propeller underwater and reduce pounding. If there is lightning, unplug the radio and electrical equipment. Stay away from metal objects and order your passengers to stay low. If you don't lose power, you should be able to ride out almost any storm.

■ How to Forecast Weather

There are dozens of signs that will give you a hint of approaching weather patterns and a whole bunch of weather axioms that will prove true most of the time. Learning how to read some basic signs is fun and it can keep you out of trouble in the outdoors, but it's still important to remember that no weather forecasting system is 100 percent accurate.

There probably isn't a boatman alive who hasn't heard the axiom, "Red sky at night, sailor's delight. Red sky in the morning, sailors take warning." The red sky in the morning may well mean rain that day because there's enough moisture in the air to redden the sky at sunrise. Because of atmospheric conditions, that prediction may come true in the northern United States, but it won't work in tropical climates where red sunrises are common.

I've also heard the axiom, "A ring around the moon means rain." If you only look for a ring around the moon, you will get rain about 50 percent of the time.

You can get better odds, however, if you're more observant. If you notice a falling barometer along with that ring around the moon, you can be sure of rain within 24 hours about 80 percent of the time.

There are other weather signs to help you in the outdoors. Birds, for example, perch on wires, rooftops, and trees more often before storms because low-pressure air is less dense, making it a lot harder to fly. Waterfowl hunters also know that ducks and geese fly a lot higher in good weather than in bad. One reason, other than visibility, is that low pressure affects their ears.

Pay attention to most clouds. Generally, the high clouds will not rain on you, no matter how threatening they look. It's those low clouds that will pound you with rain. You can also forecast impending rain by observing smoke from any smokestack. If the smoke rises, you will get fair weather. If the smoke, however, is driven downward by low pressure, rain is on the way.

If you're in the woods and you sense that smells and scents are stronger around you, there's a good chance that you will get rain. Odors held captive by high pressure escape as the barometer drops, which nearly always means bad weather.

In coastal areas, rain is more likely at low tide than at high tide. A falling tide reduces atmospheric pressure. In the country, check the trees. Leaves show their backs or undersides before a rain. Vegetation grows to prevailing winds and a change of wind direction, which also means a change in weather, turns them over.

Well-designed center consoles, such as this unsinkable 38-foot Edgewater, can easily run in 6- to 8-foot seas, but safety depends on how knowledgeable the captain is on reading and handling rough water. The major concern must always be the safety of his passengers.

Listen to the sounds of boats, gunshots, distant voices, and so on. If the sounds are loud and hollow, you could get rain. A lowering cloud ceiling acts like a sounding board and will bounce noise back to you.

If weather starts to turn bad, note the direction of lightning. If it's in the west or northwest, the storm will probably reach you. Storms to the south or east, however, will usually go past.

When you leave your cabin in the morning, look at the grass. A heavy dew on grass at night and in early morning is a sign of fair weather. Dew forms at those times only when the air is dry and the skies are clear.

Are all of these weather signs true all of the time? Not on your life! But they work most of the time, which is about all you can say for any weather forecast.

■ Lightning and Your Boat

No other kind of foul weather will make a person feel as helpless as lightning. And there's good reason to be scared. Lightning is deadly, but there are certain precautions to take to minimize the risk of being struck.

Lightning is a discharge of static electricity from a charged cloud to earth or from one cloud to another. The electric charge is created when a cumulus cloud is formed in an updraft of warm, moist air. This combination results in a huge buildup of static electricity in a big cumulonimbus cloud. The top part of the cloud holds a positive charge and the bottom part holds a negative charge from the friction of the updraft. When a thundercloud passes overhead, the negative charge induces the earth to take on a positive charge, usually at the highest points, such as tall buildings, poles, or even humans. These charges in clouds and ground are normally kept apart by air, which acts as an insulator. When the static charge becomes strong enough, however, it overcomes the resistance of the air, and lightning occurs.

When a lightning bolt with a current of more than 100,000 amps passes through the atmosphere, the air is heated and expanded, creating a strong vacuum. It's this rapid expansion and collapse of air that creates the loud shock wave known as "thunder."

Thunder can also tell you how far you are from lightning. Count the seconds between lightning and thunder, and then divide by five. The answer is the distance between you and the lightning in miles. If there's a five-second lapse between lightning and thunder, for example, the lightning is a mile or so away.

If you're in a boat on a lake or offshore, lay fishing rods down and head for cover. If you're in a cabin boat and can't reach land ahead of the storm, stay in the cabin and close all the hatches. If you're running the boat, stay as low as possible at the controls. Lower all fishing rods, antennas, and outriggers. Don't hold any gear connected with the grounding system, and don't hold lifelines or rigging. Avoid acting as a bridge between conductive objects. Never touch outriggers, radio antennas, or electrical appliances until the storm has passed. Keep the boat's bow in the wind as much as possible and head for shore. Passengers should wear life jackets and stay in the cabin or as low as possible in the boat.

■ Get Ready for Hurricanes

Don't wait for a 12-hour warning to start preparing your boat for a hurricane. Do it now! You may need more time than you think to work out a plan of action that will secure and protect your boat in a storm. Now is the time to think about extra lines and special storm gear.

Even the best plan of action, however, cannot guarantee that your boat will survive a hurricane. Some hurricanes prove so violent that boats and people are helpless in their path. Fortunately, not all hurricanes are killers and there are some precautions you can take to keep storm damage to a minimum.

Most boaters believe their real threat of damage comes from winds and waves. This isn't so. Most boat damage comes from storm surge, which means high water. In fact, storm surge accounts for nine out of 10 hurricane-related deaths.

The safest place for your boat is out of the water. If you have a trailer, load your boat on it and take it home. If the boat and trailer fit in your garage, park it there and leave your car outside. Your boat is lighter than your car and can get blown off your trailer in hurricane winds. If you must leave your boat and trailer outside, put it where it will get the best protection from the wind, trees, and electrical lines. Let some air out of the trailer tires, block the wheels, and make sure the boat is strapped securely to the trailer.

You have two options when you leave your boat on a trailer. First, if it's a heavy boat, take out the drain plug to allow rainwater to drain quickly out of the hull. If your boat is light, however, and you are concerned that it may blow off the trailer, leave the drain plug in and fill the hull with water from a garden hose to add more weight. Don't put in too much water or you will damage the hull. Remember that rain will add more water and weight.

Don't trust a storage rack, even if your marina says it's a safe place. There may be other lighter boats that could be blown off their cradle and into your boat. Tell your marina to take your boat out of the rack and block it securely in a safe area. Your marina may balk at this, but be insistent.

If you are forced to leave your boat in the water, make sure it is tied securely, which means double lines. Most boats require five lines: two bow lines, two stem lines, and one spring line. If a hurricane is approaching, you will need 10 lines. It's also wise to go up one size larger than your normal dock lines. Line your boat with as many rubber fenders as you can find to protect the craft from the dock. Always give your lines chafe protection where they will come in contact with the boat or cleats. Neoprene hose is best, but canvas wrapped in place with duct tape will do in a pinch.

If your slip is a small one, look around for a bigger one that's empty and ask your marina if you can use it. The more distance you put between your boat and the pilings and bulkhead, the safer it will be.

Reading the weather is extremely important for all fishermen. High winds and rough water can turn a pleasant day into a life-threatening nightmare. Learn how to read the weather warnings, wind, and water. A calm inlet and offshore waters can turn into a turbulent and dangerous storm in a little as 30 minutes. It's important to know when to cancel a trip.

Mooring and anchoring in a protected harbor that is not crowded is a safe way to ride out a hurricane, but only if the mooring is a permanent installation and you back it up with two additional storm anchors.

When you leave your boat, take all loose gear and electronics with you and use duct tape to seal all hatches, windows, vents, and doors. When you feel your boat is ready for a hurricane, the next step is an important one: go home! When hurricane-force winds hit your boat at 100 miles per hour, there will be nothing you can do.

You can now track a hurricane by phone, which may give you enough warning to secure your boat. When a hurricane is headed your way, you can get official hurricane advisories issued by the National Oceanic and Atmospheric Administration (NOAA) or the Weather Channel.

■ Man Overboard!

Most fishermen will have their boats in the water before warm summer temperatures arrive. They will push the season and launch for trout, flounder, and other species that will start biting in early spring. One truth that is hard to accept is the fact that many fishermen are not dedicated boatmen. Fishermen are usually interested more in fishing than boating . . . and this means a potential danger to themselves and their passengers.

One distinct danger is falling overboard into cold water. Even if you are a good swimmer, the effects of cold water may be more than your body can handle. Cold water can rob your body of heat very quickly. When your body temperature drops, hypothermia becomes a very real threat to life.

Don't be misled into believing that water has to be 35 degrees to be dangerous to someone falling overboard. Cold water is anything below 70 degrees. When the water temperature drops to as low as 35 degrees, survival is usually based on the physical condition of the victim.

Panic and shock are the first and most dangerous hazards to a fisherman falling overboard. Cold water can shock the body and sometimes induce cardiac arrest. Remember how your breath is taken away when you dive into a pool? The same reaction happens when you fall headfirst into cold water. Your first gasp for air will fill your lungs with water. You may also become disoriented for a minute or two before you realize what is happening to you.

If at all possible, get back into your boat as quickly as possible. Your life may depend on it. Unless you have a big boat, this may not be as difficult as it sounds. The majority of fatal boating accidents involve small boats

with outboard motors. Most small boats, even if capsized, can be righted and reentered.

Small boats are legally bound to have enough flotation to support all occupants. If you can, right the boat, climb back into it, and bail out the water. If you can't right the boat, climb onto the hull and hang on. It's critical that you get out of the cold water.

If the boat slips away and you can't reach it, there are certain precautions to take in the water until help arrives. Unless there is no chance for a rescue, do not try swimming. It will drain body heat and, if you're like most people, you will not be able to swim very far in cold water.

Your best bet is to remain still and get into a protective position to conserve heat and wait for a rescue. This means protecting your body's major heat-loss areas, such as your head, neck, armpits, chest, and groin. If there is more than one person in the water, huddle together to preserve body heat.

Treatment of cold-water victims varies. The first signs of hypothermia are intense shivering, loss of coordination, mental confusion, blue skin, weak pulse, irregular heartbeat, and enlarged pupils. If the victim is cold and only shivering, dry clothes and blankets may be all that is necessary.

If the victim is semiconscious, move him to a warm place and into dry clothes. Make him lie flat with his head slightly lower than his body, which will make more blood flow to the brain. You can also warm the victim with warm towels to the head, neck, chest, and groin.

Of course, it's always easier to avoid problems by taking a few simple precautions. First, wear a life jacket at all times, especially during cool weather. Whenever possible, wear several layers of wool for insulation. Wool, even when wet, will retain body heat.

If you suddenly find yourself in the water, make sure your life jacket is snug. Keep clothing buttoned up. The water trapped in your clothes will be warmed by your body heat and keep you warm.

■ Why Boats Sink

The mere thought of a boat sinking out from under its skipper and his passengers will send chills down the back of the toughest boater. Will he calmly handle the situation or will he go to pieces and panic? Why did it happen? What did he do wrong?

According to statistics, boaters should worry more about sinking at the dock than out on the water. Statistics show that three out of four recreational boat

Float Plan

File a float plan. Tell someone where you are going and when you plan to return. Tell them what your boat looks like and other information that will make identifying it easier should the need arise. Print a copy of the float plan from the Coast Guard website (www.uscgboating.org/safety/float_planning.aspx), fill it out, and leave it with a reliable person who can be depended upon to notify the Coast Guard, or another rescue organization, should you not return as scheduled. Do not, however, file float plans with the Coast Guard.

A PDF version of this form can be downloaded from the U.S. Coast Guard website.

sinkings happen right at the dock. Fortunately, most dockside sinkings can be prevented.

First, never depend completely on an automatic float switch to turn on your bilge pump when water gets into your hull. Bilge pumps and switches, because of their location, get dirty and will sometimes jam in the off position and not turn on your pump at all or get stuck in the on position and kill your battery. Both cases are bad news and could sink an unattended boat. Check your bilge pump and switches before every trip. In fact, automatic float switches should be replaced every other year. These switches are inexpensive and easy to wire to a bilge pump.

Learn how to tie your boat correctly at the dock, especially in tidal water. If your boat swings or drifts too freely at the dock, it could get stuck under the dock and get pushed under the water when the tide rises. This kind of sinking happens all too often.

Make it a point of learning every through-hull underwater fitting on your boat. Draw the locations of the fittings on a piece of paper and check them every time the boat is out of the water. Look inside the hull.

Do all the fittings have seacocks? Do they all work? Do you close them when you leave the boat unattended? Do you keep them well lubricated? It's the kind of maintenance and attention that will keep your boat afloat.

Remember that your boat can take on water from above the waterline as well as from below. Check all deck fittings, fastenings, and hatches. Not all boat manufacturers use a good sealant on fastenings and some of them leak. Hose down your cabin and decks, and then look for leaks inside and in the hull. If you see a leak, fix it. You can sink from rainwater just as easily as from a leak below the surface.

Water from washings at the dock can sometimes get trapped in the hull. To get this water out, try this trick. When your bow lifts up, just before you get on a plane, manually switch on your bilge. If you have to, keep the bow high until all the bilge water rushes to the pump and gets pumped out.

Continually check all hoses and clamps. Clamps are cheap. If they look rusty, replace them. In fact, you should keep an assortment of different size clamps in your toolbox. Pay special attention to hoses that have sharp bends. If any look stressed or kinked, replace them. Replacing a hose when your boat is on a trailer is easy. It's a panic problem, however, if it happens 5 miles from shore. It's also a good idea to double clamp all hoses.

If you're shopping for a boat, look for designs with self-bailing cockpits. This means the deck is above the waterline. Any water coming into the boat will drain out the transom scuppers and not stay in the boat or hull. This is a comforting thought in a heavy sea. Most of the tough breed of small fishing boats built for offshore fishing have this feature. Many small, less expensive ski boats, however, do not have self-bailing cockpits. Stay away from them.

Make sure your transom drains, transom wells, and scuppers are clean and not clogged with dirt. Water must be allowed to drain out. The best time to check these drains and flush them out is when you're washing your boat with a hose and good water pressure.

Maintenance of through-hull fittings, seacocks, hoses, bilge pumps, and switches is easy. Make a checklist and do it often. This is especially important if you leave your boat unattended for long periods of time.

If you leave your boat in the water, you should also get a mooring cover that protects your boat from bow to stern. This kind of full cover will give you peace of mind the next time it storms and your boat is 50 miles away at the marina where it may not get any attention.

■ Why Boats Blow Up

A day on the water can be an exhilarating experience, but when things go wrong with your boat, it can also be a frightening experience. The thought of a fire or explosion on a boat is even more terrifying. If you're far from land, there is no safe place to run.

Fires and explosions can only come from faulty fuel systems or human error. Fortunately, both are avoidable if you take certain precautions. First, let's start with the deck. Is your gas cap clearly labeled "gasoline"? As far-fetched as it sounds, there are cases on record where a clueless gas attendant has pumped gasoline into a rod holder or into a water tank.

All boats must have an overside drain or tank vent for your fuel tank. Make sure that excess fuel or fumes at the gas dock will not find their way into your boat or bilge. Make sure your vent has a mesh screen in place, which could keep fumes from igniting in the fuel line.

If your fill hose is worn or frayed, replace it. But make certain you buy the right hose. It should be stamped "USCG Type A2," which is fire resistant. Your filler cap should also be grounded with an electrical wire from the fill opening to the tank, so that any static electricity from the dock hose will flow to the ground without causing a spark.

It's critical that you run your blower to clear your bilge of gas fumes before starting your engine. Check the blower hose and make sure it's not crushed or broken or twisted. After you've run your blower, sniff the bilge with your nose, which is probably the best fuel detector of all. If you have any doubts, don't start your engine. This is especially true at the fuel dock, where most explosions and fires occur.

If you're buying a new or used boat, check the fuel tanks. Any tank over 7 gallons should have a label with the manufacturer's name, date of manufacture, capacity, and material. It should also say, "This tank has been tested under 33 CFR 183.580." If you can't find this label, avoid the boat or have the tank replaced.

Even if you have all the right fittings and parts, you can still get into trouble if you are careless. Explosions are most likely to occur at the fuel dock, when a leak in the fill or vent system may not be discovered until the tank is topped off.

When you refuel, take certain precautions. First, close all hatches and turn off the battery switch and stove. Fill the tank yourself, if you can, and never fill it to the very top. If you do, and the gas expands, you could get spillage in your boat and bilge. After refueling, run the blower for a full five minutes or longer, and then sniff the bilge with your nose before starting the engine.

If you use outboard-motor tanks, take them out of the boat and do your refueling on the dock. This is the safest procedure. Unfortunately, most inboard and stern-drive boats don't have this option.

Let's suppose, for example, that you don't notice a fuel leak until it is too late and you're out on the water with a bilge full of gas. Do you know what to do? Here's the best and only procedure. Do not start the engine or use any electrical equipment other than your VHF radio or cell phone—and this should be only after you turn off all other electrical circuits. Next, turn off your battery switch and have all your passengers put on life jackets and stay on deck. Finally, call the Coast Guard and describe your problem and situation. They will instruct you on the next step.

If you find gas has leaked into your boat at the dock, order all guests off the boat. Turn off the battery switch and shore power. Notify the marina manager and call the fire department.

Don't wreck your day or endanger your guests because you don't know how to handle a gas emergency. Most of these procedures are simple common sense.

Your Mate: That Extra PFD on a Boat

Good mates, without exception, love fishing and their jobs. Why else would they work 12-hour days, pull anchors in heavy seas on slippery bows, and tolerate squirrelly fishermen who tamper with drags? Mates never get the credit they deserve for their skills and tireless energy. They're expected to handle all jobs—from wrestling billfish into the cockpit for photos to making sure a seasick fisherman doesn't fall overboard.

In addition to helping you catch fish, a mate's job is to keep you safe on a boat and handle emergencies. His job is the same as a copilot on an airplane. I learned this the hard way several years ago when I rinsed my hands in a cockpit bucket that also held live bait and a dangling 4/0 hook. When I pulled my hands out of the bucket, I drove that hook into my forearm. The hook was too big to use the back-out method, so Marc Ellis, our mate, took over. He pushed the hook through and exposed the barb, which he cut off with his pliers. Not a pleasant day at sea for me. I got a tetanus shot when I got back to the dock. I'm still indebted to Marc.

During a lifetime of boating, I've had several emergencies in offshore waters, but one that still stands out is the time our prop got hopelessly tangled in a crab line. We were dead in the water. Again, it was our mate, Brooks Gregory, who dove under the hull in a sloppy ocean to cut the crab line loose. I also watched a mate in Key West expertly wrap a fisherman who got his hand too close to the jaws of a king mackerel. A helicopter eventually got the seriously injured fisherman off the boat, but it was the mate who quickly stopped the massive bleeding.

It's easy to describe a good mate because they do everything right. Watching a mate tie a perfect Bimini twist single-handed on a pitching deck is a pure joy to witness. They will rig a bait with the precision of a surgeon. But cockpit skills are not enough. They must also learn how to be courteous and patient with clients who get seasick, fall down, cut themselves, or drive hooks in their hands, and sometimes they are confronted with even more serious medical emergencies.

How does someone become a mate? I've spent many years along charter boats row and it's easy to spot a mate in the making. Look for a young boy, about 10 or 12 years old, who hangs around the docks. In summertime, he will be wearing flip-flops, a sun visor, and sunglasses on a string around his neck. His T-shirt will always have a fish on it. When charter boats come in, these young boys will volunteer to help the mates wash down the boats and tackle. Sometimes they will accept $10, but many times they just like to work on a boat.

Squid was one of these boys. Richard Stancyzk, who owns Bud N Mary's Marina in Islamorada, Florida, saw some potential in him and started to take Squid along on our trips as a second mate. At times, I felt sorry for Squid, a stringy little kid, when Richard would repeatedly yell, "Squid, you're standing still!" But Squid is a full mate today and he will likely be a captain with his own boat in the years to come. Squid took a beating on those early training trips with Richard, but he learned early on that a mate's work in the cockpit is never done until the boat is docked, scrubbed, and ready to sail the next morning at 6:00 a.m.

I'd like to offer some sound advice on the care and feeding of a mate. When you get onboard, extend your hand to the mate and introduce yourself. He may be working for you, but make him feel like you will be fishing buddies for the day. Share your fishing experiences and offer some help in the cockpit. Feel free to ask questions. Most mates like to show off their skills. Watch his hands and you will probably learn more about rigging and fishing techniques in one day than you would in a year of fumbling onboard your own boat. Most important, you may one day depend on him to cut a 4/0 hook out of your arm.

Vin Sparano (left) and mate Sam Worden pose with an African pompano from offshore waters of the Florida Keys.

FISHING
BASICS
FOR BOATERS

Section Five
FISHING BASICS FOR BOATERS

• SPINNING • FLY FISHING • BAITCASTING •
• SPINCASTING • LINES • FISHHOOKS • LURES •
• FRESHWATER AND SALTWATER BAITS •
• KNOTS • FISHING TACKLE •
• EASY FISH RELEASE •

SPINNING

Spinning became popular in America in the late 1940s. It is unique because the reel is mounted on the underside of the rod—rather than on top, as in other methods—and because the reel spool remains stationary (does not revolve) when the angler is casting and retrieving.

In operation, the weight and momentum of the lure being cast uncoils line (usually monofilament, fluorocarbon, or braid) from the reel spool. Unlike conventional revolving-spool reels, in which the momentum of the turning spool can cause backlashes, the spinning-reel user has no such problem, for the line stops uncoiling at the end of the cast. A beginner can learn to use spinning gear much faster than conventional tackle. Still another advantage of spinning gear is that it permits the use of much lighter lines and smaller, lighter lures than can be cast with conventional equipment.

■ The Reel

On a standard open-face spinning reel, the pickup mechanism is usually of a type called the bail—a metal arm extending across the spool's face. To cast a lure or bait, the angler opens the bail by swinging it out and down. This frees the line, which, as a rule, the angler momentarily controls with his index finger. He casts and then cranks the reel handle—not a full turn but just a small fraction of a turn. This snaps the bail closed, engaging the line.

Other devices on a spinning reel include the drag and the antireverse lock. The drag, an adjustable mechanism usually consisting of a series of discs and friction washers, is fitted on the outer (forward) face of the spool or at the rear of the gear housing in most reels. The drag permits a hooked fish to take out line without breaking off, while the reel handle remains stationary. The anti-reverse lock, usually a lever mounted on the gear-housing cover, prevents the reel handle from turning in reverse at such times as when a hooked fish is running out or when you are trolling.

Spinning reels are designed for all types of fishing. How does the beginner select the right one for his particular needs? A reel's weight and line capacity are the major determining factors. For ultralight fishing with tiny lures (1/16 to 5/16 ounce), a reel weighing 5 to 8 ounces and holding about 100 yards of 2- to 4-pound-test line is the ticket. Reels for light freshwater use weigh 8 to 10 ounces and hold up to 200 yards of 6- to 8-pound-test line. Reels for general freshwater and light saltwater use weigh 12 to 16 ounces and hold up to 250 yards of 8- to 15-pound-test line. Heavy offshore and surf-spinning reels weigh upwards of 25 ounces and hold a minimum of 250 yards of 15-pound-test line. These yardage capacities are for monofilament or fluorocarbon line. Smaller-diameter braid line will usually increase these capacities on most reels.

In addition to the open-face spinning reel, there is a closed-face design. This type, too, is mounted under the rod. Its spool and working parts are enclosed in a hood, with the line running through an opening at the front. The pickup mechanism is normally an internal pin, and there's no need for a bail since the line control is accomplished by other means. In some of these reels, which were fairly common at one time, line was disengaged from the pickup by backing the handle a half turn. In others, it was accomplished by pushing a button, working a lever or disc, or pressing the front reel plate. Closed-face reels are still available, but are no longer common.

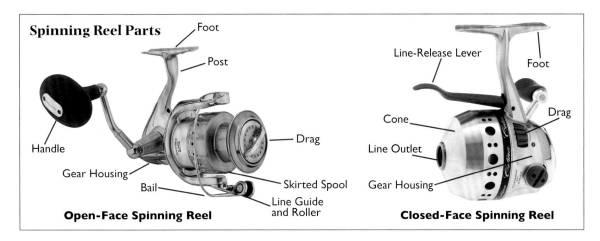

Spinning Reel Parts

Foot

Post

Handle

Gear Housing

Bail

Open-Face Spinning Reel

Drag

Skirted Spool

Line Guide and Roller

Line-Release Lever

Foot

Cone

Drag

Line Outlet

Gear Housing

Closed-Face Spinning Reel

Besides eliminating the bail, closed-faced reels give the spool and other parts some protection from the elements and help to keep out sand, dirt, and the like. Some fishermen, however, dislike the fact that the line is choked through the constriction at the point of the cone, feeling that this arrangement somewhat limits casting range and accuracy. Another drawback is that the hood enclosing the spool hides the line from the angler's view, preventing him from seeing line tangles and whether or not the line is uncoiling smoothly.

Mainly because of the simplicity of spinning reels, there has been little gadgeteering by manufacturers. However, some unusual features have appeared over the years. These have included bails that open automatically, self-centering (self-positioning) bails, rear drags, and skirted spools, which prevent line from getting behind the spool.

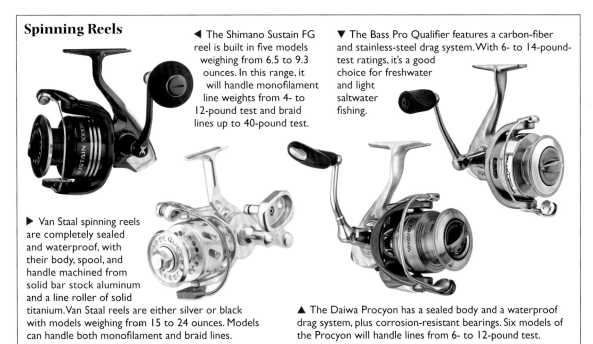

Spinning Reels

◀ The Shimano Sustain FG reel is built in five models weighing from 6.5 to 9.3 ounces. In this range, it will handle monofilament line weights from 4- to 12-pound test and braid lines up to 40-pound test.

▼ The Bass Pro Qualifier features a carbon-fiber and stainless-steel drag system. With 6- to 14-pound-test ratings, it's a good choice for freshwater and light saltwater fishing.

▶ Van Staal spinning reels are completely sealed and waterproof, with their body, spool, and handle machined from solid bar stock aluminum and a line roller of solid titanium. Van Staal reels are either silver or black with models weighing from 15 to 24 ounces. Models can handle both monofilament and braid lines.

▲ The Daiwa Procyon has a sealed body and a waterproof drag system, plus corrosion-resistant bearings. Six models of the Procyon will handle lines from 6- to 12-pound test.

How to Match Up Spinning Tackle

This chart is meant only as a general guide aimed at helping you put together, in proper balance, the basic elements of a spinning outfit tailored for fish of a particular weight category. Specific conditions—and your ability and personal preferences—should also be considered.

Species of Fish	Reel	Rod Action, Length (feet)	Line (pound test)	Lure Weights (ounces)
Trout, small bass, grayling, panfish	Ultralight	Ultralight, 4 to 6	2, 3	$\frac{1}{16}$ to $\frac{5}{16}$
Smallmouth, largemouth, and white bass, pickerel, trout, grayling	Light	Light, 5½ to 6½	4 to 8	$\frac{1}{4}$ to $\frac{3}{8}$
Large bass and trout, walleye, pickerel, pike, snook, landlocked salmon	Medium	Medium, 6 to 7½	6 to 10	$\frac{3}{8}$ to $\frac{5}{8}$
Salmon, lake trout, muskellunge, pike, bonefish, tarpon, striped bass, bluefish	Heavy	Heavy, 7 to 8½	10 to 15	½ to 1½
General saltwater use (surf and boat)	Extraheavy	Extraheavy, 9 to 13	12 and up	1 and up

▪ The Rod

There are spinning rods designed for every conceivable kind of sport fishing. They come in lengths from 4 to 13 feet and weigh from 2 to 30 ounces. Most are constructed of fiberglass, graphite, carbon, or Kevlar. Construction is usually one, two, or three pieces; however, some spinning rods designed for backpackers may have as many as a half-dozen sections.

Spinning rods fall into five general categories: ultralight, light, medium, heavy, and extraheavy. They are further broken down according to the type of reel and design of the hand grip.

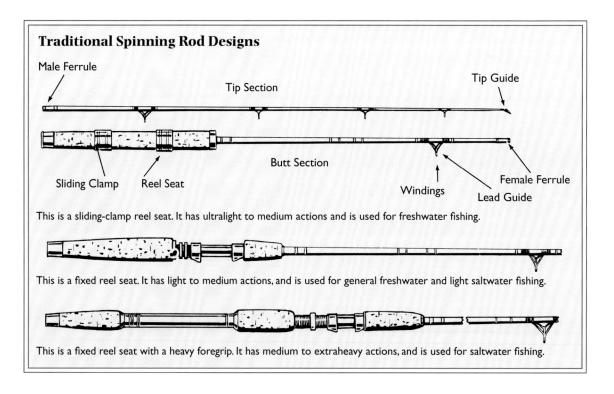

Traditional Spinning Rod Designs

Male Ferrule

Tip Section

Tip Guide

Sliding Clamp   Reel Seat

Butt Section

Windings

Female Ferrule

Lead Guide

This is a sliding-clamp reel seat. It has ultralight to medium actions and is used for freshwater fishing.

This is a fixed reel seat. It has light to medium actions, and is used for general freshwater and light saltwater fishing.

This is a fixed reel seat with a heavy foregrip. It has medium to extraheavy actions, and is used for saltwater fishing.

FLY FISHING

The art of fly fishing dates back to at least the third century AD and so is one of the oldest forms of sport fishing. Its adherents—and they are legion—say that it is also the most artistic form of the sport.

Fly fishing is unique in two basic ways. In all other forms of fishing, the weight of the lure or bait is what enables the angler to cast; in fly fishing, the weight of the line itself enables the cast. In spinning, spincasting, and baitcasting, a natural bait or a lure or plug imitating a natural bait is offered to the fish; a fly fisherman's offering is a near-weightless bit of feathers and hair that imitates an insect in one of its forms of life (though some flies—streamers and bucktails—imitate baitfish).

■ The Reel

It is generally agreed that the reel, with the exception of saltwater fly fishing, is the least important item of fly-fishing tackle, and yet without it, the angler would find himself amid a tangle of line and leader. The fly reel is mounted below the rod grip and close to the butt end of the rod. In most kinds of fishing, the reel's main function is to store line that is not being used. In handling large fish, however, the workings and drag of the fly reel come into play.

There are two basic types of fly reels: the single action and the automatic.

The single-action reel, which is best when the quarry is either small or quite heavy fish, is so named because the spool makes one complete turn for each turn of the handle. The spool is deep and narrow. A beginner should make sure that the reel has a strong click mechanism to prevent the line from overrunning, and if he'll be tangling with sizable, strong-running fish, such as striped bass, tarpon or salmon, he should get a reel with a good smooth adjustable drag.

The standard (trout size) single-action fly reel weighs 3 to 5 ounces and has a spool diameter of 3 to 4 inches. The spool should be filled with enough line (the fly line itself, usually 30 yards, plus sufficient "backing" line) to reach within about ⅛ inch of the reel's cross braces. Many of the best fly fishermen like 15- to 30-pound-test braid or monofilament line as backing. For most freshwater fishing, 20-pound-test braid backing is fine, but 30-pound test is recommended for species such as striped bass, bonefish, and salmon. The chief advantages of the single-action fly reel are that it weighs considerably less than the automatic and it can hold much more backing, an important factor in handling large fish. The automatic fly reel has a spring-operated spool

How to Match Up Fly Tackle

This chart is meant only as a general guide aimed at helping you put together, in proper balance, the basic elements of a fly-fishing outfit tailored for fish of a particular weight category. Specific conditions—and your ability and personal preference—should also be considered. The line sizes below are meant only as a general guide, and a newcomer to fishing should note that there is a wide range of conditions and circumstances that determines the correct line weight for a given rod. Level and double-taper fly lines may still be available, but the best advice for easy casting is to use weight-forward lines.

Species of Fish	Reel	Rod Length (feet)	Lines		
			Level	Double Taper	Weight Forward
Trout, small bass, grayling, panfish	Single-action, automatic	6½ to 7½	L4 or L5	DT4F or DT5F; DT6S	WF4F; WF6S
Smallmouth, largemouth, and white bass, pickerel, trout, grayling	Single-action, automatic	7½ to 8½	L6 or L7	DT6F or DT7F; DT8S	WF6F; WF8S
Large bass and trout, landlocked salmon, walleye, pickerel, pike	Single-action	8½ to 9	L8 or L9	DT8F or DT9F; DT9S	WF9F; WF10S
Salmon, lake trout, muskellunge, pike, bonefish, tarpon, striped bass, bluefish	Single-action	9½	L10	DT10F	WF10F; WF10S

KEY TO LINE DESIGNATIONS: L—LEVEL DT—DOUBLE TAPER WF—WEIGHT FORWARD F—FLOATING S—SINKING

Basic Types of Fly Reels

◀ The Orvis Battenkill Bar Stock is a typical fly reel design. Depending on the Orvis model, the Battenkill can handle any species from trout to billfish with line weights of 1 to 11.

▶ The Pflueger Automatic fly reel has a spring-operated spool that retrieves line automatically when an angler activates the lever. A one-time favorite with some fly fishermen, it has decreased in popularity.

▲ The World Wide Sportsman Gold Cup is a fly reel designed for big fish. Two models are built for fly lines up to WF12F with 300 yards of 30-pound-test backing. It features a heat-resistant carbon drag.

▲ The Sage 1600 is an all-aluminum fly reel with a quick-release spool change and a sealed graphite drag. It is built for line weights of 4 to 9. In the model with a line weight range of 4 to 6, the Sage 1600 weighs only 5⅞ ounces. It is a good freshwater choice.

▲ The White River Kingfisher fly reel, machined from cold-forged aluminum with a sealed drag system, has an open-frame design and offers a wide range of models for freshwater and saltwater fishing. These models handle fly line weights from 3 to 10 with room for backing.

that retrieves line automatically when the angler activates the spool-release lever. The spring is wound up as line is pulled from the reel, but line may be stripped from the reel at any time, even when the spring is tightly wound. Though heavier than the single action (the weight range is 5 to 10 ounces), the automatic greatly facilitates line control. Instead of having to shift the rod from the right to the left hand (assuming the user is right-handed) to reel in line—as the user of the single-action reel must do—the automatic user simply touches the release lever with the little finger of his right hand.

Fly Rod Parts

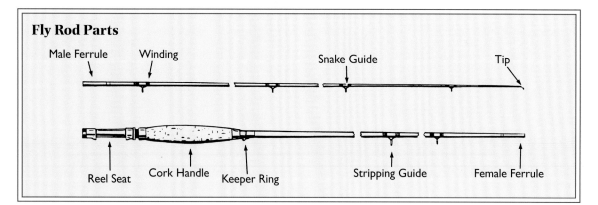

Male Ferrule   Winding   Snake Guide   Tip

Reel Seat   Cork Handle   Keeper Ring   Stripping Guide   Female Ferrule

How to Wade a River

Wading looks easy enough, but it can turn into a dangerous situation if you are swept off your feet in the swift current. The rules for safe wading are simple. First, never take a step in any direction unless your rear or anchor foot is firmly planted. Next, slide your lead foot forward until it is secure. When your lead foot is firmly planted, then slide your anchor foot ahead. Never try to wade by lifting your feet. The current will swing your leg out from under you and throw you off balance. Avoid wading big, wide stretches of river. It is safer to wade from pool to pool, taking advantage of slower current to rest.

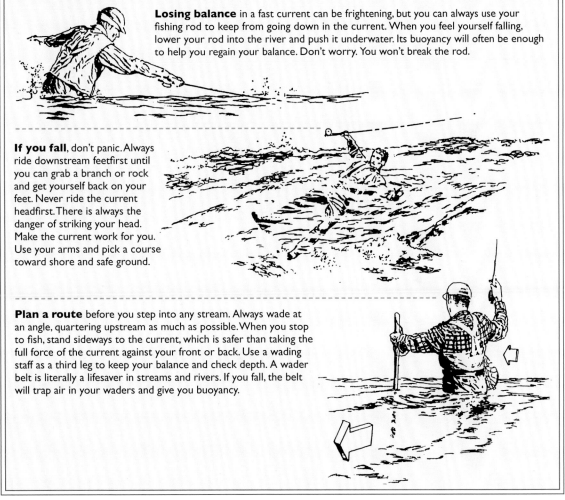

Losing balance in a fast current can be frightening, but you can always use your fishing rod to keep from going down in the current. When you feel yourself falling, lower your rod into the river and push it underwater. Its buoyancy will often be enough to help you regain your balance. Don't worry. You won't break the rod.

If you fall, don't panic. Always ride downstream feetfirst until you can grab a branch or rock and get yourself back on your feet. Never ride the current headfirst. There is always the danger of striking your head. Make the current work for you. Use your arms and pick a course toward shore and safe ground.

Plan a route before you step into any stream. Always wade at an angle, quartering upstream as much as possible. When you stop to fish, stand sideways to the current, which is safer than taking the full force of the current against your front or back. Use a wading staff as a third leg to keep your balance and check depth. A wader belt is literally a lifesaver in streams and rivers. If you fall, the belt will trap air in your waders and give you buoyancy.

■ The Rod

The rod is of paramount importance to the fly caster. It must be suited to the kind of fishing he does (saltwater, trout, bass bugging, and so on), and it must be matched with the proper fly line.

Fly rods can be made of fiberglass, graphite, or bamboo. Graphite fly rods are faster and more sensitive than fiberglass rods. And, ounce for ounce, graphite is twice as strong as glass. What length rod should the beginner select?

According to the recommendations of several casting instructors and tackle manufacturers, a good all-purpose length is 8 to 8½ feet with a weight of about 5 ounces. Such a rod should have fast action.

Action, briefly, is a measure of a rod's flexibility, and it determines the use for which the rod is suited. In fast-action rods, best suited for dry-fly fishing, most of the flex (or bend) is at the tip. Medium-action rods bend down to the middle and are designed to perform over a wide range of conditions. They are probably the best choice for an all-purpose fly rod. Slow-action rods, a traditional design that works well for fishing streamers, bass bugs, and the like, bend well down to and even into the butt.

Good fly rods have a screw-lock reel seat, which holds the reel securely. Line guides are usually made of stainless steel, except that the tip guide and sometimes the stripper guide (the one nearest to the reel) may be chrome or highly durable carboloy steel. The largest fly rods, those designed for taking tarpon and other large saltwater fish, have an extension butt or a fore-end grip, which gives the angler more leverage.

BAITCASTING

Baitcasting is a method of fishing distinguished by the use of a revolving-spool reel. Originally intended by its 19th-century creators as a means of casting live baitfish, baitcasting tackle today is used to present all sorts of offerings—from worms and minnows to spoons and huge jointed plugs—to game fish in both fresh and salt water. This method is also known as plugcasting.

Before the advent of spinning gear, baitcasting was the universally accepted tackle for presenting baits or lures. Even today, many anglers—especially those who grew up with a baitcasting outfit in their hands—prefer this method, even though the revolving-spool reel is more difficult to use than fixed-spool spinning and spincasting reels. The baitcaster feels that his gear gives him more sensitive contact with what is going on at the end of his line. He feels that he can manipulate a lure better on baitcasting gear and have better control over a hooked fish. Most fishermen agree that when the quarry is a big, strong fish such as a muskie, pike, or saltwater fish, baitcasting outfits get the nod over spinning or spincasting tackle.

Baitcasting tackle is often preferred for trolling, too, for the revolving-spool reel makes it easy to pay out line behind the moving boat, and the rod has enough backbone to handle the big, water-resistant lures used in many forms of trolling.

■ The Reel

The reel is by far the most important part of a baitcasting outfit, and the budding baitcaster would do well to buy the best reel he can afford.

How to Match Up Baitcasting Tackle

This chart is meant only as a general guide aimed at helping you put together, in proper balance, the basic elements of a baitcasting outfit. Specific conditions—and your ability and personal preferences—should also be considered.

Species of Fish	Reel	Rod Action, Length (feet)	Line (pound test)	Lure Weights (ounces)
Panfish, small bass, pickerel, trout	Multiplying gear with level-wind	Ultralight, 6 to 6½	6 to 8	⅛ to ¼
Bass, pickerel, walleye, small pike, trout	Multiplying gear with level-wind	Light, 5½ to 6½	6 to 12	¼ to ½
Large bass, walleye, pike, lake trout, muskie, striped bass	Multiplying gear with star drag	Medium, 5 to 6	10 to 20	⅝ to ¾
Muskie, steelhead, lake trout, salmon, striped bass, bluefish, tarpon, snook	Multiplying gear with star drag	Heavy, 4½ to 7	18 to 25	¾ and up

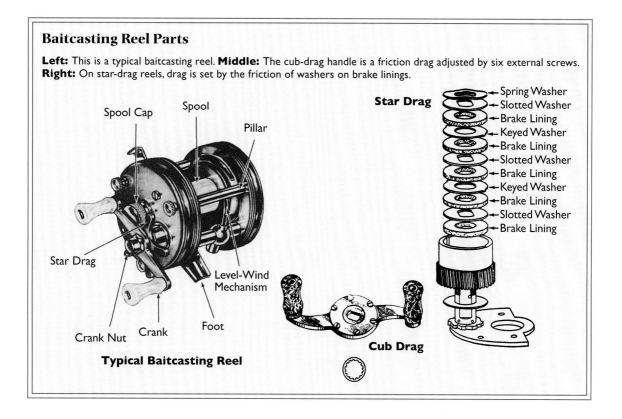

Baitcasting Reel Parts

Left: This is a typical baitcasting reel. **Middle:** The cub-drag handle is a friction drag adjusted by six external screws. **Right:** On star-drag reels, drag is set by the friction of washers on brake linings.

Star Drag

Spring Washer
Slotted Washer
Brake Lining
Keyed Washer
Brake Lining
Slotted Washer
Brake Lining
Keyed Washer
Brake Lining
Slotted Washer
Brake Lining

Spool Cap
Spool
Pillar
Star Drag
Level-Wind Mechanism
Crank Nut
Crank
Foot

Typical Baitcasting Reel

Cub Drag

The main distinguishing feature of baitcasting reels is that the spool revolves when line is cast out or reeled in, while in spinning and spincasting reels the spool remains stationary.

Baitcasting reels have a relatively wide, shallow spool, and most have multiplying gears that cause the spool to revolve several times (usually four) for each complete turn of the reel handle. There is also some kind of drag mechanism, which is helpful in fighting big fish. These range from a simple click mechanism to a screw-down nut to a star drag. Some older reels have what is called a cub drag, which is adjusted by turning six screws on the base of the handle.

Almost all of today's good baitcasting reels have an important device called a level-wind. It usually takes the form of a U-shaped loop of heavy wire attached to a base that travels from one side of the spool to the other by means of a wormlike gear. The device permits line to be wound evenly on the spool and thus is a big help in preventing backlashes, which are often caused by line "lumping up" on the spool. A backlash occurs when the speed of the revolving spool is faster than that of the outgoing line, resulting in a "bird's nest."

Most baitcasting reels are being made with anti-backlash devices. These employ either centrifugal force or pressure on the spool axle or flange to slow down the spool during a cast. Some reels use magnets to accomplish this process. However, though these antibacklash devices are helpful, the user of a baitcasting reel must still learn to apply thumb pressure to the spool if he is to prevent backlashes under all conditions. Only experience can teach how much thumb pressure is needed under any given set of circumstances.

Another development in baitcasting is the free-spool reel. Without this feature, the cast lure not only pulls out line and turns the spool, but also turns the gears, the level-wind, and the reel handle. All these moving parts tend to shorten the cast. But in the free-spool reel, most of the gearing is disconnected from the spool before a cast is made, and only the spool (and sometimes the level-wind) turns. This makes it easier to start and stop the turning of the spool and so permits the use of lighter lures than can be cast with a standard baitcasting reel. Longer casts are also possible. A turn of the handle reengages the gears of the free-spool reel so that the retrieve can be made.

■ The Rod

Most baitcasting rods are now made of fiberglass or graphite. Rod lengths range from about 4 to more than 7 feet. Some, obviously, are more suitable for specific purposes. The most popular length—because it works well for many kinds of fishing—is about 6 feet. Manufacturers generally classify their rods according to their action, which refers to the lure weights that a rod handles efficiently. Generally, ultralight rods can handle lures weighing ¼ ounce or less. Light rods can handle ¼ to ½ ounce. Medium rods are better at handling ⅝ to ¾ ounce, and heavy rods are for ¾ ounce or more.

Baitcasting rods have either a straight handle or a pistol-grip handle. No longer common is the double-offset handle, in which the reel seat is depressed and the butt grip is canted downward. Other features of baitcasting rods are a finger hook on the underside of the reel seat and a reel-holding screw lock.

Baitcasting rods are of one- or two-piece construction. Some have ferrules about midway up the rod, while others may have a detachable handle. The most popular baitcasting rods have a straight handle, a long butt section, a foregrip usually made of cork, and a rubber butt cap. These rods, sometimes called popping rods, have become so popular that lighter-action models are now commonly used for freshwater fishing. The longer straight handle makes it more comfortable and less tiring for casting and fighting fish. Well suited for freshwater and light saltwater use, these rods can also handle an extensive range of lure weights for various species of fish.

Baitcasting Reels

▶ The Johnny Morris Signature Series Baitcast Reel is built on a solid aluminum frame with a carbon-titanium finish. This reel has an 11-bearing system and a carbon drag with up to 14 pounds of drag pressure. Five different models weigh from 8.3 to 9.6 ounces. The line capacity is 160 yards of 12-pound-test monofilament.

▶ The Daiwa PX Type-R Baitcast Reel is a lightweight reel at 5.8 ounces. It's designed for light lures on light lines, and the capacity is 95 yards of 6-pound-test monofilament. The maximum drag is 13 pounds.

▲ The Abu Garcia Revo MGX is a featherweight baitcasting reel for light-tackle freshwater fishing. Weighing only 5.4 ounces with a gear ratio of 7:1 and a maximum drag pressure of 24 pounds, the reel features 10 stainless-steel bearings and a line capacity of 115 yards of 12-pound-test monofilament.

▲ The Browning Midas Low-Profile Baitcast Reel has a one-piece aluminum frame, V-shaped spool of forged aluminum, and nine stainless-steel bearings. It also has a magnetic cast control and heavy thumb-bar release. It will hold 120 yards of 12-pound-test line.

▲ The Abu Garcia 5600 is designed to handle most species of freshwater and inshore saltwater fish. A familiar reel for generations, the Abu Garcia Ambassadeur series features stainless-steel ball bearings, a carbon star-drag system, and line capacities of up to 245 yards of 14-pound-test monofilament.

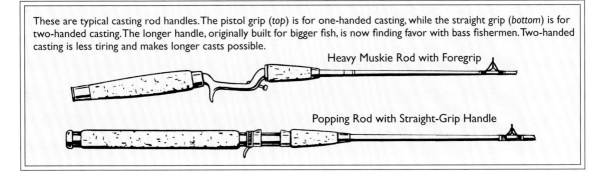

These are typical casting rod handles. The pistol grip (*top*) is for one-handed casting, while the straight grip (*bottom*) is for two-handed casting. The longer handle, originally built for bigger fish, is now finding favor with bass fishermen. Two-handed casting is less tiring and makes longer casts possible.

Heavy Muskie Rod with Foregrip

Popping Rod with Straight-Grip Handle

Typical Casting Rod Designs

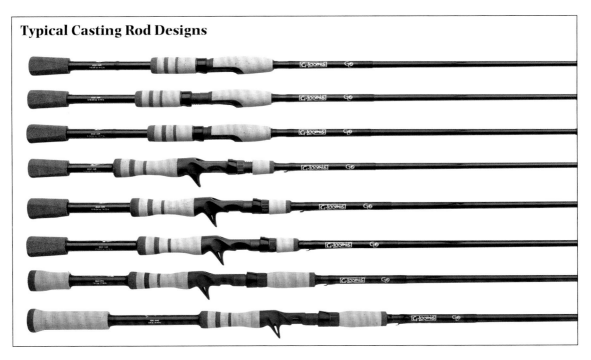

▣ Flipping

Flipping is an effective technique for bass fishermen. It's a simple but deadly approach for presenting a lure in and around brush, standing timber, grass, logs, lily pads, and heavy vegetation.

For flipping, most bass fishermen prefer 7- to 8-foot casting rods with 25- to 30-pound-test line. Lure selections are usually sparse—jigs and plastic worms. The fisherman ties on a black, blue, or brown ½-ounce "living rubber" jig. He protects the large hook with a fiber guard, and tips it with an Uncle Josh Pork Frog. This is especially deadly in the cooler springtime waters.

Flipping allows you to keep the lure close to cover constantly, thus allowing the fish to bite with very little effort or movement. Start with about 8 to 9 feet of line from rod tip to lure. Then, strip off an arm's length of line. Using your wrist and not your shoulder or elbow, begin swinging the lure like a pendulum. Never let the lure come too far back. The swing should be smooth. When the lure reaches the back of its arc closest to you, a slight flick of the wrist (pretend

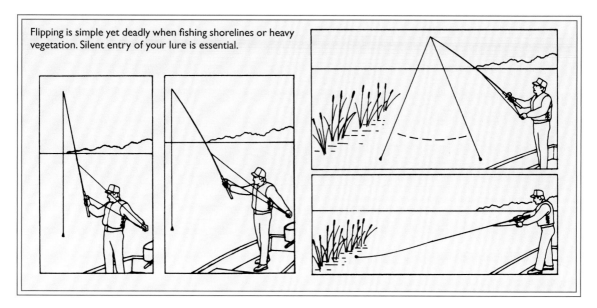

Flipping is simple yet deadly when fishing shorelines or heavy vegetation. Silent entry of your lure is essential.

you're only using the rod tip to do the work) will aim the lure toward the target. At this point, the line should be allowed to slide through your hand and the rod tip should be lowered to steer the lure to the desired spot. A silent entry is essential. Never release the line until the lure reaches the water, because you want to control the lure. Once in the water, the jig or worm should fall freely to the bottom. Then, your task is to climb and wriggle the lure up and over every limb, root, and stem, carefully watching the line for the slightest nibble.

SPINCASTING

Spincasting is a method of fishing that, in effect, combines a push-button type of spinning reel with a baitcasting rod. This tackle efficiently handles lures and baits of average weights from ¼ to ¾ ounce. With lighter or heavier lures, its efficiency falls off sharply. Spincasting is ideal for newcomers to fishing, for it is the easiest casting method to learn and is the ticket for lots of trouble-free sport.

■ The Reel

Spincasting reels, like spinning reels, operate on the fixed-spool principle—that is, the weight of the lure or bait being cast uncoils the line from the stationary spool. Most spincasting reels are of the closed-face type, the spool and gearing being enclosed in a cone-shaped hood.

The major factor distinguishing the spincasting reel from the spinning reel is that spincasting action is controlled by a thumb-activated "trigger," a push button mounted on the reel. In operation, the spincaster holds his thumb down on the trigger until the rod is about half-way through the forward-cast motion. He then releases thumb pressure on the trigger, which frees the line and feeds it through a small hole in the center of the cone, sending the lure on its way.

There are two kinds of spincasting reels, those mounted atop the rod and those mounted below it. Most spincasting reels are of the top-mounted type and are designed for rods having an offset reel seat. They can be mounted on straight-grip rods, but this combination is uncomfortable to use since the caster must reach up with his thumb to activate the reel trigger.

Below-the-rod spincasting reels are a much different design. They combine the balance of a spinning reel with the ease of a spincast reel. The line aperture in the cone is also larger than on a spincast reel. A lever activates the casting mechanism, much the same as on a push-button spincast reel.

Spincasting reels have various kinds of adjustable drag mechanisms. In one kind, the drag is set by rotating

Fishing Pliers

For many years, the only tool on a fisherman's belt was a small pair of pliers with spring-loaded handles and a wire cutter on the side of the jaws. To make mine slip-proof, I put pieces of surgical tubing over the handles. The pliers measured only 4½ inches long, probably too short when dislodging big hooks from big fish with sharp teeth. I used mine mostly to pull knots tight, cut monofilament and wire, and rig baits. These pliers worked fine for one or two seasons, but then the cutters got dull and the spring-loaded handles always had to be oiled regularly to keep them working freely.

A lot has happened over the years! Today, fishermen now have a choice of dozens of fishing tools to hang on their belts, ranging from pliers made from titanium and aircraft aluminum to plastic. The new multipurpose pliers will also do a variety of jobs. Most models will crimp, cut braid and wire, and are totally corrosion proof. And those long-nose models will keep your fingers safely away from sharp teeth and hooks.

The price tags on some of these pliers are a real enigma. They range from $12 to more than $300. Are the inexpensive models good? Can fishermen justify dropping hundreds of dollars on a pair of pliers? Are they worth the money? Is it easier to buy $12 pliers and throw them away at the end of the season? Those expensive titanium pliers may well outlive you. These are tough questions to answer. Let your fishing budget be your guide.

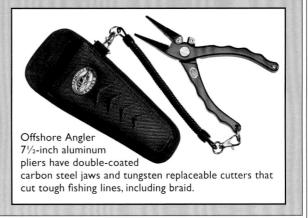

Offshore Angler 7½-inch aluminum pliers have double-coated carbon steel jaws and tungsten replaceable cutters that cut tough fishing lines, including braid.

---

the cone that surrounds the spool. Other reels have star drags like those found on baitcasting reels. The drag in still other reels is activated by turning the reel handle. Spincast reels are ideal for night fishing because of their trouble-free operation. However, besides the fact that they can handle a rather limited range of lure weights, if very light line is used on these reels, the line has a tendency to foul in the housing.

The Pflueger Cetina, a typical spincast reel, comes in five models with pre-spooled monofilament ranging from 6- to 10-pound test.

The grip for the spincasting reel is similar to the grip used for the baitcasting reel. The thumb depresses the control lever during the backcast, checking the line, and releases pressure as the rod whips forward.

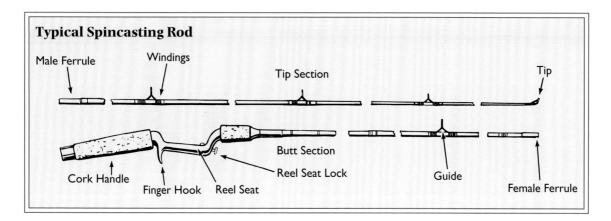

Typical Spincasting Rod

Male Ferrule · Windings · Tip Section · Tip · Cork Handle · Finger Hook · Reel Seat · Reel Seat Lock · Butt Section · Guide · Female Ferrule

■ The Rod

Spincasting rods are basically the same as those designed for baitcasting, but there are a few differences. In general, spincasting rods average a bit longer than baitcasting rods. (The most popular lengths are 6 and 6½ feet.) They have flexible tips that are more responsive, and guides that are usually of the larger, spinning-rod type.

How to Match Up Spincasting Tackle

This chart is meant only as a general guide aimed at helping you put together, in proper balance, the basic elements of a spincasting outfit tailored for fish of a particular weight category. Specific conditions—and your ability and personal preferences—should also be considered.

Species of Fish	Reel	Rod Action, Length (feet)	Line (pound test)	Lure Weights (ounces)
Panfish, small trout and bass, pickerel	Light	Light, 6½ to 7	4 to 8	⅛ to ⅜
Trout, bass, pickerel, pike, landlocks, walleye	Medium	Medium, 6 to 7	6 to 12	⅜ to ⅝
Pike, lake trout, steelhead, muskie, salmon, striped bass, snook, bonefish	Medium-Heavy, with star drag	Medium-Heavy, 6 to 6½	10 to 15	½ to ¾

CONVENTIONAL TACKLE FOR SALTWATER TROLLING AND CASTING

A host of saltwater game fish—from half-pound snapper bluefish to 40-pound yellowtails to blue-fin tuna weighing nearly a ton—draws millions of fishermen to the briny each year. They stand in crashing surf and on jetties and piers, and they sail for deeper waters aboard boats of almost every description.

Because of the great differences in weights of saltwater fish, it is important for the fisherman to be armed with balanced tackle that is suited for the particular quarry he is after. Just as the freshwater muskie angler wouldn't use bluegill tackle, the person who is trolling for, say, blue marlin wouldn't use a jetty outfit designed for striped bass.

Balanced tackle—in which the rod, reel, line, and other items are all in reasonable proportion to one another—is important. A properly balanced outfit—for example, a 9-foot surf rod with a good casting reel and 15- to 25-pound-test line—is a joy to use. Conversely, if

How to Match Up Saltwater Casting Tackle

This chart is meant only as a general guide aimed at helping you put together, in proper balance, the basic elements of a spincasting outfit tailored for fish of a particular weight category. Specific conditions—and your ability and personal preferences—should also be considered.

Species of Fish	Reel	Rod Type, Length (feet)	Line (pound test)	Lure Weights (ounces)
Small stripers, bluefish, weakfish, snook, bonefish, redfish, salmon, pompano, jacks	Light, with star drag	Popping, 6 to 7	8 to 15	½ to 1
Stripers, big bluefish, school tuna, albacore, bonito, salmon, dolphin, wahoo	Medium	Medium, 6½ to 8	12 to 30	¾ to 3
Channel bass, black drum, tarpon, dolphin, big kingfish, sharks	Heavy, with star drag	Heavy, 7 to 8½	15 to 40	1½ to 3
Surf species (bluefish, stripers, drum, channel bass, etc.)	Squidding (surf casting)	Surf, 7 to 10	15 to 45	1½ to 6

you substituted a 5-foot boat rod for the 9-footer in the above outfit and tried to cast, you would soon be turning the air blue. Besides the casting advantage, properly balanced gear makes hooking and playing a fish easier and more effective.

Let's take a detailed look at the various kinds of conventional saltwater gear and how to match up the component parts.

■ Trolling Reels

Trolling is a method of fishing in which a lure or bait is pulled along behind a moving boat. It is also a method in which the reel is of paramount importance.

At one time, saltwater trolling reels were designated by a simple but not completely reliable numbering system. This system employed a number followed by a diagonal (/) and then the letter O, which merely stood for "ocean." The numbers ran from 1 to 16, with each one representing the line capacity of the reel. The higher the number, the larger the reel's line capacity. It should be noted, however, that these numbers were not standardized—that is, one manufacturer's 4/O trolling reel may have had a smaller capacity than another maker's 4/O.

Trolling reels today are typically classified by line class and line capacity. For example, reels are classified as 12-pound test, 20-pound test, 50-pound test, 80-pound test, and so on. Weighing from 18 ounces up to nearly 10 pounds, these reels are designed primarily for handling the largest game fish (sailfish, marlin, bluefin tuna, and swordfish), but are also effective for

bluefish, striped bass, channel bass, albacore, dolphins, and the like. Generally, 12- and 20-pound class is considered light tackle, 30- to 50-pound class is medium weight, and 80- to 130-pound class is for the heaviest saltwater species.

Saltwater Reel Parts

The Daiwa Seagate is a typical saltwater conventional reel for general offshore fishing. Various models of the Seagate weigh from 14 to 21 ounces. The heaviest model will hold 630 yards of 50-pound-test braid line and 310 yards of 40-pound-test monofilament. For unlimited big-game fishing, reels get bigger and stronger to withstand powerful runs. They also cost more.

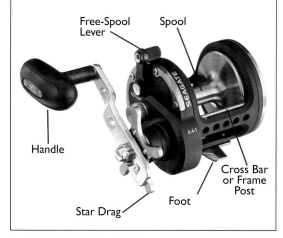

Free-Spool Lever　　Spool

Handle

Cross Bar or Frame Post

Star Drag　　Foot

These reels have no casting features (such as anti-backlash devices) since their sole function is trolling. Spools are smooth running, usually operating on ball bearings. The reels are ruggedly built and, of course, corrosion resistant. Unique features include lugs on the upper part of the sideplate for the attachment of a big-game fishing harness worn by the fisherman, a U-shaped clamp for a more secure union of rod and reel, and, in the largest reels, a lug-and-brace arrangement for extra rigidity.

By far the most important feature on a trolling reel is the drag. If a reel is to handle the sizzling runs and line-testing leaps of fish weighing hundreds of pounds, its drag must operate smoothly at all times. And the drag must not overheat or it may bind, causing the line to break.

Inexpensive reels of this type have the star type of drag consisting of a series of alternating metal and composition (or leather) washers. In some trolling reels, the drag is an asbestos composition disc that applies pressure directly to the reel spool.

Some expensive trolling reels have not one but two drag controls. One is a knob-operated device that lets you preset drag tension to a point below the breaking strength of the line being used. The other is a lever, mounted on the sideplate, that has a number of positions and permits a wide range of drag settings, from very light up to the safe maximum for the line in use. This lever, when backed off all the way, throws the reel into a free spool.

Trolling-reel spools are made of metal, usually either machined bronze or anodized aluminum, and range in width from 1⅝ inches to 5 inches (for the 80- to 180-pound-test outfits).

Some trolling reels are designed especially for wire and lead-core lines. They have narrow but deep spools and extrastrong gearing.

Other features of trolling reels include a free-spool lever mounted on the sideplate, a line-counting feature, a single oversize handle grip, and high-speed gear ratios ranging to as much as 40 inches of line retrieved for every single turn of the handle.

■ Trolling Rods

Big-game trolling rods have the strength and fittings to withstand the power runs and magnificent leaps of such heavyweights as marlin, sailfish, and giant tuna. The great majority of these rods are of fiberglass and graphite composite construction.

Almost all blue-water rods have a butt section and a tip section—that is, they seldom have ferrules fitted midway along the working length of the rod. In most rods, the tip section is about 5 feet long, while butt lengths vary from 14 to 27 inches, depending on the weight of the tip. Tip sections are usually designated by weight, ranging from about 3 ounces to as heavy as 40 ounces, depending on the line that is being used and the fish that is being sought.

Trolling rods are rated according to the line-strength classes of the International Game Fish Association. The 11 IGFA classes are: 2-pound-, 4-pound-, 6-pound-, 8-pound-, 12-pound-, 16-pound-, 20-pound-, 30-pound-, 50-pound-, 80-pound-, 130-pound-, and 180-pound-test line. No rod used in catching a fish submitted for an IGFA record can have a tip length of less than 40 inches and the rod butt cannot exceed 27 inches in length. These measurements do not apply to surfcasting rods.

The fittings on trolling rods include strong, high-quality guides. The first guide above the reel (called the stripping guide) and the tip guide are of the roller type (either single-roller or double-roller). The middle guides,

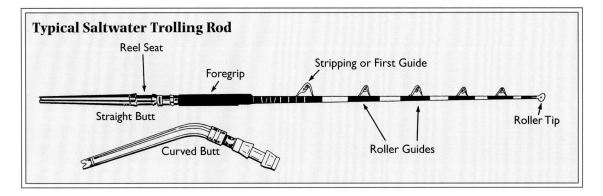

Typical Saltwater Trolling Rod

Reel Seat

Foregrip

Stripping or First Guide

Straight Butt

Curved Butt

Roller Guides

Roller Tip

usually numbering four or five, are of the ring type and are made either of heavily chromed stainless steel or of tungsten carbide (carboloy), which is the most durable material. In some rods, all of the guides are rollers. Most roller guides have self-lubricating bearings that can be disassembled for cleaning.

Other features of trolling rods include extrastrong, locking reel seats, and gimbal fittings in the end of the butt that enable the rod to be fitted into a socket on a boat's fighting chair or into a belt harness worn by the fisherman.

Casting and Boat Reels

Conventional (revolving-spool) reels in this category are widely used by saltwater fishermen who cast lures and baits from piers, bridges, jetties, and in the surf, and by sinker-bouncers (bottom fishermen) in boats. Actually an outgrowth and refinement of freshwater baitcasting reels, these reels fill the gap between those freshwater models and big-game trolling reels.

Many surf and jetty casters, especially those who are after big fish, prefer a conventional reel (and rod) over a spinning outfit because the conventional rig is better able to handle heavy lures and sinkers. And a vast majority of experienced bottom fishermen lean toward the revolving-spool reel.

Conventional reels designed for casting, often called squidding reels, have wide, light spools (a heavy spool makes casting difficult) of either metal or plastic (metal is preferred for most uses), and gear ratios ranging from 2:1 to 6:1. Weights range from about 12 to 22 ounces. In most models, the drag is of the star type and there is a free-spool lever mounted on the sideplate. Some of these reels have level-wind mechanisms.

Depending on the model, line capacities can range from about 250 yards of 12-pound-test monofilament to 350 yards of 30-pound-test mono. Line capacity can also be dramatically increased with braided line. For most surf, jetty, and pier situations, 250 yards of line is sufficient.

Most of these reels have a mechanical brake, magnets, or a device to help prevent the spool from overrunning during a cast and causing a backlash. In all models, however, as in freshwater baitcasting reels, thumb pressure against the spool is required to control the cast.

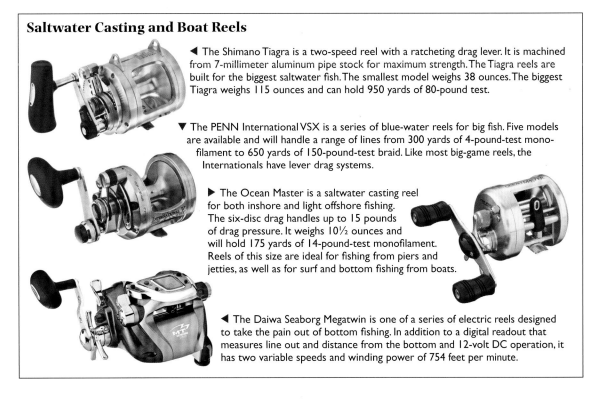

Saltwater Casting and Boat Reels

◄ The Shimano Tiagra is a two-speed reel with a ratcheting drag lever. It is machined from 7-millimeter aluminum pipe stock for maximum strength. The Tiagra reels are built for the biggest saltwater fish. The smallest model weighs 38 ounces. The biggest Tiagra weighs 115 ounces and can hold 950 yards of 80-pound test.

▼ The PENN International VSX is a series of blue-water reels for big fish. Five models are available and will handle a range of lines from 300 yards of 4-pound-test monofilament to 650 yards of 150-pound-test braid. Like most big-game reels, the Internationals have lever drag systems.

▶ The Ocean Master is a saltwater casting reel for both inshore and light offshore fishing. The six-disc drag handles up to 15 pounds of drag pressure. It weighs 10½ ounces and will hold 175 yards of 14-pound-test monofilament. Reels of this size are ideal for fishing from piers and jetties, as well as for surf and bottom fishing from boats.

◄ The Daiwa Seaborg Megatwin is one of a series of electric reels designed to take the pain out of bottom fishing. In addition to a digital readout that measures line out and distance from the bottom and 12-volt DC operation, it has two variable speeds and winding power of 754 feet per minute.

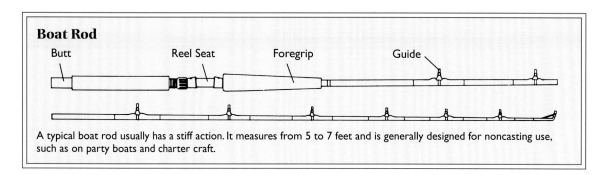

Boat Rod

Butt   Reel Seat   Foregrip   Guide

A typical boat rod usually has a stiff action. It measures from 5 to 7 feet and is generally designed for noncasting use, such as on party boats and charter craft.

Conventional reels designed for deep-sea bottom fishing are quite similar to the casting models, but they are sometimes heavier and have deeper spools. They may also have larger capacities and take heavier lines.

◼ Casting and Boat Rods

In choosing a conventional casting rod, more so than with a boat (bottom-fishing) rod, the type of fishing to be done and the fish being sought are critical factors. For casting in the surf, for example, the rod must be long enough so that the fisherman can make lengthy casts and hold the line above the breakers. A rod for jetty use, on the other hand, need not be so long. And if you'll be fishing mainly from piers and bridges, you'll need a rod with enough backbone to lift heavy fish from the water and up over the rail.

However, a beginning fisherman can get a casting rod that will handle most of the situations he'll be facing. A good choice would be one that is 8 to 9 feet in overall length and has a rather stiff tip. The stiff tip of a conventional rod lets the angler use a wide range of lure weights and enables him to have more control over big fish.

Conventional casting rods are available in lengths from 8 to 12 feet and even longer. Developments in graphite show that rods of this material can carry an exceptionally wide range of lure weights. In tests, weights of 18 ounces were cast with graphite rods. A majority of these rods are of two-piece construction, breaking either at the upper part of the butt or about midway up the working length of the rod.

These rods are distinguished by the number and arrangement of their guides. In most models, there are only three or four guides, including the tip guide, and all are located in the upper half of the tip section. Why this arrangement? Since these rods are stiffer than most others, fewer guides are required to distribute the strain along the length of the rod. The guides are bunched

Who Was Responsible for the First Circle Hook?

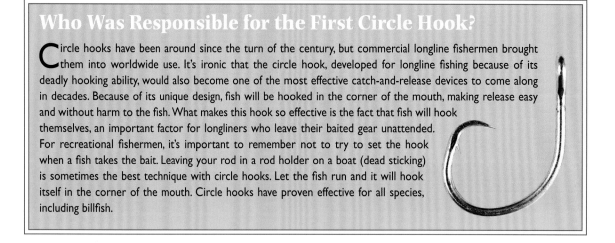

Circle hooks have been around since the turn of the century, but commercial longline fishermen brought them into worldwide use. It's ironic that the circle hook, developed for longline fishing because of its deadly hooking ability, would also become one of the most effective catch-and-release devices to come along in decades. Because of its unique design, fish will be hooked in the corner of the mouth, making release easy and without harm to the fish. What makes this hook so effective is the fact that fish will hook themselves, an important factor for longliners who leave their baited gear unattended. For recreational fishermen, it's important to remember not to try to set the hook when a fish takes the bait. Leaving your rod in a rod holder on a boat (dead sticking) is sometimes the best technique with circle hooks. Let the fish run and it will hook itself in the corner of the mouth. Circle hooks have proven effective for all species, including billfish.

near the tip because that's where most of the bend occurs when a fish is being played.

Boat, or bottom-fishing, rods, as their name implies, are designed for noncasting use aboard boats—party boats, charter craft, and private boats. They are also used on piers and bridges in situations in which a lure or bait is simply dropped down to the water.

Boat rods are considerably shorter than casting rods, running from about 5 to 7 feet in overall length, with a good average length being about 6 feet. Their shortness makes them highly maneuverable, a factor of more than a little importance aboard a crowded party boat, and makes it easier to handle, say, a 30-pound cod while trying to remain upright on a pitching deck.

As with most other modern rods, boat rods are mostly made of fiberglass or graphite. Most are one-piece or two-piece construction with a tip section and detachable butt. The number of guides on a boat rod depends on the length, but there are seldom more than six or eight. Some of these rods designed for large fish have a roller tip. Other boat-rod features are similar to those of casting rods.

KITE FISHING

No one seems to know for sure where fishing with a kite originated. The best guess is that this unique technique was first used in China, and then in New Guinea and the Pacific Islands. The technique was also used in New Zealand, where surf fishermen flew kites to get their baits beyond the breakers. Regardless of where it was invented, kite fishing is now a well-established technique to fish live baits for tuna, billfish, king mackerel, dolphin, and any species that can be attracted to take a bait on the surface.

The concept is simple enough, but it takes a skilled captain and mate to fish live baits off one or two kites. The kites are generally made of ripstop nylon and flown on 80- or 100-pound-test line connected to a short kite rod. Kite rods are typically about 3 feet with one or two guides. Kites come in various models to handle winds up to 25 miles per hour. The kites can be flown at distances up to 100 feet or more, depending on wind conditions.

Attached to the kite are one or more release clips, the same as the clips used on outriggers. Each clip is

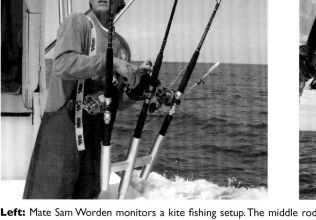

Left: Mate Sam Worden monitors a kite fishing setup. The middle rod flies the kite. The rods with live bait on either side are attached to the kite line with release clips. The baits are lowered and fished on the surface. Aggressive surface feeders will often jump clear of the water to hit a bait. **Right:** Mate Sam Worden gets a bait ready to attach to a release clip on the kite line. The red kite, already high in a blue sky, is clearly visible in this photo.

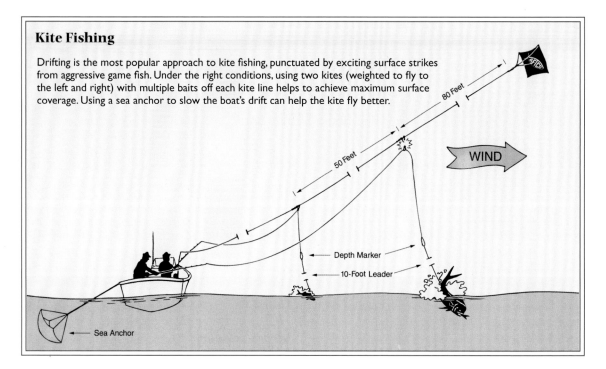

Kite Fishing

Drifting is the most popular approach to kite fishing, punctuated by exciting surface strikes from aggressive game fish. Under the right conditions, using two kites (weighted to fly to the left and right) with multiple baits off each kite line helps to achieve maximum surface coverage. Using a sea anchor to slow the boat's drift can help the kite fly better.

80 Feet

WIND

50 Feet

Depth Marker

10-Foot Leader

Sea Anchor

assigned to a rod and reel baited with live pilchards, cigar minnows, goggle eyes, blue runners, or any other bait available. Dead baits can be used, but live baits are preferred. The line is passed through the release clips on the kite, fed out along the kite line, and lowered until the bait is literally dancing on the surface.

Two rods, rigged the same way, can also be fished off one kite. Some skilled captains and mates can actually launch two kites and simultaneously run as many as six baits, three off each kite. Styrofoam markers are sometimes used above the baits to keep track of them.

Generally, the kite rod and two fishing rods are placed in a three-way rod holder with the short kite rod in the middle holder. The mate must constantly monitor all three rods, keeping the kite flying and raising or lowering the baits to keep them active on the surface. Some mates use electric reels on the kite rod to make it easier to retrieve the kites.

Kite fishing is exciting and very productive. Under the right conditions, it is not uncommon for tuna and king mackerel to come completely out of the water to hit a bait skipped on the surface. Captain Bob Lewis played a major role in developing kite fishing in southern waters, especially Florida, where kite fishing often accounts for double-digit sailfish catches.

HOW TO SET DRAG

Drag is what keeps a fish from breaking your line. That sounds simple, but fishermen sometimes lose big fish because they do not know or understand a few basic facts about the drag on their reel. Many anglers, for example, tighten their drag when a big fish makes a long run and strips off a lot of line. This is wrong. The drag should actually be lightened, because a lot of line in the water as well as a smaller spool diameter will increase the drag. Often the result is a lost trophy.

Drag is the resistance of a reel against the fighting pull of a fish, and it is set at a strain the line can endure without breaking. The drag mechanism usually consists of a series of metal (stainless steel, aluminum, or chromed brass) and composition (leather, cork, plastic, or fiber) washers. The washers are stacked, alternating

Minimum and Maximum Range of Drag

Line	Minimum Drag (pounds)	Maximum Drag (pounds)
6-pound test	1½	4
8-pound test	2	5
10-pound test	3	6
12-pound test	4	8
20-pound test	6	12
30-pound test	8	15
50-pound test	12	25
80-pound test	20	40
130-pound test	30	50

the water, and the amount of line remaining on the reel spool after a long run.

In addition, not all drags are created equal. They should be smooth, but many are sticky and jerky. In fact, it often takes as much as double the force of the drag setting to get the drag moving. For example, a drag set at 5 pounds may actually take up to 10 pounds of pull before the drag starts moving. It's obvious, therefore, that if you're using 8-pound-test line you should set your drag at about 2 pounds to allow for "starting your drag."

The amount of line on your spool is another factor. When the outside diameter of line on your spool is reduced by half, the drag tension is doubled. For example, if your drag is set at 2 pounds with a full spool, it will be increased to 4 pounds when a fish makes a long run and strips off half your line.

Long, fast runs will also generate friction and heat between the drag washers. This will frequently tighten a drag and add even more tension.

It's also important to remember that a rod held at about 45 degrees will add about 10 percent to the drag you get with the rod pointed directly at the fish. This increased drag is due to friction between your line and the rod guides. If the rod is held at about 90 degrees, drag will increase to about 35 percent of the initial setting.

This is why it is important to lighten the drag and, when possible, point the rod at the fish when it is about to

metal and composition, and the friction between the surface areas of the washers creates "drag."

When an angler tightens the drag on his reel, he compresses these washers, creates more friction, and increases drag. Conversely, when he backs off the drag, he lessens friction and decreases drag.

If the size of a fish was the only factor in setting drag, the job would be easy. But there are other considerations, such as the friction of the line against the rod guides, resistance of the line being pulled through

Left: Setting drag on your reel is easy with the help of a friend. The angler puts pressure on a 30-pound-test outfit while his friend checks the indicator on a fish scale. For 30-pound-test line, the drag should be set at a minimum of 8 pounds and a maximum of 15 pounds. **Right:** Any fishing scale can be used to set drag as well as weigh fish. The indicator and numbers should be large enough to read without getting close.

be netted or gaffed. If you hold your rod high and keep a tight drag, a sudden lunge by a fish could break your line. But if you point the rod tip at the fish, the line will run off the spool more easily, even with the same drag setting.

This technique of lowering the rod is also used when handling thrashing or jumping fish, such as tarpon and marlin. Lowering the rod will lighten drag tension and "cushion" the line from the shock of a jumping fish. This is called "bowing." It's part of the technique that makes it possible to land 100-pound tarpon on 10-pound-test line.

Taking all the above factors into consideration, how does an angler set his drag so that he can feel reasonably secure when he hooks a trophy fish? The first step is to determine the minimum and maximum range of drag for the various pound-test lines (see chart on previous page). By minimum drag, I mean "starting drag," the amount of pull needed to get the drag moving. If the minimum drag seems light for the pound-test line, remember that there will be other factors increasing your drag beyond this setting, such as rod angle, spool diameter, and the amount of line in the water. Maximum drag means the heaviest setting you should use while fighting a fish. Never go beyond the maximum for your line class.

Let's take 12-pound-test line and see what factors come into play. Minimum drag is set at 4 pounds, but 8 pounds of pull will likely be required to get that drag started. If the angler holds his rod at 45 degrees or higher, he can add another 10 percent, which brings the drag to 9 pounds. To this figure you also have to add water resistance or line drag, which varies according to the amount of line in the water, line diameter, and the speed of the fish. With 12-pound-test line and a fast fish, it can amount to as much as 2 pounds, which brings the total up to 11 pounds of drag on 12-pound-test line. With only 1 pound of drag to spare, a big fish would likely break the line. It's obvious that you're far better off with a very light drag setting.

The first step is to set your drag at the minimum setting. This is easily done at dockside with a reliable fish scale and the help of a friend. Run your line through the guides and tie it to the scale. Ask your friend to hold the scale and back off about 30 feet. Tighten your drag and begin to apply pressure as you would when fighting a fish. Now, adjust the drag so that it comes into play when the scale reads the correct minimum drag weight. For example, if you're using 12-pound-test line, the drag should begin to slip when you apply enough pressure to pull the scale indicator to the 4-pound mark.

Now, with your drag set at 4 pounds, slowly tighten your drag until it comes into play at 8 pounds, which is the maximum setting. Note how many turns of the star drag or spool cap are required to bring your drag to the maximum setting. Play with the drag, setting it back and forth from 4 to 8 pounds. Do this several times and get the feel of the resistance and pressure you're putting on the line. With enough practice, you'll be able to safely lighten and tighten the drag while fighting a fish.

An easier technique is to leave your drag set at the minimum setting and use your hand or fingers to apply more drag. This is a method many anglers use and it works well. You can practice with your buddy and the scale. With drag at the minimum setting, cup your hand around the spool (assuming you're using an open-face spinning reel), grip it so that the drag does not slip, and apply just enough pressure to pull the scale indicator to the maximum figure. Practice this technique and you'll soon be able to bear down on a fish and gain line without even touching the drag knob.

As mentioned above, you can also cup your hand around the spool of an open-face spinning reel to apply more drag. With conventional reels, use your thumb against the spool and hold the lines against the rod. Make sure you lift your finger when a big fish begins to run, or else you'll get a bad line burn.

Learn to combine this hand technique with "pumping" and you will be able to land big fish on light lines. Pumping a big fish in is not difficult. Let's assume you're using an open-face spinning reel with a light drag. Put your hand around the spool, apply pressure, and ease your rod back into a vertical position. Now drop the rod tip and quickly reel in the slack. Repeat the process and you'll eventually have your fish at boatside. Always be ready, however, to lower the rod tip and release hand pressure from the spool when you think the fish is about to make a run. When it stops, you begin to pump once again. A common mistake with new fishermen is they will try to reel against a big fish without moving their rod, which will quickly tire you out. "Pumping" your rod is also the only effective way to land a big fish, even if you are only able to retrieve a few feet of line when you drop the rod and crank in the slack line. The technique is especially effective on those big bottom feeders.

One last point: At the end of the day, back off the drag and release all pressure on the washers, or they will lose their physical characteristics and take a set. If this happens, the drag will become jerky and unpredictable. If the washers do take a set, replacing them is the only solution.

LINES

No fisherman is stronger than the line that connects him and his quarry. Fishing lines are made of a wide variety of natural and synthetic materials and, as a result, differ widely in their characteristics and the uses to which they can be put. No two types of lines, for example, have the same degree of elasticity, abrasion resistance, water absorption, weight, and diameter.

Let's take a look at the physical characteristics of the various types of lines and the uses for which they are best suited.

MONOFILAMENT (SINGLE-STRAND NYLON): By far the most widely used fishing line today, monofilament is suitable for everything from blue-water trolling to surf-casting to freshwater spinning, and it is the universal material for leaders in both fresh water and salt because of its near-invisibility in water. It is extremely strong and light for its diameter, and it absorbs very little water (3 to 12 percent of its own weight). About the only drawback of monofilament is its relatively high rate of stretch (15 to 30 percent when dry, 20 to 35 percent when wet). For that reason, it is not the best choice for such uses as deep-water bottom fishing, during which large fish must be reeled up from considerable depths.

FLUOROCARBON: Fluorocarbon looks like monofilament, but it has different features. First, it's stiffer than monofilament and makes a better leader material. It also does not absorb water and is more resistant to oils, sunscreen,

Fishing Line Troubleshooting

This chart was designed to help you quickly find and correct line troubles when you can least afford to have them—on the water. Copy this page and keep this handy chart in your tackle box.

Symptoms	Possible Causes	Recommended Cures
Unexplained line breaks under low-stress loads.	a. Nicks or abrasions. If the surface is smooth and shiny, failure may be line fatigue.	a. Strip off worn line or re-tie line more frequently.
	b. If surface is dull, faded, and fuzzy, failure is due to sunlight or excessive wear.	b. Replace line.
	c. Wear or stress points on guides or reel.	c. Replace worn guides.
Line is unusually sticky and stretchy.	Line stored in area of high heat or damaged by chemicals.	Replace line and change storage areas.
Line has kinks and flat spots.	a. Line spooled under excessive tension.	a. Use lower spooling tension. Make one final cast and rewind under low tension.
	b. Line stored on reel too long without use.	b. Strip out and soak last 50 yards in water.
Line has excessive curls and backlashes.	Using mono that is too heavy for reel spool diameter.	Use a more flexible mono or one with a lower pound test or smaller diameter.
Mono is stiff and brittle, and has a dry, powdery surface.	Improper storage in either wet or too warm conditions.	Replace line and change storage area.
Line looks good, but is losing too many fish.	Faulty or improperly set reel drag. Using too light a breaking strength for conditions.	Check reel drag. Lubricate or replace washers. Refill with line of higher breaking strength.
Reel casts poorly.	Not enough line on spool or line is too heavy for reel.	Fill spool with additional line. Use lighter, more limp monofilament.
Line is hard to see.	a. Line has faded due to excessive exposure to sunlight.	a. Replace line.
	b. Using wrong color line.	b. Switch to high-visibility line.

and other substances that may deteriorate monofilament. Fluorocarbon is actually a product of fluorine, carbon, and hydrogen. It's also tougher, sinks faster, and is more resistant to abrasion than monofilament.

DACRON: A DuPont trademark for a synthetic fiber that is made into a braided line, Dacron is nearly as strong as monofilament but does not stretch so much (about 10 percent). It has virtually the same characteristics whether wet or dry. Its visibility in water is greater than that of monofilament. Dacron's widest use is as trolling line.

LINEN: This is a braided line made from natural fibers and rated according to the number of threads, with each thread having a breaking strength of 3 pounds (six-thread linen has a breaking strength of 18 pounds, 15-thread linen has a breaking strength of 45 pounds, and so on). This material absorbs considerable amounts of water and is stronger when wet. Linen line is subject to deterioration and is heavy and bulky. Very little linen fishing line is made or used today.

CUTTYHUNK: This is a braided linen line originally created in the 1860s for the Cuttyhunk Fishing Club on Cuttyhunk Island, Massachusetts. The word cuttyhunk is often used to denote any linen line.

SILK: Before World War II, fly-fishing lines were made of silk and had an oily coating to make them water resistant. Modern materials have made the silk line obsolete, and very few are in use today.

LEAD-CORE: This type of line is made by sheathing a flexible lead core in a tightly braided nylon sleeve. It's suitable for deep trolling in both fresh and salt water, and is especially useful for quickly getting a bait or lure down deep without bulky, heavy sinkers or planers. It's color-coded in 10-yard segments for precise depth control.

WIRE: These lines, too, are designed for deep trolling in both fresh and salt water. They're made of stainless steel, Monel (nickel alloy), bronze, or copper. Wire is popular for downrigger fishing, but because it's heavy enough to sink on its own, it's also used without downriggers and in many cases eliminates the need for a cumbersome drail weight or planer. Since it has no stretch, the angler can jig the rod and give movement to a bait or lure. However, wire is somewhat tricky until a fisherman gets used to it. Kinks can develop, causing weak spots or possibly cutting an unwary angler's hand. Wire line is generally available in a wider range of test weights than lead-core line. Wire leaders, usually sleeved in plastic, are widely used to prevent line cutting when fishing for such toothy battlers as pike, muskellunge, and many saltwater species.

◾ Braided Fishing Lines

Braided fishing line has a small diameter, minimum stretch, and a good knot strength. The new, high-tech synthetic braided lines get a high score on all counts. There are more than a dozen manufacturers of these new space-age braided lines, and they all claim their lines are three times as strong as monofilament lines of the same diameter. This means, of course, that you can get three times as much line on your reel, which is one of the biggest advantages of braided line. You no longer need big reels to make sure you have enough line, an important consideration for saltwater fishermen. The smaller diameter also means easier casting with lighter lures.

Braided lines have a stretch factor of less than 5 percent and some manufacturers even claim zero stretch. Monofilament has a stretch factor of about 25 percent, depending on the manufacturer. Minimal stretch is a big deal in fishing. It means sensitivity and fast hook-ups.

Braided lines have a lot going for them, including the sensitivity to transmit the slightest nibble. Braided lines are also sharp and hard. But they do present some problems. Nearly all braided lines float and easily get tangled in rigs and lures. In fact, many party or head boats prohibit braided lines because of tangles and the danger of cut fingers from these small-diameter, tough lines. If a caster gets a serious backlash and braided line digs into the spool, it may be nearly impossible to free the line.

◾ Fly Lines

Ever since the time of Izaak Walton, anglers have been using special lines designed to present insect imitations to trout, salmon, and other fish. The earliest fly lines were made of braided horsehair. Then came oiled silk lines, which were standard until the late 1940s.

Today's fly lines are basically a synthetic coating over a braided core. They are made in various shapes and weights. Some are constructed so that they float (primarily for dry-fly fishing), and others are made to sink (for streamer and nymph fishing). Another development is the floating-sinking, or intermediate, line, the first 10 to 30 feet of which sinks while the rest of it floats. Several

When making a cast with a fly rod, it's important to remember not to aim directly at the point where you want the fly to land. Aim a few feet above that point, so the fly will stop above the target and fall gently to the surface.

manufacturers offer fly lines designed with special tapers for various conditions and species. Tarpon, bonefish, and billfish anglers now have access to fly lines that make casting to these species easier.

It is impossible to overemphasize the importance to the fly fisherman of balanced tackle, and the most vital element in a fly-fishing outfit is the line. It must "fit" the rod if casting is to be accurate and efficient. A line that is too heavy for the rod causes sloppy casts, poor presen-

tation of the fly, and lack of accuracy, and it makes it difficult to manipulate the fly once it is on the water. An angler who uses a line that's too light for his rod must flail the rod back and forth during repeated backcasts in order to get out enough line to make his cast, and even then his forward cast might not "turn over" and the line may fall onto the water in a jumbled mass of coils.

Before 1961, fly lines were identified by a system of letters—A to I—with each letter representing a line diameter. For example, an A line measured .060 inch in diameter, and an I line measured .020 inch. But when modern fly lines replaced silk after World War II, weight, rather than diameter, became the critical factor in matching a fly line with a rod. So, in 1961, manufacturers adopted a universally accepted fly-line identification code. Its three elements give a complete description of a fly line.

The first part of the code describes the line type: L means level, DT means double taper, and WF means weight forward. The second element, a number, denotes the weight of the line's first 30 feet. The third element tells whether the line is floating (F), sinking (S), or floating-sinking (F/S). Therefore, a DT6F, for example, is a double-taper, weight-6 floating line.

Many fly-rod manufacturers today are eliminating the angler's problem of proper line choice by imprinting on the rod itself, usually just above the butt, the proper line size for that particular rod. However, there are other general ways to pick the right fly line. The general recommendations in the accompanying chart may help.

Choosing the Correct Fly Line

Rod Length (feet)	Proper Line
7½	DT4F or WF4F to WF6F
8	DT5F or WF5F to WF8F
8½	DT6F or WF6F to WF9F
9 and 9½	DT8F or WF8F to WF12F

Type of Water	Suitable Line Weights
Very small streams	4 to 5
Small and medium streams	5 to 8
Large streams	7 to 11
Lakes (light outfits)	5 to 7
Lakes (heavy outfits)	8 to 11
Salt water	9 to 15

FISHHOOKS

Modern hook design and manufacturing has come a long way since the first Stone Age bone hooks found by archaeologists and dating back to more than 5,000 BC. Today's fishhooks come in hundreds of sizes, shapes, colors, and special designs. They're made from carbon steel, stainless steel, or some rust-resistant alloy. They're hardened and tempered, then plated or bronzed to meet special specifications. Some are thin steel wire for use in tying artificial flies; others are thick steel for big-game fish that prowl off-shore waters.

There is no such thing as an all-purpose hook. Fishermen must carry a variety of patterns and sizes to match both the tackle and size of fish being hunted. Let's start from the beginning by learning the basic nomenclature of a typical fishhook (see accompanying illustration).

Even the parts of a typical fishhook may vary in design to meet certain requirements. There are sliced shanks to better hold bait on the hook, forged shanks for greater strength in marine hooks, tapered eyes to reduce the weight of hooks used in tying dry flies, and so on.

■ Hook Wire Size

The letter X and the designations "Fine Wire" or "Heavy Wire" are used to indicate the weight or diameter of a hook. For example, a 2X Heavy Wire means the hook is made of the standard diameter for a hook two sizes larger, and a 3X Heavy Wire is made of the standard diameter for a hook three sizes larger.

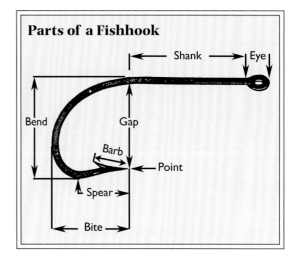

Parts of a Fishhook

For lightweight hooks, the designations are reversed. For example, a 2X Fine Wire means that the hook is made of the standard diameter for a hook two sizes smaller, and so on. These designations, however, vary from manufacturer to manufacturer.

Obviously, an angler seeking a big fish should lean toward the heavy hooks, which are not apt to bend or spring when striking the larger fish that swim the waters, particularly salt water.

Fishermen who use live bait will want to use fine-wire hooks, which will not weigh down the bait. The use of flies, particularly dry flies, also requires fine-wire hooks, since their light weight will enable a fly to float more easily.

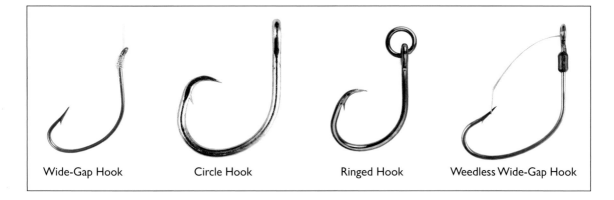

Wide-Gap Hook   Circle Hook   Ringed Hook   Weedless Wide-Gap Hook

■ Shank Length

The letter X and the designations "Long" or "Short" are used to specify the shank length of a hook. One manufacturer lists shank lengths from extrashort to extralong. The formula for determining shank length is similar to that used for wire sizes. A 2X Long means the shank of the hook is the standard length for a hook two sizes larger, and a 4X Long is the standard length for a hook four sizes larger. A 2X Short has a shank as short as the standard length of a hook two sizes smaller, and a 4X Short for a hook four sizes smaller, and so on. Again, these designations might vary from manufacturer to manufacturer.

Picking a hook with the correct shank length depends on the type of fishing you plan to undertake. A short-shank hook is preferred for baitfishing, since it can be hidden in the bait more easily. A long-shank hook is at its best when used for fish with sharp teeth.

A bluefish, for example, would have a tough time getting past the long shank and cutting into the leader. Long-shank hooks are also used in tying streamers and bucktails.

■ Hook Characteristics

In addition to size and shank length, there are other characteristics to consider when selecting a hook for a specific purpose. The barb, obviously, is a critical part of the hook. A short barb is quick to set in the mouth of a fish, but it also gives a jumping fish a greater chance of dislodging it. A long barb, on the other hand, is more difficult to set but it also makes it a lot tougher for a fish to shake it loose.

So what guidelines should an angler follow? Let's list some basic recommendations. The all-around saltwater

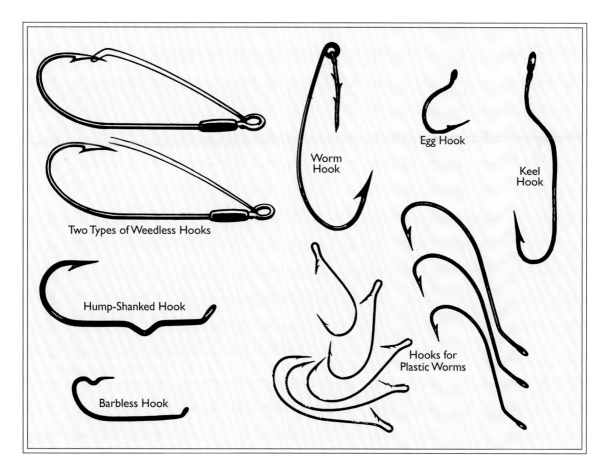

Two Types of Weedless Hooks

Hump-Shanked Hook

Barbless Hook

Worm Hook

Egg Hook

Keel Hook

Hooks for Plastic Worms

fisherman can't go wrong with the O'Shaughnessy, Kirby, Wide Gap, or Circle Hook patterns. And if you happen to have some salmon hooks, they're perfectly all right to use with a wire leader for barracuda and other toothy fish.

If you're a flounder fisherman, you'll find that the Chestertown and Carlisle patterns are your best bet. The long-shanked Chestertown makes it especially easy to unhook flounders.

If you're a bait fisherman, use the sliced-shanked Mustad Beak or Eagle Claw patterns. Those extra barbs on the shanks do a good job of keeping natural baits secured to the hook.

Fishermen can also become confused when they see hooks with straight-ringed eyes, turned-up eyes, and turned-down eyes. This should not present a problem. If you're replacing hooks on lures or attaching hooks to spinners, use a straight-ringed eye. If you're tying short-shanked artificial flies, pick the turned-up eye, which will provide more space for the hook point to bite into the fish. The turned-down eye is the best bet for standard flies and for baitfishing, since it brings the point of the hook closest to a straight line of penetration when striking a fish.

Curved shanks also lead to some confusion. A curved shank—curved right or left—has its place in

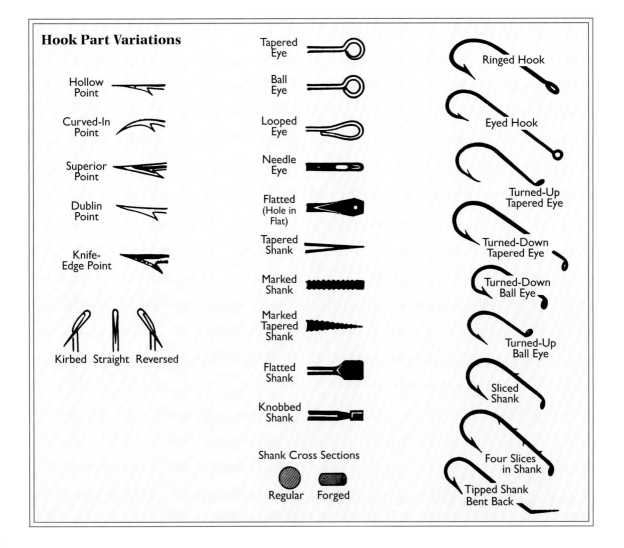

baitfishing. The offset point has a better chance of hitting flesh when a strike is made. When you are casting or trolling with artificial lures or spinners, however, the straight-shanked hook is a better choice, since it does not have a tendency to spin or twist, which is often the case with curved-shanked hooks.

Hooks for Fly Fishing

HOOK EYES

Ball Eye: A strong, untapered eye, the ball eye is the simplest form. It is available turned up and turned down. Considered too heavy for dry flies, hooks with ball eyes are used for wet flies.

Tapered Eye: This type of eye is also produced turned up and turned down. The tapered eye is made to maintain a full inner diameter while at the same time featuring a reduced outer diameter. This is achieved by the diameter of the wire decreasing as the eye closes. The larger diameter makes for easier insertion of leader material in the eyes of the hooks. The tapered eye also lightens the weight of the hook and, when turned up, faces away from the point of the hook, leaving the gap clear and enhancing the chances of the small hook setting firmly and quickly when hit. Tapered eye hooks are used for dry flies, wet flies, and streamers.

Looped Eye: Properly referred to as the looped eye because of its construction, this eye is a traditional characteristic of salmon fly hooks. It is a strong fly hook, easily tied to leaders, and it is less likely to fray them than ball and tapered eyes. In addition to dry and wet salmon hook patterns, the looped eye is available in a barbless dry-fly pattern and in a long-shanked streamer hook. It is available turned up and turned down.

Oval Eye: This eye takes its name from its obvious shape. It is a characteristic found on many traditional salmon fly hooks as well as numerous treble hooks. The oval eye is used to achieve a slimmer profile than an eyed hook.

HOOK SIZES

Every fly has a size number that is determined by the hook pattern (name) and that is stated in terms of the width of the gap between the hook point and the hook shank. The gap width of the given size in one particular pattern or family of hooks (e.g., the Viking) for the most part does not vary. Between different hook families, however, there is little compatibility in gap width.

HOOK SHAPES AND BENDS

Here are some examples of the variations in shapes and bends that help identify hook patterns used in fly tying.

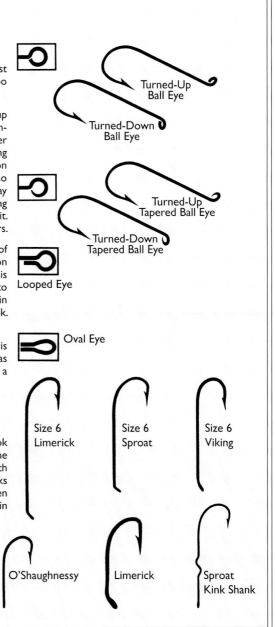

Turned-Up Ball Eye

Turned-Down Ball Eye

Turned-Up Tapered Ball Eye

Turned-Down Tapered Ball Eye

Looped Eye

Oval Eye

Size 6 Limerick

Size 6 Sproat

Size 6 Viking

O'Shaughnessy

Limerick

Sproat Kink Shank

ARTIFICIAL LURES

Fishing with bait is enjoyable, certainly, but there's something about fooling a fish with an artificial lure that gives most anglers a special charge.

A neophyte fisherman who visits a well-stocked sporting-goods store or tackle shop is confronted with a bewildering array of plugs, spoons, spinners, jigs, flies, bugs, and others. Some artificials look like nothing that ever swam, crawled, or flew, and yet they catch fish.

Let's look at each type of artificial lure and see how and why it works and how it should be fished.

■ Plugs

Plugs are lures designed to imitate small fish for the most part, though some plugs simulate mice, frogs, eels, and other food on which game fish feed. Plug action—meaning the way the lure moves when retrieved by the angler—is important and is something on which manufacturers expend much money and time. These lures are called crankbaits because every crank of the reel handle imparts some sort of diving or darting action.

The type, size, and weight of the plug you select is determined by the fish you are after and the kind of fishing tackle you are using. The charts found at the beginning of this section on how to match up various kinds of fishing tackle will help the beginner choose the right weight plugs.

There are five basic types of plugs: popping, surface, floating-diving, sinking (deep running), and deep diving.

POPPING: These plugs float on the surface and have concave, hollowed-out faces. The angler retrieves a popping plug by jerking the rod tip back so that the plug's face digs into the water, making a small splash, bubbles, and a popping sound. Some make a louder sound than others. This sound is especially attractive to largemouth bass, pike, muskies, and some inshore saltwater species, such as striped bass and bluefish. Most popping plugs (and most other plugs) have two sets of treble hooks. Popping plugs are most productive when the water surface is calm or nearly so. They should usually be fished slowly.

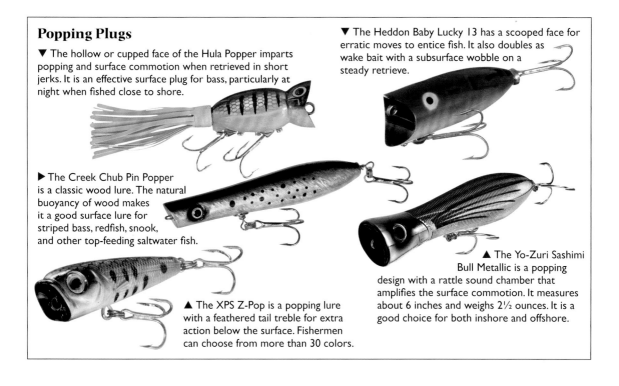

Popping Plugs

▼ The hollow or cupped face of the Hula Popper imparts popping and surface commotion when retrieved in short jerks. It is an effective surface plug for bass, particularly at night when fished close to shore.

▶ The Creek Chub Pin Popper is a classic wood lure. The natural buoyancy of wood makes it a good surface lure for striped bass, redfish, snook, and other top-feeding saltwater fish.

▲ The XPS Z-Pop is a popping lure with a feathered tail treble for extra action below the surface. Fishermen can choose from more than 30 colors.

▼ The Heddon Baby Lucky 13 has a scooped face for erratic moves to entice fish. It also doubles as wake bait with a subsurface wobble on a steady retrieve.

▲ The Yo-Zuri Sashimi Bull Metallic is a popping design with a rattle sound chamber that amplifies the surface commotion. It measures about 6 inches and weighs 2½ ounces. It is a good choice for both inshore and offshore.

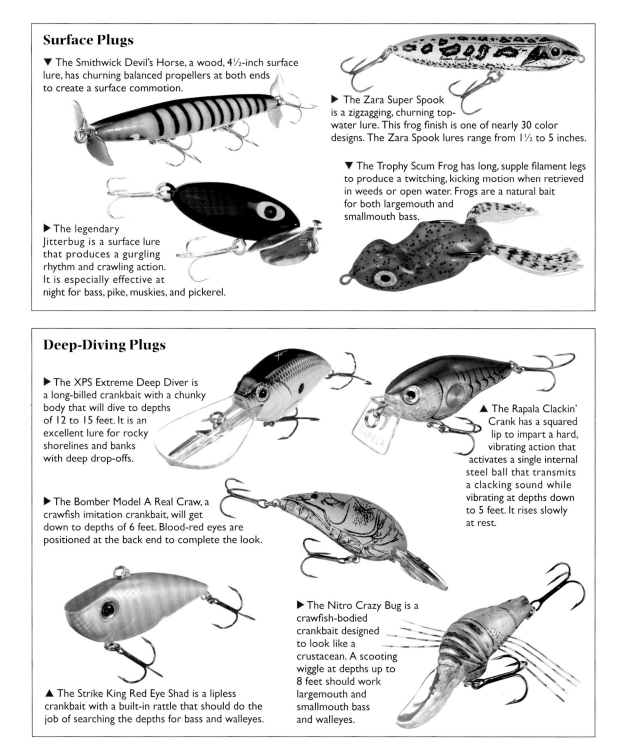

Surface Plugs

▼ The Smithwick Devil's Horse, a wood, 4½-inch surface lure, has churning balanced propellers at both ends to create a surface commotion.

▶ The Zara Super Spook is a zigzagging, churning top-water lure. This frog finish is one of nearly 30 color designs. The Zara Spook lures range from 1½ to 5 inches.

▼ The Trophy Scum Frog has long, supple filament legs to produce a twitching, kicking motion when retrieved in weeds or open water. Frogs are a natural bait for both largemouth and smallmouth bass.

▶ The legendary Jitterbug is a surface lure that produces a gurgling rhythm and crawling action. It is especially effective at night for bass, pike, muskies, and pickerel.

Deep-Diving Plugs

▶ The XPS Extreme Deep Diver is a long-billed crankbait with a chunky body that will dive to depths of 12 to 15 feet. It is an excellent lure for rocky shorelines and banks with deep drop-offs.

▲ The Rapala Clackin' Crank has a squared lip to impart a hard, vibrating action that activates a single internal steel ball that transmits a clacking sound while vibrating at depths down to 5 feet. It rises slowly at rest.

▶ The Bomber Model A Real Craw, a crawfish imitation crankbait, will get down to depths of 6 feet. Blood-red eyes are positioned at the back end to complete the look.

▶ The Nitro Crazy Bug is a crawfish-bodied crankbait designed to look like a crustacean. A scooting wiggle at depths up to 8 feet should work largemouth and smallmouth bass and walleyes.

▲ The Strike King Red Eye Shad is a lipless crankbait with a built-in rattle that should do the job of searching the depths for bass and walleyes.

Floating-Diving Plugs

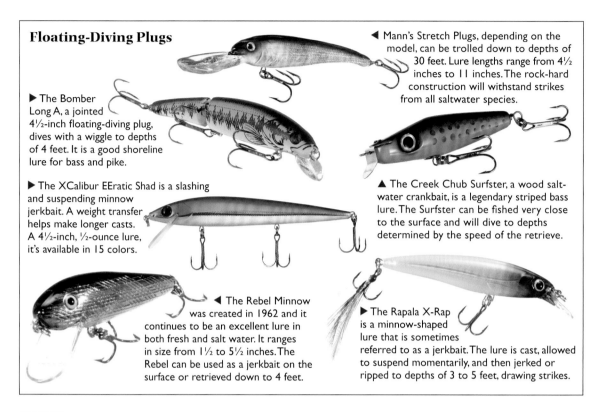

▶ The Bomber Long A, a jointed 4½-inch floating-diving plug, dives with a wiggle to depths of 4 feet. It is a good shoreline lure for bass and pike.

▶ The XCalibur EEratic Shad is a slashing and suspending minnow jerkbait. A weight transfer helps make longer casts. A 4½-inch, ½-ounce lure, it's available in 15 colors.

◀ The Rebel Minnow was created in 1962 and it continues to be an excellent lure in both fresh and salt water. It ranges in size from 1½ to 5½ inches. The Rebel can be used as a jerkbait on the surface or retrieved down to 4 feet.

◀ Mann's Stretch Plugs, depending on the model, can be trolled down to depths of 30 feet. Lure lengths range from 4½ inches to 11 inches. The rock-hard construction will withstand strikes from all saltwater species.

▲ The Creek Chub Surfster, a wood salt-water crankbait, is a legendary striped bass lure. The Surfster can be fished very close to the surface and will dive to depths determined by the speed of the retrieve.

▶ The Rapala X-Rap is a minnow-shaped lure that is sometimes referred to as a jerkbait. The lure is cast, allowed to suspend momentarily, and then jerked or ripped to depths of 3 to 5 feet, drawing strikes.

SURFACE: These plugs float on the surface, but they can be fished with various kinds of retrieves and create a different kind of surface disturbance than poppers do. Designed with an elongated, or bullet-shaped, head, they create surface disturbance by various means, including propellers (at the head or at both head and tail), a wide metal lip at the head, or hinged metal "wings" just behind the head. They can be twitched so that they barely nod, retrieved steadily so that they chug across the water, or skimmed across the top as fast as the angler can turn his reel handle. The proper retrieve depends on the lure's design and, of course, on the mood of the fish. It's best to try different retrieves until you find one that produces.

FLOATING-DIVING: These plugs are designed to float when at rest and dive when retrieved. Some float horizontally, while others float with the tail hanging down beneath the surface. They are made to dive by an extended lip at the head. The speed of the retrieve determines the depth of the dive. The faster the retrieve, the deeper the dive. Most of these plugs have a side-to-side

Freshwater vs. Saltwater Lures

A long time ago, I stopped labeling lures as "freshwater" and "saltwater." There is really no difference. Size no longer matters. I've caught 40-pound dolphin on 1-ounce bucktails and a 10-inch farm pond bass on a 7-inch Rapala. My favorite Creek Chub darter caught dozens of pike and so many bluefish that I retired the lure. The same is true for flies. My Clouser Minnows are equally productive on rainbow trout as they are on striped bass. Some lures have corrosion-resistant hooks and some have bronze hooks that will rust, but I never worry about hooks rotting away because they are easy to replace. With very few exceptions, all lures will work both in fresh and salt water.

wobbling action. An erratic retrieve—dive, surface, dive, surface—is often productive, and these plugs are also effective when made to swim just above a submerged weed bed, rock pile, and so on.

SINKING (DEEP RUNNING): These plugs sink as soon as they hit the water and are designed for deep work. Some sink slower than others and can be fished at various depths, depending on how long the angler waits before starting his retrieve. Most of these plugs have some sort of wobbling action, and some fairly vibrate when retrieved. Some have propellers fore and aft.

These plugs are excellent fish-finders: the fisherman can start by bouncing them along the bottom, and if that doesn't work, he can work them at progressively shallower depths until he finds at what depth the fish

Saltwater Diving and Trolling Lures

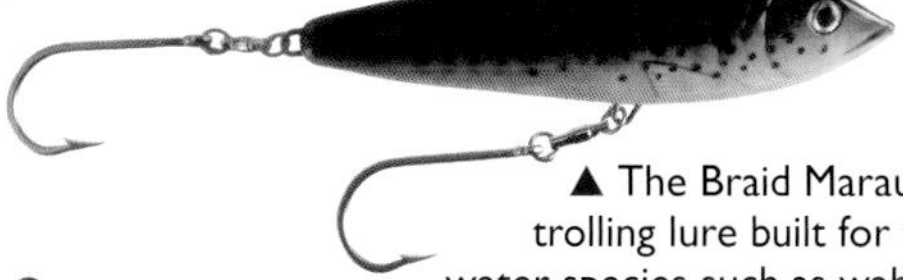

▲ The Braid Marauder is a saltwater trolling lure built for the toughest blue-water species such as wahoo, king mackerel, tuna, and billfish. It has a diving face and internal ballast that keeps it running true when rolled deep. Sizes run from 6 to 11 inches and weights run from 3 to 18 ounces.

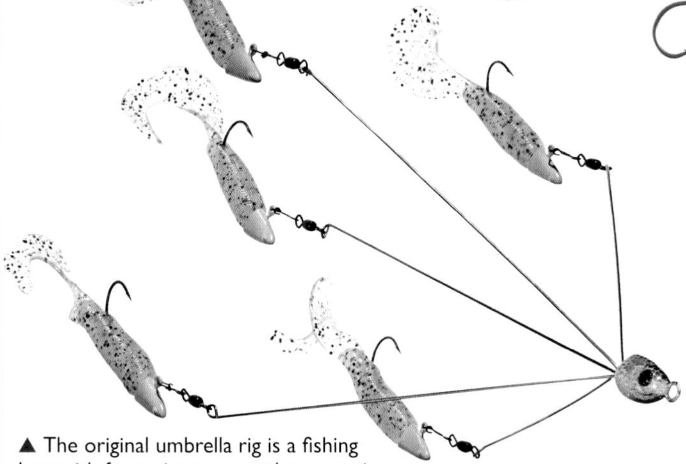

▼ The MirrOlure Deep 25'+ is a floating-diving plug that will get down to depths of 25 feet or more. The lure's tight wiggling action can be maintained when trolled at speeds up to 7 knots. It is a good lure for both offshore and inshore species.

▲ The original umbrella rig is a fishing lure with four wire arms, each supporting two or three surgical tube lures. A single tube is trailed from the center. It is designed to imitate a school of sand eels or baitfish. It was especially effective along the East Coast for bluefish and striped bass. Modified designs on the umbrella rig have now found their way into fresh water and offshore waters for tuna and other pelagic species. The Bass Pro Deadly 5 Shad Rig, shown here, is a good example of new designs of the umbrella rig.

▶ The Offshore Angler Blue Water Bait has a flat head to create turbulence when trolled for nearly all offshore species. Shown rigged, the lure comes with 100-pound-test mono-filament and a 7/0 hook.

▼ The Williamson Live Little Tunny is trolled at 7 to 9 knots. Built to catch big fish, the lure is rigged with a single 11/0 hook and a 10-foot leader of 400-pound-test monofilament. It is built from soft plastic.

▼ The Sea Striker Rigged Cedar Plug is a proven bluewater lure for tuna. This lure is rigged with 8 feet of 130-pound-test monofilament leader. Cedar plugs are typically trolled bouncing on the crest of the boat's wake.

are feeding. It should be remembered that deep-running plugs don't have to be fished in deep water; for example, in small sizes they're great for river smallmouths.

DEEP DIVING: These plugs may float or sink, but they all are designed with long or broad lips of metal or plastic that cause the plugs to dive to depths of 30 feet or more as the angler reels in. As with other diving plugs, the faster the retrieve, the deeper the dive. Most of these lures have some sort of wobbling action. They are ideally suited for casting or trolling in deep lakes and at the edges of drop-offs, and they work best in most waters when the fish are holding in deep holes, as fish usually do during midday in July and August.

■ Spoons

Spoons are among the oldest of artificial lures. If you cut the handle off a teaspoon, you'd have the basic shape of this lure.

Spoons are designed to imitate small baitfish of one kind or another, so flash is an important feature in many of these lures. Most spoons have a wobbling, side-to-side action when retrieved.

Many spoons have a silver or gold finish, while others are painted in various colors and combinations of colors. Most have a single free-swinging treble hook at the tail; others have a single fixed hook. Weedless arrangements are becoming more and more popular on both types.

Spoons

▼ The Bass Pro Nitro Flash is a 5-inch spoon that can be cast and retrieved at different speeds. The lure can also be cast, allowed to drop, then jerked up to the surface much like a jig. It is a good lure for bass, pike, and muskies.

▲ The Kastmaster, machined from solid brass with weights ranging from $\frac{1}{12}$ ounce to 1 ounce, is a proven lure for fresh and salt water. This lure will cast like a bullet. A jerk retrieve is best on inshore species.

▶ The Clarkspoon has been around for generations. The smaller sizes, tipped with a strip of pork rind, are excellent lures for bass, pike, and muskies. In the bigger sizes, it's an effective lure for striped bass, bluefish, barracuda, king mackerel, and a host of inshore species.

▲ The Mepps Little Wolf is a solid brass spoon with a reverse curve design that has 10 reflective surfaces. Its intense side-to-side wobbling will catch literally every freshwater species. The Little Wolf is available in 20 designs.

◀ This Eagle Claw collection of spoons in familiar patterns should be in every angler's tackle box. These lures will catch every freshwater species. Change the speed of retrieves until you find one that will catch fish.

In general, the smaller spoons are better in streams and ponds, while the larger ones are a good choice for lakes. However, the angler must remember that with two spoons of equal weight but different sizes, the smaller one will cast easier in wind and sink faster, while the larger one will sink slower and swim at shallower depths.

What's the best retrieve for a spoon? Again, that depends on weather and water conditions and other circumstances, including the mood of the fish. But generally, an erratic retrieve, with twitches and jerks of the rod tip, is better than a steady retrieve because it makes the spoon look like an injured baitfish. Attaching a strip of pork rind to a spoon often adds to its fish appeal.

■ Spinners

Spinners, like spoons, are designed to imitate baitfish, and they attract game fish by flash and vibration. A spinner is simply a metal blade mounted on a shaft by means of a revolving arm or ring called a clevis. Unlike

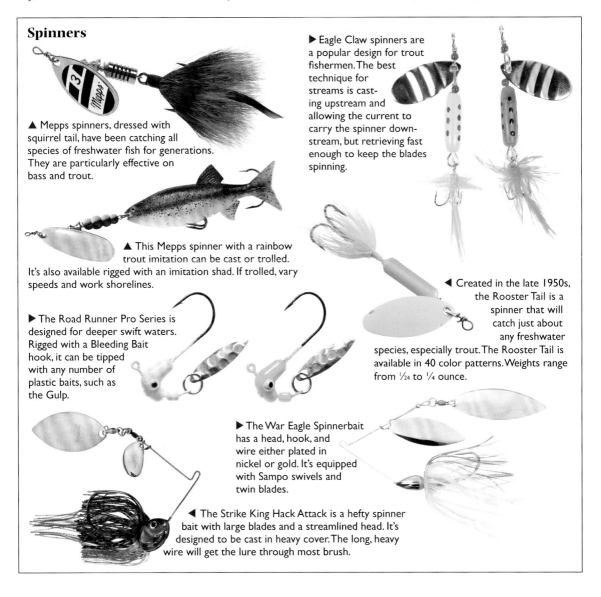

Spinners

▲ Mepps spinners, dressed with squirrel tail, have been catching all species of freshwater fish for generations. They are particularly effective on bass and trout.

▲ This Mepps spinner with a rainbow trout imitation can be cast or trolled. It's also available rigged with an imitation shad. If trolled, vary speeds and work shorelines.

▶ The Road Runner Pro Series is designed for deeper swift waters. Rigged with a Bleeding Bait hook, it can be tipped with any number of plastic baits, such as the Gulp.

▶ Eagle Claw spinners are a popular design for trout fishermen. The best technique for streams is casting upstream and allowing the current to carry the spinner downstream, but retrieving fast enough to keep the blades spinning.

◀ Created in the late 1950s, the Rooster Tail is a spinner that will catch just about any freshwater species, especially trout. The Rooster Tail is available in 40 color patterns. Weights range from $1/24$ to $1/4$ ounce.

▶ The War Eagle Spinnerbait has a head, hook, and wire either plated in nickel or gold. It's equipped with Sampo swivels and twin blades.

◀ The Strike King Hack Attack is a hefty spinner bait with large blades and a streamlined head. It's designed to be cast in heavy cover. The long, heavy wire will get the lure through most brush.

a spoon, which has a wobbling action, a spinner blade rotates around the shaft when retrieved.

Other parts of a simple spinner include a locking device to accommodate a hook at one end of the shaft, a metal loop to which the line is tied at the other end of the shaft, and a series of metal or plastic beads that separate the blade from the locking device and loop. In some spinners, notably the Colorado, the blade is mounted on a series of swivels instead of on a shaft.

Most spinners have either one or two blades. However, in some forms of fishing, particularly deep-water trolling for lake trout, eight or more spinner blades are mounted in tandem on a length of wire.

Most spinner blades have either a silver or gold finish. Some, however, are painted in various colors, including black, yellow, and white, while others are striped and still others are made of simulated pearl. In general, the brighter finishes are best in shaded or discolored water and on overcast days, while the darker finishes are better in very clear water under bright skies.

Spinner blades have various shapes and other physical characteristics. Both shape and thickness determine how the blade reacts when retrieved. To illustrate this point, let's take a look at a few types of simple spinners, often used with bait, that have proven their worth over the years.

COLORADO: This spinner has a wide, nearly round blade that rotates well out from the shaft. Because it has considerable water resistance and spins relatively slowly, it is best suited for use in lakes and in streams with slow currents. A Colorado spinner used with a worm is a proven taker of trout, walleyes, and other fish.

WILLOW LEAF: This spinner has a long, narrow blade that spins fast and close to the shaft. Having minimum water resistance, it is well suited for use in fast-flowing water. A willow-leaf spinner is often used with a worm, minnow, or other natural baits.

JUNE BUG: Unusual in that the blade is attached directly to the shaft (there is no clevis), this spinner has a sort of "leg" that braces the blade against the shaft, and has a hole in the middle. A June Bug spinner with its hook sweetened by a night crawler is a potent combination for trout, walleyes, and many other game fish. The June Bug comes in various designs.

Spinner-blade sizes are usually classified by numbers, but the numbers vary with the manufacturers and are not a reliable guide for the buyer. It's easy enough to simply look over a selection of spinners and select the size that seems right for your particular purpose.

Many spinner-type lures are produced today and are extremely popular, especially among freshwater fishermen. In all of them, the basic attracting element is a revolving spinner blade. Most have some sort of weight built in along the shaft and a treble hook at the tail. In many, the treble hook is hidden or at least disguised with bucktail, feathers, squirrel tail, or a skirt of rubber or plastic strands. Weedless hooks are also becoming increasingly popular on these lures.

■ Buzz Baits

Buzz baits are spinner baits that incorporate a wide propeller and jig that churn a substantial commotion as the bait is retrieved across the surface, leaving a bubble trail. Buzz baits can be fished fast or slow, depending on water conditions and the mood of the fish. Try various retrieves until you find one that catches fish.

Buzz Baits

Booyah Counter Strike buzz baits have counter-rotating blades for stability and to create a distinct sound. Vary the retrieves with these lures to create a bubble trail.

■ Jigs

Generally speaking, a jig is any lure with a weighted head (usually lead), a fixed hook, and a tail of bucktail, feathers, nylon, or similar material. Jigs are made in sizes of ⅟₁₆ ounce to 6 ounces and even heavier, and they will take just about any fish that swims in fresh water or salt. Jigs imitate baitfish, crustaceans, and other game-fish forage. In some jigs, the hook rides with the point up to minimize the chance of snagging. Jigs, and related lures, take many forms. Here's a look at the most popular types.

FEATHERED JIG: Often called Japanese feathers, this jig is commonly used in saltwater trolling and casting. It consists of a heavy metal head with eyes. Through the head runs a wire leader, to the end of which the hook is attached. Running from the head down to the hook is a long tail, usually of feathers. A plastic sleeve covers the feathers for about half their length. This jig is typically used in trolling for tuna, billfish, dolphin, and other pelagic species.

BUCKTAIL JIG: This jig consists of a lead head, embedded hook, and trailing tail of bucktail. The head is painted, with the most popular colors being white, red, yellow, or combinations of these colors. The most

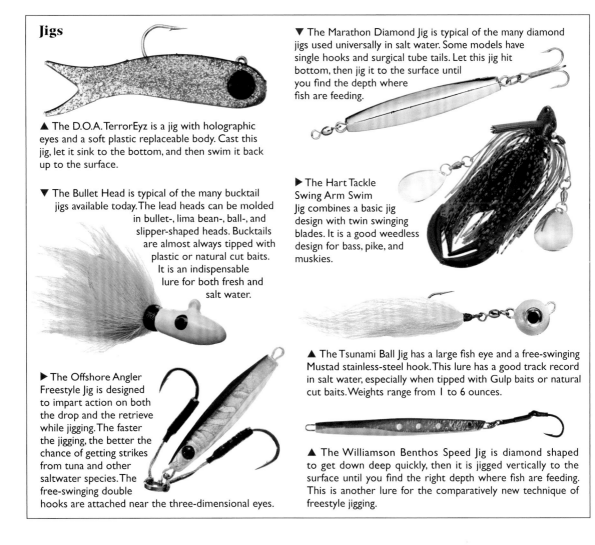

Jigs

▲ The D.O.A. TerrorEyz is a jig with holographic eyes and a soft plastic replaceable body. Cast this jig, let it sink to the bottom, and then swim it back up to the surface.

▼ The Bullet Head is typical of the many bucktail jigs available today. The lead heads can be molded in bullet-, lima bean-, ball-, and slipper-shaped heads. Bucktails are almost always tipped with plastic or natural cut baits. It is an indispensable lure for both fresh and salt water.

▶ The Offshore Angler Freestyle Jig is designed to impart action on both the drop and the retrieve while jigging. The faster the jigging, the better the chance of getting strikes from tuna and other saltwater species. The free-swinging double hooks are attached near the three-dimensional eyes.

▼ The Marathon Diamond Jig is typical of the many diamond jigs used universally in salt water. Some models have single hooks and surgical tube tails. Let this jig hit bottom, then jig it to the surface until you find the depth where fish are feeding.

▶ The Hart Tackle Swing Arm Swim Jig combines a basic jig design with twin swinging blades. It is a good weedless design for bass, pike, and muskies.

▲ The Tsunami Ball Jig has a large fish eye and a free-swinging Mustad stainless-steel hook. This lure has a good track record in salt water, especially when tipped with Gulp baits or natural cut baits. Weights range from 1 to 6 ounces.

▲ The Williamson Benthos Speed Jig is diamond shaped to get down deep quickly, then it is jigged vertically to the surface until you find the right depth where fish are feeding. This is another lure for the comparatively new technique of freestyle jigging.

popular member of the jig family, bucktail jigs are used on a wide variety of freshwater and saltwater game fish, especially largemouth and smallmouth bass, walleyes, pike, striped bass, bluefish, and many other bottom-feeders.

SHAD DART: This is a small jig (usually weighing about ¼ ounce) with a relatively long, narrow head, flat face, and short tail of bucktail or similar material. It is usually painted in two colors, with the most popular combinations being red and white, yellow and white, and red and yellow. It is an extremely popular lure for American (white) shad in East Coast rivers.

METAL (BLOCK-TIN) SQUIDS: Falling under the general category of jigs are these lures, which are used mostly in salt water for striped bass, bluefish, tuna, and the like. Made to resemble baitfish, they have a long, narrow body of block tin, stainless steel, chrome, or nickel-plated lead and either a single fixed hook or a free-swinging treble hook, with or without a tail of bucktail. Most metal squids range in length from 3 to 6 inches. All have bright finishes, usually silvery; in some, the finish is smooth, while others have a hammered finish that gives a scale-like appearance. Among the most popular metal squids are types such as the Hopkins (which has a hammered finish, a long, narrow, flat body, and a free-swinging treble hook), the diamond jig (which has a four-sided body and a treble hook), and the sand eel (which has a long, rounded, undulating body). A strip of pork rind often adds to the effectiveness of metal squids.

JIG AND EEL: This jig consists of a small metal squid on which is rigged a common eel, either the real McCoy (usually dead and preserved) or a plastic artificial. These rigged eels range in length from about 6 inches up to a foot or longer. The jig and eel is a deadly combination for striped bass, big snook, redfish, and sea trout. The best retrieve depends on various conditions, but usually a slow, slightly erratic swimming motion is best.

Vertical jigging is a productive technique for a variety of species, especially in salt water. The most effective jigging method is to cast, let the jig drop to the bottom, and then begin retrieving with an up-and-down jigging motion. Once you determine where the fish are, concentrate on jigging at that depth. Most fish will strike when the jig is fluttering down to the bottom. Jigging speed will range from very rapid to slow and works best with braided line. Vertical jigging can be deadly on all species, especially striped bass, tuna, and grouper.

Hot Lures for Salmon

The most consistent key to catching salmon is color! Millions of salmon return each year to their birthplace to deposit billions of salmon eggs. Some of these eggs will eventually become salmon, but most will sink to the bottom and provide a food source for all Alaska game fish. Salmon eggs vary in color from pink to shades of red and orange. It's these reddish hues that trigger a feeding response.

What should be in your tackle box? A spin fisherman needs only spoons and jig heads with red or pink swimming plastic tails. Curly tails seem to work best. Cover the hook of the jig head and fish it slow with occasional twitches.

Pixie Spoon

Chris Batin's BBL

For fishermen who prefer to cast spoons, the same color rule applies. For several years, I've used Pixie spoons in weights from ¼ to ½ ounce. These chromed spoons have red or orange plastic insets molded to look like salmon egg clusters.

When I arrived in Alaska, Chris Batin also gave me a handful of his special flies. He calls them BBLs, which stands for Batin Bunny Leeches. The fly is a bright fuchsia-colored streamer with a barbell lead eye.

■ Plastic Lures

Hundreds of years from now the history books may refer to our era as the Age of Plastic. And fishermen haven't escaped the gaze of plastic manufacturers.

On the market today are soft-plastic lures that imitate just about anything a fish will eat. There are plastic worms, eels, snakes, crickets, crawfish, minnows, shrimp, hellgrammites, mullet, flies, beetles, grasshoppers, frogs, and many, many more. Even salmon eggs! Many manufacturers impregnate these lures with secret formulas, attractants, and scents, claiming fish will strike these baits and not let go.

Surprisingly, a good many of these synthetic creations catch fish. A prime example is the plastic worm, which came into its own in the mid- and late 1960s. It has accounted for some eye-popping stringers of large-

Rigging Plastic Worms

The plastic worm can be fished on the bottom, above the bottom, on the surface, and through thick weeds. It comes in different lengths, shapes, colors, flavors, and scents. The fake night crawler is so versatile it has spawned specialized hooks and a separate vocabulary. Here's how to tie the basic worm rigs, as well as when and where to fish them—and, just so there's no confusion, what they're called.

Floating Worm Rig: This is the simplest of all worm rigs. Thread a worm on a hook, push it up to the hook eye, and the rig is complete. You can buy floating worms (usually molded with air chambers), or you can make any worm a floater by threading a piece of cork on your line in front of the hook. You can also try "larding" the worm with bits of Styrofoam (cut from a plate or coffee cup). Some fishermen buy injectors—they look like miniature basketball pumps—to float worms, lizards, or any other soft-plastic lure. A floating worm works best at dusk or dawn. It's especially effective during spawning season, when bass are protective of their beds: cast the worm near a bass bed, swim it slowly, pause, and allow it to hang directly above the bed . . . and hang on.

Carolina Rig: This rig is designed to be fished deep, but not on the bottom. The principal difference between the Carolina and Texas rigs is that in the Carolina the sinker, usually a slip sinker, is placed 2 and 3 feet ahead of a floating worm. The sinker is held in position with a swivel (and often a bead). Use a bullet- or egg-shaped sinker; either will slide over most obstructions. The rig allows a bass to pick up the bait without immediately feeling the weight of a sinker, and it makes the worm more visible to suspended fish. The Carolina rig is another good summer lure for deep water. Depending on the amount of vegetation, the hook can be left exposed or buried in the worm.

Swivel

3/0 Hook

Slip Sinker (½ to 1 ounce) Leader (2 to 3 feet)

Texas Rig: The Texas rig is a brush-buster. In its most common variant, a bullet-shaped sinker is threaded on the line just ahead of the worm, and the point of the hook is buried in it. This requires that the worm be carefully measured so it will hang straight when the hook point is inserted (it takes some practice). If the worm is "scrunched" on the shank of the hook, it won't be nearly as effective. The Texas rig is designed to be fished through weeds and brush and around stumps, and crawled along snag-infested bottoms. It's particularly effective on hot summer days when bass seek out brushy, shaded shorelines or hang very deep in cool water.

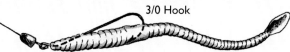

3/0 Hook

Slip Sinker (½ to 1 ounce)

Worm Hooks

This hook has a weighted shank with a free-swinging keeper at the eye to hold the worm.

This is a wide-gap hook with a weighted keeper. The worm is snugged against the eye; the point is buried.

The kink in the shank of this hook holds the worm securely and helps it hang straight.

The worm is threaded on the keeper. The ultrawide gap reduces the chance of a thrown hook.

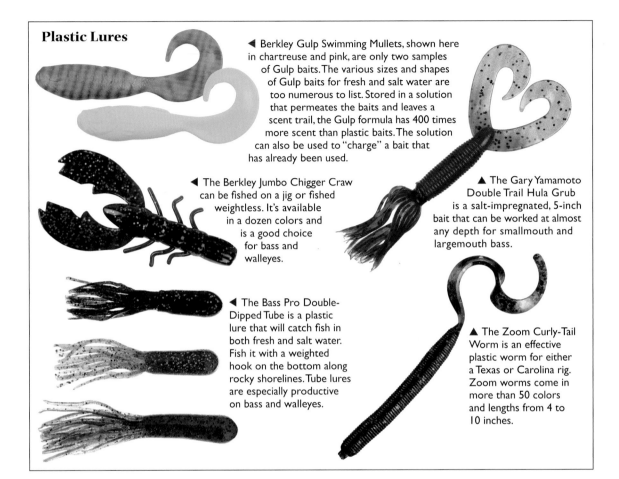

Plastic Lures

◄ Berkley Gulp Swimming Mullets, shown here in chartreuse and pink, are only two samples of Gulp baits. The various sizes and shapes of Gulp baits for fresh and salt water are too numerous to list. Stored in a solution that permeates the baits and leaves a scent trail, the Gulp formula has 400 times more scent than plastic baits. The solution can also be used to "charge" a bait that has already been used.

◄ The Berkley Jumbo Chigger Craw can be fished on a jig or fished weightless. It's available in a dozen colors and is a good choice for bass and walleyes.

▲ The Gary Yamamoto Double Trail Hula Grub is a salt-impregnated, 5-inch bait that can be worked at almost any depth for smallmouth and largemouth bass.

◄ The Bass Pro Double-Dipped Tube is a plastic lure that will catch fish in both fresh and salt water. Fish it with a weighted hook on the bottom along rocky shorelines. Tube lures are especially productive on bass and walleyes.

▲ The Zoom Curly-Tail Worm is an effective plastic worm for either a Texas or Carolina rig. Zoom worms come in more than 50 colors and lengths from 4 to 10 inches.

mouth bass, especially in big southern lakes. A plastic worm threaded on a weedless hook and slithered through lily pads or an underwater weed bed is a real killer. Some plastic worms come with a weighted jig-type head or a spinner at the front.

■ Pork Rind

Pork rind, as used by fishermen, is the skin from the back of a hog. It is sold in jars containing a liquid preservative to prevent spoilage and to retain the rind's flexibility.

It used to be that pork rind was used only as an addition to a spoon or other lure. For example, a single-hook spoon with a 2- or 3-inch strip of pork rind was—and still is—a popular combination for pickerel, pike, and the like. Pork rind is still widely used that way today. It is sold in many shapes and sizes, from tiny half-inch V-strips for panfish up to 6-inch strips for muskies and salt-water game fish. Pork-rind baits come in many colors and shapes, such as lizards, frogs, worms, and eels.

■ Flies

An artificial fly is a combination of feathers, hair, floss, tinsel, and other materials tied to a hook to imitate a natural insect (dry and wet flies, including nymphs) or a baitfish (streamer flies and bucktails). Flies are used to take many freshwater and saltwater game fish, but most were originally designed for trout and salmon. There are four basic kinds of artificial flies: dry, wet (including nymph), streamer, and bucktail.

DRY FLIES: The dry fly, designed to imitate a floating insect, is tied so that the fibers of the hackles (feathers)

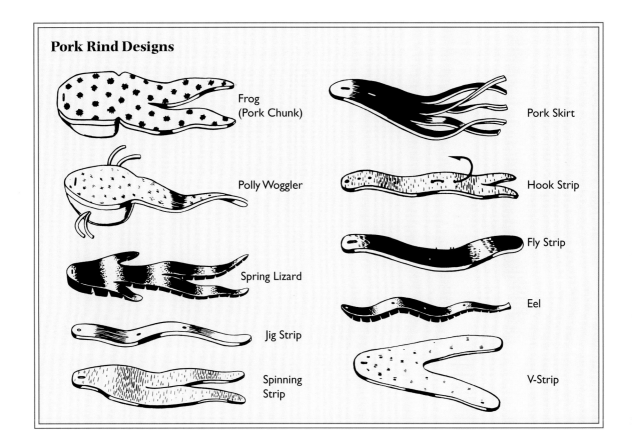

Pork Rind Designs

Frog (Pork Chunk)

Pork Skirt

Polly Woggler

Hook Strip

Spring Lizard

Fly Strip

Jig Strip

Eel

Spinning Strip

V-Strip

stick out at approximately right angles to the shank of the hook. A properly tied dry fly sits high and lightly on the tips of its hackles, riding the surface of the water.

There are countless dry-fly patterns, but almost all of them fall into one of 10 basic types. Here is a brief description of each type:

- **Downwing (or Sedge):** This fly has a built-up body, hackle, and wings lying flat along the shank of the hook. It floats with the hook underwater.

- **Divided Wing:** This is the standard dry-fly type. It has two erect separated wings of feather fibers, hackle, tapered body, and a stiff, slender tail. It floats with the hook above or partly underwater.

- **Hairwing:** This fly has upright wings made of deer hair, as well as hackle, a tapered body, and stiff tail. It floats with the hook above or partly underwater.

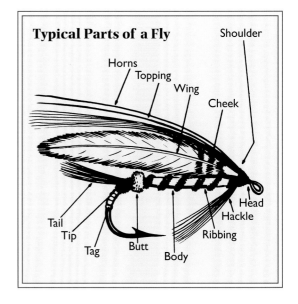

Typical Parts of a Fly

Shoulder

Horns

Topping

Wing

Cheek

Tail

Tip

Tag

Butt

Body

Ribbing

Hackle

Head

Basic Dry Flies

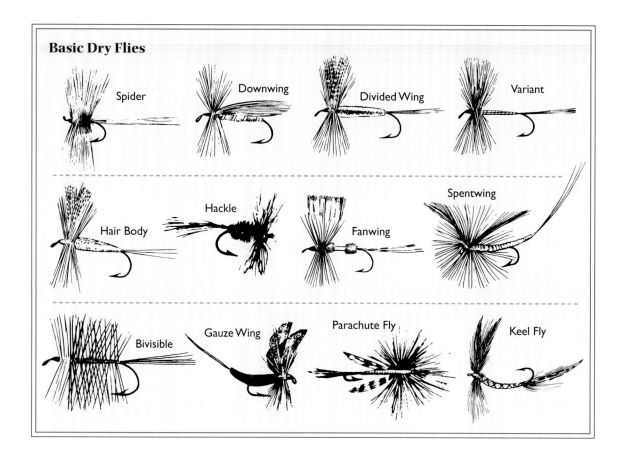

- **Fanwing:** This fly has large, flat, erect wings, hackle, body, and a stiff tail. It floats with the hook above or partly underwater. The large wings make this fly readily visible to an angler.

- **Bivisible:** This fly has no wings. White hackle is wound on the body at the fly's head, and hackle of another color (brown, gray, or black are the most popular) covers most of the remainder of the body. The tail is stiff. It floats high, with the hook above water, and is highly visible to an angler.

- **Spentwing:** This fly has slender wings that stick out horizontally from the tapered body, hackle, and stiff tail. It floats on its wings and body with the bend of the hook underwater.

- **Spider:** This fly has no wings. The hackle is extralong and stiff. There is no body in the smaller sizes, a tinsel or herl body in the larger sizes. It has a stiff, extralong tail. It floats on its hackle tips and tail with the hook well out of the water.

- **Variant:** This fly has upright divided wings, extralong and stiff hackle, a very light body (or none at all), and a stiff, extralong tail. It floats on its hackle tips and tail with the hook well out of the water.

- **Hair Body:** This fly has upright divided wings, hackle, a body of clipped deer hair or similar material, and a stiff tail. It floats with the hook partly underwater.

- **Keel Fly:** The shank of the hook is weighted, causing the fly to ride upright in the water. The keel principle also has been applied to wet flies and streamers.

The budding fly fisherman who walks into a fishing-tackle store is sure to be overwhelmed by the display of artificial flies. Which patterns are best for his particular needs? Only experience can answer that question.

Basic Wet Flies

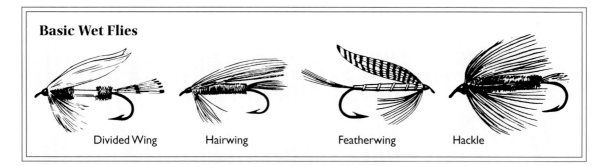

Divided Wing   Hairwing   Featherwing   Hackle

However, here are 10 basic dry-fly patterns—and the most productive sizes—that should be found in every trout fisherman's fly box:

◦ Light Cahill, Size 16
◦ Gray Midge Hackle, Size 20
◦ Black Flying Ant, Size 20
◦ Red Variant, Size 14
◦ Black Gnat, Size 12
◦ Gray Wulff, Size 10
◦ Blue Dun, Size 16
◦ Adams, Size 12
◦ Quill Gordon, Size 14
◦ Jassid, Size 20

WET FLIES: Wet flies are tied to imitate submerged insects, either those that have fallen to the surface and drowned or those that are rising from the stream or lake bottom to the surface to hatch. Nymphs, which are classified as wet flies, are imitations of the larval or nymphal states of underwater insects that rise to the surface before hatching.

As with dry flies, there is a bewildering number of wet-fly patterns. However, most of them fall into one of four basic types. Here's a brief description of each type:

- **Divided Wing:** Two prominent separated wings are tied at about a 30-degree angle from the shank of the hook. This type also has a wisp of hackle, body, and a stiff tail.

- **Hairwing:** A wing of deer hair extends over the shank of the hook, a wisp of hackle, body, and a tail.

- **Featherwing:** This type of fly has a swept-back wing of feather fibers, soft hackle, tapered body, and a sparse tail.

- **Hackle:** This fly has soft hackle tied on at the head, which extends back over the built-up body all around the fly. It has a sparse tail.

Here are 10 wet-fly patterns that should produce well for the trout fisherman:

◦ Gray Hackle, Yellow Body, Size 10
◦ Brown Hackle, Size 10
◦ Coachman, Size 12
◦ Royal Coachman, Size 12
◦ Black Gnat, Size 14
◦ Quill Gordon, Size 14
◦ Blue Dun, Size 16
◦ Light Cahill, Size 16
◦ March Brown, Size 12
◦ Ginger Quill, Size 16

Other Wet Flies

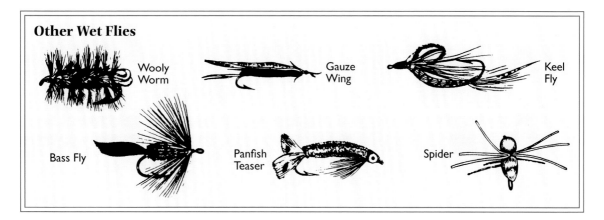

Wooly Worm   Gauze Wing   Keel Fly

Bass Fly   Panfish Teaser   Spider

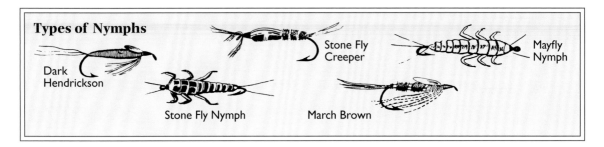

Types of Nymphs

Dark Hendrickson

Stone Fly Nymph

Stone Fly Creeper

March Brown

Mayfly Nymph

NYMPHS: It is impossible to break down the various nymph patterns into broad classifications. However, most nymphs have the following basic characteristics: no wings, wisps of soft hackle at the head, a tapered body, usually of dubbed fur, and a sparse tail of a few feather fibers.

Here are 10 nymph patterns that no trout fisherman should be without:

◦ March Brown, Size 12
◦ Ginger Quill, Size 14
◦ Yellow May, Size 12
◦ Freshwater Shrimp, Size 8
◦ Light Mossback, Size 6
◦ Large Stone Fly, 2X long shank, Size 8
◦ Large Mayfly, 2X long shank, Size 10
◦ Caddis, 2X long shank, Size 10
◦ Dark Olive, 2X long shank, Size 12
◦ Montana, Size 4

STREAMERS AND BUCKTAILS: Streamer flies and bucktails are tied to imitate a minnow or other baitfish on which game fish feed. They are widely used in both fresh and salt water. Many saltwater streamers and bucktails, and some used in fresh water, have two hooks—the main hook, on which the dressings are tied, and a trailer hook. Streamers and bucktails are well known for producing big fish.

Streamers are tied with long wings of feathers. Bucktails are similar, but more durable, flies tied with wings of hair, usually deer hair. Most streamers and bucktails are tied on Size 8 and Size 10 longshank hooks. Some have bodies that hide the shank of the hook, but in others the bare shank shows.

Here is a list of 10 of the most productive streamer patterns and 10 top bucktail patterns (best hook sizes are 6 to 12, unless otherwise noted):

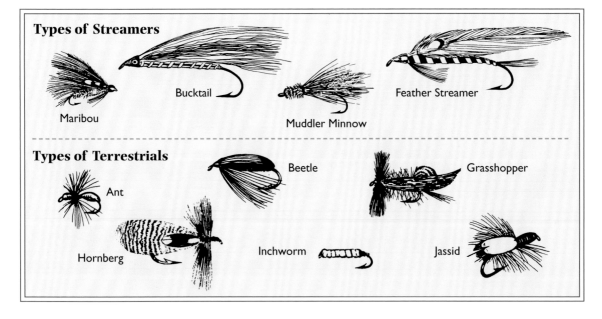

Types of Streamers

Maribou

Bucktail

Muddler Minnow

Feather Streamer

Types of Terrestrials

Ant

Beetle

Grasshopper

Hornberg

Inchworm

Jassid

Streamers
- Black Ghost
- Gray Ghost
- Supervisor
- Mickey Finn
- Black-Nosed Dace
- Red and Yellow
- Clouser Minnow
- Red and White
  Multiwing, Size 1
- Black Marabou
- White Marabou

Bucktails
- Black Prince
- Brown and White
- Black and White
- Red and White
- Mickey Finn
- Platinum Blonde, Size 1/0
- Strawberry Blonde, Size 1/0
- Brown Muddler Minnow,
  Sizes 1/0 to 10
- Black Woolly Bugger,
  Sizes 6 to 10
- White Marabou Muddler,
  Sizes 1/0 to 6

Streamers

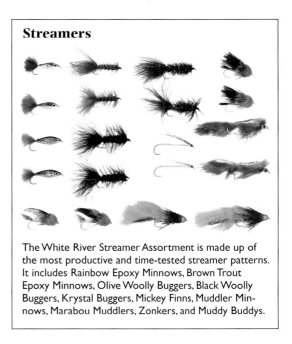

The White River Streamer Assortment is made up of the most productive and time-tested streamer patterns. It includes Rainbow Epoxy Minnows, Brown Trout Epoxy Minnows, Olive Woolly Buggers, Black Woolly Buggers, Krystal Buggers, Mickey Finns, Muddler Minnows, Marabou Muddlers, Zonkers, and Muddy Buddys.

TERRESTRIALS: A class of artificial flies that is unique and deserves special mention is terrestrials—a group of flies, both wet and dry, that are tied to imitate insects that are born on land and then fly, jump, fall, crawl, or are blown into the water and become food for trout and other fish. Such insects include ants, grasshoppers, inchworms, beetles, houseflies, and others.

Among the most popular and productive terrestrial patterns are the Inchworm, the Black Ant (especially in very small sizes), and the Jassid, a fly that was developed in Pennsylvania and is particularly effective in limestone streams. It is tied on tiny hooks, with the best sizes being 18, 20, and 22.

BASS BUGS: If any form of fly fishing approaches the thrill of taking a wary trout on a dry fly, it is having a belligerent largemouth or smallmouth bass burst through the surface and engulf an enticingly twitched bass bug.

Bass bugs are fly-rod lures created to imitate such bass morsels as frogs, bees, dragonflies, mice, and anything else that looks like it would taste good to a bass or

pike. Because of the size of a bass's mouth, these surface lures are tied on large hooks—size 4 to 2/0 in most cases. However, smaller versions of these bugs are made for panfish.

Most bass bugs fall into one of two categories: those with solid bodies (usually of cork, plastic, or balsa wood) and those with bodies of deer hair.

Many cork or balsa bugs have some hackle or bucktail at the tail to partly disguise the hook. Some have a perpendicular, hollowed-out surface so that when the angler jerks the rod tip the bug makes a popping sound that often brings a bass charging out of its lair. These bugs are called poppers. Others have a more stream-

Bass Bugs and Poppers

Classic Frog

Sneaky Pete Popper

Bluegill Bug

Hair Bass Bug

lined body and are really designed to be twitched slowly rather than jerked.

Deer-hair bugs are, as you might expect, made of deer hair that is wound onto a hook and clipped to form the body shape of a mouse, large insect, and the like. These bugs are best fished very slowly. Weedless arrangements, usually stiff monofilament or light wire, are sometimes used.

NATURAL FRESHWATER BAITS

Live bait is the real thing! Even the most avid purist would concede that live bait, when properly presented, is one of the deadliest of all lures. Many times, however, live bait is incorrectly rammed onto a hook. When this happens, the bait does not act naturally, may die quickly, and will likely turn away lunkers that grew big by learning how to recognize food that doesn't look right.

Live bait will only appear natural if placed on the hook correctly, and this depends on how you plan to fish it. You wouldn't, for example, hook a minnow behind the dorsal fin if you plan on trolling. Minnows just don't swim backward. Let's take a look at the popular baits and learn how to hook them.

Even though garden worms and night crawlers will take most species of fish, they must still be presented differently. A worm washed into a stream, for example, would drift with the current, so it should be fished that way. Hook it once through the collar or girdle with both ends free to drift naturally, fish it with no line drag, and let the current do the work. The worm should look strung out, bouncing along quickly through riffles and slowly through pools.

Using worms for panfish requires a different tack. Generally, the panfish angler is still-fishing, so natural presentation is less important. A single worm should be used and threaded about three times on the hook. If you're bothered by nibblers, use only a piece of worm and thread it on the hook, covering the point and barb completely.

Night crawlers are effective on bass, and many fishermen still-fish for bass with the big worms the same way they would for panfish. Actually, bass prefer a moving bait and anglers would catch more big bass if they cast and retrieved night crawlers slowly along the bottom. Hook the worm by running the point of the hook into its head, bringing the point and barb out an inch below the head. Rigged this way and retrieved slowly, a night crawler will appear to be crawling on the bottom.

Next on the list of most common live baits are minnows, from 1-inchers for panfish to 8-inchers for big fish.

There are two ways of hooking a live minnow, and how an angler intends to fish determines which one to use.

When trolling or fishing from a drifting boat, run the hook upward and through both lips of the minnow. The lip-hooked bait will move through the water on an even keel and look natural.

If you're still-fishing from an anchored boat or shoreline, hook the minnow just behind the dorsal fin. Be careful not to run the hook too deep or it will hit the spine and kill the bait. Hooked just behind the fin, a minnow can swim freely and for a surprisingly long time. There is no hook weight near its head or tail to throw off its balance.

Frogs rank as another excellent bait. Stick with the small frogs, however, such as leopard and green frogs. An old sock makes a fine frog carrier, and frogs are easy to find along any shoreline or riverbank during the summer. There is only one good way to hook a live frog and that is under the jaw and up through both lips. Cast it out and let the frog swim freely, or use a twitch-and-pause retrieve. A lip-hooked frog will stay alive for a long time. A frog can also be hooked through one of its hind legs. A hook through a frog's leg, however, will destroy some leg muscles, limiting its natural movement.

The crayfish, often called crawfish, is another top bait for bass and trout. The problem is that crayfish are often difficult to find. The best way to hunt them is at night in shallow water that has a rocky or gravel bottom. A crayfish's eyes will glow reddish in the beam of a flashlight. The light seems to freeze them and they can be easily picked up. The best way to hook a crayfish is to run the hook up, through, and out the top of its tail. Cast into rocky shorelines or streams, they'll account for big trout, bass, and walleyes.

Salamanders or newts also take bass, trout, and similar species. Finding salamanders isn't hard. They like small springs and streams. They're active at night and easily spotted with a flashlight. Salamanders are fragile and must be hooked carefully. Use a fine-wire hook and run it through the lips or the tail. Salamanders produce best when drifted along stream and river bottoms.

Natural Freshwater Baits

Natural Baits	Species of Fish
Minnows	Largemouth and smallmouth bass, trout, pickerel, pike, walleyes, perch, crappies, rock bass
Earthworms	Trout, white bass, rock bass, perch, crappies, catfish, sunfish, whitefish
Night crawlers	Largemouth and smallmouth bass, trout, pickerel, pike, walleyes, muskies, catfish, sturgeon
Crickets	Trout, crappies, perch, rock bass, sunfish
Grubs	Trout, crappies, perch, rock bass, sunfish
Caterpillars	Trout, largemouth and smallmouth bass, crappies, perch, rock bass, sunfish
Crayfish	Smallmouth bass, walleyes, trout, catfish
Hellgrammites	Trout, largemouth and smallmouth bass, walleyes, catfish, rock bass
Nymphs (mayfly, caddis fly, stone fly, and others)	Trout, landlocked salmon, perch, crappies, sunfish
Grasshoppers	Trout, largemouth and smallmouth bass, perch, crappies
Newts and salamanders	Largemouth and smallmouth bass, trout, pickerel, rock bass, walleyes, catfish
Frogs	Largemouth and smallmouth bass, pickerel, pike, muskies, walleyes
Wasp larvae	Perch, crappies, sunfish, rock bass
Suckers	Pike, muskies, smallmouth and largemouth bass
Mice	Largemouth and smallmouth bass, pike, muskies
Freshwater shrimp (scud)	Trout, smallmouth and largemouth bass, perch, crappies, rock bass, sunfish
Dragonflies	Largemouth and smallmouth bass, crappies, white bass, rock bass
Darters	Trout, largemouth and smallmouth bass, walleyes, pickerel, crappies, rock bass
Sculpins	Largemouth and smallmouth bass, walleyes, pickerel, rock bass
Salmon eggs	Trout, salmon
Cut bait (perch belly, etc.)	Pickerel, pike, muskies, largemouth and smallmouth bass, walleyes
Doughballs	Carp, catfish

The most popular live baits have been covered here, but there are still others worth mentioning. The hellgrammite, for example, ranks high with bass and trout. Water insects, hellgrammites average 1 to 2 inches long and can be caught in most streams by simply turning over rocks and holding a net just downstream from the rock. The hellgrammite has a hard collar just behind the head and this is where the hook should be inserted.

The nymph, an underwater stage of the aquatic fly, is still another top bait, particularly for trout. Nymphs differ in the way they behave. Some crawl on rocks, others climb shoreline growths, and still others float downstream. They will all eventually hatch into flies, but it is during this nymphal period that they can be effectively used as bait. There are two ways to put nymphs on a hook. They can be completely threaded—running the hook from the rear, through the body, and up to the head—or they can be simply hooked once just behind the head.

Grasshoppers also work well, and finding them is no problem. Most grassy fields are loaded with 'hoppers. Using a butterfly net, you should be able to fill a box quickly. It's easier to catch them at dawn and dusk. During midday, they are most active and spooky. There are several varieties of grasshoppers and nearly all of them take fish. It's best to use a fine-wire hook, running it down and through, behind the head.

Baiting Game

Worms, earthworms, and night crawlers are the most popular baits. Night crawlers come to the surface at night. They like warm and damp and dewy weather. Prowl around your lawn, a golf course, or a park after dark. Use a flashlight, but not one with a bright beam, which will spook worms. Cover the lens with red cellophane if necessary. Usually worms you will spot will only be partly out of their holes. Quickly press your finger at the spot where the tail enters the ground and grab the worm with the other hand.

Natural Freshwater Baits

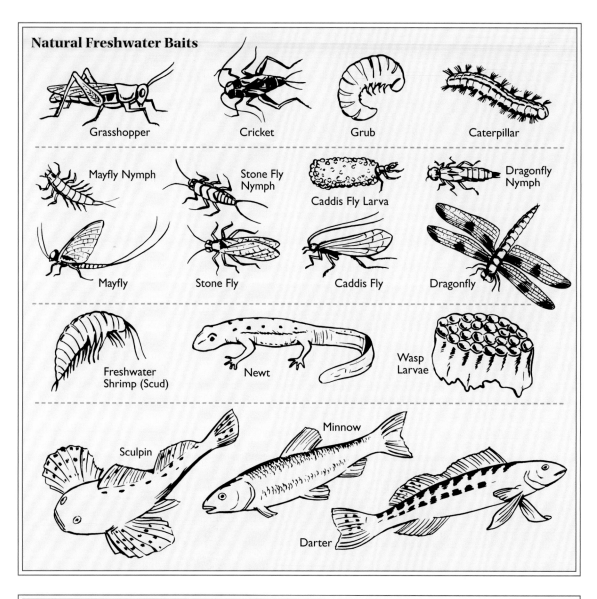

Grasshopper

Cricket

Grub

Caterpillar

Mayfly Nymph

Stone Fly Nymph

Caddis Fly Larva

Dragonfly Nymph

Mayfly

Stone Fly

Caddis Fly

Dragonfly

Freshwater Shrimp (Scud)

Newt

Wasp Larvae

Sculpin

Minnow

Darter

Crayfish and Hellgrammite Rigs

Tail-Hook Rig for Crawfish

Hellgrammite Hooked through Collar

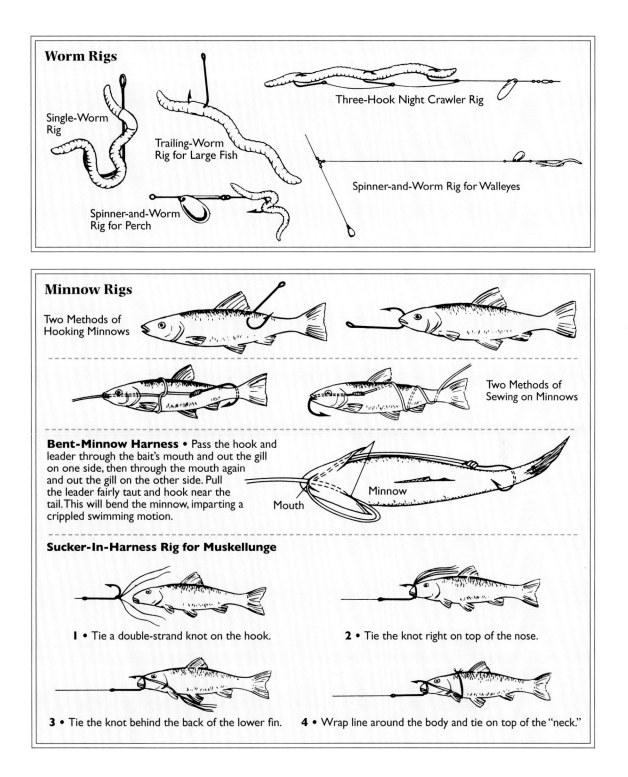

Worm Rigs

Single-Worm Rig

Trailing-Worm Rig for Large Fish

Three-Hook Night Crawler Rig

Spinner-and-Worm Rig for Walleyes

Spinner-and-Worm Rig for Perch

Minnow Rigs

Two Methods of Hooking Minnows

Two Methods of Sewing on Minnows

Bent-Minnow Harness • Pass the hook and leader through the bait's mouth and out the gill on one side, then through the mouth again and out the gill on the other side. Pull the leader fairly taut and hook near the tail. This will bend the minnow, imparting a crippled swimming motion.

Mouth

Minnow

Sucker-In-Harness Rig for Muskellunge

I • Tie a double-strand knot on the hook.

2 • Tie the knot right on top of the nose.

3 • Tie the knot behind the back of the lower fin.

4 • Wrap line around the body and tie on top of the "neck."

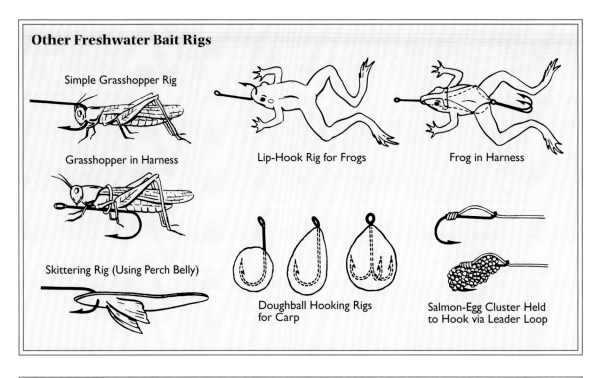

Other Freshwater Bait Rigs

Simple Grasshopper Rig

Grasshopper in Harness

Lip-Hook Rig for Frogs

Frog in Harness

Skittering Rig (Using Perch Belly)

Doughball Hooking Rigs for Carp

Salmon-Egg Cluster Held to Hook via Leader Loop

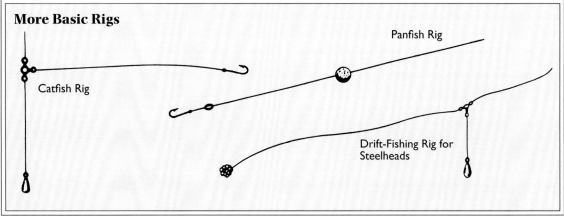

More Basic Rigs

Panfish Rig

Catfish Rig

Drift-Fishing Rig for Steelheads

■ Big Shiners for Big Bass

Nearly all bass experts agree that fishing a live shiner is one of the most effective ways to catch the biggest bass of your life. Like most things, however, it's not as easy as it sounds.

Your first problem may be finding 10- to 12-inch shiners. If your bait shop doesn't have them, you'll have to catch them in back bays and river pools. You can chum for shiners with oatmeal and bread crumbs and catch them with doughballs on a No. 12 or 14 hook. You'll need at least two dozen for a day of bass fishing.

Shiners are most productive when fished along shorelines or close to floating vegetation such as lily pads or hyacinths. The standard rig will have two hooks—a treble hook through the lips of the shiner, and a trailing single or treble hook in the tail of the bait or held along-

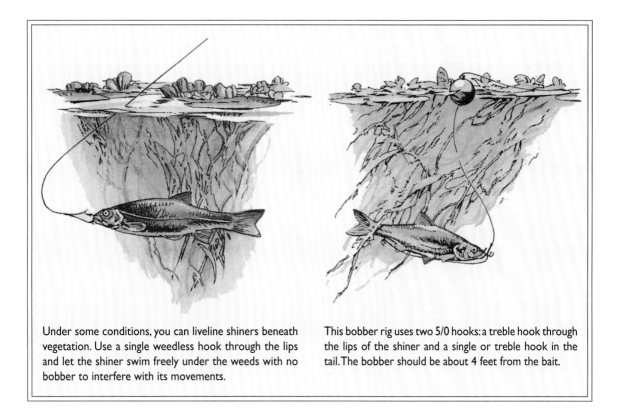

Under some conditions, you can liveline shiners beneath vegetation. Use a single weedless hook through the lips and let the shiner swim freely under the weeds with no bobber to interfere with its movements.

This bobber rig uses two 5/0 hooks: a treble hook through the lips of the shiner and a single or treble hook in the tail. The bobber should be about 4 feet from the bait.

side the tail with a rubber band. A bobber big enough to keep an active shiner from dragging it under water should be placed 3 to 4 feet above the bait.

Don't try to cast this half-pound bait overhand. Lob it underhand against shoreline vegetation and let the shiner take over. The fish will try to seek cover in the growth, and its movements will be telegraphed through the action of the bobber. When your shiner is motionless, jerk it back into action with a twitch or two of your rod tip.

The Best Tracking Line

Here's a neat trick: You may find it easier to track a shiner if you use a leader and a white level floating fly line with some backing on your conventional reel. The white fly line will be much more visible than monofilament. It will also be easier to track a bass when it picks up your bait.

If the bobber starts to bounce and jump on the surface, you'll know a big bass is after the shiner. Do nothing until that bobber goes down and stays down. A bass will grab the shiner around the middle and slowly swim away.

Begin counting as you watch your line move toward open water. As you count, slowly begin to reel in all slack until your rod tip is pointing in the direction the line is moving. Use your judgment here, but when your count is between 20 and 30 and all slack is out of your line, set the hook solidly.

Don't try to set the hook too quickly—you'll jerk the bait away from the bass. You have to allow enough time for the bass to pick up the shiner, swim away from the weed growth, and turn the shiner around in its mouth. Bass, like most other fish species, will swallow a live bait headfirst. You can also use circle hooks and you won't have to set the hook. As your line tightens, just lift your rod and the bass will hook itself.

You're after big bass, so leave your light tackle at home. Your best bet is a medium-weight rod with a conventional reel loaded with 20- to 30-pound-test line.

NATURAL SALTWATER BAITS

Natural baits are no less important in salt water than they are in fresh water. That fact is well known to anyone who has seen a school of bluefish slash viciously into a horde of mossbunkers or a tuna or sailfish ravaging a ballyhoo bait.

What natural saltwater baits should you use and when? Those are questions that only time and experience can help you answer accurately. Generally, you will find that it pays to use any bait that is prevalent when and where you are fishing. A few discreet questions at a bait shop in the fishing area will go a long way toward helping you choose a productive bait.

How you rig a saltwater bait can be a vital factor. The primary consideration in rigging most baits is to make them appear as lifelike as possible, whether they are to be trolled, cast out and retrieved, or bounced on the bottom.

The accompanying illustrations show proven ways to prepare and rig the most popular baits used in salt water.

Florida Bait Bomb

One of the most exciting and productive ways to fish the inshore waters of Florida is to chum the patches of coral for yellowtail snappers, groupers, or the dozens of other species that live and hunt for food in these reefs. Every catch is a colorful surprise.

Captain Glen Miller, a charter captain for more than 30 years in the Florida Keys, and his mate, Brooks Gregory, are masters at chumming these patches. Glen knows how to position and anchor his boat so that the current will carry his chum to the fish living on the coral. If the current is too strong, the chum might pass over the patch and might not get close enough to pull fish into the chum. Once Glen has his position and current figured out, he starts to chum with a mixture of sand, chum, and oats. Within 10 or 15 minutes, small fish begin to appear, darting in and out of the chum.

Glen cautions about over-chumming. Put out too much chum and you will end up feeding the fish instead of catching them. Ladle out a handful of chum, and then wait until all the chum is out of sight before tossing out more. You can also place a frozen chum block in a mesh bag and hang it near the transom. Wave action will gradually thaw and release the chum automatically.

Now is the time to use Florida bait bombs. Some Florida captains call them bait balls or chum balls instead. Call them whatever you want, but these bombs are deadly and catch fish. Once Glen has a good slick working, he puts a piece of cut bait on a hook and centers it in the mixture of water, sand, chum, and oats. The mix is now formed into a snowball shape and packed firmly. The bait bomb is ready for fish.

Glen strips off about 12 yards of line from the reel, so there is no drag when he tosses the bait ball into the slick. The ball is allowed to drop slowly back into the slick. The ball puts out a small cloud of chum with the piece of cut bait in the middle. The fish will follow the chum and find the bait when the ball finally breaks apart in the current. A fish, usually a yellowtail snapper or one of many species of grouper, will invariably hit the bait. These Florida reefs harbor a great variety of fish. It is not uncommon to catch a dozen different species on one coral patch.

The bait bomb is only one trick Florida captains use to bring fish to the boat. While building a chum slick, some fishermen will also have two live grunt baits on the bottom and two live pilchards, one off an outrigger and another on a kite rod. More often than not, a big grouper will take a grunt on the bottom rig near the surface and a kingfish will nail the live pilchards.

This technique for using bait or chum balls is a strategy that should work anywhere a fisherman is trying to entice fish into a chum slick. It's so effective that commercial yellowtail fishermen use it in Florida. In northern coastal waters, weakfish and bluefish are two good targets for the Florida bait bomb.

Natural Saltwater Baits

Species of Fish	Natural Baits and Lures	Recommended Methods	Hooks
Albacore	Feather lures	Trolling	7/0
Amberjack	Strip baits, feathers, spoons, plugs	Trolling, casting	6/0 to 9/0
Barracuda	Baitfish, plugs, feathers, spoons	Trolling, casting	1/0 to 8/0
Bass, channel	Mullet, mossbunker, crabs, clams, spoons, plugs	Casting, still-fishing, trolling	6/0 to 10/0
Bass, sea	Squid, clams, sea worms, crabs, killie	Drifting, still-fishing	1/0 to 5/0
Bass, striped	Sea worms, clams, eels, metal squids, plugs, jigs, live mackerel	Casting, trolling, drifting, still-fishing	2/0 to 8/0
Billfish (sailfish, marlin, swordfish)	Balao, mackerel, squid, bonito, strip baits, feathered jigs	Trolling	4/0 to 12/0
Bluefish	Rigged eel, cut bait, butterfish, plugs, spoons, feathers	Trolling, casting, drifting, still-fishing	3/0 to 8/0
Bonefish	Cut bait (mainly sardines and conch), flies, plugs, spoons	Casting, drifting, still-fishing	1/0 to 4/0
Bonito	Feather lures, spoons	Trolling	4/0 to 6/0
Codfish	Clams, crabs, cut bait	Still-fishing, drifting	7/0 to 9/0
Dolphin	Baitfish, feather lures, spoons, plugs, streamer flies	Trolling, casting	2/0 to 6/0
Eel	Killie, clams, crabs, sea worms, spearing	Still-fishing, drifting, casting	6 to 1/0
Flounder, summer	Squid, spearing, sea worms, clams, killie, smelt	Drifting, casting, still-fishing	4/0 to 6/0
Flounder, winter	Sea worms, mussels, clams	Still-fishing	6 to 12 (long shank)
Grouper	Squid, mullet, sardines, balao, shrimp, crabs, plugs	Still-fishing, casting	4/0 to 12/0
Haddock	Clams, conch, crabs, cut bait	Still-fishing	1/0 to 4/0
Hake	Clams, conch, crabs, cut bait	Still-fishing	2/0 to 6/0
Halibut	Squid, crabs, sea worms, killie, shrimp	Still-fishing	3/0 to 10/0
Jack Crevalle	Baitfish, cut bait, feathers, metal squid, spoons, plugs	Trolling, still-fishing, casting, drifting	1/0 to 5/0
Mackerel	Baitfish, tube lures, jigs, spinners, streamer flies	Trolling, still-fishing, casting, drifting	3 to 6
Perch, white	Sea worms, shrimp, spearing, flies, spoons	Still-fishing, casting	2 to 6
Pollack	Squid strip, clams, feather lures	Still-fishing, trolling	6/0 to 9/0
Pompano	Sand bugs, jigs, plugs, flies	Trolling, casting, drifting, still-fishing	1 to 4
Porgy	Clams, squid, sea worms, crabs, mussel, shrimp	Still-fishing	4 to 1/0
Rockfish, Pacific	Herring, sardine, mussels, squid, clams, shrimp	Still-fishing, drifting	1/0 to 8/0
Snapper, mangrove	Cut bait, shrimp	Trolling, still-fishing, drifting	1/0 to 6/0
Snapper, red	Shrimp, mullet, crabs	Trolling, still-fishing, drifting	6/0 to 10/0
Snapper, yellowtail	Shrimp, mullet, crabs	Trolling, still-fishing	4 to 1/0
Snook	Crabs, shrimp, baitfish, plugs, spoons, spinners, feathers	Casting, drifting, still-fishing	2/0 to 4/0
Sole	Clams, sea worms	Still-fishing	4 to 6
Spot	Crabs, shrimp, baitfish, sea worms	Still-fishing	8 to 10
Tarpon	Cut bait, baitfish, plugs, spoons, feathers	Trolling, casting, drifting, still-fishing	4/0 to 10/0
Tautog (blackfish)	Clams, sea worms, crabs, shrimp	Still-fishing	6 to 2/0
Tomcod	Clams, mussels, shrimp	Still-fishing	6 to 1/0
Tuna, bluefin	Mackerel, flying fish, bonito, squid, dolphin, herring, cut bait, feathered jigs	Trolling	6/0 to 14/0
Wahoo	Baitfish, feathered jigs, spoons, plugs	Trolling, casting	4/0 to 8/0
Weakfish	Shrimp, squid, sea worms	Still-fishing, casting, drifting, trolling	1 to 4/0
Whiting, northern	Sea worms, clams	Still-fishing, drifting, casting	4 to 1/0
Yellowtail	Herring, sardine, smelt, spoons, metal squids, feather lures	Trolling, casting, still-fishing	4/0 to 6/0

How to Rig Saltwater Baits

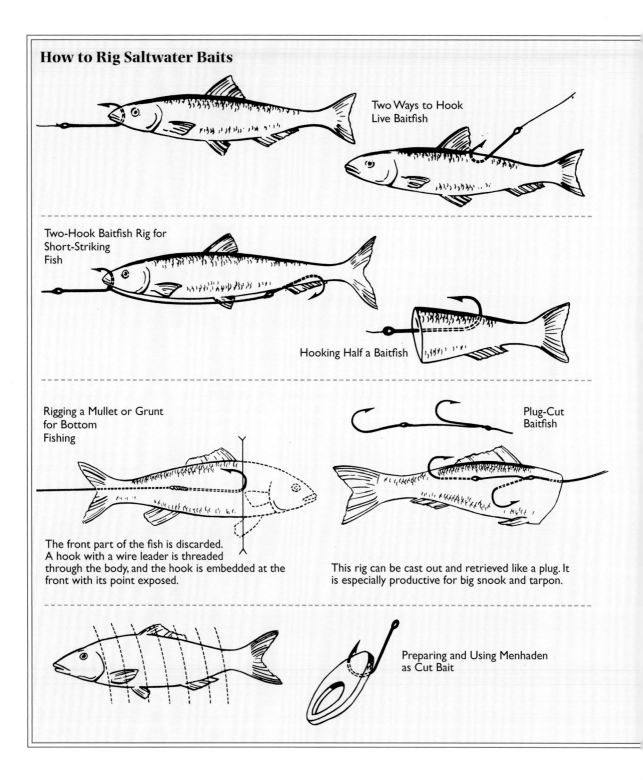

Two Ways to Hook
Live Baitfish

Two-Hook Baitfish Rig for
Short-Striking
Fish

Hooking Half a Baitfish

Rigging a Mullet or Grunt
for Bottom
Fishing

Plug-Cut
Baitfish

The front part of the fish is discarded.
A hook with a wire leader is threaded
through the body, and the hook is embedded at the
front with its point exposed.

This rig can be cast out and retrieved like a plug. It
is especially productive for big snook and tarpon.

Preparing and Using Menhaden
as Cut Bait

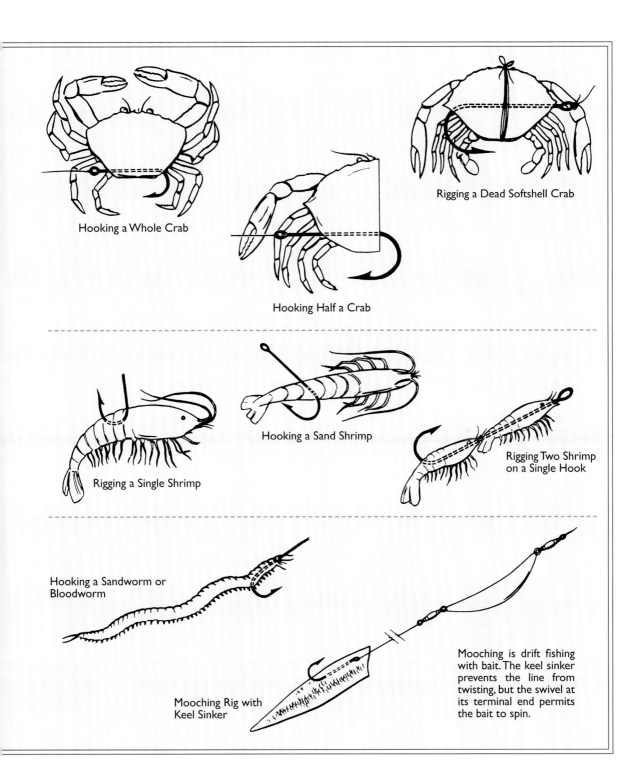

Hooking a Whole Crab

Rigging a Dead Softshell Crab

Hooking Half a Crab

Rigging a Single Shrimp

Hooking a Sand Shrimp

Rigging Two Shrimp on a Single Hook

Hooking a Sandworm or Bloodworm

Mooching Rig with Keel Sinker

Mooching is drift fishing with bait. The keel sinker prevents the line from twisting, but the swivel at its terminal end permits the bait to spin.

Saltwater Bait Rigs

Rigging a Whole Unweighted Eel

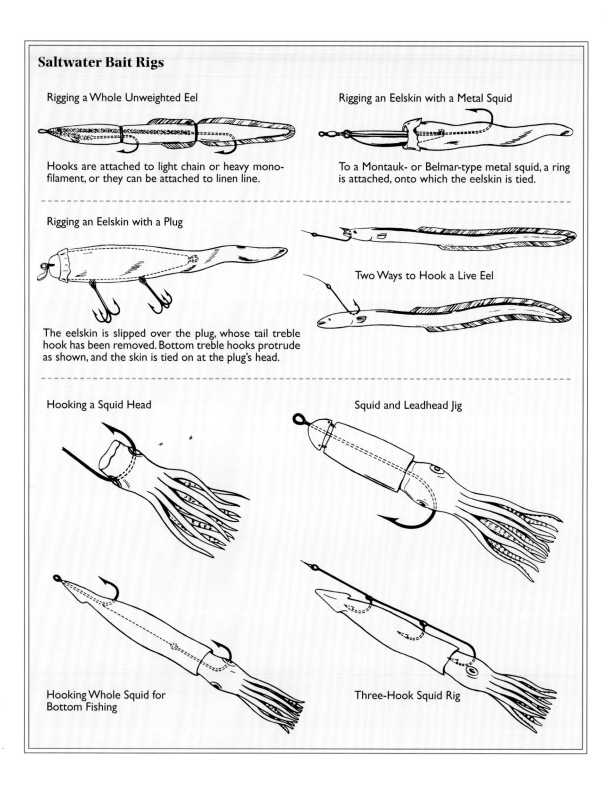

Hooks are attached to light chain or heavy mono-filament, or they can be attached to linen line.

Rigging an Eelskin with a Metal Squid

To a Montauk- or Belmar-type metal squid, a ring is attached, onto which the eelskin is tied.

Rigging an Eelskin with a Plug

The eelskin is slipped over the plug, whose tail treble hook has been removed. Bottom treble hooks protrude as shown, and the skin is tied on at the plug's head.

Two Ways to Hook a Live Eel

Hooking a Squid Head

Squid and Leadhead Jig

Hooking Whole Squid for Bottom Fishing

Three-Hook Squid Rig

Saltwater Trolling Rigs

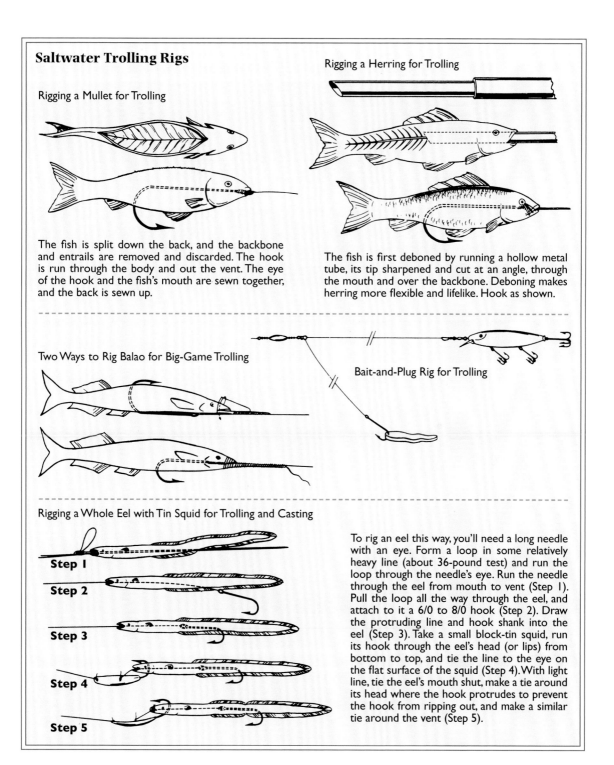

Rigging a Mullet for Trolling

The fish is split down the back, and the backbone and entrails are removed and discarded. The hook is run through the body and out the vent. The eye of the hook and the fish's mouth are sewn together, and the back is sewn up.

Rigging a Herring for Trolling

The fish is first deboned by running a hollow metal tube, its tip sharpened and cut at an angle, through the mouth and over the backbone. Deboning makes herring more flexible and lifelike. Hook as shown.

Two Ways to Rig Balao for Big-Game Trolling

Bait-and-Plug Rig for Trolling

Rigging a Whole Eel with Tin Squid for Trolling and Casting

Step 1

Step 2

Step 3

Step 4

Step 5

To rig an eel this way, you'll need a long needle with an eye. Form a loop in some relatively heavy line (about 36-pound test) and run the loop through the needle's eye. Run the needle through the eel from mouth to vent (Step 1). Pull the loop all the way through the eel, and attach to it a 6/0 to 8/0 hook (Step 2). Draw the protruding line and hook shank into the eel (Step 3). Take a small block-tin squid, run its hook through the eel's head (or lips) from bottom to top, and tie the line to the eye on the flat surface of the squid (Step 4). With light line, tie the eel's mouth shut, make a tie around its head where the hook protrudes to prevent the hook from ripping out, and make a similar tie around the vent (Step 5).

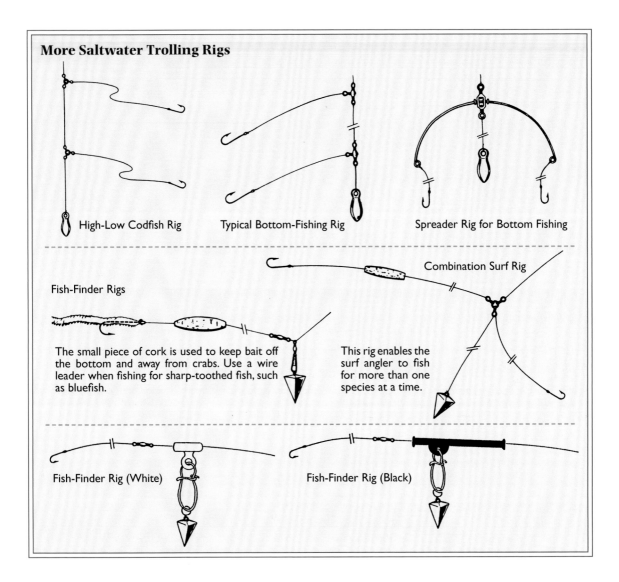

More Saltwater Trolling Rigs

High-Low Codfish Rig   Typical Bottom-Fishing Rig   Spreader Rig for Bottom Fishing

Fish-Finder Rigs

Combination Surf Rig

The small piece of cork is used to keep bait off the bottom and away from crabs. Use a wire leader when fishing for sharp-toothed fish, such as bluefish.

This rig enables the surf angler to fish for more than one species at a time.

Fish-Finder Rig (White)   Fish-Finder Rig (Black)

HOW TO CATCH BAIT AND KEEP IT FRESH

Anglers are often puzzled if they have to catch and keep something other than a dozen worms for a day's fishing. Catching the various baits and keeping them alive and kicking is not difficult, and sometimes catching bait is as much fun as the fishing. Only the popular baits are covered here. As you collect these, you'll soon discover that there are other baits available, such as grasshoppers, crickets, hellgrammites, lizards, and so on.

■ Worms

Worms, whether earthworms or night crawlers, are the most popular live baits. Night crawlers get their name from the fact that they come to the surface at night. They like warm and wet weather. Wait until it has been dark at least two to three hours, then prowl around your lawn, a golf course, or a park. Use a flashlight, but not one with a bright beam. If the beam is too bright, cover

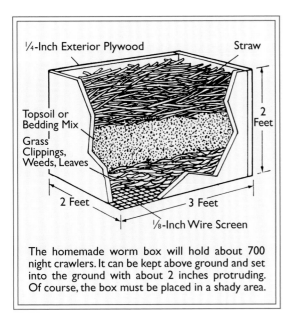

1/4-Inch Exterior Plywood

Straw

Topsoil or Bedding Mix

Grass Clippings, Weeds, Leaves

2 Feet

2 Feet

3 Feet

1/8-Inch Wire Screen

The homemade worm box will hold about 700 night crawlers. It can be kept above ground and set into the ground with about 2 inches protruding. Of course, the box must be placed in a shady area.

above ground. Damp and cool are the key words in keeping worms fresh. A wet burlap bag over some straw will work well. You might also try spreading out a few handfuls of ice cubes on the straw every two or three days. The ice will keep the soil damp and cool as it melts. Food is no problem, since worms eat almost anything. You can feed them coffee grounds, breadcrumbs, and cornmeal.

Ice cubes, incidentally, can also be used effectively when transporting and keeping worms on an extended fishing trip. Try the following method on your next trip. In the center of your bait box, which should measure about 12 inches by 12 inches by 8 inches if you're carrying 400 or so worms, clear a space in the bedding. Next, fill a glass jar or plastic container with ice cubes, screw the cap back on, and put it in a plastic bag. Place the container in the center of the box and push the bedding or soil around it. The ice will keep the soil cool and damp and it will stay that way until the cubes melt. In hot weather, worms will actually crowd around the jar. The purpose of the plastic is to seal in condensation. Without the plastic, the soil would become too soggy for the worms.

■ Sea Worms

Sea worms, such as bloodworms and sandworms, are delicate and should be kept in damp seaweed. If they are to be kept for a week or so, spread them out in seaweed and keep them refrigerated. Bloodworms and sandworms are enemies and should be kept separate. Use a wood partition to divide your bait box into two compartments.

■ Minnows

Minnows rank as the second-most popular bait, and they can be caught almost as easily as worms. There are several ways to collect minnows: minnow traps, drop or umbrella nets, minnow seines, or cast nets.

Caution: A fishing license is usually required to take bait in fresh water, and many states set limits on the number of baitfish that may be kept. Check the fishing regulations of your state before netting or trapping.

The minnow trap requires the least skill to use. It works on the principle that a small fish will swim into the funnel-like openings after food and be unable to find its way out. For bait, you should wet oatmeal or cornmeal and roll it into balls the size of golf balls. The meal will break up gradually in the trap and provide bait for long periods. The best place to set the trap is in shallow

the lens with red cellophane. When you spot a worm, grab it by the head (the thicker end) with your fingers. If the worm tries to shoot back into the hole, hold onto one end until the worm releases tension and is free of the hole.

If you can't find night crawlers at night, it's probably too dry for them to come to the surface. You can wait for rain or water your lawn in the afternoon and go worm hunting that night.

If you're after the common earthworm, which is smaller than a night crawler, you'll have to dig for them. Concentrate on compost heaps, vegetable gardens, and stream banks.

A day's supply of worms can be carried in a few inches of damp soil in a coffee can from which both ends have been removed. Punch holes in the plastic lids that come with the cans. With two of these lids in place, it can be opened from either end for easy access to the worms on the bottom. If you keep this container in a burlap pouch and dip it occasionally in a cool creek, the worms will stay fresh all day.

Commercial boxes for worms, as well as other baits, are available. Most are made of porous fiberboard, which insulates the box and keeps the inside cool and humid.

If you want to keep a good supply of worms on hand, you can build a worm box. In a box of 2 feet by 3 feet by 2 feet, you can house 600 or 700 night crawlers. Sink the box in a shady spot, allowing 2 inches of it to be water near a dock or boathouse. In streams, set it near the head or side of a pool where the current is slow.

The drop or umbrella net, which measures 36 by 36 inches, gets more immediate results but may be more difficult to use. Lower it into the water just deep enough so that you can still lift it fast. Sprinkle breadcrumbs over it and let them sink. When minnows begin to feed on the crumbs, lift the net fast. With practice, you'll make good hauls every time.

A minnow seine not only produces a lot of bait, but also is fun to use, especially in bays and tidal rivers. A seine is usually 4 feet high and anywhere from 10 to 50 feet long, with lead weights along the bottom and floats on top. A 20-footer is a good size for most purposes. Seining is easy. Two people carry the seine about 100 feet from the shore or until the depth hits 4 feet or so. Keeping the weighted end of the seine on the bottom, the people sweep toward shore. The seine will belly out, catching everything in its path and carrying bait up on shore, where it can be picked up.

The cast net is one of the most useful tools of both the freshwater and saltwater angler, because he can use it to get the bait that he can't buy and to obtain forage baitfish native to the waters that he's fishing—which is the best bait to use under most circumstances. Mono-filament nets, because their nylon strands are stiff, open better than nets made of braided threads. Mono nets also sink faster and are less visible after they're thrown into the water. Generally, they catch more fish, but they're also more expensive. Cast nets are available in various sizes and types. Experts throw 16-foot and larger nets, but anglers who would only use them occasionally are better off getting one that measures 8 to 10 feet. Bridge nets, popular in the Florida Keys, are short nets with extra lead weights around the bottom. When the net is dropped off a bridge into deep water, its added weight allows it to sink quickly and hold baitfish before they dive and escape. A plastic bucket is the best storage container for a net. All nets should routinely be rinsed with clean, fresh water and cleared of debris.

The next problem is keeping the minnows alive and fresh. The water must be aerated to keep enough oxygen in the bucket for survival, and this can be done in several ways. Water can be aerated by battery-powered devices, or you can aerate the water manually with a tin can. Scoop up a canful of water and pour it back into the bucket from a height of 2 feet. Doing this a dozen times every 15 minutes should provide sufficient oxygen for a couple dozen minnows.

If you plan to troll, keep bait in a bucket designed for trolling. This bucket, built to float on its side, will take water at an angle and aerate it.

If you're still-fishing, use the traditional bucket, which is actually two buckets. The outer bucket is used when transporting minnows. When you start fishing, lift out the insert and lower it into the water. The insert, which floats upright, is vented so that water is constantly changed.

Bait water must be kept at a constant temperature. In summer, add ice cubes to the water before transporting it. As the ice melts, it will cool the water and add oxygen. Take care, however, not to cool the water too fast. It is important to avoid abrupt temperature changes, which will kill minnows.

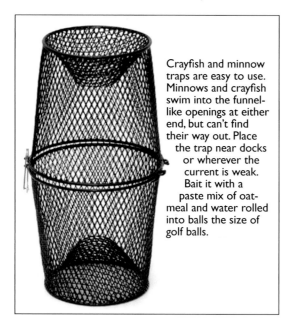

Crayfish and minnow traps are easy to use. Minnows and crayfish swim into the funnel-like openings at either end, but can't find their way out. Place the trap near docks or wherever the current is weak. Bait it with a paste mix of oatmeal and water rolled into balls the size of golf balls.

A cricket basket is also handy for other baits, such as grasshoppers, lizards, and hellgrammites.

How to Throw a Cast Net

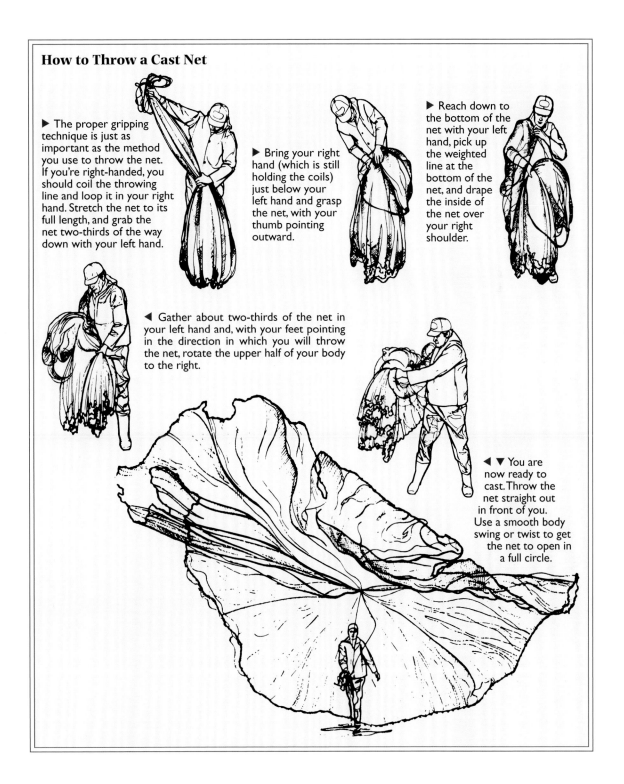

▶ The proper gripping technique is just as important as the method you use to throw the net. If you're right-handed, you should coil the throwing line and loop it in your right hand. Stretch the net to its full length, and grab the net two-thirds of the way down with your left hand.

▶ Bring your right hand (which is still holding the coils) just below your left hand and grasp the net, with your thumb pointing outward.

▶ Reach down to the bottom of the net with your left hand, pick up the weighted line at the bottom of the net, and drape the inside of the net over your right shoulder.

◀ Gather about two-thirds of the net in your left hand and, with your feet pointing in the direction in which you will throw the net, rotate the upper half of your body to the right.

◀ ▼ You are now ready to cast. Throw the net straight out in front of you. Use a smooth body swing or twist to get the net to open in a full circle.

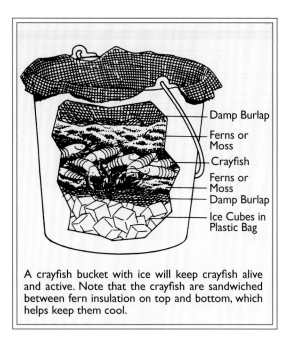

Damp Burlap

Ferns or Moss

Crayfish

Ferns or Moss

Damp Burlap

Ice Cubes in Plastic Bag

A crayfish bucket with ice will keep crayfish alive and active. Note that the crayfish are sandwiched between fern insulation on top and bottom, which helps keep them cool.

■ Crayfish

Crayfish make excellent bait, but they can sometimes be difficult to find. You'll do best at night along gravel shorelines. Crayfish feed in the shallows and you can spot them with a flashlight. Their eyes reflect reddish in the beam. When you locate one, hold a dip net behind it and touch its head with your hand or a stick. If you are lucky, it will swim backward into the net. If you are fast, you can try grabbing a crayfish from behind with your hand.

Keeping crayfish fresh in hot weather can be a problem. You can use an ice-bucket setup. In the bottom of a pail, place two dozen ice cubes in a plastic bag. Cover the ice with a layer of burlap, followed by a few inches of moss or ferns. Next, spread out the crayfish and cover them with another layer of moss or ferns. Cover this top layer with another piece of wet burlap. Crayfish will stay in fine shape in this insulated pail during the hottest weather. Keep the top piece of burlap wet.

■ Frogs

Few anglers will question the value of a lively frog as a bait. Look for frogs along the grassy banks of creeks, ponds, and lakes. Catching them is not hard. You can catch a fair number during the day, but you can collect more at night with a flashlight and a long-handled, small-mesh net. Frogs will remain still in the beam of a flashlight and you should have no trouble netting them. Keeping a day's supply of frogs is no problem. Commercial frog boxes are available, or you can make your own (see accompanying illustration).

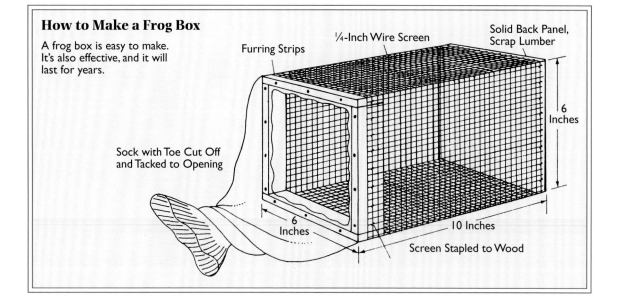

How to Make a Frog Box

A frog box is easy to make. It's also effective, and it will last for years.

Furring Strips

¼-Inch Wire Screen

Solid Back Panel, Scrap Lumber

Sock with Toe Cut Off and Tacked to Opening

6 Inches

6 Inches

10 Inches

Screen Stapled to Wood

TERMINAL-RIG ACCESSORIES

The items of fishing gear covered in this section are various components of the rigs shown in previous sections. These accessories are as important as links in a chain, so buy the best you can afford. A well-constructed snap swivel of the correct size, for example, won't come apart at the seams under the surge of a big fish.

Swivels come in many forms and sizes, but basically a swivel consists of two or three round metal eyes connected in such a way that each eye can rotate freely and independently of the others. Swivels perform such func-

tions as preventing or reducing line twist, enabling the angler to attach more than one component (sinker and bait, for example) to his line, and facilitating lure changes.

Sinkers, like swivels, come in many shapes and weights. Usually made of lead, they are used to get a bait (or lure) down to the desired depth.

Floats are lighter-than-water devices that are attached to the line. They keep a bait at a predetermined distance above the bottom and signal the strike of a fish. Floats are usually made of cork or plastic and come in many forms.

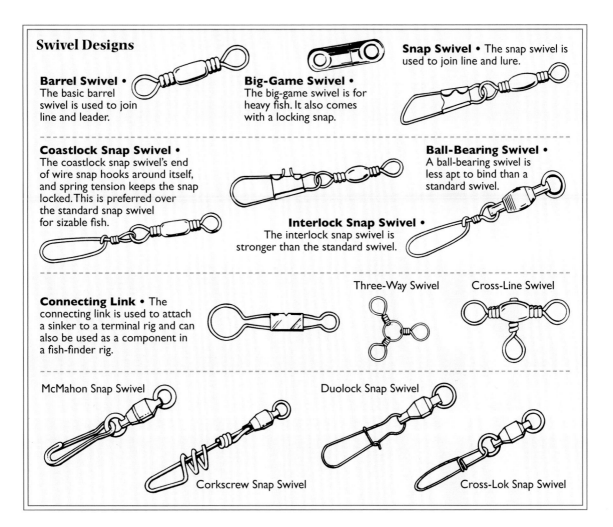

Swivel Designs

Barrel Swivel • The basic barrel swivel is used to join line and leader.

Big-Game Swivel • The big-game swivel is for heavy fish. It also comes with a locking snap.

Snap Swivel • The snap swivel is used to join line and lure.

Coastlock Snap Swivel • The coastlock snap swivel's end of wire snap hooks around itself, and spring tension keeps the snap locked. This is preferred over the standard snap swivel for sizable fish.

Interlock Snap Swivel • The interlock snap swivel is stronger than the standard swivel.

Ball-Bearing Swivel • A ball-bearing swivel is less apt to bind than a standard swivel.

Connecting Link • The connecting link is used to attach a sinker to a terminal rig and can also be used as a component in a fish-finder rig.

Three-Way Swivel

Cross-Line Swivel

McMahon Snap Swivel

Duolock Snap Swivel

Corkscrew Snap Swivel

Cross-Lok Snap Swivel

Sinker Designs

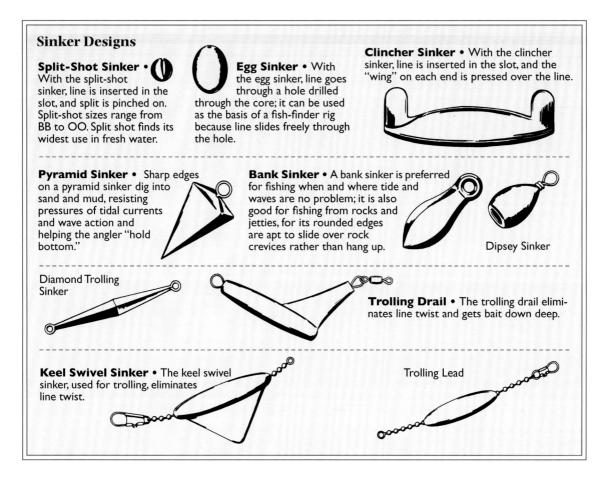

Split-Shot Sinker • With the split-shot sinker, line is inserted in the slot, and split is pinched on. Split-shot sizes range from BB to OO. Split shot finds its widest use in fresh water.

Egg Sinker • With the egg sinker, line goes through a hole drilled through the core; it can be used as the basis of a fish-finder rig because line slides freely through the hole.

Clincher Sinker • With the clincher sinker, line is inserted in the slot, and the "wing" on each end is pressed over the line.

Pyramid Sinker • Sharp edges on a pyramid sinker dig into sand and mud, resisting pressures of tidal currents and wave action and helping the angler "hold bottom."

Bank Sinker • A bank sinker is preferred for fishing when and where tide and waves are no problem; it is also good for fishing from rocks and jetties, for its rounded edges are apt to slide over rock crevices rather than hang up.

Dipsey Sinker

Diamond Trolling Sinker

Trolling Drail • The trolling drail eliminates line twist and gets bait down deep.

Keel Swivel Sinker • The keel swivel sinker, used for trolling, eliminates line twist.

Trolling Lead

Trolling Devices

The trolling planer is a heavily weighted device with metal or plastic "wings" that permit trolling at considerable depths. The bait-walker sinker keeps the bait moving near, but not dragging on, the bottom. The downrigger assembly shown has a terminal rig with a cable, cannonball, and release mechanism.

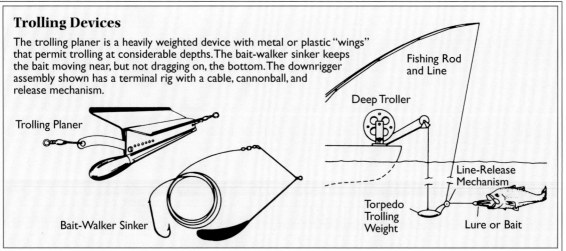

Trolling Planer

Bait-Walker Sinker

Fishing Rod and Line

Deep Troller

Line-Release Mechanism

Torpedo Trolling Weight

Lure or Bait

Float Designs

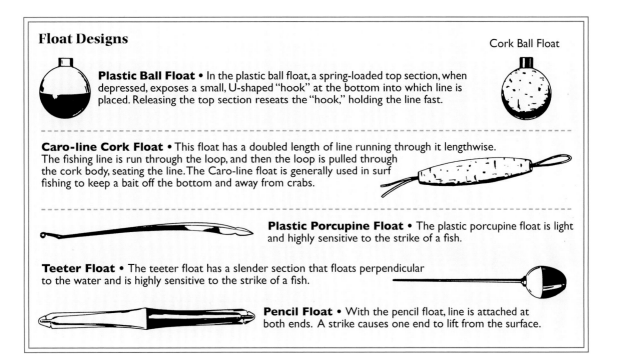

Cork Ball Float

Plastic Ball Float • In the plastic ball float, a spring-loaded top section, when depressed, exposes a small, U-shaped "hook" at the bottom into which line is placed. Releasing the top section reseats the "hook," holding the line fast.

Caro-line Cork Float • This float has a doubled length of line running through it lengthwise. The fishing line is run through the loop, and then the loop is pulled through the cork body, seating the line. The Caro-line float is generally used in surf fishing to keep a bait off the bottom and away from crabs.

Plastic Porcupine Float • The plastic porcupine float is light and highly sensitive to the strike of a fish.

Teeter Float • The teeter float has a slender section that floats perpendicular to the water and is highly sensitive to the strike of a fish.

Pencil Float • With the pencil float, line is attached at both ends. A strike causes one end to lift from the surface.

Panfish Are for Big People, Too

Every fisherman agrees that panfish are a perfect species for children. I agree, but I also think it's a great fish for big people, too. Bluegills and crappies are not difficult to catch and they are literally everywhere. In fact, many waters are overpopulated and overrun with stunted panfish. My favorite technique is with a fly rod and almost any kind of black or brown dry fly or small popper. Whether you're in a boat or fishing from shore, cast the fly as close as you can to the edge of a dock and twitch it a few times. If you don't get a hit, don't waste your time. Move to the next dock.

Not into fly fishing? You can do just as well with spinning tackle. You can catch panfish on small jigs and spoons, but, as a rule, bait works better than most lures. Worms and small minnows, especially for crappies, are the most consistent baits. Other baits that work include crickets, grubs, caterpillars, grasshoppers, and hellgrammites. Stick with ultralight tackle and 2- or 4-pound-test line. You can fish these baits deep with some split shot or with a bobber about 2 or 3 feet above your bait. With children, the bobber is probably more effective in shallow water close to shore. It's also fun for children to watch a bobber dance when a bluegill begins its attack.

Bluegills will eat just about anything you put in front of them, and you can find them in any shallow area of a lake or near structures such as docks and stumps. If you're looking for platter-size bluegills and crappies, there are a couple of factors to keep in mind. If you're fishing from shore, cast out a little farther and fish your bait deeper. Small bluegills will take bait anytime, but those bigger panfish concentrate their feeding at dawn and dusk.

Cleaning and cooking bluegills is easy. Fillet the two small slabs of meat from both sides of the fish. Dip the fillets in flour, egg, and bread crumbs, and then fry them golden brown in peanut or olive oil. It's that simple!

KNOTS

Anyone who aspires to competence as a fisherman must have at least a basic knowledge of knots. Most anglers know and use no more than half a dozen knots. However, if you fish a lot, you are sure to run into a situation that cannot be solved efficiently with the basic ties. The aim of this section is to acquaint you with knots that will help you handle nearly all line-tying situations.

All knots reduce—to a greater or lesser degree, depending on the particular knot—the breaking strength of the line. Loose or poorly tied knots reduce line strength even more. For that reason, and to avoid wasting valuable fishing time, it is best to practice tying the knots at home. In most cases, it's better to practice with cord or rope; the heavier material makes it easier to follow the tying procedures.

It is important to form and tighten knots correctly. They should be tightened slowly and steadily for best results. In most knots requiring the tyer to make turns around the standing part of the line, at least five such turns should be made.

Now let's take a look at the range of fishing knots. Included are tying instructions, as well as the uses for which each knot is suited.

■ BLOOD KNOT

This knot is used to connect two lines of relatively similar diameter. It is especially popular for joining sections of monofilament in making tapered fly leaders.

1 • Wrap one strand around the other at least four times, and run the end into the fork thus formed.

2 • Make the same number of turns, in the opposite direction, with the second strand, and run its end through the opening in the middle of the knot, in the direction opposite that of the first strand.

3 • Hold the two ends so they do not slip (some anglers use their teeth). Pull the standing part of both strands in opposite directions, tightening the knot.

4 • Tighten securely, clip off the ends, and the knot is complete. If you want to tie on a dropper fly, leave one of these ends about 6 to 8 inches long.

■ STU APTE IMPROVED BLOOD KNOT

This knot is excellent for joining two lines of greatly different diameter, such as a heavy monofilament shock leader and a light leader tippet.

1 • Double a sufficient length of the lighter line, wrap it around the standing part of the heavier line at least five times, and then run the end of the doubled line into the fork thus formed.

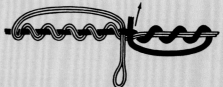

2 • Wrap the heavier line around the standing part of the doubled lighter line three times in the opposite direction, and run the end of the heavier line into the opening in the direction opposite that of the end of the doubled line.

3 • Holding the two ends to keep them from slipping, pull the standing parts of the two lines in opposite directions. Tighten the knot completely, using your fingernails to push the loops together if necessary, and clip off the ends.

DOUBLE SURGEON'S KNOT

This knot is used to join two strands of greatly unequal diameter.

1 • Place the two lines parallel, with the ends pointing in opposite directions. Using the two lines as a single strand, make a simple overhand knot, pulling the two strands all the way through the loop, and then make another overhand knot.

2 • Holding both strands at each end, pull the knot tight, and clip off the ends.

IMPROVED CLINCH KNOT

This knot is used to tie flies, bass bugs, lures, and bait hooks to line or leader. This knot reduces line strength only slightly.

1 • Run the end of the line through the eye of the lure, fly, or hook, and then make at least five turns around the standing part of the line. Run the end through the opening between the eye and the beginning of the twists, and then run it through the large loop formed by the previous step.

2 • Pull slowly on the standing part of the line, being careful that the end doesn't slip back through the large loop and that the knot snugs up against the eye. Clip off the end.

DOUBLE-LOOP CLINCH KNOT

This knot is the same as the improved clinch knot except that the line is run through the eye twice at the beginning of the tie.

DOUBLE IMPROVED CLINCH KNOT

This is the same as the improved clinch knot except that the line is used doubled throughout the entire tie.

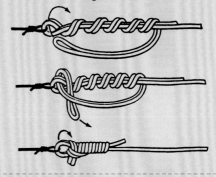

TRILENE KNOT

Used in joining line to swivels, snaps, hooks, and artificial lures, the Trilene knot is a strong, all-purpose knot that resists slippage and premature failures. It is easy to tie and retains 85 to 90 percent of the original line strength. The double wrap of monofilament line through the eyelet provides a protective cushion for added safety.

1 • Run the end of the line through the eye of the hook or lure and double back through the eye a second time.

2 • Loop around the standing part of the line five or six times.

3 • Thread the tag end back between the eye and the coils as shown.

4 • Pull up tight and trim the tag end.

SHOCKER KNOT

This knot is used to join two lines of unequal diameter.

ARBOR KNOT

The arbor knot provides the angler with a quick, easy connection for attaching line to the reel spool.

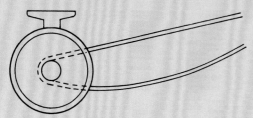

1 • Pass line around the reel arbor.

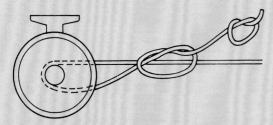

2 • Tie an overhand knot around the standing line. Tie a second overhand knot in the tag end.

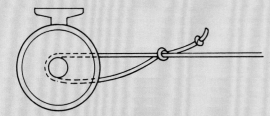

3 • Pull tight and snip off the excess. Snug down the first overhand knot on the reel arbor.

MULTIPLE CLINCH KNOT

This knot is used to join line and leader, especially in baitcasting. This knot slides through rod guides with a minimum of friction.

A loop is tied in the end of the line. Then, the leader is run into the loop, around the entire loop four times, and then back through the middle of the four wraps.

PALOMAR KNOT

This is a quick, easy knot to use when tying your line directly to a hook.

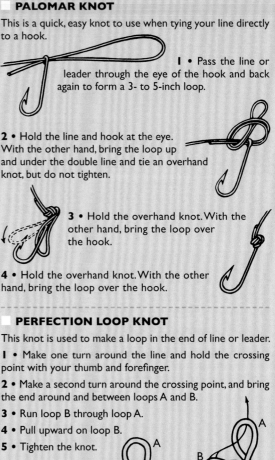

1 • Pass the line or leader through the eye of the hook and back again to form a 3- to 5-inch loop.

2 • Hold the line and hook at the eye. With the other hand, bring the loop up and under the double line and tie an overhand knot, but do not tighten.

3 • Hold the overhand knot. With the other hand, bring the loop over the hook.

4 • Hold the overhand knot. With the other hand, bring the loop over the hook.

PERFECTION LOOP KNOT

This knot is used to make a loop in the end of line or leader.

1 • Make one turn around the line and hold the crossing point with your thumb and forefinger.

2 • Make a second turn around the crossing point, and bring the end around and between loops A and B.

3 • Run loop B through loop A.

4 • Pull upward on loop B.

5 • Tighten the knot.

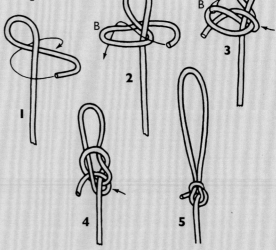

KING SLING KNOT

This knot offers the angler an easy-to-tie end loop knot that is used primarily as a connection for crankbaits. This knot allows the lure to work freely, making it more lifelike, and resulting in more strikes.

1 • Insert the tag end of the line through the artificial bait so that it extends 8 to 10 inches.

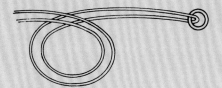

2 • Hold the tag end and the standing line in your left hand and form a loop.

3 • With the bait in your right hand, make four turns around the tag end and the standing line above the loop.

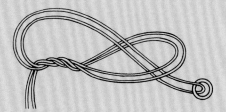

4 • Bring the bait down and through the loop.

5 • To tighten, hold the line above the bait at the desired loop length and pull the tag end and the standing line at the same time. Trim the tag end.

DOUBLE SURGEON'S LOOP

This is a quick, easy way to tie a loop in the end of a leader. It is often used as part of a leader system because it is relatively strong.

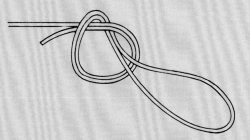

1 • Double the tag end of the line. Make a single overhand knot in the double line.

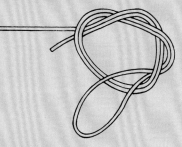

2 • Hold the tag end and standing part of the line in your left hand and bring the loop around and insert through the overhand knot again.

3 • Hold the loop in your right hand. Hold the tag end and standing line in your left hand. Moisten the knot (don't use saliva) and pull to tighten.

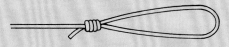

4 • Trim off the tag end.

WORLD'S FAIR KNOT

This is an easy-to-tie terminal tackle knot for connecting line to swivel or lure.

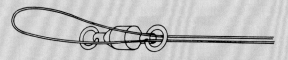

1 • Double a 6-inch length of line and pass the loop through the eye.

2 • Bring the loop back next to the doubled line and grasp the double line through the loop.

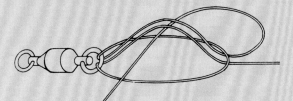

3 • Put the tag end through the new loop formed by the double line.

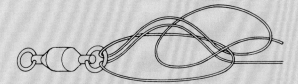

4 • Bring the tag end back through the new loop created by Step 3.

5 • Pull the tag end snug, and slide the knot up tight. Clip the tag end.

TUCKED SHEET BEND

This knot joins fly line and leader when the leader has an end loop.

1 • Run the fly line through the leader loop and around the loop as shown.

2 • Run the line back through the loops.

3 • Smoothly start to draw up the knots.

4 • Pull on both ends until the knot is tight.

DROPPER LOOP KNOT

This knot is frequently used to put a loop in the middle of a strand of monofilament.

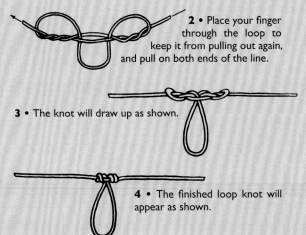

1 • Make a loop in the line and wrap one end overhand several times around the other part of the line. Pinch a small loop in the middle and thrust it between the turns as shown by the simulated, imaginary needle.

2 • Place your finger through the loop to keep it from pulling out again, and pull on both ends of the line.

3 • The knot will draw up as shown.

4 • The finished loop knot will appear as shown.

OFFSHORE SWIVEL KNOT

This knot is used to attach your line to a swivel.

1 • Slip a loop of double-line leader through the eye of the swivel. Rotate the loop a half turn to put a single twist between the loop and swivel eye.

2 • Pass the loop with the twist over the swivel. Hold the loop end, together with both strands of double-line leader, with one hand. Let the swivel slide to the other end of the double loops now formed.

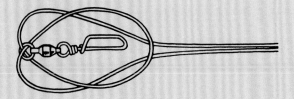

3 • Still holding the loop and lines, use your other hand to rotate the swivel through the center of both loops. Repeat at least five times.

4 • Continue holding the strands of double-line leader tightly, but release the end of the loop. As you pull on the swivel, loops of line will begin to gather.

5 • To draw the knot tight, grip the swivel with pliers and push the loops toward the eye with your fingers, still keeping the strands of leader pulled tight.

NAIL KNOT

This is the best knot for joining the end of a fly line with the butt end of a fly leader. The knot is smooth, streamlined, and will run freely through the guides of the fly rod. Caution: This knot is designed for use with modern synthetic fly lines; do not use it with an old silk fly line, for the knot will cut the line.

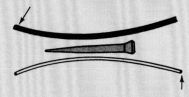

1 • Place the end of the fly line and the butt end of the leader—pointing in opposite directions—along the length of a tapered nail. Allow sufficient overlap.

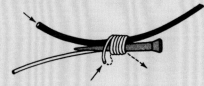

2 • Wrap the leader five or six times around itself, the nail, and the fly line, keeping the windings up against one another. Run the butt end of the leader back along the nail, inside the wraps.

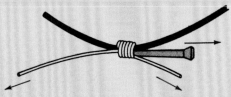

3 • Pull both ends of the leader tight, and then remove the nail and tighten again by pulling on both ends of the leader.

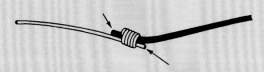

4 • Pull on both line and leader to test the knot, and clip off the ends, completing the knot.

■ NAIL KNOT (Alternate)

Tying procedures for this knot are the same as for the standard nail knot, except that in place of the nail, use an air-inflation needle like those used to inflate basketballs and footballs. The tip of the needle must be cut or filed off so that the tube is open at both ends. A large hypodermic needle with its point snipped off also works well. In tying Step 3 (third illustration from the top), the butt end of the leader—after having been wrapped five or six times around the fly line, leader, and tube—is simply run back through the tube (needle). Then, the knot is tightened, the tube is removed, and the final tightening is done.

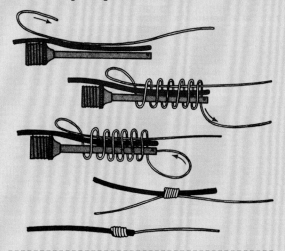

■ DOUBLE NAIL KNOT

This knot is used to join leader sections of the same or slightly different diameters. This is especially useful in saltwater fly fishing and in making heavy salmon leaders.

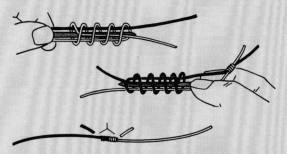

The tying procedure involves making two nail knots, one around each of the two leader sections. As each knot is formed, it is tightened only enough to prevent it from unraveling. When both are formed, each leader is pulled slowly so that the knots tighten together securely.

■ TURLE KNOT

This knot is used to tie a dry or wet fly to a leader tippet. It is not as strong as the improved clinch knot, but it allows a dry fly's hackle points to sit high and jauntily on the surface of the water.

1 • Run the end of the leader through the eye of the hook toward the bend, and tie a simple overhand knot around the standing part of the line, forming a loop.

2 • Open the loop enough to allow it to pass around the fly, and place the loop around the neck of the fly, just forward of the eye.

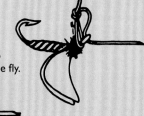

3 • Pull on the end of the leader, drawing the loop up tight around the neck of the fly.

4 • Tighten the knot completely by pulling on the main part of the leader.

■ LOOP KNOT

This knot is used to tie on a lure.

Tie an overhand knot in the line, leaving the loop loose and a sufficient length of line below the loop to tie the rest of the knot. Run the end through the hook eye and back through the loop in the line, and then tie another overhand knot around the standing part. Pull tight.

END LOOP

This knot is used to form a loop in the end of a line.

1 • Double the end of the line for about 6 or 8 inches.

2 • Wrap the double line around itself at least six times.

3 • Take the end of the doubled line and pass it through the first loop as shown.

4 • Now tighten the knot by pulling on the loop and the tag end at the same time.

BUFFER LOOP

This knot is used to attach a lure to line or leader via a nonslip loop.

1 • Tie a simple overhand knot in the line, leaving the loop loose and leaving the end long enough to complete the knot, and then run the end through the eye of the lure.

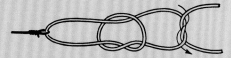

2 • Run the end back through the loose loop and make another overhand knot, using the end and standing part of the line.

3 • Tighten the overhand knot nearest to the lure eye, and then tighten the second overhand knot, which, in effect, forms a half hitch against the first knot.

4 • The finished knot appears as shown.

KNOTTING BACKING LINE TO FLY LINE

This knot is used to join backing line to fly line.

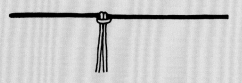

1 • Double the end of the backing line, make one wrap around the fly line, and pull all of the backing line through the loop at its doubled end so the lines appear as shown.

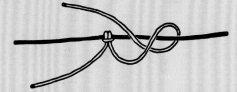

2 • With the end of the backing line, make a half hitch around the fly line, and pull it tight against the original knot.

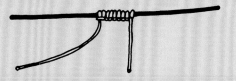

3 • Continue making such half hitches (eight or 10 should be enough) until the tie appears as shown.

4 • Wrap the entire tie with nylon thread, including part of the end of the backing line. This step is simplified by placing the fly line in a fly-tying vise.

5 • Give the entire tie a good coat of lacquer.

ALBRIGHT KNOT (MONO TO MONO)

This knot is used to join lines of dissimilar diameter, such as a fly line to a leader or heavy shock leader to a finer leader tippet.

1 • Double the end of the heavier line, forming a long U shape. Bring the lighter line up into the U, and make about 10 wraps—in the direction of the bottom of the U—around the U and the standing part of the lighter line, bringing the end of the lighter line out of the bottom of the U.

2 • Pull slowly and evenly until the knot is tight.

ALBRIGHT KNOT (MONO TO WIRE)

This knot is used when a short length of wire leader is needed below monofilament leader tippet to prevent sharp-toothed fish from biting through the leader. The fly is attached to the wire leader with a brass crimping sleeve. It is also used to tie mono leader to wire or lead-core line so that the knot will pass through guides and tip tops smoothly. It eliminates the need for a swivel.

1 • Bend the end of a wire leader into a U or open-end loop. Run the end of monofilament into the tip of the U, make about seven wraps around the doubled wire, and run the end of the monofilament back out through the tip of the U.

2 • Hold both leaders to prevent the knot from slipping, and slowly draw the wraps of monofilament tight.

3 • Clip off the ends, and the knot is finished.

FLY-LINE SPLICE

This splice is used to join two fly lines.

1 • Remove the coating from 2¼ inches of the end of each line, and fray about 1 inch.

2 • Enmesh the frayed ends of one line with those of the other, and wrap most of this joint with nylon thread.

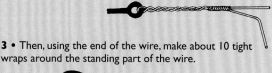

3 • Make another series of wrappings over the entire splice. Finish the job with coats of varnish.

HAYWIRE TWIST

This knot is used to tie wire to the hook, lure, or swivel, or make a loop in the end of the wire.

1 • Run about 4 inches of the end of the leader wire through the eye of the hook, lure, or swivel, and then bend the end across the standing part of the wire.

2 • Holding the two parts of the wire at their crossing points, bend the wire around itself, using hard, even, twisting motions. Both wire parts should be twisted equally.

3 • Then, using the end of the wire, make about 10 tight wraps around the standing part of the wire.

4 • Break off or clip the end of the wire close to the last wrap so that there is no sharp end, and the job is complete.

BIMINI TWIST

This knot is used to create a loop or double line without appreciably weakening the breaking strength of the line. It is especially popular in bluewater fishing for large saltwater fish. Learning this knot requires practice.

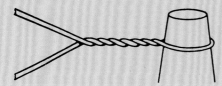

1 • Double the end of the line to form a loop, leaving yourself plenty of line to work with. Run the loop around a fixed object, such as a cleat or the butt end of a rod, or have a partner hold the loop and keep it open. Make 20 twists in the line, keeping the turns tight and the line taut.

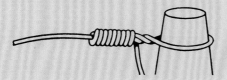

2 • Keeping the twists tight, wrap the end of the line back over the twists until you reach the V of the loop, making the wraps tight and snug up against one another.

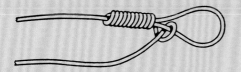

3 • Make a half hitch around one side of the loop and pull it tight.

4 • Then, make a half hitch around the other side of the loop, and pull this one tight, too.

5 • Now make a half hitch around the base of the loop, tighten it, clip off excess line at the end, and the bimini twist is complete.

SPIDER HITCH

This knot serves the same function as the bimini twist, but many anglers prefer the spider hitch because it's easier and faster to tie—especially with cold hands—and requires no partner to help, nor any fixed object to keep the loop open. Plus, it's equally strong.

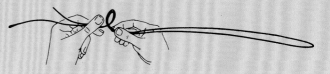

1 • Make a long loop in the line. Hold the ends between your thumb and forefinger, with the first joint of the thumb extending beyond your finger. Then, use your other hand to twist a smaller reverse loop in the doubled line.

2 • Slide your fingers up the line to grasp the small reverse loop together with the long loop. Most of the small loop should extend beyond your thumb tip.

3 • Wind the doubled line from right to left around both your thumb and the small loop, taking five turns. Then, pass the remainder of the doubled line (large loop) through the small loop.

4 • Pull the large loop to make the five turns unwind off the thumb, using a fast, steady pull—not a quick jerk.

5 • Pull the turns around the base of the loop tight and then trim off the tag end.

The Uni-Knot System

The Uni-Knot System consists of variations on one basic knot that can be used for most needs in fresh water and salt water. The system was developed by Vic Dunaway, editor of *Florida Sportsman* magazine and author of numerous books. Here's how each variation is tied, step by step.

TYING TO TERMINAL TACKLE

1 • Run the line through the eye of the hook, swivel, or lure at least 6 inches and fold it back to form two parallel lines. Bring the end of the line back in a circle toward the eye.

2 • Turn the tag end six times around the double line and through the circle. Hold the double line at the eye and pull the tag end to snug up turns.

3 • Pull the running line to slide the knot up against the eye.

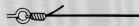

4 • Continue pulling until the knot is tight. Trim the tag end flush with the last coil of the knot. This basic Uni-Knot will not slip.

LOOP CONNECTION

Tie the same basic Uni-Knot as shown above—up to the point where the coils are snugged up against the running line. Then, slide the knot toward the eye only until the desired loop size is reached. Pull the tag end with pliers to tighten. This gives a lure or fly free, natural movement in the water. When a fish is hooked, the knot slides tight against the eye.

JOINING LINES

1 • With two lines of about the same diameter, overlap ends for about 6 inches. With one end, form a Uni-Knot circle and cross the two lines at about the middle of the overlap.

2 • Tie a basic Uni-Knot, making six turns around the lines.

3 • Pull the tag end to snug the knot.

4 • Use the loose end of the overlapped line to tie a second Uni-Knot and snug it up in the same manner.

5 • Pull the two lines in opposite directions to slide the two knots together. Pull tight and snip the tag ends to the outermost coils.

JOINING LEADER TO LINE

1 • Using a leader no more than four times the pound test of the line, double the end of the line and overlap with the leader for about 6 inches. Make a Uni-Knot circle with the doubled line.

2 • Tie a Uni-Knot around the leader with the doubled line, but use only three turns. Snug up.

3 • Now tie a Uni-Knot with the leader around the doubled line, again using only three turns.

4 • Pull knots together tightly. Trim the tag ends and loop.

JOINING SHOCK LEADER TO LINE

1 • Using a leader of more than four times the pound test of the line, double the ends of both leader and line back about 6 inches. Slip the line loop through the leader loop far enough to permit tying a Uni-Knot around both strands of the leader.

2 • With doubled line, tie a Uni-Knot around the doubled leader, using only four turns.

3 • Put a finger through the loop of line and grasp both the tag end and running line to pull the knot snug around the leader loop.

4 • With one hand, pull the long end of the leader (not both strands). With the other hand, pull both strands of line. Pull slowly until the knot slides to the end of the leader loop and slippage is stopped.

DOUBLE-LINE SHOCK LEADER

1 • As a replacement for a bimini twist or spider hitch, first clip off the amount of line needed for the desired length of loop. Tie the two ends together with an overhand knot.

2 • Double the end of the running line and overlap it 6 inches with the knotted end of the loop piece. Tie a Uni-Knot with the tied loop around the double running line, using four turns.

3 • Now, tie a Uni-Knot with the doubled running line around the loop piece, again using four turns.

4 • Hold both strands of double line in one hand, both strands of loop in the other. Pull to bring the knots together until they barely touch.

5 • Tighten by pulling both strands of the loop piece, but only the main strand of running line. Trim off both loop tag ends, eliminating the overhand knot.

SNELLING A HOOK

1 • Thread line through the hook eye for about 6 inches. Hold the line against the hook shank and form a Uni-Knot circle. Make as many turns as desired through the loop and around the line and shank. Close the knot by pulling on the tag end.

2 • Tighten by pulling the running line in one direction and the hook in the other. Trim off the tag end.

AVOIDING LINE TWIST

Winding new line on your reel is a fairly simple job, but if you do it wrong you'll end up with twists that will pose big problems from your first cast.

■ Open-Face Spinning Reel

First, attach the reel to a rod. Any rod will do, but never try winding line on a spool by holding the reel in your hands. Next, string the line through the guides, open the bail, and knot the line to the spool. Finally, flip the bail closed.

The line should spiral off the supply spool in the same direction it is going onto the reel spool. Keep the rod tip several feet from the supply spool and maintain tension on the line by holding it between the thumb and forefinger of your rod-holding hand.

If you're alone, place the spool label side up on the floor and wind about 10 feet of line under tension on your reel. Now, drop the rod tip. If the slack line between the rod tip and reel immediately starts to twist, you're putting the line on wrong. Flip the spool label side down and start again. The line should now wind on your reel correctly.

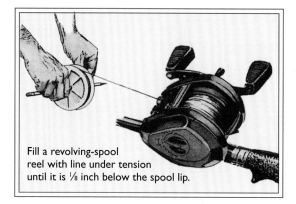

Fill a revolving-spool reel with line under tension until it is 1/8 inch below the spool lip.

You should fill an open-face spinning reel slightly below the spool lip. When the line drops more than 1/4 inch below the spool lip, it's time to put on new line.

■ Revolving-Spool Reel

If you're filling a revolving-spool reel, start by pushing a pencil through the center of the supply reel. Have a friend hold both ends of the pencil and exert pressure

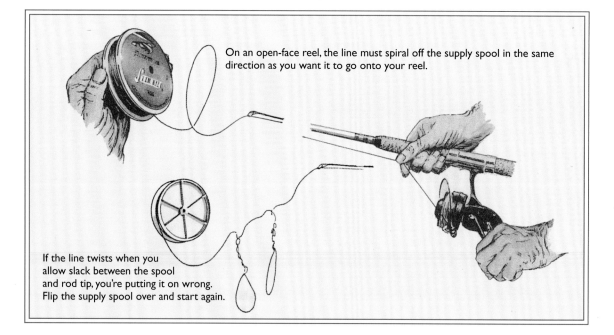

On an open-face reel, the line must spiral off the supply spool in the same direction as you want it to go onto your reel.

If the line twists when you allow slack between the spool and rod tip, you're putting it on wrong. Flip the supply spool over and start again.

inward on the supply spool with his hand to put tension on the line.

The line will go on evenly from side to side if the reel has a level-wind. If not, make sure you wind the line on evenly. You can also use your index finger and thumb of your holding hand to maintain additional tension. Fill the spool to within ⅛ inch of the spool lip.

Spincast Reel

With closed-face spincast reels, use nearly the same method as for open-face spinning reels, except remove the nose cone and hold it in front of the reel while winding on line. Most spincast reels have narrow, deep spools,

which means you'll lose casting distance if the line level drops below ⅛ inch on the spool.

When filling a spincast reel, slip the nose cone forward as you wind line, exposing the spool. Don't overfill the spool.

CARE AND REPAIR OF FISHING TACKLE

There's more than a germ of truth in the old saying, "A fisherman is no better than his tackle." It pays in more ways than one to keep your gear in good working order. For one thing, proper maintenance can add a good many years to the working life of rods, reels, and other tackle on which hard-earned money has been spent. And legions of fishermen have discovered, to their chagrin, that un-oiled reels can "freeze up," neglected rods can snap, and rusty lure hooks can give out—just when that record-breaking fish comes along. The following tackle-care tips should help to prevent such problems.

Care of Rods

Today's rods are designed for long life, but they still require some basic maintenance. The steps recommended below should keep any rod in good working order. How often they should be applied depends upon how often the rods are used and whether they are used in fresh or salt water. Remember that saltwater rods—in fact, all saltwater gear—require much more care than freshwater rods. Even the best of tackle cannot withstand the corrosive action of salt.

1. Wash the rod, including the guides, thoroughly with soap and fresh water, rinse it with hot water, and let it dry completely. If the rod is used in salt water, this step should be taken after each use.

2. If the rod is two pieces or more, thoroughly clean the ferrules. If the ferrules are metal, give them a very light coating of grease to help prevent oxidation.

3. Apply a light coating of wax (automobile wax does a good job) to the entire rod—excluding the cork handle, if the rod has one, and guides.

4. If your rod is starting to show signs of wear, you may want to varnish it. Two thin coats are better than one heavy coat. To avoid creating bubbles in the varnish, apply it with a finger or a pipe cleaner.

5. Store your rod in a dry, safe place. If the rod is bamboo, it must be placed so that it lays flat; if stored on end, it may develop a "set" or permanent bend. Caution: Never store a wet cork-handled rod in a rod case. Mildew will surely form on the cork.

Care of Lines

Check each line for cracking, aging, wear, and rot. If the entire line is no longer serviceable, discard it. If one end has taken all the use, reverse the line. Fly lines tend to crack at the business end after considerable use. If the cracking is confined to the last foot or so, clip off the damaged section or, if the line is a double taper, reverse it. If the damage is more widespread, replace the line.

Check particularly for nicks and other weak spots in monofilament and fluorocarbon, and test the line's breaking strength. If it's weak, replace it. With braided line, check for dark spots, which signify rot, and test the breaking strength. Replace if weak.

■ Care of Reels

Reels are the most important item of fishing gear and must be cared for properly. The following checklist should be followed:

1. Rinse the reel thoroughly with hot, fresh water. If used in salt water, do this after each trip and use soap. Let dry completely.

2. Oil sparingly.

3. Release drag tension to eliminate spring fatigue.

4. Check the reel's operation. Replace worn or missing parts, and send the reel to the manufacturer for repair if necessary.

5. Cover the reel with a very light coating of oil, and store it in a safe, dry place, preferably in a cloth bag (cloth permits air to enter and escape). Leather cases lock out air.

■ Care of Tackle Accessories

Accessory equipment deserves equal time from the fisherman. Saltwater lures, for example, are expensive, so take a few minutes to rinse them off with soapy, fresh water after each use so that they don't corrode. The same applies to swivels, hooks, and other saltwater accessories.

The following checklist covers a general overhaul of a tackle box and its contents:

1. Remove the contents of the box, and place the items in some kind of order on a table rather than simply dumping them in a pile. This will help you remember where everything goes when it's time to put your accessories away after cleaning.

2. Use a vacuum cleaner to remove dust and dirt and other loose particles. If the box is metal, wipe the inside with an oily rag, and lubricate the hinges. If it is plastic, wash it with soap and water.

3. Examine the hooks and lures, and discard rusty hooks and all lures that are beyond repair. Make a list of those lures you'll need to restock the box while they are fresh in your mind.

4. Repair salvageable lures. A soft-wire soap pad can be a great help in sprucing up dingy crankbait blades

and spoons. Check for broken, rusty, or dull lure hooks, replacing the hooks if necessary or sharpening them with a small whetstone.

5. Sharpen all hooks, and give them a light coating of oil to prevent rust.

6. Wash the bag of your landing net with a mild detergent.

7. Patch all holes and weak spots in hip boots and waders, and store them in a dark, cool spot. The best way to store boots is to hang them upside down by the boot feet. A sturdy, heavy-wire coat hanger, cut in the middle of the bottom section and bent judiciously, makes an excellent and inexpensive boot-hanger.

■ Rod-Wrapping Tricks of the Trade

GUIDES AND TENSION: Guides should be purchased in matched sets to ensure uniformity. The feet of guides should be dressed with a file to a fine taper. Next, sight your rod. If you notice a slight bend or offset, apply guides opposite the bend; this will bring it into a straight position. Guides should be affixed with snug wrapping tension, so that you may sight after wrapping and make slight guide adjustments before applying the color preserver. Do not wrap guides to the absolute breaking point of the thread. Remember, 10 or 20 wraps of thread exert very heavy pressure on the feet of the guides. It is possible to damage a blank by wrapping too tight.

THREADS: Sizes 2/0 to E are the most commonly used threads. Sizes 2/0 or A are used for fly, casting, or spinning rods. Sizes D or E are used for the heavier freshwater spinning or saltwater rods. Naturally, the finer size 2/0 thread will make a neater job, but, being lighter, it is not quite as durable.

TRIM: You may trim the basic color of your wrap with five to 10 turns of another color of thread. This is done just as outlined in the instructions for a basic wrap.

COLOR PRESERVER AND ROD VARNISH: Good color preserver has plastic in it, and should be quite thin in order to penetrate the wrappings. Good-grade varnish is essential to the durability of the finish. Most custom rod builders prefer two-part rod finishes. A brush may be used to apply both the color preserver and rod varnish; however, air bubbles are usually present when a brush is used. To maintain a smooth finish, make certain these

How to Wrap Guides

1 • Start by wrapping over the end of the thread toward the guide so the thread end is held down by the wrapping. Using the tension from whatever type of tension device you are using to hold the wrapping tight, continue to turn the rod so that each thread lies as close as possible to the preceding turn.

2 • About five to eight turns from the finish of the wrap, insert the loop of the tie-off thread. (This can be 6 inches of heavier thread or a fine piece of nylon leader material.) Finish the wrap over this tie-off loop.

3 • Holding the wrap tightly, cut the wrapping thread about 4 inches from your rod. Insert this cut end through the tie-off loop. Still holding onto the wrapping thread, pull the cut-off thread under the wraps with the tie-off loop.

4 • With a razor blade, trim the cut-off end as close as possible to the wrap. With the back of a knife or your fingernail, push the wrapping up tight so that it appears solid, and none of the rod or guide shows through.

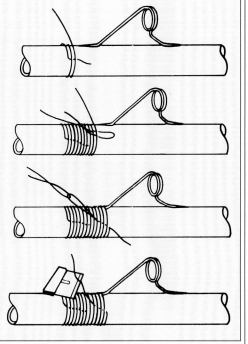

bubbles are out. A very satisfactory method of minimizing air bubbles is to apply both the color preserver and rod varnish with your index finger. This will prevent any shading of the wrapping color.

■ Selecting the Tip Top and Other Guides

The rod builder, like just about everyone else, gets what he pays for. It doesn't pay to skimp on rod guides, especially if the rod is to be used in salt water or for heavy freshwater fish such as pike, muskies, and salmon. Guides are made of various metals, including hardened stainless steel, chrome (or chrome-plated Monel), Fuji Hardloy, agate, and tungsten carbide, with the carbide types being the most durable. Silicone carbide or titanium carbide are recommended for abrasive lines, such as braid or Dacron. Roller guides for heavy saltwater fishing are usually made of stainless steel, Monel, or nickel alloy. The rod builder should note that guides are available in sets tailored to particular rod types and lengths.

The tip top must fit snugly over the end of the rod, and so its selection is sometimes a problem. The accompanying chart will help the rod builder overcome this problem. It shows the actual sizes, in 64ths of an inch, of the inside diameters of a wide range of tip-top guides.

Rod Guide Diameters

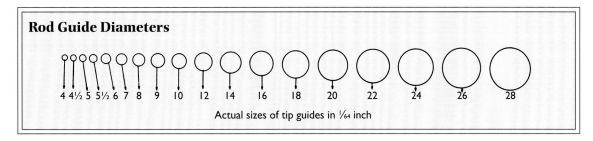

4 4½ 5 5½ 6 7 8 9 10 12 14 16 18 20 22 24 26 28

Actual sizes of tip guides in 1/64 inch

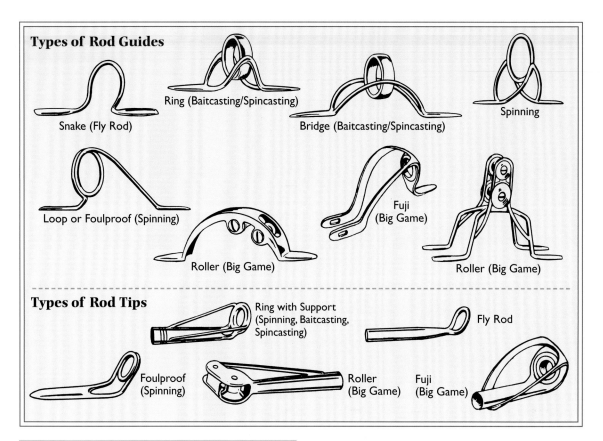

Types of Rod Guides

Snake (Fly Rod)

Ring (Baitcasting/Spincasting)

Bridge (Baitcasting/Spincasting)

Spinning

Loop or Foulproof (Spinning)

Roller (Big Game)

Fuji (Big Game)

Roller (Big Game)

Types of Rod Tips

Ring with Support (Spinning, Baitcasting, Spincasting)

Fly Rod

Foulproof (Spinning)

Roller (Big Game)

Fuji (Big Game)

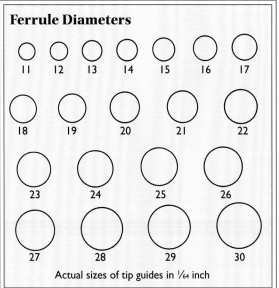

Ferrule Diameters

11   12   13   14   15   16   17

18   19   20   21   22

23   24   25   26

27   28   29   30

Actual sizes of tip guides in 1/64 inch

To determine what size tip top you need, simply place the end of the rod tip over the circles until you find the correct size.

■ Selecting Rod Ferrules

Most rods today that break down into two or more pieces avoid any kind of ferrule, preferring to use the tapers themselves to form a smooth integral connection and an action that comes close to a one-piece rod. Some rods, however, still use a ferrule system—joint-like devices inserted along the working length of a fishing rod that enables the rod to be dismantled into two or more sections. Ferrules are generally made of metal (nickel, brass, or aluminum), or a synthetic material. A ferrule set consists of two parts, the male ferrule and the female ferrule. The male section should fit snugly into the female section.

What size ferrule do you need for your rod? The accompanying chart will help you find out. It shows

Suggested Guide Spacing

All measurements are from the tip of the rod down. Figures indicate measurements at the guide ring.

Rod Length	Lure-Weight Range (ounces)	Fly-Line Weights	Measurements at the Guide Ring (inches)							
			1st	2nd	3rd	4th	5th	6th	7th	8th
SPINCASTING, BAITCASTING										
5½ ft.	⅛ to ⅓		4½	12	23	36				
6 ft.	⅛ to ⅜		4	10	18	28	40			
6 ft.	¼ to ¾		4	8¼	13	18	24½	32⅛	42	
6 ft.	⅜ to 1¼		3½	7½	12	17⅜	23⅝	31⅞	42½	
6 ft., 4 in.	1/16 to ¼		4	10	18½	28½	41			
6 ft., 4 in.	⅜		4	10	18½	28½	41			
6 ft., 4 in.	⅛ to ½		4	10	18½	28½	41			
6 ft.	⅜ to ⅝		4	10	18	28	40			
6 ft., 4 in.	¼ to ⅝		4	10	18½	28½	41			
FLY RODS										
5 ft., 5 in.		5F, 6S	5	13	25	40				
6 ft.		5F, 6S	3	7½	12	17¾	25	33	42½	
7½ ft.		6F, 7S	6	13	21	30	41½	60		
7 ft., 8 in.		6 or 7F, 7S	6	13	21	30	43	62		
8 ft.		6 or 7F, 7S	6	13	21	30	41	52	66	
8 ft.		7F, 7S	6	13	21	30	40	53	66	
8 ft.		7 or 8F, 7 or 8S	6	13	21	30	41	53	66	
8½ ft.		7 or 8F, 7 or 8S	6	13	21	30	40	56	73	
8½ ft.		7F, 7S	6	13	21	30	40	56	73	
8½ ft.		8 or 9F, 8 or 9S	6	13	21	30	40	56	73	
9 ft.		7 or 8F, 7 or 8S	5	11	18	26	35	45	58½	73
9 ft.		8 or 9F, 8 or 9S	5	11	18	26	35	45	58½	73
10 ft.		9 or 10F, 9 or 10S	6	13	22	32	43	54½	66½	80½
SPINNING ROD										
6 ft.	up to ¼		5½	15½	27½	40½				
6 ft.	up to ⅜		3½	10	19	29¼	41½			
6½ ft.	1/16 to ¼		3½	8½	15	23	33	46		
6½ ft.	⅛ to 1		5	10⅜	16⅜	23⅜	31⅞	44		
6½ ft.	⅛ to ⅜		3½	8½	15	23	33	46		
6½ ft.	¼ to ⅝		3½	8½	15	23	33	46		
7 ft. *	1/16 to ⅜	5 or 6F, 6S	4	10	18	27½	38½	52½		
7 ft.	1/16 to ⅜		4	10	18	27½	38½	52½		
7 ft.	up to 1½		4	10	18	27½	38	51		

KEY: F—FLOATING   S—SINKING   *—COMBINATION SPIN/FLY ROD

the actual sizes, in 64ths of an inch, of the inside diameters of a wide range of ferrules. To determine the correct ferrule for your rod, simply place the upper end of the butt section (if it is a two-piece rod) over the circles until you find the right fit.

■ Spacing of Rod Guides

Whether you are building a fishing rod from scratch (that is, taking a fiberglass blank and adding a butt, reel seat, and guides) or refinishing an old favorite, you must pay close attention to the placement of the guides along the working length of the rod.

Putting too many or too few guides on a rod, or placing them improperly along the rod, may detract from proper rod action and put undue strain on the line and the rod.

The accompanying chart gives the correct number of guides—and exact spacing measurements—for most spinning, baitcasting, spincasting, and fly rods.

How to Hold a Fish

You want to release the fish you just caught unharmed, but do you know where to hold it without damaging any of its vital organs so that you can remove the hook safely?

It really depends on the fish. Some have sharp teeth, while others have gill plates that will cut you like a knife. Fin spines are other obstacles to avoid. Bass—including stripers and members of the black bass family—are the easiest to hold because their lower jaws make perfect handles. You should lift a bass with your thumb inside its lower lip, and your curled index finger pinching firmly against it from the outside. Big crappies also can be handled in the same manner.

Unlike bass and crappies, walleyes have very sharp teeth and sharp gill plates. Don't even think about trying a lip hold on a walleye—you'll regret it. Instead, grab it behind the head and across the back. Always start your grip in front of the dorsal fin and carefully slide your hand to the rear, pushing down the sharp dorsal spines with the heel of your hand.

Panfish and some varieties of perch likewise have sharp dorsal spines and should be held in the same manner as walleyes. The dorsal fin of a bluegill can inflict a painful puncture if it's not held down with your hand.

Trout and salmon might not have sharp dorsal fins, but they do have mouths full of teeth. When you hold a trout or salmon, first wet your hands and then cradle the fish in the palms of both hands. Trout are slippery, so you will need a firm grip. Don't squeeze too tightly, however, if you plan to release the fish. Squeeze a trout too hard and you might rupture its organs, which is fatal.

Many species of freshwater and saltwater fish have sharp teeth and require special handling. Bluefish and barracuda, for example, can inflict painful bites if not handled carefully. The best way to hold one of these toothy critters is to get a firm grip behind the top of its head and hold on tightly while you remove hooks with needle-nose fishing pliers. You're holding the fish in an area of its body that is virtually impervious to injury. The same technique will work for muskies, pike, and pickerel.

Catfish have spines in the dorsal and pectoral fins that can puncture skin and inflict a nasty wound. When you hold a catfish, grip it from the front and slide your hand carefully toward the tail, pushing down the fins and sharp spines. Catfish are tough and can usually survive a firmer grip than might be employed for trout.

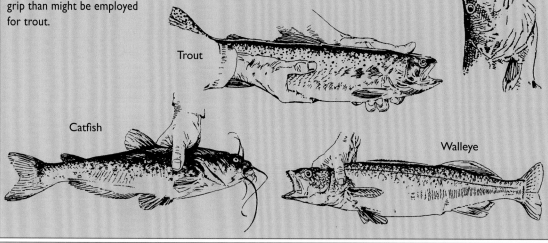

Barracuda

Bass

Trout

Catfish

Walleye

ESTIMATING FISH WEIGHT

You've just caught a big pike. In fact, it measures 40 inches, according to the stick-on tape measure you received free from the bait shop. Now you want to know how much the pike weighs, but you don't have a scale.

Over the years, fishermen have come up with several ways to estimate fish weight without a scale. Some have proved to be fairly accurate; some didn't even come close. Eventually, the generally accepted formula became:

Length times Girth squared divided by 800 equals Weight,
or L x G² ÷ 800 = W

Using this formula is supposed to bring you within 10 percent of a fish's actual weight. The only problem is that the formula doesn't differentiate between fat fish (such as bass or tuna) and elongate fish (such as pike or barracuda).

Doug Hannon, a renowned Florida bass fisherman, has developed a more precise calculation specifically for bass and similarly shaped round fish. In addition to being more accurate, it requires only one measurement. Hannon's formula is:

Length cubed divided by 1,600 equals Weight,
or L³ ÷ 1,600 = W

If you caught a 20-inch bass, for example, the math would be 20 times 20 times 20 (8,000), divided by 1,600. Congratulations, that's a nice 5-pounder.

With the widespread adoption of catch-and-release fishing, fishermen have developed modifications of the length-cubed formula that work well with other species, too. For pike, muskies, and other elongate fish, use this formula:

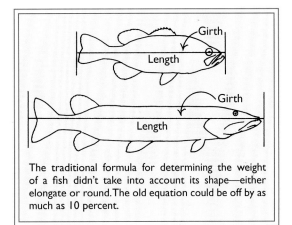

The traditional formula for determining the weight of a fish didn't take into account its shape—either elongate or round. The old equation could be off by as much as 10 percent.

$$L^3 ÷ 3,500 = W$$

In other words, that 40-inch pike that you caught would weigh about 18.3 pounds. (Actually, it's 18.28 pounds, but any fisherman is allowed to round up to the higher tenth.)

If you're a panfish specialist, the formula to use is:

$$L^3 ÷ 1,200 = W$$

An 8-inch bluegill, for example, would weigh 0.42 pounds. And if walleyes are your target, the formula changes slightly to:
$$L^3 ÷ 2,700 = W$$

This means the 22-inch walleye you boasted was a 10-pounder really only weighed about 4 pounds.

EASY FISH RELEASE

Effective catch-and-release fishing is a critical factor for the future of fish stocks in both fresh and salt water. A simple wire dehooker device is amazingly effective in releasing lip-hooked fish without harm and in a matter of seconds. The device, shown on page 208, is a wire with an L-shaped hook formed on the end. Using this type of dehooker, you can release a fish over water without touching it. The fish will drop safely back into the water.

If you must touch or net a fish, wear wet cotton gloves and always avoid touching the gills. If you regularly net your fish before release, use a smooth rubber mesh net, such as the nets used in fish hatcheries. Avoid nets with knots, which will break through the fish's

10 Tips for Proper Catch and Release

With virtually every species of food and game fish regulated by size and bag limits these days, knowing how to release your catch has never been more important. Whether you fish for marlin or striped bass, here are some "best practice" tips for improving a fish's post-release survival.

1. Land 'Em Fast • Due to stress and exhaustion, the longer a fish is fought, the less chance it has of surviving after being released. If you're serious about catch and release, try to land the fish as quickly as possible.

2. Don't Go Too Light • This goes hand-in-glove with tip number one. Using tackle that's too light for the species you're targeting leads to prolonged fights and exhausted fish that are either unable to recover from the fight or end up as easy targets for predators. Also, light line is more likely to break during the fight, leaving the fish with a plug or hook in its mouth that may hamper its ability to survive.

3. Keep 'Em Wet • Keeping a fish in the water while you remove the hook will improve its chances of survival. Not only does the water keep the fish's skin moist and provide more oxygen to its gills, it provides support for the fish's internal organs, which could be damaged if the fish (especially a big fish) is hefted onboard or accidentally dropped.

4. Minimize Handling Time • If you must bring a fish onboard to measure it or remove the hook, do so as quickly as possible and get it back in the water. The longer you keep a fish out of water, the more stress it endures due to lack of oxygen and exhaustion. Also, handling a fish can remove its mucous coating, which guards against parasites and disease, or damage its internal organs.

5. Water Temperature Matters • When the water temperature climbs above the normal comfort level for a particular species, the fish will have a harder time recovering from a fight, especially a prolonged one. In midsummer, this makes it even more important to land the fish quickly, remove the hook, and release it as soon as possible.

6. Use Circle Hooks with Bait • It is now widely recognized that circle hooks can reduce fish mortality when used with natural bait. Circle hooks feature a clever design that allows the hook to slide out of the fish's throat and "lock" around the jaw hinge as the line tightens. Other hook styles tend to lodge more frequently in the fish's stomach, throat, or gills, especially if the fish is allowed to run with the bait for a long time. Circle hooks aren't a guaranteed cure against deep hooking, of course, and some anglers feel that using them reduces the number of fish they catch; however, circles do work in terms of causing less damage to fish. In fact, some states now mandate the use of circle hooks when fishing bait for certain species.

7. Use Single Hooks with Lures • Rigging your artificial lures with single hooks also improves the odds of the fish recovering after release. Plugs armed with two or even three treble hooks often cause a lot of damage, especially if the dangling hooks lodge in the

If you bring a fish onboard to remove a hook, do it quickly. The longer you keep a fish out of water, the more stress it endures.

fish's eyes or gills. And cuts on the fish's body caused by the hooks can lead to infection. Using single hooks not only causes less damage to the fish, it also makes it easier to release, thus reducing the amount of time it spends out of the water. Crushing or removing the barbs on your hooks will also facilitate a fast release.

8. **Net Results** · As mentioned, handling a fish can remove its protective mucous coating, as can a net. Nets made of stiff, scratchy material can also remove scales and tangle with the lure or line, further prolonging the amount of time the fish spends out of water. If you do use a net, buy one made especially for catch and release. These nets feature a shallower "bag" and smooth, plastic-coated mesh that causes less damage to the fish and makes it harder for hooks to get caught in the material.

9. **Different Techniques for Different Fish** · Not every fish should be released in the same way. For example, an exhausted striped bass, snook, redfish, seatrout, tarpon, or bluefish may need to be revived by holding it by the mouth (using a lip-gripping device such as the Boga-Grip) or tail and gently "swimming" it back and forth to push oxygenated water across its gills until it has time to recover and swim off on its own. False albacore, bonito, and similar tuna-type fish, on the other hand, should be released by dropping them headfirst into the water, giving them a sort of jump start. As for tautog, scup, and sea bass, these remarkably hardy species seem to have little trouble returning to the bottom, even after being kept out of the water for long periods. Deep-water species such as snapper, cod, grouper, and rockfish that suffer barotrauma (extended swim bladders) often must be released by lowering them back to the bottom with a special weighted device so the gas inside their bodies can decompress. With billfish, holding the fish alongside a slow-moving boat can help it recover.

10. **Know When to Quit** · Don't spend too much time trying to remove a hook that is hopelessly lodged in the throat or stomach of a fish. While an attempt should be made to remove the hook with special tools, it's sometimes best to cut the line as close to the hook as possible and let the fish go rather than stressing it further. It's a gamble, of course, but fish have been known to survive with deeply embedded hooks.

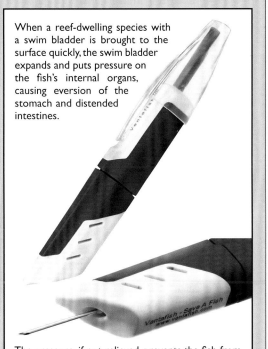

When a reef-dwelling species with a swim bladder is brought to the surface quickly, the swim bladder expands and puts pressure on the fish's internal organs, causing eversion of the stomach and distended intestines.

The pressure, if not relieved, prevents the fish from returning to the depths. If the fish is not vented properly, the fish will either die due to the pressure on its organs or be eaten by predator fish. In most instances, proper venting will ensure the fish's distended stomach and intestines will return to their normal state and the fish can safely return to its normal depths. Properly used, the Ventafish gives the fish its best chance of survival. The Ventafish includes a 16-gauge needle with a 45-degree entry. The entry point for the needle is 1 to 2 inches from the base of the pectoral fin. Venting a fish is especially important for gag and red groupers, red snappers, black sea bass, and any other species with closed swim bladders.

This sidebar was written by Tom Richardson and used with his permission.

Easy Fish Release

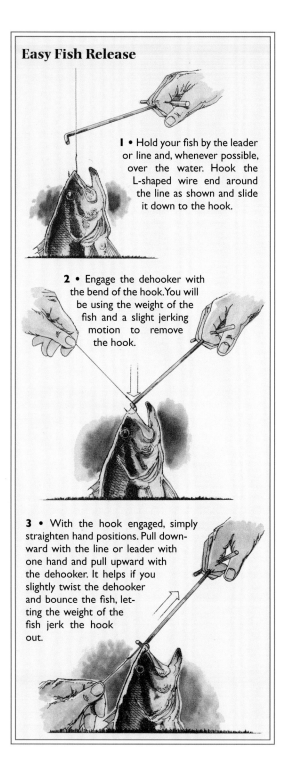

1 • Hold your fish by the leader or line and, whenever possible, over the water. Hook the L-shaped wire end around the line as shown and slide it down to the hook.

2 • Engage the dehooker with the bend of the hook. You will be using the weight of the fish and a slight jerking motion to remove the hook.

3 • With the hook engaged, simply straighten hand positions. Pull downward with the line or leader with one hand and pull upward with the dehooker. It helps if you slightly twist the dehooker and bounce the fish, letting the weight of the fish jerk the hook out.

protective coat of slime and make it vulnerable to fungus infection.

You can make your own catch-and-release device for lip-hooked fish from a length of heavy wire or you can buy one of the many inexpensive dehookers available from your local tackle dealer.

FISHING BY THE BIRDS

The modern angler has a multitude of fishing aids arrayed before him when he goes to sea, and they can greatly increase his chances of making a good catch. Yet all too often, these same fishermen fail to use the powers of observation that were the only stock-in-trade of their predecessors. Though few fishermen are also birders, we'd be well advised to become more acquainted with our feathered friends, as they'll often lead us to fish we'd otherwise be unaware of.

The most important aspect of successful saltwater fishing is being at the right place at the right time. The water volume we cover is huge, and every clue must be considered in order to narrow down the search. No matter how high the tower of the boat, your visibility is of little consequence when compared to that of any bird—and you can bet their sight is a lot better too. Best of all, their services in leading us to fish are completely free.

Whether you're fishing for stripers and blues or marlin and tuna, the assistance provided by seabirds can make or break your effort on many occasions. The trick is to learn which birds will prove helpful for various species in your area and how to interpret their behavior.

The frigate, more commonly known as the man-o-war, is one of the most reliable fish-finders in the ocean. Oddly enough, the frigate is unable to dive for fish, but it will track a single billfish until it pushes bait to the surface, where it can be plucked up by the swooping bird.

If you see a commercial trawler surrounded by flying and diving seabirds, it's a sure bet that there's a school of fish feeding on baitfish and trash that falls from nets into the water.

■ Frigates

Among the most reliable fish indicators in tropical and semitropical seas is the frigate, also known as the man-o-war. This bird, which can have a wing spread of up to 8 feet, is unable to dive for fish. However, there is no better fish spotter in the world. The frigate hovers far up in the sky and will track a single billfish until it pushes a baitfish to the surface, where it can be plucked off by the swooping bird. If there are no other signs, I'll always steer toward any frigate spotted.

Years ago, frigates put me into some of the most exciting striped marlin fishing I've ever seen off the coast of Salinas, Ecuador, as the birds targeted marlin balling baitfish. More recently, those birds led to action with marlin off the coast of La Guaira, Venezuela, as they dove on schools of bait driven so far up on the surface that the frigates could fly in one after another and easily pick off a fish on each pass. On another day off La Guaira, large dolphin were scattered over a wide area offshore of the bank, but our skipper was able to race to each pair as they chased bait to the surface by watching the actions of the frigates. That timing was critical, as the balao were blasted immediately and after the fish were boated it was time to race to another swooping frigate for a sure hookup.

Feeding isn't usually easy for frigates, and they are notorious pirates—stealing fish from lesser birds. That propensity has to be accounted for, as the birds may end up well away from the predator fish you're seeking in the course of a fight for an already captured bait.

Frigates aren't usually much of a problem for fishermen, but that's not the case at Christmas Island. That mid-Pacific bonefishing hot spot has its own species of frigate (*Fregata andrewsi*) that is extremely aggressive. They would dive on plugs trolled along the surface of the lagoon, and while casting plugs I'd have to watch out on my backcast as frigates would swoop down to grab the plug from the tip of the rod. After the cast was made, it became a question of whether a giant trevally would hit before a frigate nabbed the popper.

■ Blue-Footed Boobies

Frigates aren't the only birds that can be a hindrance to anglers at times. Blue-footed boobies can be a real pain when trolling bait in the tropics, as they don't give up easily. There were many occasions in the Galapagos Islands when we had to stop trolling balao because boobies wouldn't stay off them. After first picking up a balao and having it pulled away, they'd typically fly off far ahead of the boat as if they were leaving—but would then make a big circle and sneak back in for the same bait. However, boobies don't seem to be as aggressive on plugs as the frigates that often feed with them in the same areas. Boobies are found in most tropical seas and are related to gannets. They also can plunge

Blue-footed boobies can sometimes be a hindrance to fishermen. Found mostly in the tropics, boobies have a nasty habit of swooping down and picking up trolled balao baits.

Shearwaters are excellent fish indicators when diving on actively feeding fish. Shearwaters have no need to dive to get below the surface. They can sit on the water in flocks and swim down to baitfish like a winged fish.

below the surface to pick off fish, but make shallower, more angled dives than gannets.

Petrels

The most fascinating and widespread seabird is the tiny storm petrel. Actually there are 22 species of these small web-footed seabirds that are better known to sailors as Mother Carey's chickens. According to David Saunders in his *Sea Birds*, petrels were probably named after St. Peter because they seem to walk on the surface while feeding. Saunders suspects that the popular name may

have evolved from the words *Mater Cara*, which is an appellation of the Blessed Virgin Mary.

Wilson's petrel is the most common species of storm petrel, and they may well be the most numerous birds in the world. Shark fishermen of the Northeast see these constantly flying birds picking at the tiniest scraps in their shark chum slicks, but few realize that the 6-inch petrels migrate north all the way from the Antarctic. Though they have no meaning while in chum slicks, petrels have earned their nickname of "tuna birds" by leading fishermen to everything from schools of smaller tuna up to a single feeding giant. Never overlook a concentration of petrels while trolling!

Shearwaters

Sharkers have no problem with storm petrels, but they're occasionally plagued with shearwaters. Those long-winged slender seabirds are great divers and can pick off baits at considerable depths. Most of the time you'll just see one or two fly by and check out any chunks that may be in the slick. However, there are times when flocks will sit around the boat and defy you to get a bait in the water. Unlike gannets and pelicans, shearwaters have no need to dive out of the air in order to get below the surface. They can sit on the water and spot a bait well below before swimming down to it like a winged fish.

Shearwaters are excellent tuna indicators when diving on actively feeding fish, and even when sitting in the water in flocks. It has been my experience that shear-

Petrels, more commonly known as Mother Carey's chickens, may be the most numerous shorebird in the world. There are more than 20 species of petrels. Never overlook a concentration of petrels when trolling. They may lead you to a giant tuna.

Pelicans are sometimes not a reliable guide to feeding fish, but they are worth a look when you see them diving in deeper water, especially when fishing for pelagic species.

waters rarely rest for long, and a flock on the water indicates very recent action in the area.

Pelicans

Pelicans were once considered threatened, but it would be hard to prove that point in Florida, where these big-billed birds hang around boats to grab baits and try to push fishermen aside at cleaning tables in order to swallow anything not protected. I've seen them in the summer as far north as Sandy Hook, New Jersey, and they've become a permanent winter resident in Hatteras, North Carolina, even when water temperatures drop into the 40s. Pelicans aren't very reliable guides to predators in shal-

low waters because they have the ability to dive on baitfish, sticking their heads underwater in order to scoop up the prey without the aid of a predator fish chasing them to the surface. In both the Atlantic and Pacific, I've often spotted masses of diving pelicans near shore only to find they were happily feeding in skinny water. Under such circumstances, it's likely the crashing of these awkward-looking birds as they hit the water would probably scare off fish anyway.

On the other hand, pelicans diving in deeper waters are always worth a look for a variety of coastal and oceanic game fish. Off Cabo San Lucas, at the tip of Mexico's Baja California, pelicans dive on baits chased up by striped marlin and the entire fleet will start a high-speed chase toward even a single diving pelican.

Seagulls

Seagulls are the seabird most familiar to shorebound fishermen, and they can be very effective fish spotters. Like the frigate, gulls can't dive and must look for easy pickings. In the case of the gull, those pickings can be literally anything and they've earned the nickname "flying rats." Yet gulls are pretty reliable indicators of feeding fish, since they have to wait for dead and dying baitfish pushed up by predators.

Seagulls are particularly important to striped bass and bluefish anglers in the Northeast. Even a novice fisherman would realize that gulls are probably over feeding fish, but those sitting on the water also may provide a valuable clue that something has recently gone on or is about to happen.

Seagulls are probably the most common fish-finders in the ocean. Like the frigate, seagulls can't dive and they typically show up for easy pickings on the surface. Gulls have to wait for dead or dying baitfish pushed up by big predator fish, such as a striped bass or bluefish.

Terns, close relatives of seagulls, are good indicators of fish. When terns are in the area, they will find fish long before the gulls arrive. They are agile enough to partly plunge beneath the surface for baitfish.

A valuable example occurred during a November striper run in Raritan Bay. As the birds got active after sunup, they clued us in to the portion of the open bay where bass would briefly chase bunkers. However, after the action was over, Tony Arcabascio of Staten Island noted that the sitting birds were also a good indicator—and almost every time we dropped a live bunker near even a few sitting gulls we raised at least one bass from seemingly dead water.

On the negative side, gulls can be a big problem for anglers attempting to cast lures at breaking fish. Not only do they often try to grab surface plugs, but the cast line may get tangled in their wings. As with all seabirds that get tangled in lines or hooks, it's important to avoid being bitten by sharp beaks. The trick is to drop a cloth over the bird's eyes. Without sight, they usually remain quite calm and you'll be able to get everything cleared so the bird can fly away unharmed.

It was on Cape Cod that I learned how seagulls can help in navigation. At the time, I was running a Mako 19 and fishing for stripers in the fall off Monomoy Island at Chatham. Rather than running the dangerous inlet, I would return on the calm back side of Monomoy. However, fog was a regular problem and, combined with darkness, it was difficult to follow the winding channel through the flats. Yet I found it was possible to do so in practically zero visibility by stopping to listen for and smell the seagulls standing on the exposed flats I had to avoid.

■ Terns

Terns are close relatives of gulls, but these slender birds with long wings and forked tails are much more active. They are very good fish indicators, but can fool you when bait is close to the surface since they're agile enough to plunge partly beneath the surface in order to nab sand eels, rainfish, etc., without any help from predators. Though terns have webbed feet, they prefer to stand on shore or floating objects rather than resting on the water. When terns are in the area, they'll find bluefish long before the gulls arrive, so keep an eye on them.

Since terns can feed on tiny objects, they're often attracted to weed lines. Anything different in the ocean is always worth checking out, as weed lines often indicate contrasting currents and temperature variations. However, terns may be actively picking away in weed lines when there are no predators around. By observing them closely, you'll soon be able to tell at a glance when terns are picking on undisturbed baitfish or working over baits being pushed to the surface—at which time they fly and dip much more erratically.

An illustration of that occurred after the perfect combination of a northeaster followed by a cool, clearing northwester during a recent October when I joined Captain Frank Rose on his Miss Diane from Point Pleasant as Stu Wilk and other marine biologists from the Sandy Hook Marine Lab sought out specimens of fall bluefish for analysis of possible contaminants. There was plenty of bait being marked on Rose's fish-finder in the Shrewsbury Rocks area, but we were surprised to

Fishing by the Birds

Bird	Fish Indicated	Behavior
Frigate	Oceanic predators	Check out area they circle over
Pelican	Oceanic predators	Race to diving birds
Gannet	Striped bass	Diving from great heights
Shearwater	Tuna	Troll by even sitting flocks
Petrel	Tuna	Flock to tuna on surface
Seagull	All predators	Raucous and erratic

Note: Seabirds may react differently in various areas, depending on the bait and predators involved. This chart only reflects personal observations of bird behavior in many areas around the world where I've fished. In every case, the angler must decipher the behavior of seabirds in his area—which could be quite different.

find no bluefish where they should have been thick—a preview of what turned out to be the first fall without a real bluefish migration in decades.

By noon there was considerable tern action on that bait, but it didn't look frantic enough. Purple clouds of bait could be spotted just under the surface and the terns would dive on them every time the school moved just a bit higher and within reach. Seagulls were also sitting on the water, which normally wouldn't be the case if bluefish were feeding.

Though seabirds know enough to stay clear of the sharp-toothed, ravenous blues, which may hit anything in the course of wild feeding, they're probably unaware of their real enemies. Goosefish (or anglerfish or monkfish) gained their name by making meals of sitting birds, and tiger sharks seem to be fond of seagulls. In the course of releasing a 600-pounder from my boat off Montauk, I watched it spit up hundreds of gull feathers while I was holding it on the leader for photos—and Captain Bob Rocchetta saw a tiger eat a seagull off the surface the next day.

Gannets

Gannets are the coldwater, high-diving relatives of the tropical boobies. Measuring up to 3 feet in length, the North Atlantic gannet circles 100 feet above the water before diving headlong with folded wings to nail the prey well below the surface. Those spectacular dives are punctuated with 3-foot splashes that look like bombs being dropped into the water from a distance. Gannets can handle large prey, and should prosper now that the herring population is rebuilding after being decimated by foreign trawlers. These birds become abundant in the fall, and can clue anglers in to migrating schools of striped bass from great distances.

I used to run across to Nantucket with the late Captain Bud Henderson, and we'd spot gannets from a mile or more away. Gulls and gannets made it look like a garbage dump at sea as they fed on herring and squid driven to the surface by acres of stripers. There are no longer such vast schools of bass, and these days there's usually a lot more bait than predators, but gannets will still find those subsurface bait concentrations that may well have bass below them.

Off the New Jersey coast, we usually start seeing gannets in November. There's no greater assurance that bait is available, though most of the time they're feeding without help from the striped bass we seek. As with the terns, there's a more erratic pattern to the gannet's

Gannets are high-diving birds, sometimes diving 100 feet to feed on prey well below the surface. Three feet in length, gannets are big enough to feed on big baitfish like herring. Look for gannets in the Northeast when fishing for striped bass.

movements when they're actually on feeding fish—and seagulls tend to join them quickly when easy pickings are available.

The height of the dive is another indication with gannets—as well as with many other birds—as to how high the bait and predators are. When birds are flying high, they're broadening their range of vision as well as the depth they can see below the surface—a good indication that baitfish are deep. On the other hand, birds fly lower and dive shallower when bait is close to the surface and, hopefully, being pushed to the surface by the fish we seek.

Though I have a reputation to protect and even in my most desperate hours of fishlessness have never slipped to such depths, I must note that the unwary can also be fooled by birds with just a bit of help from certain fishermen who carry bread, oatmeal, or a few dead baits that can be spread upon the waters to create a feeding flurry—drawing boats to an otherwise dead area while they slip off to the real hot spot.

This overview only briefly touches on the many seabirds that are far better fishermen than any human being, and whose skills can be used by anglers to make themselves look a lot smarter. Keep your eyes peeled whenever you're at sea or on the beach, and there'll be many occasions when you'll be thanking seabirds for saving the day.

This text section was written by Al Ristori and used with his permission.

WATER TEMPERATURE AND FISH

There is no doubt left in anglers' minds of the importance of water temperature and its direct bearing on the activities of fish. Water temperature will tell you where the fish gather and where they feed at various times of the year.

It is a scientifically proven fact that every species of fish has a preferred temperature zone or range and it will stay and generally feed in this zone. Smallmouth bass, for example, prefer water that is 65 to 68°F. During spring, this temperature range may be in shallow water, and in hot, midsummer weather, this range may be in depths of 30 feet or more. In other words, locate the depth that reads 65 to 68°F and you're sure to find smallmouths.

Taking temperature readings of water is not difficult, whether you use a sophisticated electronic thermometer or an inexpensive water thermometer lowered into the water on a fishing line. One electronic thermometer has a probe attached to a cable that is marked at regular intervals, so depth and temperature can be read simultaneously.

The inexpensive water thermometers can also do the job, and many also indicate depth by inserting a water pressure gauge in the thermometer tube. With these thermometers, allow at least 30 seconds to one minute for a reading. Also, the fishing line attached to it should be marked off in regular intervals, say 5 feet, so you can determine just how deep you are lowering the thermometer in the water.

The accompanying chart shows popular fresh- and saltwater game fish and baitfish and their preferred temperature zones. Look up the fish you are seeking and the water temperature it prefers. Then, begin taking temperature readings from the surface on down, at 5-foot intervals, until you locate the correct zone and depth. Concentrate your efforts at that depth and you'll soon come to discover how important this water temperature business is.

Preferred Temperature

Note: Celsius temperatures are rounded to the nearest degree.

FRESHWATER GAME FISH

Species	Lower Avoidance	Optimum	Upper Avoidance
American shad (*Alosa sapidissima*)		66°F (19°C)	86°F (30°C)
Atlantic salmon (*Salmo salar*)		62°F (17°C)	
Atlantic sturgeon (*Acipenser oxyrhynchus*)	56°F (13°C)	66°F (19°C)	70°F (21°C)
Black crappie (*Pomoxis nigromaculatus*)	60°F (16°C)	70°F (21°C)	75F° (24°C)
Bloater (*Coregonus hoyi*)	43°F (6°C)		50°F (10°C)
Bluegill (*Lepomis macrochirus*)	58°F (14°C)	69°F (21°C)	75°F (24°C)
Brook trout (*Salvelinus fontinalis*)	44°F (7°C)	59°F (15°C)	70°F (21°C)
Brown bullhead (*Ictalurus nebulosus*)		74°F (23°C)	
Brown trout (*Salmo trutta*)	44°F (7°C)	55–65°F (13–18°C)	75°F (24°C)
Buffalo species (*Ictiobus sp.*)	81°F (27°C)		94°F (34°C)
Burbot (*Lota lota maculosa*)		52°F (11°C)	
Carp (*Cyprinus carpio*)	75°F (24°C)	84°F (29°C)	88°F (31°C)
Chain pickerel (*Esox niger*)	60°F (16°C)	66°F (19°C)	74°F (23°C)
Channel catfish (*Ictalurus punctutatus*)	55°F (13°C)	82–89°F (28–32°C)	
Chinook salmon (*Oncorhynchus tshawytscha*)	44°F (7°C)	54°F (12°C)	60°F (16°C)
Chum salmon (*Oncorhynchus keta*)		57°F (14°C)	
Cisco (*Coregonus artedii*)		52–55°F (11–13°C)	
Coho salmon (*Oncorhynchus kisutch*)	44°F (7°C)	54°F (12°C)	60°F (16°C)

FRESHWATER GAME FISH (continued)

Species	Lower Avoidance	Optimum	Upper Avoidance
Flathead catfish (*Pylodictis olivaris*)	81°F (27°C)		90°F (32°C)
Freshwater drum (*Aplodinotus grunniens*)		74°F (23°C)	
Grass pickerel (*Esox americanus vermiculatus*)		78°F (26°C)	
Grayling (*Thymallus arcticus*)			64°F (18°C)
Green sunfish (*Lepomis cyanellus*)	73°F (23°C)	87°F (31°C)	91°F (33°C)
Goldeye (*Hiodon alosoides*)	72°F (22°C)		83°F (28°C)
Kamloops trout (*Salmo gairdneri*)	46°F (8°C)	47–54°F (8–12°C)	
Kokanee (*Oncorhynchus nerka*)		52–55°F (11–13°C)	
Lake trout (*Salvelinus namaycush*)	42°F (6°C)	50–59°F (10–15°C)	
Lake whitefish (*Coregonus clupeaformis*)	43°F (6°C)	51°F (11°C)	
Landlocked Atlantic salmon (*Salmo salar sebago*)		50–58°F (10–14°C)	65°F (18°C)
Largemouth bass (*Micropterus salmoides*)	60°F (16°C)	80°F (27°C)	
Longnose gar (*Lepisosteus osseus*)		92°F (33°C)	
Longnose sucker (*Catostomus catostomus*)		53°F (12°C)	
Mooneye (*Hiodon tergisus*)	72°F (22°C)		81°F (27°C)
Muskellunge (*Esox masquinongy*)	55°F (13°C)	63°F (17°C)	72°F (22°C)
Northern pike (*Esox lucius*)	56°F (13°C)	63°F (17°C)	74°F (23°C)
Pink salmon (*Oncorhynchus gorbuscha*)		49°F (9°C)	
Pumpkinseed (*Lepomis gibbosus*)		82°F (28°C)	
Rainbow trout (*Salmo gairdneri*)	44°F (7°C)	48–65°F (9–18°C)	75°F (24°C)
Redhorse suckers (*Moxostoma sp.*)	72°F (22°C)		79°F (26°C)
Rock bass (*Ambloplites rupestris*)		70°F (21°C)	
Round whitefish (*Prosopium cylindraceum*)		63°F (17°C)	
Sauger (*Stizostedion canadense*)	55°F (13°C)	67°F (19°C)	74°F (23°C)
Shortnose gar (*Lepisosteus platostomus*)	81°F (27°C)		94°F (34°C)
Smallmouth bass (*Micropterus dolomieui*)	60°F (16°C)	65–68°F (18–20°C)	73°F (23°C)
Sockeye salmon (*Oncorhynchus nerka*)		55°F (13°C)	
Spotted bass (*Micropterus punctulatus*)	71°F (22°C)	75°F (24°C)	80°F (27°C)
Steelhead trout (*Salmo gairdneri*)	38°F (3°C)	48–52°F (9–11°C)	
Sunfishes (*Centrarchidae*)	50°F (10°C)	58°F (14°C)	68°F (20°C)
Tench (*Tinca tinca*)			79°F (26°C)
Walleye (*Stizostedion vitreum*)	50°F (10°C)	67°F (19°C)	76°F (24°C)
White bass (*Morone chrysops*)	62°F (17°C)	70°F (21°C)	78°F (26°C)
White crappie (*Pomoxis annularis*)		61°F (16°C)	
White perch (*Morone americana*)		89°F (32°C)	
White sucker (*Catostomus commersoni*)		72°F (22°C)	
Yellow bass (*Morone mississippiensis*)		81°F (27°C)	
Yellow bullhead (*Ictalurus natalis*)		83°F (28°C)	
Yellow perch (*Perca flavescens*)	58°F (14°C)	65°F (18°C)	74°F (23°C)

FRESHWATER BAITFISH

Species	Lower Avoidance	Optimum	Upper Avoidance
Alewife (*Alosa pseudoharengus*)	48°F (9°C)	54°F (12°C)	72°F (22°C)
Bitterling (*Rhodeus sericeus*)		77°F (25°C)	

FRESHWATER BAITFISH (continued)

Species	Lower Avoidance	Optimum	Upper Avoidance
Bluehead chub (*Nocomis leptocephalus*)	50°F (10°C)	59°F (15°C)	63°F (17°C)
Bluntnose minnow (*Pimephales notatus*)	70°F (21°C)	84°F (29°C)	88°F (31°C)
Desert pupfish (*Cyprinodon macularius*)	71°F (22°C)		78°F (26°C)
Emerald shiner (*Notropis atherinoides*)		61°F (16°C)	
Fathead minnow (*Pimephales promelas*)	77°F (25°C)	84°F (29°C)	90°F (32°C)
Fourhorn sculpin (*Myoxocephalus quadricornis*)	39°F (4°C)		
Gizzard shad (*Dorosoma cepedianum*)		69°F (21°C)	
Golden shiner (*Notemigonus crysoleucas*)		70°F (21°C)	
Goldfish (*Carassius auratus*)		77°F (25°C)	
Guppy (*Poecilia reticulata*)		84°F (29°C)	
Lake chub (*Couesius plumbeus*)		48–52°F (9–11°C)	
Longjaw mudsucker (*Gillichthys mirabilis*)	48°F (9°C)	72°F (22°C)	
Moapa dace (*Moapa coriacea*)		85°F (29°C)	
Mosquitofish (*Gambusia affinis*)		81°F (27°C)	85°F (29°C)
Mottled sculpin (*Cottus bairdi*)		48–52°F (9–11°C)	
Mozambique mouthbrooder (*Tilapia mossambica*)		83°F (28°C)	92°F (33°C)
Ninespine stickleback (*Pungitius pungitius*)		48–52°F (9–11°C)	
Quillback (*Carpiodes cyprinus*)		72°F (22°C)	
Rainbow smelt (*Osmerus mordax*)	43°F (6°C)	50°F (10°C)	57°F (14°C)
River carpsucker (*Carpoides carpio*)	79°F (26°C)		94°F (34°C)
Rosyface shiner (*Notropis rubellus*)	70°F (21°C)	80°F (27°C)	88°F (31°C)
Slimy sculpin (*Cottus cognatus*)	39°F (4°C)		43°F (6°C)
Spotfin shiner (*Cyprinella spiloptera*)	79°F (26°C)	85°F (29°C)	95°F (35°C)
Spottail shiner (*Notropis hudsonius*)		54°F (12°C)	
Stonecat (*Notorus flavus*)		59°F (15°C)	
Stoneroller (*Campostoma anomalum*)	75°F (24°C)	84°F (29°C)	91°F (33°C)
Trout-perch (*Percopsis omiscomaycus*)	50°F (10°C)		61°F (16°C)
White River killfish (*Crenichthys baileyi*)		85°F (29°C)	

SALTWATER GAME FISH

Species	Lower Avoidance	Optimum	Upper Avoidance
Albacore (*Thunnus alalunga*)	59°F (15°C)	64°F (18°C)	66°F (19°C)
Amberjack (*Seriola dumerili*)	60°F (16°C)	65°F (18°C)	72°F (22°C)
Atlantic bonito (*Sarda sarda*)	60°F (16°C)	64°F (18°C)	80°F (27°C)
Atlantic cod (*Gadus morhua*)	31°F (-1°C)	44–49°F (7–9°C)	59°F (15°C)
Atlantic croaker (*Micropogon undulatus*)			100°F (38°C)
Atlantic mackerel (*Scomber scombrus*)	45°F (7°C)	63°F (17°C)	70°F (21°C)
Barracuda (*Sphyraena barracuda*)	55°F (13°C)	75–79°F (24–26°C)	82°F (28°C)
Bigeye tuna (*Thunnus obesus*)	52°F (11°C)	58°F (14°C)	66°F (19°C)
Blackfin tuna (*Thunnus atlanticus*)	70°F (21°C)	74°F (23°C)	82°F (28°C)
Black marlin (*Makaira indica*)	68°F (20°C)	75–79°F (24–26°C)	87°F (31°C)
Bluefin tuna (*Thunnus thynnus*)	50°F (10°C)	68°F (20°C)	78°F (26°C)
Bluefish (*Pomatomus saltatrix*)	50°F (10°C)	66–72°F (19–22°C)	84°F (19°C)
Blue marlin (*Makaira nigricans*)	70°F (21°C)	78°F (26°C)	88°F (31°C)

SALTWATER GAME FISH (continued)

Species	Lower Avoidance	Optimum	Upper Avoidance
Bonefish (*Albula vulpes*)	64°F (18°C)	75°F (24°C)	88°F (31°C)
Dolphinfish (*Coryphaena hippurus*)	70°F (21°C)	75°F (24°C)	82°F (28°C)
Fluke or summer flounder (*Paralichthys dentatus*)	56°F (13°C)	66°F (19°C)	72°F (22°C)
Haddock (*Melanogrammus aeglefinus*)	36°F (2°C)	47°F (8°C)	52°F (11°C)
Horn shark (*Heterodontus francisci*)		75°F (24°C)	
Kelp bass (*Paralabrax clathratus*)	62°F (17°C)	65°F (18°C)	72°F (22°C)
King mackerel (*Scomberomorus cavalla*)	70°F (21°C)		88°F (31°C)
Opaleye (*Girella nigricans*)		79°F (26°C)	86°F (30°C)
Permit (*Trachinotus falcatus*)	65°F (18°C)	72°F (22°C)	92°F (33°C)
Pollock (*Pollachius virens*)	33°F (1°C)	45°F (8°C)	60°F (16°C)
Red drum (*Sciaenops ocellatus*)	52°F (11°C)	71°F (22°C)	90°F (32°C)
Red snapper (*Lutjanus blackfordi*)	50°F (10°C)	57°F (14°C)	62°F (17°C)
Sailfish (*Istiophorus platypterus*)	68°F (20°C)	79°F (26°C)	88°F (31°C)
Sand seatrout (*Cynoscion arenarius*)	90°F (32°C)	95°F (35°C)	104°F (40°C)
Sea catfish (*Arius felis*)			99°F (37°C)
Skipjack tuna (*Euthynnus pelamis*)	50°F (10°C)	62°F (17°C)	70°F (21°C)
Snook (*Centropomus undecimalis*)	60°F (16°C)	70–75°F (21–24°C)	90°F (32°C)
Spotted seatrout (*Cynoscion nebulosus*)	48°F (9°C)	72°F (22°C)	81°F (27°C)
Striped bass (*Morone saxatilis*)	61°F (16°C)	68°F (20°C)	77°F (25°C)
Striped marlin (*Tetrapturus audax*)	61°F (16°C)	70°F (21°C)	80°F (27°C)
Swordfish (*Xiphias gladius*)	50°F (10°C)	66°F (19°C)	78°F (26°C)
Tarpon (*Megalops atlantica*)	74°F (23°C)	76°F (24°C)	90°F (32°C)
Tautog (*Tautoga onitis*)	60°F (16°C)	70°F (21°C)	76°F (24°C)
Weakfish (*Cynoscion regalis*)		55–65°F (13–18°C)	78°F (26°C)
White marlin (*Tetrapturus albidus*)	65°F (18°C)	70°F (21°C)	80°F (27°C)
White sea bass (*Cynoscion nobilis*)	58°F (14°C)	68°F (20°C)	74°F (23°C)
Winter flounder (*Pseudopleuronectes americanus*)	35°F (2°C)	48–52°F (9–11°C)	64°F (18°C)
Yellowfin tuna (*Thunnus albacares*)	64°F (18°C)	72°F (22°C)	80°F (27°C)
Yellowtail (*Seriola dorsalis*)	60°F (16°C)	65°F (18°C)	70°F (21°C)

SALTWATER BAITFISH

Species	Lower Avoidance	Optimum	Upper Avoidance
Atlantic silverside (*Menidia menidia*)			90°F (32°C)
Atlantic threadfin (*Polydactylus octonemus*)			92°F (33°C)
Bay anchovy (*Anchoa mitchilli*)		82°F (28°C)	92°F (33°C)
California grunion (*Leuresthes tenuis*)	68°F (20°C)	77°F (25°C)	93°F (34°C)
Gulf grunion (*Leuresthes sardina*)	68°F (20°C)	89°F (32°C)	98°F (37°C)
Gulf menhaden (*Brevoortia patronus*)			86°F (30°C)
Pacific silversides (jacksmelt and topsmelt) (*Atherinopsis sp.*)	72°F (22°C)	77°F (25°C)	82°F (28°C)
Rough silverside (*Membras martinica*)			91°F (33°C)
Skipjack herring (*Alosa chrysochloris*)	72°F (22°C)		84°F (29°C)
Spot (*Leiostomus xanthurus*)			99°F (37°C)
Tidewater silverside (*Menidia beryllina*)			93°F (34°C)

FRESHWATER GAME FISH

Section Six
FRESHWATER GAME FISH

▦ Atlantic Salmon *(Salmo salar)*

DESCRIPTION: Atlantic salmon are anadromous fish, meaning that they are spawned in freshwater rivers and then migrate to the ocean to spend most of their lives before returning to fresh water to spawn themselves. When fresh from the sea, Atlantics are steel blue on top and silver on the sides and belly, and have dark spots on their sides. As their stay in fresh water lengthens, the colors become darker, with the sides taking on a pinkish hue as spawning time arrives. Very young salmon are called parrs. Parrs have distinctive dark vertical bars called parr markings. Unlike Pacific salmon, all of which die after spawning, about 15 percent of Atlantic salmon survive the spawning act and return to sea.

RANGE: The highly prized Atlantic salmon once ranged from Delaware north through Quebec and the Canadian Maritime provinces to Greenland, and in the western Atlantic Ocean to the British Isles and parts of Scandinavia. But today, because of "progress"—meaning dams, pollution, and urban and suburban sprawl—the range of the Atlantic salmon in the United States is restricted to a handful of rivers in Maine, though efforts are being made to restore this fine game fish to the Connecticut River and other northeastern rivers.

HABITAT: In fresh water, the Atlantic salmon must have clean, flowing, cold water. In upstream spawning areas, fish can create "redds," or spawning beds. When in the ocean, these salmon range over vast areas but tend to concentrate on feeding grounds, which are only recently being discovered.

SIZE: Mature Atlantic salmon weigh from 9 to 75 pounds, with the average being 12 pounds. Their size depends on how many years they have spent in the sea, where their growth is fast. Salmon that return to fresh water after only one or two years at sea are called grilse and weigh up to about 6 or 8 pounds.

FOOD: These fish feed on small baitfish and the like when in the ocean, but upon entering fresh water, they stop feeding almost completely. And yet they can be induced to strike an artificial lure, particularly dry and wet flies.

FISHING METHODS: Casting from shore or boats, mostly in tidal waters of rivers and river mouths during spawning migration

BAITS: Artificial lures (especially spoons) and dry, wet, and streamer flies

▦ Landlocked Salmon *(Salmo salar sebago)*

COMMON NAMES: Landlocked salmon, Sebago salmon, landlock, and ouananiche

DESCRIPTION: The landlocked salmon is very similar in coloration and general appearance to the Atlantic salmon, of which the landlock is a subspecies. It is assumed that the subspecies descended from Atlantic salmon trapped in freshwater lakes thousands of years ago. As their name suggests, landlocks do not spawn

Atlantic Salmon

in the sea. They either spawn in their home lakes or descend to outlet streams to spawn.

RANGE: Landlocks range over much of New England (they are most numerous in Maine), Quebec and other parts of eastern Canada, and north to Labrador. They have been introduced in New York and other eastern states and in South America.

HABITAT: The landlock survives best in deep, cold lakes that have a high oxygen content.

SIZE: Most landlocks average 2 to 3 pounds, but a 6-pounder is not unusual and an occasional 10-pounder is caught. The maximum weight is about 30 pounds.

FOOD: Landlocks feed mostly on small baitfish, particularly smelt.

FISHING METHODS: Casting and trolling

BAITS: Baitfish, smelt, artificial lures, and streamers

■ Chinook Salmon
(Oncorhynchus tshawytscha)

COMMON NAMES: Chinook salmon, king salmon, tyee salmon, and blackmouth (immature stage)

DESCRIPTION: The chinook, like all other Pacific salmon, is anadromous and seems to prefer the largest of Pacific coast rivers for spawning. Chinooks have a dark-blue back that shades to silver on the sides and white on the belly. Small, dark spots—barely noticeable in fish fresh from the sea—mark the upper part of the body.

RANGE: Chinook salmon range from southern California to northern Alaska, being more numerous in the northern part of that area. They often travel enormous distances upriver to spawn; in the Yukon River, for example, chinooks have been seen 2,000 miles from the sea.

HABITAT: Chinooks prefer large, clean, cold rivers, but often enter small tributary streams to spawn in shallow water over gravel bottoms.

SIZE: The chinook is the largest of the Pacific salmon, reaching weights of more than 100 pounds. Rarely,

Chinook Salmon

however, does a sportfisherman catch one of more than 60 pounds, and the average size is about 18 pounds.

FOOD: Chinook salmon eat ocean baitfish (herring, sardines, candlefish, and anchovies), freshwater baitfish, and fish roe.

FISHING METHODS: Casting and trolling

BAITS: Baitfish, egg sacks, spoons, spinners, and flies

■ Dog Salmon (Oncorhynchus keta)

COMMON NAMES: Dog salmon and chum salmon

DESCRIPTION: The dog salmon closely resembles the chinook salmon, but has black-edged fins and lacks the chinook's dark spots on the back, dorsal fin, and tail. During spawning, the male dog salmon often exhibits red or green blotches on its sides. The dog salmon is rarely taken by sportfishermen.

RANGE: One of five species of Pacific salmon, the dog salmon is found from central California north to Alaska,

Dog Salmon

Dog Salmon Spawning

but is far more numerous in Alaska than farther south. In their sea migrations, dog salmon travel as far as the Aleutians, Korea, and Japan.

HABITAT: Like all other salmon, the dog spawns in gravel in freshwater rivers, usually in the lower reaches of the parent streams, but occasionally far upstream.

SIZE: Dog salmon reach weights of 30 pounds or a bit more, but they average 6 to 18 pounds.

FOOD: The diet of dog salmon consists mainly of baitfish and crustaceans.

FISHING METHODS: Casting and trolling

BAITS: Baitfish, spoons, spinners, and flies, especially those in red

■ Sockeye Salmon
(Oncorhynchus nerka)

COMMON NAMES: Sockeye salmon, red salmon, and blueback salmon

DESCRIPTION: The sockeye is similar to the chinook, but it has a small number of gill rakers and tiny spots along its back. When spawning, sockeye males turn dark red, with the forward parts of their body being greenish. Females range in color from olive to light red. Sockeyes are more

Sockeye Salmon

often caught by sportfishermen than dog salmon, and they will take artificial flies and are good fighters.

RANGE: Sockeyes are found from California to Japan, but few are encountered south of the Columbia River. A landlocked strain of the sockeye (see Kokanee Salmon), originally found from British Columbia south to Oregon and Idaho, is being stocked in freshwater lakes in various areas of the United States.

HABITAT: This species spawns over gravel in freshwater lakes, especially those fed by springs.

SIZE: Sockeyes reach a maximum weight of about 15 pounds, but the average weight is 4 to 9 pounds.

FOOD: Sockeyes feed mainly on crustaceans, but also eat small baitfish.

FISHING METHODS: Casting and trolling

BAITS: Crustaceans, baitfish, spoons, and streamer flies

■ Humpback Salmon
(Oncorhynchus gorbuscha)

COMMON NAMES: Humpback salmon and pink salmon

DESCRIPTION: Similar to other salmon but smaller, the humpback has small scales and its caudal fin (tail) has large, oval, black spots. At maturity, or at spawning time, the males develop a large, distinctive hump on their backs. The humpback is among the most commercially valuable of the Pacific salmon and is becoming more popular with sportfishermen.

RANGE: The humpback is found from California to Alaska and as far away as Korea and Japan.

HABITAT: This species spawns over gravel in freshwater rivers, usually near the sea.

Humpback Salmon

Humpback Salmon Spawning

SIZE: The smallest of the Pacific salmon, the humpback averages 3 to 6 pounds, attaining a maximum weight of about 10 pounds.

FOOD: Humpbacks subsist largely on a diet of crustaceans, baitfish, and squid.

FISHING METHODS: Casting and trolling

BAITS: Crustaceans, baitfish, spoons, spinners, and flies

■ Coho Salmon *(Oncorhynchus kisutch)*

COMMON NAMES: Coho salmon, silver, and hooknose

DESCRIPTION: The coho is generally silvery with a bluish back and has small, dark spots along the upper part of the sides and tail. When the spawning urge takes hold, the males assume a reddish coloration, but when they enter fresh water they become almost black. The coho is highly prized as a sport fish, striking artificials readily and leaping breathtakingly when hooked.

RANGE: The coho is found from California to Alaska and as far from the West Coast of the United States as Japan. It has also been transplanted with unprecedented success in all of the Great Lakes and in many landlocked reservoirs throughout the United States.

HABITAT: This fish spawns in gravel in freshwater rivers, either near the sea or far upstream.

SIZE: Cohos reach weights approaching 30 pounds, but they average 6 to 12 pounds.

FOOD: A coho's diet is mainly baitfish, squid, crustaceans, and crab larvae.

FISHING METHODS: Casting and trolling

BAITS: Baitfish, squid, crustaceans, spoons, and flies

Kokanee Salmon

Kokanee Salmon Spawning

■ Kokanee Salmon *(Oncorhynchus nerka kennerlyi)*

COMMON NAMES: Kokanee salmon, silver trout, blueback, little redfish, Kennerly's salmon, landlocked sockeye, redfish, and silversides

DESCRIPTION: The kokanee is a landlocked strain of the anadromous sockeye salmon. Biologically identical with the true sockeye (though much smaller), the kokanee is silvery on its sides and belly, but during spawning the males have reddish sides and the females have slate-gray sides. Kokanees resemble some trout, but differ from all trout in that they have more than 12 rays in the anal fin. The kokanee is the only Pacific salmon that matures in fresh water. It is much prized by fishermen.

RANGE: The kokanee's original range extended from Idaho and Oregon north to Alaska, but it has been introduced in recent years in lakes as far south as New Mexico and as far east as New England.

HABITAT: The kokanee spawns in gravel, both in lakes and in tributary streams, and ranges throughout lakes at other times.

SIZE: Much smaller than the true sockeye salmon, the kokanee reaches a maximum weight of about 4 pounds. The average length varies greatly, depending upon water and food conditions. In some places they never exceed 10 inches, while in other places—California's Donner Lake, for example—their average length is more than 18 inches.

Coho Salmon

Brook Trout

FOOD: Kokanees feed almost exclusively on tiny forage—minute crustaceans and other plankton.

FISHING METHODS: Casting and trolling

BAITS: Small crustaceans, artificial lures, and flies

■ Arctic Char *(Salvelinus alpinus)*

COMMON NAMES: Arctic char, Arctic trout, alpine trout, and Quebec red trout

DESCRIPTION: The Arctic char is a far-north salmonid whose colors vary greatly. Sea-run char are quite silvery as they enter freshwater rivers, but their freshwater colors soon predominate, turning the char into a stunning fish with sides ranging in color from pale to very bright orange and red. Char are usually spotted in red, pink, or cream, and have the white-edged fins of brook trout, but they lack the brook trout's vermiculations (wormlike markings) on the back. There are both anadromous and landlocked strains of Arctic char.

RANGE: Arctic char are found in northern Canada, Alaska, Iceland, Greenland, Scandinavia, England, Ireland, Scotland, Europe, and the Soviet Union.

HABITAT: As its range indicates, the char thrives in very cold, clean water, preferring fast, shallow river water near the mouths of tributary streams. Relatively little is known about the nomadic movements of anadromous char, but they apparently spend the summer near the mouths of rivers, where they feed heavily before moving inland.

SIZE: Arctic char reach weights of nearly 30 pounds, but the average weight is 2 to 8 pounds.

FOOD: Char feed on a species of smelt called capelin and on sand eels, various baitfish, some crustaceans, and occasionally on insects.

Arctic Char

FISHING METHODS: Casting

BAITS: Small baitfish, crustaceans, spoons, spinners, and flies

■ Brook Trout *(Salvelinus fontinalis)*

COMMON NAMES: Brook trout, speckled trout, speck, and squaretail

DESCRIPTION: This best-loved American native fish is not a true trout but actually a member of the char family. It is a beautiful fish, having a dark back with distinctive vermiculations (wormlike markings), sides marked with yellow spots and with red spots encircled in blue, a light-colored belly (bright orange during spawning), and pink or red lower fins edged in white. Wherever they are found, brook trout willingly take the offerings of fly, bait, and lure fishermen alike, a fact that has contributed to their decrease in many areas, though pollution has done far more to decimate populations of native brookies.

RANGE: Originally native only to northeastern North America from Georgia to the Arctic, the brook trout is now found in suitable waters throughout the United States, Canada, South America, and Europe. Stocking maintains brook trout in many waters, but true native brookies are becoming rare.

HABITAT: Brook trout must have clean, cold water, seldom being found in water warmer than 65°F. They spawn both in lakes and in streams, preferring small, spring-fed brooks.

SIZE: Though the rod-and-reel record for brook trout is 14½ pounds, fish half that size are a rarity today. In fact, a 5-pounder is an exceptional brook trout, and fish of that size are seldom found anywhere but in Labrador, northern Quebec and Manitoba, and Argentina. Native brook trout caught in streams average about 6 to 12 inches in length.

Sunapee Trout

FOOD: Brook trout eat worms, insects, crustaceans, and various kinds of baitfish.

FISHING METHODS: Casting, trolling, and streamers

BAITS: Baitfish, worms, insects, spoons, spinners, and flies

Sunapee Trout *(Salvelinus aureolus)*

COMMON NAMES: Sunapee trout and Sunapee golden

DESCRIPTION: This attractive fish—which may be a member of the char family or a distinct species of trout (there is some disagreement on the subject)—has a dark-bluish back that lacks the wormlike markings of the brook trout. Its sides have spots of pinkish white, yellow, or red, and the yellowish or orange fins are edged in white.

RANGE: Originating in New Hampshire, principally in Sunapee Lake, the Sunapee trout is exceedingly rare, being found only in Sunapee Lake and in a few lakes and ponds in northern New England. The introduction of lake trout in Sunapee and other lakes has had a deteriorating effect on populations of Sunapee trout.

HABITAT: Little is known about the wanderings of this attractive fish, but it is known that in Sunapee Lake these trout move into the shallows in spring and fall, while in summer they are found in the deepest parts of the lake—way down to 60 to 100 feet, where the water is quite cold.

SIZE: Many years ago, 10- and 12-pound Sunapees were taken in the lake from which they derive their name, but today a fisherman is lucky to catch a 15-incher.

FOOD: Smelt makes up the majority of the Sunapee trout's diet.

FISHING METHODS: Casting

BAITS: Baitfish, smelt, spoons, spinners, and flies

Dolly Varden Trout *(Salvelinus malma)*

COMMON NAMES: Dolly Varden trout, Dolly, western char, bull trout, salmon trout, and red-spotted trout

DESCRIPTION: This member of the char family somewhat resembles the brook trout, but it lacks the brookie's wormlike back markings and is usually more slender. It has red and yellow side spots and the white-edged fins typical of all chars. In salt water, the Dolly is quite silvery. The Dolly, said to have been named after a Charles Dickens character, is not as popular in some parts of its range as other trout species, possibly because it is not as strong a fighter.

RANGE: Occurring from northern California to Alaska and as far from the United States as Japan, the Dolly is found in both fresh water and, in the northern part of its range, in salt water.

HABITAT: Dolly Vardens spawn in gravel in streams. At other times of the year, stream fish are likely to be found in places similar to those preferred by brook trout, such as under rocks, logs, and other debris and lying in deep holes. In lakes, they are likely to be found near the bottom near reefs and drop-offs. They are seldom found near the surface.

SIZE: Dolly Vardens reach weights of upwards of 30 pounds. The average size is 8 to 18 inches in some places (usually streams), and 3 to 6 pounds in others (usually lakes).

FOOD: These fish are primarily bottom-feeders, though in streams they feed heavily on insects and may be taken on flies. Large fish feed heavily on baitfish, including the young of trout and salmon. It has been said that these

Dolly Varden Trout

trout will eat anything, which may be true considering that in some areas fishermen shoot ground squirrels, remove and skin the legs, and use the legs for Dolly Varden bait!

FISHING METHODS: Casting, trolling, and streamers

BAITS: Baitfish, spoons, spinners, and flies

■ Lake Trout *(Salvelinus namaycush)*

COMMON NAMES: Lake trout, togue, mackinaw, gray trout, salmon trout, forktail, and laker

DESCRIPTION: More somberly hued than most other trout, the laker is usually a fairly uniform gray or bluish gray, though in some areas it is a bronze green. It has irregular, pale spots over its head, back, and sides and also has the white-edged fins that mark it as a char.

RANGE: The lake trout is distributed throughout Canada and in the northern United States, principally in New England, and New York's Finger Lakes, the Great Lakes, and many large western lakes. Stockings have widened the laker's range considerably and have restored the species to portions of the Great Lakes, where an incursion of lamprey eels decimated the laker populations in the 1950s and early 1960s.

HABITAT: Lake trout are fish of deep, cold, clear lakes, though in the northern part of their range they are also found in large streams. Lakers prefer water temperatures of about 45°F and are rarely found where water rises above 70°F. In the southern part of their range, they are usually found only in lakes that have an adequate oxygen supply in the deeper spots.

SIZE: The lake trout is the largest of the trout species, reaching weights of more than 100 pounds. Its average size often depends on the size, depth, and water quality of a given lake.

Lake Trout

Rainbow Trout

FOOD: Though the young feed on insects and crustaceans, adult lake trout eat primarily fish, such as smelt, small kokanee salmon, ciscoes, whitefish, and sculpin.

FISHING METHODS: Casting and trolling

BAITS: Baitfish, crustaceans, deep-running spoons, and plugs

■ Rainbow Trout *(Oncorhynchus mykiss)*

COMMON NAMES: Rainbow trout, steelhead, Kamloops rainbow, Kamloops trout, and redsides

DESCRIPTION: This native American trout takes three basic forms: the nonmigratory rainbow, which lives its entire life in streams or lakes; the steelhead, which is spawned in freshwater rivers, migrates to the sea, and returns to the rivers to spawn itself (large rainbows that live in the Great Lakes and elsewhere in the eastern United States are also called steelheads but are not true members of the steelhead clan); and the Kamloops rainbow, a large subspecies found mostly in interior British Columbia. Though the rainbow's colors vary greatly depending upon where it is found, the fish generally has an olive or lighter-green back shading to silvery or white on the lower sides and belly. There are numerous black spots on the upper body from head to tail and a distinctive red stripe along the middle of each side. Sea-run and lake-run rainbows are usually quite silver, with a faint or nonexistent red stripe and few spots. The rainbow is an extremely important sport fish and will take flies, lures, and bait willingly. It usually strikes hard and is noted for its wild leaps.

RANGE: The natural range of the rainbow trout is from northern Mexico to Alaska and the Aleutian Islands, but stocking programs have greatly widened that range so that it now includes most of Canada, all of the northern and central states of the United States, and some of the colder waters in such southern states as Georgia, Tennessee, Arkansas, and Texas.

HABITAT: The rainbow, like all trout, must have cold, clean water, though it does fairly well under marginal conditions. It is found in shallow lakes and deep lakes, in small streams and large ones. It may be found at the surface one day, and feeding on the bottom the next. The rainbow's universality is due partly to the fact that it can do well in a wide variety of environments.

SIZE: The average nonmigratory stream rainbow runs from 6 to 18 inches in length, though some much larger specimens are occasionally taken. Nonmigratory lake fish tend to run considerably larger—up to 50 pounds or more. An average migratory steelhead runs from 8 to 12 pounds, but this strain reaches 35 pounds or so.

FOOD: Rainbows feed heavily on insect life, but they also eat baitfish, crustaceans, worms, and the roe of salmon and trout. The diet of the Kamloops rainbow is mainly kokanee salmon.

FISHING METHODS: Casting and trolling

BAITS: Baitfish, worms, salmon eggs, spoons, spinners, and flies

Cutthroat Trout *(Salmo clarki)*

COMMON NAMES: Cutthroat trout, coastal trout, cut, native trout, mountain trout, Rocky Mountain trout, black-spotted trout, harvest trout, Montana black-spotted trout, Tahoe cutthroat, and Yellowstone cutthroat

DESCRIPTION: Occurring in both nonmigratory and anadromous forms, the cutthroat trout gets its common name from the two slashes of crimson on the underside of its lower jaw. Its scientific name honors William Clark of the famed Lewis and Clark expedition. The cutthroat is often mistaken for the rainbow, but it lacks the rainbow's bright-red side stripe, and its entire body is usually covered with black spots, while the rainbow's spots are usually limited to the upper half of the body. The cutthroat usually has a greenish back, colorful gill plates, sides of yellow or pink, and a white belly. Coastal cutthroats are greenish blue with a silvery sheen on the sides and heavy black spots. The cutthroat is a fine sport fish, taking flies—particularly wet flies—readily and showing an inordinate liking for flashy spoons.

RANGE: The cutthroat is found from northern California north to Prince William Sound, Alaska, and inland throughout the western United States and Canada.

HABITAT: A fish of clean, cold water, the cutthroat frequents places like those preferred by the brook trout—undercut banks, deep holes, logs, and other debris. They prefer quiet water, generally, in streams. Unlike other trout that go to sea, anadromous cutthroats do not range widely in the ocean depths. Instead, they remain in bays at the mouths of their home streams or along the nearby ocean shores.

SIZE: Though cutthroats of up to 41 pounds have been caught by anglers, they seldom exceed 5 pounds and average 2 to 3 pounds. A fish weighing 4 pounds is considered large for a sea-run cutthroat.

FOOD: Young cutthroats feed mainly on insect life, while adults eat insects, baitfish, crayfish, and worms.

FISHING METHODS: Casting and trolling

BAITS: Insects, crayfish, worms, spoons, spinners, and flies

Golden Trout *(Salmo aquabonita)*

COMMON NAMES: Golden trout, Volcano trout, and Sierra trout

DESCRIPTION: This rare jewel of the western high country is the most beautiful of all trout. The golden trout has an olive back and crimson gill covers and side stripes, while the remainder of the body ranges from orangish yellow to gold. The dorsal fin has orange tips, and the anal and ventral fins have white edges. Each side

Cutthroat Trout

Golden Trout

contains about 10 black parr markings. The coloring differs from lake to lake. The golden is a rarely caught but highly prized sport fish.

RANGE: Originally found only in the headwaters of California's Kern River, the golden is now present in high-mountain lakes in many western states, including California, Wyoming, Idaho, and Washington. Modern fish-breeding and stocking techniques have extended the range of the golden—or, rather, a golden-rainbow trout cross—to the eastern states, including West Virginia and New Jersey.

HABITAT: The true golden trout is found in small, high lakes and their tributary streams at elevations of 9,000 to 12,000 feet. The water in these lakes is extremely cold, and weed growth is minimal or nonexistent. Because of the golden's spartan habitat, it can be extremely moody and difficult to catch.

SIZE: Golden trout are not large, a 2-pounder being a very good one, though some lakes hold fair numbers of fish up to 5 pounds. The maximum size is 11 pounds.

FOOD: Golden trout feed almost exclusively on minute insects, including terrestrial insects, but also eat tiny crustaceans and are sometimes caught by bait fishermen using worms, salmon eggs, and grubs.

FISHING METHODS: Casting and trolling

BAITS: Insects, worms, salmon eggs, spinners, and flies

Brown Trout

◼ Brown Trout *(Salmo trutta)*

COMMON NAMES: Brown trout, German brown trout, and Loch Leven trout

DESCRIPTION: Introduced in North America in the 1880s, the brown trout is a top-notch dry-fly fish, and yet its daytime wariness and whimsy can drive fishermen to the nearest bar. The brown trout is generally brownish to olive brown, shading from dark brown on the back to dusky yellow or creamy white on the belly. The sides, back, and dorsal fin have prominent black or brown spots, usually surrounded by faint halos of gray or white. Some haloed red or orange spots are also present. Sea-run browns and those in large lakes are often silvery and resemble landlocked salmon.

RANGE: The brown is the native trout of Europe and is also found in New Zealand, parts of Asia, South America, and Africa. It is found in the United States from coast to coast and as far south as New Mexico, Arkansas, and Georgia.

HABITAT: The brown trout can tolerate warmer water and other marginal conditions better than other trout species can. It is found in both streams and lakes, preferring hiding and feeding spots similar to those of the brook trout. It often feeds on the bottom in deep holes, coming to the surface at night.

SIZE: Brown trout have been known to exceed 40 pounds, though one of more than 10 pounds is exceptional. Most browns caught by sportfishermen weigh ½ to 1½ pounds.

FOOD: Brown trout feed on aquatic and terrestrial insects as well as worms, crayfish, baitfish, and fish roe. Large specimens will eat such tidbits as mice, frogs, and small birds.

FISHING METHODS: Casting and trolling

BAITS: Baitfish, insects, worms, salmon eggs, spoons, spinners, and flies

◼ Grayling *(Thymallus arcticus)*

COMMON NAMES: Grayling, Montana grayling, and Arctic grayling

Grayling

DESCRIPTION: Closely related to trout and whitefish, the grayling's most distinctive feature is its high, wide dorsal fin, which is gray to purple and has rows of blue or lighter dots. Its back is dark blue to gray, and the sides range from gray to brown to silvery, depending upon where the fish lives. The forepart of the body usually has irregularly shaped dark spots. The grayling is a strikingly handsome fish and a fly fisherman's dream.

RANGE: The grayling is abundant in Alaska, throughout northern Canada from northern Saskatchewan westward, and northward through the Northwest Territories. It is less common in the United States, ranging in high areas of Montana, Wyoming, and Utah. Recently developed grayling-breeding procedures are extending the range of this fish into Idaho, California, Oregon, and other mountain states.

HABITAT: The grayling is found in both lakes and rivers, but is particularly at home in high and isolated timberline lakes. In lakes, schools of grayling often cruise near the shore. In rivers, the fish are likely to be found anywhere, but they usually favor one type of water in any given stream.

SIZE: The maximum weight of the grayling is 20 pounds or a bit heavier, but in most waters, even in the Arctic, a 2-pounder is a good fish. In U.S. waters, grayling seldom top 1½ pounds.

FOOD: The grayling's diet is made up almost entirely of nymphs and other insects and aquatic larvae. However, this northern fish will also readily eat worms and crustaceans.

FISHING METHODS: Casting

BAITS: Nymphs, insects, worms, and flies

Rocky Mountain Whitefish
(*Prosopium williamsoni*)

COMMON NAMES: Rocky Mountain whitefish, mountain whitefish, and Montana whitefish

DESCRIPTION: The Rocky Mountain whitefish resembles the lake whitefish, though its body is more cylindrical. Coloration shades from brown on the back to silver on the sides to white on the belly. The dorsal fin is large, but not nearly as large as that of the grayling. Where it competes with trout in a stream, the Rocky Mountain whitefish is considered a nuisance by many anglers, though it fights well and will take dry and wet flies, spinning lures, and bait.

RANGE: The Rocky Mountain whitefish is endemic to the western slope of the Rocky Mountains from northern California to southern British Columbia.

HABITAT: Found in cold, swift streams and in clear, deep lakes, these whitefish school up in deep pools after spawning in the fall and feed mostly on the bottom. In spring, the fish move to the riffles in streams and the shallows in lakes.

SIZE: Rocky Mountain whitefish reach 5 pounds, but a 3-pounder is an exceptional one. The average length is 11 to 14 inches and the average weight is 1 pound.

FOOD: These fish feed almost entirely on such insects as caddis and midge larvae and stone fly nymphs. They also eat fish eggs, their own included.

FISHING METHODS: Casting and fly fishing (not an important game fish)

BAITS: Insects, nymphs, fish eggs, and flies

Lake Whitefish
(*Coregonus clupeaformis*)

COMMON NAMES: Lake whitefish, common whitefish, Great Lakes whitefish, Labrador whitefish, and Otsego bass

Rocky Mountain Whitefish

Lake Whitefish

DESCRIPTION: Similar in appearance—though only distantly related—to the Rocky Mountain whitefish, the lake whitefish has bronze or olive shading on the back, with the rest of the body being silvery white. It has rather large scales, a small head and mouth, and a blunt snout. Large specimens appear humpbacked. Lake whitefish, because they spend much of the year in very deep water, are not important sport fish.

RANGE: Lake whitefish are found from New England west through the Great Lakes area and throughout much of Canada.

HABITAT: These fish inhabit large, deep, cold, clear lakes and are usually found in water from 60 to 100 feet deep, though they will enter tributary streams in spring and fall. In the northern part of their range, however, lake whitefish are often found foraging in shallow water, and they will feed on the surface when mayflies are hatching.

SIZE: Lake whitefish reach weights of a bit more than 20 pounds, but their average size is less than 4 pounds.

FOOD: Lake whitefish feed primarily on small crustaceans and aquatic insects, but they will also eat baitfish.

FISHING METHODS: Casting (not an important game fish)

BAITS: Small baitfish, insects, and crustaceans

■ Cisco *(Coregonus artedii)*

COMMON NAMES: Cisco, herring, lake herring, common cisco, lake cisco, bluefin, Lake Erie cisco, tullibee, shortjaw chub, and grayback

DESCRIPTION: Though the cisco superficially resembles members of the herring family, it is not a herring but rather a member of the whitefish family. The cisco has a darker back (usually bluish or greenish) than the true whitefish. The body is silvery with large scales. There are more than 30 species and subspecies of ciscoes in the Great Lakes area alone, and all of them look and act alike. Ciscoes occasionally provide good sport fishing, particularly on dry flies, but they are more important commercially.

RANGE: The various strains of ciscoes occur from New England and New York west through the Great Lakes area and range widely through Canada. Their center of concentration seems to be the Great Lakes area.

HABITAT: Ciscoes prefer large, cold, clear lakes, usually those having considerable depth. Little is known of the wanderings of these fish; some species are found from the surface to several hundred feet down. They spawn in July and August over hard bottoms. In summer, ciscoes often come to the surface to feed on hatching insects, usually at sundown.

SIZE: The size of a cisco depends on its species. Some average only a few ounces in weight, while the largest attain a maximum weight of about 7 pounds. The average length is about 6 to 20 inches.

FOOD: Insect life—mainly bottom-dwelling types—is the blue-plate special of the cisco, though it sometimes feeds on surface insects and on minute crustaceans and worms as well.

FISHING METHODS: Fly fishing

BAITS: Insects, worms, and flies

■ American Shad *(Alosa sapidissima)*

DESCRIPTION: The American shad is an anadromous fish—meaning one that ascends coastal rivers to spawn but spends much of its life in salt water. A member of the herring family, the shad has a greenish back, with the remainder of the body being silvery. There are usually a few indistinct markings on the forebody. Shad put up a no-holds-barred battle on hook and line and are important sport and commercial fish, though pollution is putting a dent in their population in some areas.

RANGE: American shad were originally native only to the Atlantic, but they were introduced in the Pacific in

American Shad

the 1870s. On the Atlantic coast, they are found from Florida to the Gulf of St. Lawrence, while on the Pacific coast, they range from San Diego, California, to southern Alaska. They are also found in Scandinavia, France, Italy, Germany, Russia, and elsewhere.

HABITAT: American shad swarm up large, coastal rivers to spawn in the spring—from March to May, depending upon the location of the river. They are particularly susceptible to anglers below dams and in holes and slow runs just upstream of riffles, where they tend to rest before continuing upriver. They generally spawn in the main river.

SIZE: The average weight of an American shad is 3 to 5 pounds, while the maximum weight is 12 to 13 pounds. Egg-laden females are usually heavier than males.

FOOD: While in the ocean, American shad feed almost exclusively on plankton, so far as is known. After they enter fresh water on the spawning runs, these fish apparently do not feed at all. Curiously, however, they will strike at a small variety of artificial lures, including small, sparsely dressed wet flies and leadhead jigs tied on a gold hook and having a wisp of bucktail at the tail.

FISHING METHODS: Casting, jigs, and shad darts

BAITS: Artificial lures, small jigs, spinners, and spoons

■ Largemouth Bass
(*Micropterus salmoides*)

COMMON NAMES: Largemouth bass, bigmouth bass, black bass, green trout, Oswego bass, and green bass

DESCRIPTION: The largemouth bass is among the most important of this continent's freshwater game fish. In physical makeup it is a chunky fish, with coloration ranging from nearly black or dark green on the back, through varying shades of green or brownish green on the sides, to an off-white belly. The largemouth's most distinctive marking, however, is a horizontal, dark band running along its side from head to tail. In large, old bass particularly, the band may be almost invisible. There are two reliable ways to distinguish the largemouth from its close relative and look-alike, the smallmouth bass: the largemouth's upper jaw (maxillary) extends back behind the eye, while the smallmouth's does not; and the spiny part of the largemouth's dorsal fin is almost completely separated from the softer rear portion, while in the smallmouth the two fin sections are connected in one continuous fin.

RANGE: The largemouth is native to or stocked in every state in the Lower 48 and is found as far south as Mexico and as far north as southern Canada.

HABITAT: Largemouths are found in slow-moving streams large and small and in nonflowing waters ranging in size from little more than puddles to vast impoundments. They thrive best in shallow, weedy lakes and in river backwaters. They are warm-water fish, preferring water temperatures of 70°F to 75°F. Largemouths never venture too far from such areas as weed beds, logs, stumps, and other sunken debris, which provide both cover and food. They are usually found in water no deeper than 20 feet.

SIZE: Largemouth bass grow biggest in the southern United States, where they reach a maximum weight of a little more than 20 pounds and an 8- to 10-pounder is not a rarity. In the north, largemouths rarely exceed 10 pounds and a 3-pounder is considered a good catch.

FOOD: The largemouth's diet is as ubiquitous as the fish itself. These bass eat minnows and any other available baitfish, worms, crustaceans, a wide variety of insect life, frogs, mice, and ducklings.

Largemouth Bass

FISHING METHODS: Casting and trolling

BAITS: All baitfish, worms, crustaceans, frogs, artificial lures, and flies

■ Smallmouth Bass
(*Micropterus dolomieui*)

COMMON NAMES: Smallmouth bass, black bass, and bronzeback

DESCRIPTION: A top game fish and a flashy fighter, the smallmouth bass is brownish, bronze, or greenish brown in coloration, with the back being darker and the belly being off-white. The sides are marked with dark, vertical bars, which may be indistinguishable in young fish. (For physical differences between the smallmouth bass and its look-alike relative, the largemouth bass, see Largemouth Bass.) The smallmouth is not as common as, and is a wilder fighter than, the largemouth.

RANGE: The smallmouth's original range was throughout New England, southern Canada, and the Great Lakes area, and in large rivers of Tennessee, Arkansas, and Oklahoma. However, stocking has greatly widened this range so that it now includes states in northern and moderate climates from coast to coast.

HABITAT: Unlike the largemouth bass, the smallmouth is a fish of cold, clear waters (preferring water temperatures of no higher than 65°F or so). Large, deep lakes and sizable rivers are the smallmouth's domain, though it is often found in streams that look like good trout water—that is, those with numerous riffles flowing over gravel, boulders, or bedrock. In lakes, smallmouths are likely to be found over gravel bars, between submerged weed beds in water 10 to 20 feet deep, along drop-offs near shale banks, on gravel points running out from shore, and near midlake reefs or shoals. In streams, they often

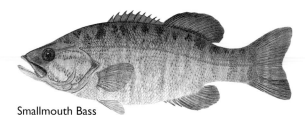
Smallmouth Bass

hold at the head of a pool where the water fans out, and in pockets having moderate current and nearby cover.

SIZE: The maximum weight attained by smallmouth bass is about 12 pounds. In most waters, however, a 4- or 5-pounder is a very good fish, and the average weight is probably 1½ to 3 pounds.

FOOD: Smallmouths eat baitfish and crayfish mainly, though they also feed on hellgrammites and other insect life, worms, small frogs, and leeches.

FISHING METHODS: Casting and trolling

BAITS: All baitfish, worms, crustaceans, crayfish, frogs, artificial lures, and flies

■ Redeye Bass (*Micropterus coosae*)

COMMON NAMES: Redeye bass, Coosa bass, shoal bass, and Chipola bass

DESCRIPTION: Given full status as a distinct species in about 1940, the redeye bass is a relative of the smallmouth. Though this fish is often difficult to identify positively, especially in adult form, the redeye young have dark, vertical bars that become indistinct with age and brick-red dorsal, anal, and caudal fins. This fin color and the red of its eyes are the redeye's most distinctive physical traits. The redeye is a good fighter and is good eating.

RANGE: An inhabitant of the southeastern states, the redeye bass is found mainly in Alabama, Georgia, and South Carolina. It is also found in the Chipola River system in Florida.

HABITAT: The redeye bass is mainly a stream fish, usually inhabiting upland parts of drainage systems. It often feeds at the surface.

SIZE: The maximum weight of the redeye bass is

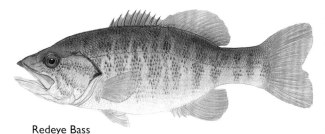
Redeye Bass

6 pounds, but, in Alabama at least, the average weight is about 12 ounces.

FOOD: A large portion of the redeye's diet is insects, but it also feeds on worms, crickets, and various baitfish.

FISHING METHODS: Casting and drift fishing

BAITS: Worms, crickets, small baitfish, spinners, spoons, and flies

Spotted Bass
(Micropterus punctulatus)

COMMON NAMES: Spotted bass, Kentucky bass, Kentucky spotted bass, and Alabama spotted bass

DESCRIPTION: The spotted bass, recognized as a distinct species only since 1927, is quite similar in appearance to the largemouth bass and has characteristics of both the largemouth and the smallmouth. The spotted bass is olive green on the back with many dark blotches, most of which are diamond shaped. A series of short blotches form a horizontal, dark band along the sides that is somewhat more irregular than that of the largemouth. Spots below the lateral line distinguish the spotted bass from the largemouth, and that spotting, plus the lack of vertical side bars, distinguishes it from the smallmouth bass.

RANGE: The spotted bass is found in the Ohio-Mississippi drainage from Ohio south to the states bordering the Gulf of Mexico and western Florida, and west to Texas, Oklahoma, and Kansas.

HABITAT: In the northern part of its range, the spotted bass prefers large, deep pools in sluggish waters. Its preferred habitat in the southern part of its range is quite different, consisting of cool streams with gravel bottoms and clear spring-fed lakes. In lakes, spotted bass are sometimes found in water as deep as 100 feet.

SIZE: The maximum weight of spotted bass is 8 pounds, but few specimens top 4 or 5 pounds.

FOOD: Spotted bass, like most other members of the bass family, feed on various baitfish and insects, frogs, worms, crustaceans, grubs, and the like.

FISHING METHODS: Casting and drift fishing

BAITS: Baitfish, worms, frogs, artificial lures, and flies

Bluegill *(Lepomis macrochirus)*

COMMON NAMES: Bluegill, bluegill sunfish, bream, sun perch, blue perch, blue sunfish, copperbelly, red-breasted bream, copperhead bream, and blue bream

DESCRIPTION: Many fishermen cut their angling teeth on the bluegill, the most widely distributed and most popular of the large sunfish family. The color of the bluegill varies probably more than that of any other sunfish, ranging in basic body color from yellow or orange to dark blue. The shading goes from dark on the back to light on the forward part of the belly. The sides of a bluegill are usually marked by six to eight irregular, vertical bars of a dark color. A bluegill's prominent features are a broad, black gill flap, and long, pointed pectoral fins. Bluegills are excellent fighters, and if they grew to largemouth-bass size, they would break a lot of tackle.

RANGE: The bluegill's range just about blankets the entire 48 contiguous states.

HABITAT: The bluegill prefers habitat very much like that of the largemouth bass—that is, quiet, weedy waters, in both lakes and streams, where it can find both cover and food. In daytime, the smaller bluegills are usually close to shore in coves, under overhanging trees, and around

Spotted Bass

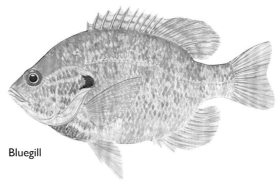

Bluegill

docks. The larger ones are usually nearby but in deeper water, moving into the shallows early and late in the day.

SIZE: The maximum size of bluegills is about 4½ pounds in weight and 15 inches in length, but the average length is 4 to 8 inches.

FOOD: A bluegill's food consists chiefly of insect life and vegetation. Other items on the menu include worms, grubs, small baitfish, crustaceans, small frogs, grasshoppers, and the like.

FISHING METHODS: Casting, still-fishing, fly fishing

BAITS: Small baitfish, worms, insects, crickets, grasshoppers, and flies

■ Redear Sunfish
(*Lepomis microlophus*)

COMMON NAMES: Redear sunfish, redear, shellcracker, stumpknocker, yellow bream, and chinquapin

DESCRIPTION: A large and very popular sunfish in the South, the redear has a small mouth, large and pointed pectoral fins, and a black gill flap with a whitish border (the bluegill lacks the white gill-flap border). The body color is olive with darker olive spots, and the sides have five to 10 dusky vertical bars. The redear is distinguishable from the pumpkinseed—the member of the sunfish family it most closely resembles—by the lack of spots on the dorsal fin.

RANGE: The redear sunfish ranges from southern Illinois and southern Indiana south to Florida and the other Gulf states and westward to Texas and New Mexico. Its heaviest concentration is in Florida.

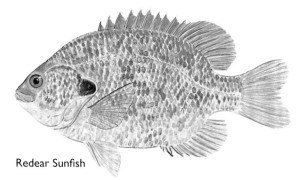
Redear Sunfish

HABITAT: The redear sunfish shows a definite liking for large, quiet waters, congregating around logs, stumps, and roots. It will, however, frequent open waters and seems to require less vegetation than other sunfish.

SIZE: The redear is more likely to run to a large size than most any other sunfish. The maximum weight seems to be 3 pounds, but 2-pounders are not uncommon.

FOOD: Redears depend mainly on snails for food, but will eat other mollusks, crustaceans, worms, and insects.

FISHING METHODS: Casting and still-fishing

BAITS: Small baitfish, worms, crickets, insects, artificial lures, and flies

■ White Crappie (*Pomoxis annularis*)

COMMON NAMES: White crappie, papermouth, bachelor perch, papermouth perch, strawberry bass, calico, calico bass, sago, and grass bass

DESCRIPTION: This popular freshwater panfish is a cousin to the true sunfish. In coloration, its back is olive green and its sides silvery olive with seven to nine dark vertical bands, while the sides of the very similar black crappie have irregular dark mottling. Another, more reliable way to tell the white crappie from the black is the number of spines in the dorsal fin: the white has six while the black has seven or eight. The white is more elongated in general shape, while the black, by comparison, has a high, rather arched back.

RANGE: The original range of the white crappie extended from Nebraska east to the Great Lakes, south through the Mississippi and Ohio River systems, and throughout most of the South as far north as North Carolina. Stocking has greatly extended that range, though the white crappie is still predominantly a southern species.

HABITAT: The white crappie can live under more turbid conditions than the black crappie—in fact, it prefers silty rivers and lakes to clear water and is common in southern impoundments and cypress bayous, warm and weedy ponds, and slow streams. The ideal home for these schooling fish is a pile of sunken brush or a submerged treetop. In summer, crappies often seek such a spot in deep holes, moving into the shallows in the evening to feed.

How to Be a Crappie Expert

It doesn't take an angling wizard to catch a few crappies, but if you want to feed dinner guests, you have to learn a few tricks.

Location is the key to productive crappie fishing. When you're working at shoreline, look for brush piles or downed trees, especially if a structure is on the edge of deep water. Pilings and docks are also hot spots for crappies. These areas typically attract baitfish.

Crappies are also dedicated school fish. Find one and you will find many. When you catch one crappie, toss a marker over the side and mark the school. You can fish the spot until they stop hitting. If you catch one and still can't locate the school, tie a balloon to the crappie and turn it loose. It will try to get back to the school and give away its location.

You can use worms, grubs, crickets, and grasshoppers, but the best bait for crappies is a small live minnow. If you're trolling slowly to locate a school, hook the minnow through both lips. If you're still-fishing, hook your bait just behind the dorsal fin. If you can't find natural baits, try using small Gulp baits. Gulp baits come in so many sizes and shapes that you will have no trouble finding one of these ascended baits that will work for you.

If you don't want to use bait, try a small jig. Crappies seem to be more sensitive to color than other species. Keep changing jig colors until you find one that works consistently. The jig should weigh $1/24$ ounce, and don't use anything heavier than 6-pound-test line. In fact, 2- or 4-pound-test line is even better.

Crappies are also year-round fish. You can catch them right in the middle of football season. But remember that during the winter months, many lakes turn over, which means the coldest water will be on the top and the warmest water will be on the bottom. This is particularly true in the South. Because crappies always seek a comfort zone, they will look for that deeper, warmer water during the cold months.

Also remember that a crappie's metabolism drops during cold weather, so you will have to fish baits and jigs slower and deeper. Crappies will not chase a bait as fast or as far as they will during spring and summer. The reverse is true during the warm months, when the warm water is on top and the colder water is on bottom.

Don't worry about catching too many crappies and hurting the resource. Crappies are prolific and can handle the pressure. It's a good species to target when you're fishing for the freezer.

Crappies are also excellent eating. Cut the fillets into bite-size pieces. Mix cornmeal, flour, and pepper in a bowl. Beat some eggs in another bowl, and then dip the fillets in the eggs and coat with the cornmeal mix. Fry in vegetable oil until the fillets are golden brown. It's as simple as that!

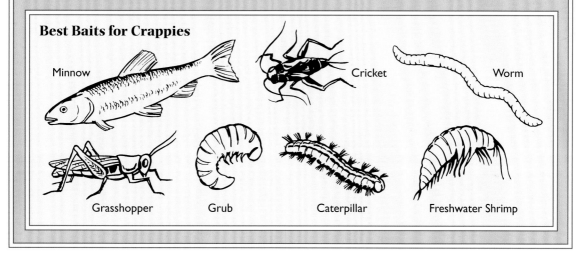

Best Baits for Crappies

Minnow

Cricket

Worm

Grasshopper

Grub

Caterpillar

Freshwater Shrimp

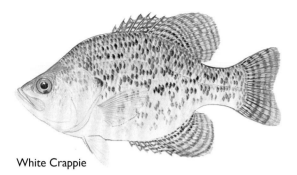

White Crappie

SIZE: White crappies average 6 to 10 inches in length and less than a pound in weight. However, individuals of more than 5 pounds have been caught by sportfishermen, and 2- or 3-pounders are not rare.

FOOD: White crappies eat baitfish for the most part—gizzard shad is their blue-plate special in southern lakes—but also feed on worms, shrimp, plankton, snails, crayfish, and insects.

FISHING METHODS: Casting and still-fishing

BAITS: Small baitfish, worms, crayfish, insects, jigs, and flies

■ Black Crappie
(Pomoxis nigromaculatus)

COMMON NAMES: Black crappie, calico bass, papermouth, and grass bass

DESCRIPTION: This near-identical twin of the white crappie is dark olive or black on the back. Its silvery sides and its dorsal, anal, and caudel fins contain dark and irregular blotches scattered in no special pattern. (For physical differences between the black and white crappie, see White Crappie.) Though it is a school fish like the white crappie, the black crappie does not seem to populate a lake or stream so thickly as does the white.

RANGE: The black crappie, though predominantly a northern U.S. fish, is found from southern Manitoba to southern Quebec, and from Nebraska to the East Coast and south to Texas and Florida. However, stocking has widened this range to include such places as British Columbia and California.

HABITAT: The black crappie prefers rather cool, clear,

weedy lakes and rivers, though it often shares the same waters as the white crappie. The black is a brush lover, tending to school up among submerged weed beds and the like. It occasionally feeds at the surface, particularly near nightfall.

SIZE: See White Crappie.

FOOD: See White Crappie.

FISHING METHODS: See White Crappie.

BAITS: See White Crappie.

■ White Bass *(Morone chrysops)*

COMMON NAMES: White bass, barfish, striped bass, and streak

DESCRIPTION: This freshwater member of the ocean-going sea-bass family has boomed in popularity among sportfishermen in recent years, thanks to its schooling habits, its eagerness to bite, tastiness of its flesh, and increase in its range. The white bass is a silvery fish tinged with yellow toward the belly. The sides have about 10 narrow, dark stripes, the body is moderately compressed, and the mouth is bass-like. The white bass may be distinguished from the look-alike yellow bass by its unbroken side stripes (those of the yellow bass are broken) and by its projecting lower jaw (the upper and lower jaws of the yellow are about even). The white bass is astonishingly prolific.

RANGE: White bass are found in the St. Lawrence River area and throughout the Mississippi and Missouri River systems, west into Texas, and in most of the other southern and southwestern states.

White Bass

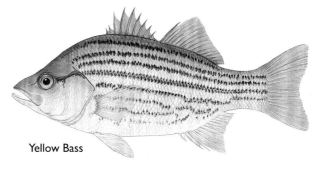

Yellow Bass

HABITAT: The white bass lives in large lakes and rivers, but it appears to prefer large lakes containing relatively clear water. The burgeoning number of large, deep reservoirs constructed recently in the South and Southwest are tailor-made for the white bass. These fish like large areas of deep water and need gravel or bottom rubble for spawning. Schools of whites can often be seen feeding voraciously on or near the surface, particularly in the evening.

SIZE: The maximum size of the white bass is about 6 pounds, but the average size is ½ to 2 pounds. A 3- or 4-pounder is an excellent specimen.

FOOD: Baitfish, particularly gizzard shad, form the main part of the white bass's diet, though it will also eat crustaceans, worms, and insect life.

FISHING METHODS: Casting and still-fishing

BAITS: Small baitfish, worms, insects, and artificial lures

■ Yellow Bass
(Morone mississippiensis)

COMMON NAMES: Yellow bass, barfish, brassy bass, stripe, striped bass, and streaker

DESCRIPTION: Quite similar in appearance to the white bass (for physical differences, see White Bass), the yellow bass has an olive-green back, silvery to golden-yellow sides with six or seven dark, horizontal, broken stripes, and a white belly. Like the white bass, the yellow bass is a member of the seabass family. It is a school fish, but its population levels tend to fluctuate drastically from year to year.

RANGE: The range of the yellow bass is quite restricted, being mainly the Mississippi River drainage from Minnesota to Louisiana and eastern Texas, plus the Tennessee River drainage, and Iowa. Even within its range, the yellow bass is found only in scattered lakes and streams.

HABITAT: One of the yellow bass's primary habitat requirements is wide, shallow, gravelly areas and rocky reefs. This fish prefers large lakes and large rivers, especially those with clear water. Yellow-bass schools tend to roam in deep water in daytime, coming into the shallows to feed late and very early.

SIZE: Most yellow bass caught by sportfishermen range from 8 to 11 inches, and from ¼ to ¾ pound. The maximum size is probably about 3 pounds.

FOOD: Yellow bass feed almost exclusively on baitfish, but occasionally take crustaceans and insects.

FISHING METHODS: Casting and still-fishing

BAITS: Small baitfish, worms, insects, jigs, and spinners

■ White Perch *(Morone americanus)*

COMMON NAMES: White perch, silver perch, and sea perch

DESCRIPTION: This fish is not a perch but rather a bass. And though it is often found in fresh water, it is not a freshwater bass. It is a member of the sea-bass family and superficially resembles one other member of that family—the saltwater striped bass—though it is much smaller. The white perch is greenish to blackish green on the back and silvery on the sides, particularly when living in salt water (freshwater individuals are usually darker). Young white perch have indistinct stripes on the sides, but adult fish lack them.

RANGE: In salt water, white perch range along the Atlantic coast from Nova Scotia to North Carolina. They are found inland as far as the Great Lakes and are especially abundant in New York State and New England.

HABITAT: In salt water, white perch are most likely to be found in brackish ponds and backwaters formed by coastal sandbars. Anadromous members of the clan run upriver to spawn. In inland lakes, these fish usually lie in deep water over a sand or gravel bottom during the day, sometimes at 50 feet or deeper, but often come into

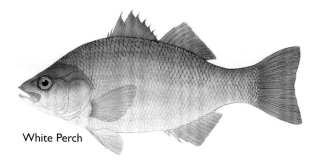

White Perch

shoreside shallows in the evening and at night to feed. At those times, and on dark days, schools of white perch may be seen breaking the surface.

SIZE: White perch seem to run larger in salt and brackish water than in fresh water. The average size, generally, is 8 to 10 inches. As for the weight, 2-pounders are not rare, but white perch seldom exceed 4 pounds.

FOOD: In salt water, white perch forage on small fish, shrimp, squid, crabs, and the like. In fresh water, their diet includes larval and other insect forms, crustaceans, baitfish, and worms.

FISHING METHODS: Casting

BAITS: Small baitfish, crabs, shrimp, crustaceans, spoons, and spinners

■ Yellow Perch *(Perca flavescens)*

COMMON NAMES: Yellow perch, ringed perch, striped perch, coon perch, and jack perch

DESCRIPTION: The yellow perch, in no way related to the white perch, is an extremely popular freshwater panfish. Though its colors may vary, the back is generally olive, shading to golden yellow on the sides and white on the belly. Six to eight rather wide, dark, vertical bands run from the back to below the lateral line. Though the body is fairly elongated, the fish has a somewhat humpbacked appearance.

RANGE: The yellow perch is a ubiquitous species, being found in most areas of the United States. It is most common from southern Canada south through the Dakotas and Great Lakes states into Kansas and Missouri, and in the East from New England to the Carolinas. Stockings have also established it in such places as Montana and the Pacific slope.

HABITAT: The yellow perch is predominantly a fish of lakes large and small, though it is also found in rivers. It prefers cool, clean water with plenty of sandy or rocky-bottomed areas, though it does well in a wide variety of conditions. As a very general rule, the best perch lakes are large and have only moderate weed growth. These fish feed at various levels, and the fisherman must experiment until he finds them.

SIZE: The average yellow perch weighs a good deal less than a pound, though 2-pounders aren't uncommon. The maximum weight is about 4½ pounds.

FOOD: Yellow perch eat such tidbits as baitfish (including their own young), worms, large plankton, insects in various forms, crayfish, snails, and small frogs.

FISHING METHODS: Casting and trolling

BAITS: Small baitfish, worms, crayfish, insects, jigs, spinners, and flies

■ Walleye *(Stizostedion vitreum)*

COMMON NAMES: Walleye, walleyed pike, pike, jack, jackfish, pickerel, yellow pickerel, blue pickerel, dore, and pikeperch

DESCRIPTION: The walleye is not a pike or pickerel, as its nicknames might indicate, but rather the largest member of the perch family. Its most striking physical characteristic is its large, almost opaque eyes, which appear to be made of glass and which reflect light eerily. The walleye's colors range from dark olive or olive brown on the back to a lighter olive on the sides and white on the belly. Here's how to tell the walleye from its look-alike relative, the sauger: the lower fork of the

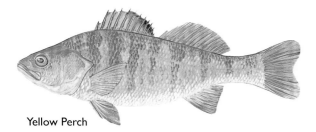

Yellow Perch

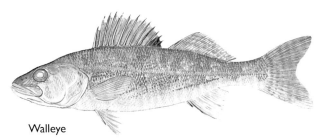

Walleye

walleye's tail has a milky-white tip, absent in the sauger; and the walleye's dorsal-fin foresection has irregular blotches or streaks, unlike the definite rows of spots found on the sauger's dorsal. The walleye isn't the best fighter among game fish, but it makes up for that shortcoming by providing delectable eating.

RANGE: The walleye is found in most of Canada as far north as Great Slave Lake and Labrador. Its original U.S. range was pretty much limited to the northern states, but stocking has greatly widened this range to include all of the East and most of the Far West and southern states.

HABITAT: The walleye loves clear, deep, cold, and large waters, both lakes and rivers, and prefers a sand, gravel, or rock bottom. It is almost always found on or near the bottom, though during evening and night hours it may move into shallow water to feed. Once you find a walleye hole, you should catch fish there consistently, for walleyes are schooling fish and are unlikely to move their places of residence.

SIZE: The top weight of walleyes is about 25 pounds, but a 6- to 8-pounder is a brag fish. Most walleyes that end up on fishermen's stringers weigh 1 to 3 pounds.

FOOD: Walleyes feed primarily on small fish and crayfish. Strangely enough, though they don't often eat worms, night crawlers are a real walleye killer, especially when combined with a spinner.

FISHING METHODS: Casting and trolling

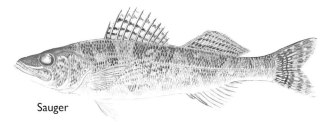

Sauger

BAITS: Baitfish, worms, frogs, crayfish, spinners, and spoons

▣ Sauger *(Stizostedion canadense)*

COMMON NAMES: Sauger, sand pike, gray pike, river pike, spotfin pike, and jack fish

DESCRIPTION: The sauger is very much like the walleye in all important respects, except that it is quite a bit smaller. It is olive or olive gray on its back and sides and has a white belly. Its large, glassy eyes are also like those of the walleye. (For physical differences between the sauger and the walleye, see Walleye.)

RANGE: The sauger's range is generally a blueprint of the walleye's. However, sauger are most common in the Great Lakes, other very large lakes in the northern United States and southern Canada, and in large rivers (and their tributaries), such as the Mississippi, Missouri, Ohio, and Tennessee.

HABITAT: In this category, too, the sauger is much like the walleye, though the sauger can tolerate siltier or murkier water than the walleye and tends to stick to deeper waters. A good place to look for sauger is in tailwaters below dams.

SIZE: The sauger's maximum weight is about 8 pounds. Its average size is 1 to 2 pounds.

FOOD: See Walleye.

FISHING METHODS: See Walleye.

BAITS: Baitfish, worms, frogs, crayfish, jigs, and spinners

▣ White Sturgeon *(Acipenser transmontanus)*

DESCRIPTION: This huge, primitive throwback to geological history is one of 16 species of sturgeon in the world, seven of which occur in the United States. It is the largest fish found in this country's inland waters and the only member of the sturgeon family that is considered a game fish. The white sturgeon does not have scales but rather five rows of bony plates along its body. It has a large, underslung, sucking mouth, and its

White Sturgeon

skeleton is cartilage rather than true bone. Sturgeon roe is better known as caviar. Though relatively few anglers fish for these behemoths, careful regulation of the fishery is necessary to prevent depletion of the populations of white sturgeon.

RANGE: The white sturgeon is found along the Pacific coast from Monterey, California, to Alaska. It is also found inland in the largest of rivers, including the Columbia and Snake.

HABITAT: Some white sturgeon are entirely landlocked, but many spend much of their lives at sea and ascend large West Coast rivers to spawn. In large rivers, they lie on the bottom in deep holes.

SIZE: The largest white sturgeon reported taken pulled the scales down to 1,800 pounds. The average size is difficult to determine.

FOOD: In fresh water, the white sturgeon uses its vacuum-cleaner mouth to inhale crustaceans, mollusks, insect larvae, and all manner of other bottom-dwelling organisms. Bait used by sturgeon anglers includes night crawlers, lamprey eels, cut bait, and even dried river moss.

FISHING METHODS: This species is not typically sought by fishermen (check regulations).

BAITS: Worms, eels, and baitfish

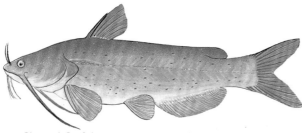

Channel Catfish

◼ Channel Catfish
(Ictalurus punctatus)

COMMON NAMES: Channel catfish and fiddler

DESCRIPTION: This sizable member of the large catfish family (which includes bullheads) is undoubtedly the most streamlined, gamest, and most agile of the whole clan. In coloration, the channel cat is steely blue on top and shades to white on the belly, though young ones may be silvery even along the back. It is the only spotted catfish (it has dark speckles on the sides, though these spots may be missing in large specimens) with a deeply forked tail.

RANGE: The channel catfish occurs from the Saskatchewan River and entire Great Lakes area southward into Mexico. Stocking has transplanted this fish far west and east of its natural range.

HABITAT: Channel catfish are found in lakes, but they are more common in rivers, especially large ones. They are likely to be found in faster, cleaner water than other catfish and seem to prefer a bottom composition of sand, gravel, or rock. Like all other catfish, they are bottom-feeders and are especially active at night.

SIZE: Channel cats are among the larger members of the catfish family, attaining weights of up to 60 pounds. The average size is 1 to 5 pounds.

FOOD: The channel cat's varied menu includes just about anything it can get its jaws around—small fish, insects, crustaceans, worms, grubs, frogs, and many other aquatic food forms.

FISHING METHODS: Still-fishing and drift fishing in rivers

BAITS: Small fish, insects, worms, frogs, crustaceans, and stink baits

◼ Blue Catfish *(Ictalurus furcatus)*

DESCRIPTION: The blue is the largest member of the catfish clan. It has a deeply forked tail, but lacks the spots of the channel catfish. In color, the blue catfish is pale blue on the back, a lighter silvery blue on the sides, and white on the belly. The most reliable way to tell the

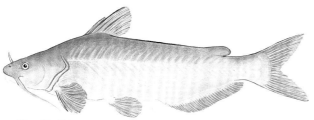

Blue Catfish

blue from other catfish is by the number of rays on its straight-edged anal fin (there are 30 to 36 rays).

RANGE: The blue catfish is found mainly in the Mississippi River system, but it occurs south into Mexico and has been introduced into some rivers on the Atlantic coast.

HABITAT: The blue is a catfish of large rivers and is likely to be found below the dams creating large impoundments, especially in the southern United States. It prefers less-turbid waters than do most other catfish and seems to do best over bottoms of rock, gravel, or sand. It feeds in rapids or fast chutes.

SIZE: This heavyweight grows to more than 100 pounds. The average size, however, is 2 to 15 pounds.

FOOD: The blue catfish feeds primarily on small fish and crayfish. A favorite bait in some areas is a whole golden shad.

FISHING METHODS: Bottom fishing and drift fishing

BAITS: Baitfish, worms, crustaceans, and stink baits

■ Brown Bullhead *(Ictalurus nebulosus)*

COMMON NAMES: Brown bullhead, horned pout, and speckled bullhead

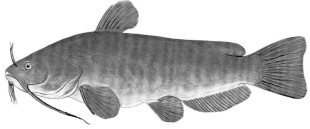

Brown Bullhead

DESCRIPTION: Probably the most popular of the catfish—at least, it's the most often caught—the brown bullhead is a rather slender catfish with typical catfish features: sharp dorsal spine and sensitive barbels (the "feelers" projecting from the mouth area). The brown bullhead's chin barbels are dark brown or black. The tail has almost no fork, and the anal fin has 22 or 23 rays. The back is yellowish brown to light chocolate brown and has vague dark mottling, the sides are lighter, and the belly is yellow to milky white.

RANGE: Brown bullheads occur from Maine and the Great Lakes south to Mexico and Florida, but stocking has greatly expanded this range.

HABITAT: Brown bullheads prefer relatively deep, weedy waters in lakes and slow-moving streams. They may be found over sand and gravel bottoms and also over mud. They are almost exclusively bottom-feeders.

SIZE: The brown bullhead seldom weighs more than 3 pounds, with its average length being 6 to 16 inches.

FOOD: Insect larvae and mollusks constitute the majority of the brown bullhead's menu, but it will eat almost anything, from worms, small fish, and frogs to plant material and even chicken livers (a favorite catfisherman's bait).

FISHING METHODS: Still-fishing and drift fishing

BAITS: Baitfish, worms, frogs, and stink baits

■ Black Bullhead *(Ictalurus melas)*

COMMON NAMES: Black bullhead and horned pout

DESCRIPTION: Quite similar in appearance to the brown bullhead, the black bullhead is black to yellow green on the back, yellowish or whitish on the sides, and bright yellow, yellow, or milky on the belly. Its chin barbels are dark or spotted, and its pectoral spines have no serrations. The body is chunky.

RANGE: The areas in which the black bullhead is most numerous are New York, west to the Dakotas, and south to Texas. However, the fish has been introduced into most other areas of the United States.

HABITAT: The black bullhead is a fish of muddy, sluggish,

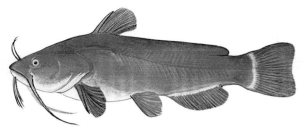

Black Bullhead

turbid streams and lakes. It seems to do well, in fact, in any kind of environment except cool, clear, deep water. It is a bottom-feeder.

SIZE: The largest black bullhead taken by sport fishing weighed 8 pounds, but this catfish seldom weighs more than 2 pounds.

FOOD: See Brown Bullhead.

FISHING METHODS: Bottom fishing and drift fishing

BAITS: Small baitfish, worms, crustaceans, and stink baits

■ Carp *(Cyprinus carpio)*

COMMON NAMES: Carp and common carp

DESCRIPTION: This big, coarse, much-maligned rough fish belongs to the minnow family and is related to the goldfish. In color, the carp is olive to light brown on the back, golden yellow on the sides, and yellowish white on the belly. At the base of each of its large scales is a dark spot. On each side of the upper jaw are a pair of fleshy barbels, and the dorsal fin has a serrated spine. Though the carp is cussed out by most sportfishermen and often poisoned out of lakes and streams, it is taken by rod and line, bow and arrow, spear, ice gig, and set line, and it can put up a whale of a battle.

RANGE: Introduced into the United States in 1876, the carp has found its way into just about every area in the nation. It is also widely distributed throughout Europe and Asia.

HABITAT: The carp can live almost anywhere and under almost any conditions—except cold, clear waters. It is almost always found on the bottom, except during spawning, when schools of carp are often seen slashing around on the surface.

SIZE: Carp reach a maximum size of about 60 pounds, but the average weight is 8 to 15 pounds.

FOOD: Carp are mainly vegetarians, feeding on aquatic plant life and plankton, though they also eat insects and are often caught by anglers on doughballs, cornmeal, and such.

FISHING METHODS: Bottom fishing

BAITS: Mostly doughball mixtures

■ Alligator Gar *(Lepisosteus spatula)*

DESCRIPTION: Exceeded in size in fresh water only by the western sturgeons, the alligator gar is the largest of the ancient gar family. It can be distinguished from its relatives by an examination of the teeth. Young alligator gars have two rows of large teeth on each side of the upper jaw; other gars have only a single row. The alligator gar has a long, cylindrical body that is olive green or brownish green along the back and lighter below. The sides and rear fins have mottling or large, dark spots. Gars are of minor importance as sport fish, though they wage a wild, no-holds-barred battle when taken on rod and line.

RANGE: The alligator gar is found mainly in the Mississippi and Ohio River systems as far north as Louisville, Kentucky, and St. Louis, Missouri, and as far south as northeastern Mexico.

HABITAT: Alligator gars prefer sluggish rivers, lakes, and backwaters over muddy, weedy bottoms. They often congregate in loose schools, usually near the surface, where they roll around.

SIZE: The largest reported alligator gar was 10 feet long and weighed 302 pounds. The average size, however, is undetermined.

FOOD: Various kinds of fish, notably the freshwater drum (or gaspergou), are the principal food of alligator gars, though anglers catch them on wire nooses baited with minnows and on bunches of floss-like material that tangle tenaciously in the gar's teeth.

FISHING METHODS: Bottom fishing and drift fishing

BAITS: Baitfish (though most fishermen catch this fish with any material that will tangle in the gar's teeth)

■ Longnose Gar *(Lepisosteus osseus)*

DESCRIPTION: The longnose gar is the most common and most widely distributed of the entire gar family. Its name derives from its long, slender beak (nose). Other distinguishing characteristics are its overlapping diamond-shaped scales and the unusual position of its dorsal fin—far back near the tail and almost directly above the anal fin. The coloration is similar to that of the alligator gar.

RANGE: The longnose gar occurs from Quebec's St. Lawrence drainage west to the Great Lakes (excluding Lake Superior) and as far as Montana, south along the Mississippi River system, and down into Mexico.

HABITAT: The longnose lives in much the same habitat as the alligator gar, though it is more likely to be found swimming and feeding in flowing water—that is, where there is a moderate current.

SIZE: Smaller by far than the alligator gar, the longnose reaches a length of 4 to 5 feet.

FOOD: The longnose, like the alligator gar, feeds mostly on other fish, though it also eats plankton and insect larvae when young.

FISHING METHODS: Drift fishing

BAITS: See Alligator Gar.

■ Muskellunge *(Esox masquinongy)*

COMMON NAMES: Muskellunge, maskinonge (and a variety of other spellings), muskie, pike, blue pike, great pike, jack, spotted muskellunge, barred muskellunge, and tiger muskellunge

DESCRIPTION: Moody, voracious, and predaceous, the muskellunge, the largest member of the pike family, presents one of the greatest challenges of any freshwater fish. Its adherents probably catch fewer fish per

Muskellunge

hour than do those who fish for any other freshwater species, and yet muskie fishermen are legion—and growing in number. The muskellunge—whose name means "ugly fish" in Ojibway dialect—is green to brown to gray in overall color, depending upon its geographical location. Side markings are usually vertical bars, though the fish may be blotched or spotted or lack any distinctive markings. The muskie has no scales on the lower part of its cheek and gill covers; other members of the pike family have scales in those areas. There are three subspecies of the muskellunge: the Great Lakes muskie, the Ohio (or Chautauqua) muskie, and the tiger (or northern) muskie.

RANGE: The Great Lakes muskie is generally a fish of the Great Lakes basin area. The Ohio (Chautauqua) muskie occurs in New York's Chautauqua Lake and through the Ohio River drainage. The tiger (northern) muskie is common in Wisconsin, Minnesota, and western Michigan. In overall distribution, the muskellunge is found as far north as the James Bay and Hudson Bay drainages in northern Canada, across the northern United States, from Wisconsin east to New York and Pennsylvania, and south into Tennessee, North Carolina, Georgia, and in much of the northern Mississippi drainage. Stocking and propagation methods are greatly widening the muskie's range.

HABITAT: Muskies live in rivers, streams, and lakes, usually only in clear waters, though they may inhabit discolored water in the southern part of their range. They prefer cold waters, but they can tolerate water as warm as 70°F to 75°F. Favorite hangouts for adult muskies are shoreline weed beds, particularly near deep water, and such items of cover as logs, stumps, and rocks. They are usually found in water shallower than 15 feet, though midsummer may find them as deep as 50 feet.

SIZE: Muskies can reach weights of more than 100 pounds. However, the biggest rod-caught specimen weighed just shy of 70 pounds, and the average is 10 to 20 pounds.

Northern Pike

FOOD: Muskies feed mainly on fish, including their own young, as well as suckers, yellow perch, bass, and panfish. They also eat crayfish, snakes, muskrats, worms, frogs, ducklings, squirrels, and just about anything else they can sink their ample teeth into.

FISHING METHODS: Casting and trolling

BAITS: Baitfish, small bass, panfish, worms, frogs, ducklings, big spoons, and plugs

■ Northern Pike *(Esox lucius)*

COMMON NAMES: Northern pike, pike, northern, snake, great northern, jackfish, and jack

DESCRIPTION: This baleful-looking predator of the weed bed is of great importance as a sport fish. In color, it is dark green on the back, shading to lighter green on the sides and whitish on the belly. Its distinctive side markings are bean-shaped light spots, and it has dark-spotted fins. The entire cheek is scaled, but only the upper half of the gill cover contains scales. The dorsal fin, as in all members of its family, is far to the rear of the body, almost directly above the anal fin.

RANGE: The pike is found in northern waters all around the globe. In North America, it occurs from Alaska east to Labrador, and south from the Dakotas and the St. Lawrence River to Nebraska and Pennsylvania. Stockings have extended this range to such states as Montana, Colorado, North Carolina, and Maryland.

HABITAT: Over its entire range, the pike's preferred living conditions are shallow, weedy lakes (large and small); shallow areas of large, deep lakes; and rivers of moderate current. In summer, pike are normally found in about 4 feet of water near cover; in fall, they are found along steep, stormy shores.

SIZE: In the best Canadian pike lakes, rod-caught pike average 5 to 25 pounds, but in most waters, a 10- to 15-pounder is a very good pike. The maximum weight is a little more than 50 pounds.

FOOD: Pike are almost entirely fish eaters, but they are as voracious and predacious as the muskie and will eat anything that won't eat them first.

FISHING METHODS: Casting and trolling

BAITS: Baitfish, small bass, perch, panfish, worms, frogs, spoons, spinners, plugs, and flies

■ Chain Pickerel *(Esox niger)*

COMMON NAMES: Chain pickerel, jack, and chainsides

DESCRIPTION: This attractive pike-like fish with chain-like markings is the largest of the true pickerels. Its body color ranges from green to bronze, darker on the back and lighter on the belly. Its distinctive dark, chain-like side markings and larger size make the chain pickerel hard to confuse with the other, less common pickerel (mud or grass pickerel and barred or redfin pickerel).

RANGE: The chain pickerel originally was found only east and south of the Alleghenies, but its range now extends from Maine to the Great Lakes in the north and from Texas to Florida in the south.

HABITAT: The pickerel is almost invariably a fish of the weeds. It lurks in or around weed beds and lily pads, waiting to pounce on unsuspecting morsels. It is usually found in water no deeper than 10 feet, although in hot weather it may retreat to depths of as much as 25 feet.

SIZE: Chain pickerel attain a maximum weight of about 10 pounds, but one of 4 pounds is bragging size. The average weight is 1 to 2½ pounds.

FOOD: Chain pickerel eat fish for the most part, although they will also readily dine on frogs, worms, crayfish, mice, and insects.

Chain Pickerel

FISHING METHODS: Casting and trolling

BAITS: Baitfish, worms, frogs, crayfish, spoons, spinners, plugs, and flies

▨ Redhorse Sucker
(Maxostoma macrolepidotum)

COMMON NAMES: Redhorse sucker, redhorse, northern redhorse, redfin, redfin sucker, and bigscale sucker

DESCRIPTION: Many anglers look at the entire sucker clan—of which the redhorse is probably the best known and most widely fished for—as pests or worse. And yet countless suckers are caught on hooks, netted, trapped, and speared every year, particularly in the spring, when their flesh is firm and most palatable. The redhorse, like all other suckers, has a large-lipped, tubelike, sucking mouth on the underside of its snout. Its overall color is silver, with the back somewhat darker. The mouth has no teeth, and the fins lack spines.

RANGE: The redhorse is found east of the Rocky Mountains from the midsouth of the United States north to central and eastern Canada.

HABITAT: Unlike some of its relatives, the redhorse prefers clean, clear waters and is at home in large and medium-size rivers, even swift-flowing ones, and in lakes. These fish seem to prefer sandy shallows in lakes, and deep holes in streams. As spawning runs begin in the spring, the redhorse congregates at the mouths of streams.

SIZE: The redhorse sucker's maximum weight is about 12 pounds. Most of the redhorses taken by anglers weigh 2 to 4 pounds.

FOOD: This bottom-feeding species eats various small fish, worms, frogs, crayfish, various insects (both aquatic and terrestrial), and insect larvae.

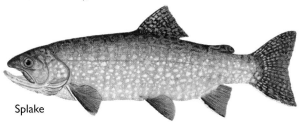
Splake

FISHING METHODS: This species is not typically sought by fishermen.

BAITS: Small baitfish, worms, insects, and fish eggs

▨ Splake
(Salvelinus namaycush x S. fontinalis)

DESCRIPTION: The splake is a trout hybrid created by crossing lake trout with brook trout. The name is a combination of *speckled* (brook) trout and *lake* trout. The first important crossing of these two trout species was done in British Columbia in 1946, and some of the new strain was stocked in lakes in Banff National Park in Alberta. The body shape of the splake is midway between that of the brook trout and lake trout—heavier than the laker, slimmer than the brookie. Like the true lake trout, the splake's spots are yellow, but its belly develops the deep orange or red of the true brook trout (see Brook Trout and Lake Trout). Splake mature and grow faster than lake trout. Unlike many other hybrids, the splake is capable of reproducing.

RANGE: The splake's range is quite spotty, including a number of lakes in western Canada, at least one of the Great Lakes, and a few lakes in the northern United States. Stockings are slowly increasing this range.

HABITAT: See Lake Trout.

SIZE: The world-record splake, caught in Georgian Bay, Ontario, Canada, was 20 pounds, 11 ounces.

FOOD: See Lake Trout.

FISHING METHODS: See Lake Trout.

BAITS: Baitfish, smelt, insects, crustaceans, spoons, spinners, and plugs

▨ Tiger Trout
(Salmo trutta x Salvelinus fontinalis)

DESCRIPTION: This hybrid is a cross between the female brown trout and the male brook trout. The tiger's most prominent physical characteristic is the well-defined vermiculations (wormlike markings) on its back and sides. Its lower fins have the white edges of the true brook trout. The tiger is an avid surface-feeder and is considerably more aggressive than either of its parent species. Under hatchery conditions, only 35 percent of the tiger's offspring develop. The tiger occasionally occurs under natural conditions, but it does not reproduce.

RANGE: The tiger, being a hybrid, has no natural range, but stockings have introduced it into a few streams in the United States. At least one state, New Jersey, has stocked this trout in its waters on an experimental basis.

HABITAT: The tiger's habitat is undetermined, but it is probably similar to that of the brook trout.

SIZE: The world-record tiger trout, caught in Lake Michigan, Wisconsin, was 20 pounds, 13 ounces.

FOOD: The tiger's food is undetermined, but it is probably similar to that of the brook trout.

FISHING METHODS: Casting and drift fishing

BAITS: Spoons, spinners, and flies

■ Rock Bass *(Ambloplites rupestris)*

COMMON NAMES: Rock bass, goggle eye, redeye, rock sunfish, black perch, and goggle-eye perch

DESCRIPTION: The rock bass isn't a bass—it's one of the sunfishes. And though it isn't much of a fighter, it is fun to catch and is sometimes unbelievably willing to gobble any lure, bait, or fly it can get its jaws around. The basic color of the rock bass is dark olive to greenish bronze, with a lighter belly. The sides contain brownish or yellowish blotches, and a dark spot at the base of each scale produces broken horizontal streaks. The mouth is much larger than that of most other sunfishes, and the anal fin has six spines, while the anal fin of most other sunfishes has only three spines. There is a dark blotch on the gill flap.

RANGE: The rock bass occurs from southern Manitoba east to New England, and south to the Gulf states. Stockings have somewhat widened this range in recent years.

HABITAT: Rock bass prefer large, clear streams and lakes and are often found in the same waters as smallmouth bass. As their name suggests, the more rocks and stones

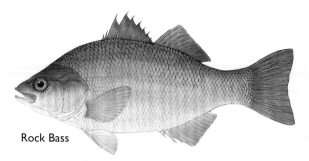

Rock Bass

on the bottom of the stream or lake, the better a fisherman's chances of finding rock bass. The species seems to prefer pools or protected waters to fast current or open waters.

SIZE: The top weight of the rock bass is a bit more than 2 pounds. Most of those caught by fishermen are 6 to 10 inches long and weigh about ½ pound.

FOOD: A voracious eater, the rock bass eats crawfish, minnows and other baitfish, worms, adult and larval insect life, and the like.

FISHING METHODS: Casting and drift fishing

BAITS: Small baitfish, worms, crayfish, spoons, spinners, and flies

■ Hickory Shad *(Alosa mediocris or Pomolobus mediocris)*

DESCRIPTION: The hickory shad—like its larger relative, the American shad—is a herring. In color, it is gray green above, with silvery sides and underparts. Behind the upper part of the gill cover is a horizontal row of dark spots, usually numbering about six. Spots on the upper rows of scales form faint horizontal lines. It has a shallow-notched upper jaw, and the lower jaw projects prominently. The hickory shad is not so important a food or sport fish as is the American shad.

RANGE: The hickory shad is found along the Atlantic coast from the Bay of Fundy south to Florida.

HABITAT: An anadromous species (it lives in salt water but ascends freshwater rivers to spawn), the hickory shad's movements in the ocean are little known. But in the spring, it goes up the rivers, often the same rivers in which American shad spawn, though its runs usually precede those of the American shad.

SIZE: Though 5-pounders have been reported, the hickory shad seldom tops 2½ pounds in weight or 24 inches in length.

FOOD: The hickory shad feeds more on fish than does the American shad, and it is often caught by anglers using artificial flies and small spoons.

FISHING METHODS: Small jigs, shad darts, small spoons, spinners, and flies

BAITS: Artificial lures

■ Freshwater Drum
(Aplodinotus grunniens)

COMMON NAMES: Freshwater drum, sheepshead, gray bass, gaspergou, white perch, croaker, crocus, jewel-head, and grunter

DESCRIPTION: This species is the only freshwater member of the drum (croaker) family, which has about three dozen saltwater members. The freshwater drum has a blunt head, rounded tail, long dorsal fin, and a humped back. Colors are pearly gray on the back and upper sides, silver on the remainder of the sides, and milky white on the belly. A rather faint lateral line runs all the way into the tail. These fish make a weird "drumming" noise that, when they feed near the surface on calm evenings, seems to come from everywhere. It is caused by repeated contractions of an abdominal muscle against the swim bladder. Another oddity: the otoliths, or ear bones, of freshwater drum were used by Indians as wampum, as lucky pieces, and to prevent sicknesses.

RANGE: Freshwater drum are found from Guatemala north through eastern Mexico and the Gulf states to Manitoba, northern Ontario, Quebec, and the Lake Champlain area. East to west, they range from the Atlantic coast to the Missouri River drainage.

HABITAT: Found principally in large lakes and large, slow rivers, this species prefers modest depths (10 to 40 feet) and silty or muddy bottoms. It is a school fish, often congregating below large dams.

SIZE: Freshwater drum attain a maximum weight of about 60 pounds, but the average size is 1 to 5 pounds.

FOOD: Primarily a bottom-feeder, this species feeds almost entirely on mollusks—clams, mussels, and snails—which it "shells" with its large, strong teeth. Other foods include crawfish and some baitfish.

FISHING METHODS: Bottom fishing and drift fishing

BAITS: Clams, mussels, crawfish, snails, and baitfish

SALTWATER GAME FISH

Section Seven
SALTWATER GAME FISH

■ Blue Shark (*Prionace glauca*)

DESCRIPTION: This large shark species, which has a reputation as a man-eater, is distinguished by its abnormally long pectoral fins and by its bright-cobalt color (the belly is white). It has the long snout of many members of the large shark family, and the dorsal fin is set well back on the back, nearly at the midpoint.

RANGE: Blue sharks are found throughout the tropical and temperate waters of the world.

HABITAT: Though often seen in shallow waters on the Pacific coast of the United States and on the surface in other northern areas, the blue shark is usually caught in deep water. It often roams in packs, while at other times it is found singly or in pairs.

SIZE: Blue sharks average less than 10 feet in length, but they have been reported to attain lengths of more than 20 feet. The largest rod-caught blue shark weighed 410 pounds.

FOOD: Blue sharks eat mainly mackerel, herring, squid, other sharks, flying fish, anchovies, and even such tidbits as seagulls and garbage deep-sixed from ships.

FISHING METHODS: Chumming and trolling from boats

BAITS: Whole or cut fish (and occasionally artificial lures)

■ Mako Shark (*Isurus oxyrinchus*)

COMMON NAMES: Mako shark and mackerel shark

DESCRIPTION: This huge, dangerous, fast-swimming, hard-fighting shark is closely related to the white shark.

Blue Shark

It differs from the white mainly in the dorsal and pectoral fins, the tips of which are rounded in the mako, rather than pointed in the white. In color, the mako is dark blue to bluish gray above, shading to silver on the belly. The mako differs from the porbeagle shark in that its second dorsal fin is positioned a bit forward of the anal fin, while the porbeagle's second dorsal is directly above the anal fin.

RANGE: The mako is an inhabitant of the tropical oceans and the warmer areas of the Atlantic Ocean. In U.S. waters, it is found as far north as Cape Cod. It seems to be most numerous around New Zealand.

HABITAT: Makos tend to stay near the surface in open-ocean areas.

SIZE: Makos reach lengths of more than 12 feet and weights of more than 1,000 pounds.

FOOD: Staples of the mako's diet include tuna, mackerel, and herring. For some reason, it often attacks, but seldom kills, swordfish.

Mako Shark

FISHING METHODS: Trolling and chumming

BAITS: Whole or cut fish and scrap meat (and occasionally artificial lures)

■ White Shark *(Carcharodon carcharias)*

COMMON NAMES: White shark, great white shark, and man-eater

DESCRIPTION: The white shark—enormous, vicious, and incredibly powerful—is one of the largest of all fish. Its usual colors are grayish brown, slate blue, or gray, while the belly is off-white. Large specimens are sometimes a general off-white color. The white shark is built blockier than the look-alike mako, having a much deeper body. The white has a pointed snout, triangular serrated teeth, and a crescent-shaped caudal fin.

RANGE: The white shark is found throughout the world in tropical and temperate waters, though it seems to prefer warm to temperate regions over tropics. It is not numerous anywhere.

HABITAT: White sharks generally stay well offshore and seem to prefer relatively cool waters.

SIZE: The white shark is a true behemoth; one specimen 36½ feet long has been captured. The weight of that fish must have been astronomical, considering that a white shark just 13 feet long weighed 2,100 pounds! Whites that are 20 feet long are not at all uncommon.

FOOD: White sharks eat such things as other sharks that are 4 to 7 feet long, sea lions, seals, sturgeon, tuna, sea turtles, squid, and refuse.

FISHING METHODS: Chumming and trolling

BAITS: Whole fish or cut baits (and occasionally artificial lures)

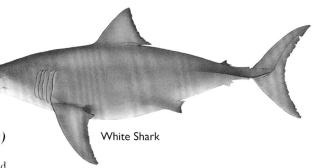

White Shark

■ Porbeagle Shark *(Lamna nasus)*

COMMON NAMES: Porbeagle shark and mackerel shark

DESCRIPTION: The porbeagle is a blocky-bodied shark that closely resembles the mako, though it is much less game. The best way to distinguish the porbeagle from both the mako and the white shark is the location of the second dorsal fin—the porbeagle is the only one whose second dorsal is directly above the anal fin. In color, the porbeagle shades from black to bluish gray on the back to white on the belly. Its anal fin is white or dusky.

RANGE: The porbeagle is found on both sides of the Atlantic as far south as the Mediterranean and Africa. On the Atlantic coast of the United States, it has been taken from South Carolina to the St. Lawrence Gulf. It is also found along most of the Pacific coast.

HABITAT: The porbeagle is a fish of temperate waters. In warm waters, it is found closer to shore and nearer to the surface, but when the water cools it may head for depths as great as 80 fathoms.

SIZE: The porbeagle apparently reaches a maximum length of about 12 feet, though the largest definitely recorded stretched 10 feet. The largest rod-caught porbeagle weighed 465 pounds.

FOOD: Porbeagles thrive on school-type fish such as mackerel and herring and on bottom-dwelling fish such as cod, hake, and flounders.

FISHING METHODS: Trolling and chumming

BAITS: Whole or cut baits

■ Thresher Shark *(Alopias vulpinus)*

DESCRIPTION: The thresher shark is nearly as large as the mako and is an excellent fighter, making breath-

Porbeagle Shark

taking jumps and long runs. The thresher has one unique physical characteristic—its inordinately long upper lobe of the tail, or caudal fin, which is at least as long as the body. The thresher shark is dark gray, bluish, brown, or even black on the back and sides, while the belly is white, sometimes with a gray mottling.

RANGE: Threshers are found from Nova Scotia to Argentina and from Ireland to the Cape of Good Hope. They occur throughout the Mediterranean, in the Pacific from Oregon to Chile, and as far from the continental United States as Hawaii, Japan, and Australia.

HABITAT: The thresher is most at home at or near the surface in subtropical to temperate waters.

SIZE: Threshers reach lengths of 20 feet and weights of half a ton.

FOOD: The thresher shark uses its long tail to herd and injure such schooling fish as mackerel, menhaden, and bluefish.

FISHING METHODS: Chumming

BAITS: Whole or cut baits

■ Tiger Shark *(Galeocerdo cuvieri)*

DESCRIPTION: One of the so-called requiem sharks, the aptly named tiger is often the culprit in attacks on swimmers. In color, it is usually a general steel gray or brownish gray with a white belly, though the young have bars and spots on the back and upper sides. The upper lobe of the tail is long and slender, and it has a short and sharp-pointed snout.

RANGE: Tiger sharks are found throughout the world's tropical and subtropical regions.

HABITAT: Though sometimes caught offshore, the tiger seems to be largely a coastal fish, and it occasionally comes into quite shallow waters. It stays near the surface.

SIZE: Tigers are reported to reach lengths of 30 feet. The maximum weight is unknown, but 13- to 14-footers tip the scales at 1,000 to 1,500 pounds.

FOOD: Tiger sharks are omnivorous and cannibalistic. They eat their own kind, as well as fish of most species,

Tiger Shark

crabs, lobsters, and even sea lions and turtles. Examinations of their stomachs have revealed such things as tin cans, parts of crocodiles, and even human remains.

FISHING METHODS: Chumming and trolling

BAITS: Whole or cut baits (and occasionally artificial lures)

■ Hammerhead Shark *(Sphyrna mokarran)*

COMMON NAMES: Hammerhead shark, hammerhead, and great hammerhead

DESCRIPTION: There's no mistaking the hammerhead shark. Its small eyes are located at each end of its unique and grotesque head, which looks as if it had been modeled after the head of a huge mallet that had been pounded nearly flat. Gray or sometimes brownish gray on its back and sides and off-white on its underparts, the hammerhead's dorsal fin is less erect than that of any of its Atlantic relatives. Though not officially classified as a game fish, the hammerhead is a large and powerful adversary. Its hide makes fine leather, and its liver contains a high-grade oil.

RANGE: In the western Atlantic, the hammerhead occurs from North Carolina to Argentina. It is found elsewhere in the tropical and subtropical areas of the Atlantic, as well as in the eastern Pacific and the Indo-Pacific.

HABITAT: Hammerheads often travel in schools and may be found both near shore and far offshore.

SIZE: The average size is difficult to determine, but hammerheads apparently reach a maximum length of about 18 feet and a maximum weight of considerably more than 1,600 pounds.

FOOD: Voracious and cannibalistic, the hammerhead eats just about anything unlucky enough to get in its way, including big tuna, tarpon, and other sharks.

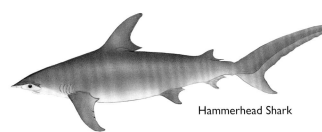

Hammerhead Shark

FISHING METHODS: Chumming and trolling

BAITS: Whole or cut fish (and occasionally artificial lures)

■ Swordfish (*Xiphias gladius*)

COMMON NAMES: Swordfish, broadbill, and broadbill swordfish

DESCRIPTION: The swordfish is one of the elite saltwater fish, much sought by both commercial and sportfishermen. It is distinguished from the other billfish (sailfish and marlin) by its much longer, flat bill (sword) and by its lack of scales and pelvic fins (the other billfish have both). The swordfish's dorsal and anal fins are sickle shaped. Its color is usually dark brown or bronze, but variations of black to grayish blue are common. The belly is usually white, but the dark colors sometimes extend right down to the fish's undersides.

RANGE: Swordfish are migratory and are found worldwide in warm and temperate waters. Their occurrence in the United States and adjacent waters extends in the Atlantic from Newfoundland to Cuba and in the Pacific from California to Chile.

HABITAT: Swordfish are open-ocean fish, usually feeding in the depths but often seen "sunning" on the surface.

SIZE: The maximum size of swordfish is a matter of some uncertainty, but specimens of nearly 1,200 pounds have been taken on rod and line. The average size is probably 150 to 300 pounds.

Swordfish

FOOD: Swordfish use their greatest weapon, the sword, to stun and capture such food as dolphins, menhaden, mackerel, bonito, bluefish, and squid.

FISHING METHODS: Night fishing was the standard technique, but now daytime methods regularly catch swordfish by placing baits at various depths from 100 feet to as deep as 1,500 feet.

BAITS: Whole squid, fish, or cut baits, such as mackerel fillets

■ Blue Marlin (*Makaira nigricans*)

DESCRIPTION: This king of the blue water is probably the most highly prized of the big-game fish, mainly because of its mammoth size and spectacular fighting abilities. In general coloration, the blue marlin is steel blue on the back, shading to silvery white on the belly. In most specimens, the sides contain light, vertical bars, which are not nearly as prominent as those of the white marlin. The dorsal and anal fins are bluish purple and sometimes have dark blotches. The blue marlin's distinguishing physical traits include a relatively short dorsal fin and a relatively long anal fin, and a body shape that is considerably rounder than other billfish.

RANGE: Blue marlin are found in warm and temperate seas throughout the world. In the United States and nearby waters, they occur from the Gulf of Maine to Uruguay in the Atlantic, and from Mexico to Peru in the Pacific.

HABITAT: Blue marlin are deep-water fish almost exclusively, and they are often seen cruising and feeding on the surface.

SIZE: The maximum size of the blue marlin is something more than 2,000 pounds, with the average being 200 to 500 pounds. Males seldom exceed 300 pounds, so those monsters often referred to as "Big Daddy" should really be called "Big Mama." Because the biggest blue marlin are thought to be in the Pacific, the International Game Fish Association separates these fish into two categories—Atlantic and Pacific.

FOOD: Blue marlin eat a broad range of fish life, including bluefish, mackerel, tuna, and bonito, as well as squid and octopus.

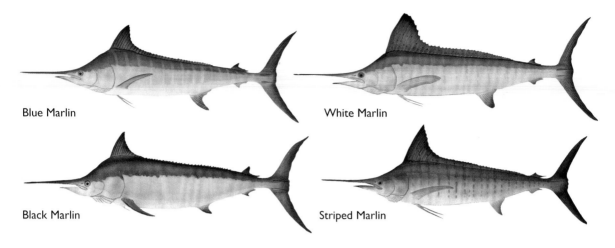

Blue Marlin

White Marlin

Black Marlin

Striped Marlin

FISHING METHODS: Trolling

BAITS: Feathers, lures, whole squid, and rigged ballyhoo

■ White Marlin
(Makaira albida or *Tetrapturus albidus)*

DESCRIPTION: The white marlin is considerably smaller and less universal than the blue marlin. Its colors are a brilliant greenish blue on the back and upper sides, changing abruptly to white at the lateral line. The sides have an irregular number of vertical bands of light blue or lavender. A unique feature of the white marlin is the rounded tips of its dorsal and anal fins. The relatively flat-sided body is slender.

RANGE: The white marlin is limited to the Atlantic, occurring from Nova Scotia to Brazil and from the Azores to St. Helena Island and South Africa. Centers of concentration at differing times of year seem to be off the coast of Ocean City, Maryland, and near Venezuela.

HABITAT: Like the blue marlin, the white marlin is a fish of warm and temperate waters and is a migrant.

SIZE: Most white marlins caught by fishermen weigh 40 to 60 pounds, but the species apparently can reach 160 pounds.

FOOD: The white is mainly a fish eater, but it will dine on anything it can capture.

FISHING METHODS: Trolling

BAITS: Feathers, lures, squids, rigged ballyhoo, and mullet

■ Black Marlin
(Makaira indica or *Istiompax indicus)*

DESCRIPTION: Possibly the largest of the marlins, the black is an ocean giant that is most easily distinguished from other marlins by the fact that its pectoral fins stick out at right angles from the body and are held rigidly in that position. The pelvic fins of the black marlin are shorter than those of other marlins, usually less than 1 foot long. The black marlin is seldom truly black, though its color varies greatly. Most are slate blue on the back and upper sides, shading to silvery white on the underparts. The sides occasionally exhibit pale-blue stripes.

RANGE: Black marlin seem to be found almost exclusively in the Pacific and Indian Oceans, being found as far north as southern California and Mexico. One area of abundance seems to be off the coast of Peru.

HABITAT: Little is known of the movements of the black marlin, though it is certainly a fish of the open oceans, and evidence indicates that it migrates only short distances if at all.

SIZE: The record rod-caught black marlin weighed 1,560 pounds, but specimens of up to 2,000 pounds have been taken commercially. The average size is probably 300 to 500 pounds.

FOOD: Various fish species (a tuna of 158 pounds was

found in a black marlin's stomach) and squid are the main items in the black marlin's diet.

FISHING METHODS: Trolling

BAITS: Whole fish, strip baits, whole squids, and artificial lures

■ Striped Marlin
(Makaira audax or *Tetrapturus audax)*

DESCRIPTION: Smaller than the blue and black marlins, the striped marlin, as its name suggests, is most easily distinguished by the stripes on its sides. These stripes vary both in number and in color, which ranges from pale blue to lavender to white. Body colors are steel blue on the back and upper sides, shading to white on the bottom areas. The striped marlin also has a high, pointed dorsal fin, which is usually taller than the greatest depth of its body. Like all other marlins, the striped variety puts up a breathtaking battle.

RANGE: Striped marlin are found in the Indian Ocean and in the Pacific from southern California to Chile.

HABITAT: Striped marlin are open-ocean fish. The fairly well-defined local populations seem to make short north-to-south migrations. Like all the other marlins, they are often seen feeding on the surface.

SIZE: The average rod-caught striped marlin weighs about 200 to 250 pounds, but the species grows to more than 500 pounds.

FOOD: Striped marlin feed on a wide variety of fish life (anchovies, bonito, mackerel, and many others), and on squid, crustaceans, octopus, and anything else that might get in their way.

FISHING METHODS: Trolling

BAITS: Whole fish, cut baits, whole squids, and artificial lures

■ Atlantic Sailfish *(Istiophorus albicans)*

DESCRIPTION: The uncommonly beautiful sailfish probably adorns more den and living-room walls than any other marine game fish. Sailfish are spectacular fighters, hurling themselves high out of the water time and time again. You can't mistake the sailfish for anything else that swims—thanks to its enormous purple (or cobalt-blue) dorsal fin, which it often seems to flaunt at fishermen. Body colors range from striking blue on the back and upper sides to silver white below the well-defined lateral line. Side markings usually consist of a variable number of pale, vertical bars or vertical rows of pale spots. The dorsal fin usually is marked with numerous black spots. A sailfish's pelvic fins are longer than those of other billfish.

RANGE: The Atlantic sailfish is commonly found in the Atlantic Ocean from Cape Hatteras to Venezuela, with winter concentrations off the east coast of Florida. This species is also found off England, France, Africa, and in the Mediterranean.

HABITAT: Sailfish are most often seen—and are almost always caught—on or near the surface. However, studies of their preferred diet indicate that they do much of their feeding in middle depths, along reefs, and even on the bottom.

SIZE: Most Atlantic sailfish caught by sportfishermen weigh 30 to 50 pounds, but the maximum size is probably a bit larger than the rod-and-reel record of 128 pounds, 1 ounce.

FOOD: According to studies made of the feeding habits of Atlantic sailfish in Florida waters, these fish feed mainly on a wide variety of fish life (tuna, mackerel, jacks, balao, needlefish, herring, and a few other species make up 83 percent of the Atlantic sailfish's diet). They also feed on squid and octopus.

FISHING METHODS: Trolling and sight casting

BAITS: Whole or cut baits, rigged ballyhoo, pilchards, and artificial lures

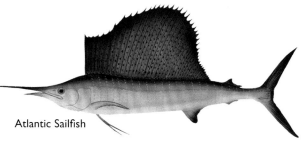

Atlantic Sailfish

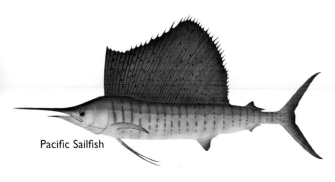
Pacific Sailfish

◼ **Pacific Sailfish** (*Istiophorus greyi*)

DESCRIPTION: It is not known for certain whether the Pacific sailfish is truly a distinct species from the Atlantic sailfish, though it does grow considerably larger than the Atlantic variety. In most other important respects, the two fish are exactly alike. The only physical difference is that the Pacific sailfish's body colors tend to be somewhat more muted. It should be noted that in sport fishing for sailfish, marlin, and all other large pelagic game fish, the trend today is toward releasing all fish.

RANGE: Pacific sailfish are found in the Pacific Ocean from about Monterey, California, south to Ecuador, and also in the vicinity of the Hawaiian Islands and elsewhere in the South Pacific.

HABITAT: See Atlantic Sailfish.

SIZE: Pacific sailfish put on a good deal more weight than their relatives in the Atlantic. The maximum weight is about 240 pounds, but the average rod-caught Pacific sailfish weighs from 60 to 100 pounds.

FOOD: See Atlantic Sailfish.

FISHING METHODS: See Atlantic Sailfish.

BAITS: Whole or cut baits, rigged baitfish, and artificial lures

◼ **Bluefin Tuna** (*Thunnus thynnus*)

COMMON NAMES: Bluefin tuna, bluefin, and horse mackerel

DESCRIPTION: The bluefin is the king of the tunas, all of which are members of the mackerel family. Bluefins—from those of school size (15 to 100 pounds) to giants of nearly half a ton—have incredible strength and tenacity, and they are much sought by both commercial and sportfishermen. The bluefin has the blocky, robust body of a typical heavyweight. The head is rather small, and the snout is pointed. The bluefin has shorter pectoral fins than any of the American tunas. It has two dorsal fins—the forward one retractable and the rearward one fixed—and a sickle-shaped tail. In color, the bluefin is steel blue on its back and upper sides, shading to light gray or creamy white on its lower parts. In small bluefins, the lower sides have vertical white lines.

RANGE: Bluefin tuna are found throughout the world, mostly in temperate and subtropical waters. In the western Atlantic, they occur in abundance from the Bahamas north to the Labrador Current. In the Pacific, they seem to be less abundant, being found in greatest numbers in the general area of Catalina Island.

HABITAT: The bluefin is generally a fish of the open ocean, though school-size bluefins occasionally come quite close to shore. In summer, bluefins show up in large numbers from New Jersey to Nova Scotia, the smaller fish showing up first and closer to shore. Atlantic areas where bluefins tend to congregate and provide good fishing include the New York Bight, New Jersey, Block Island to Rhode Island, Cape Cod Bay, Wedgeport and St. Margaret's Bay in Nova Scotia, and Conception Bay in Newfoundland.

SIZE: For all practical fishing purposes, bluefins can be grouped into two size categories: school fish (those weighing 15 to 100 pounds) and adult fish (those weighing more than 100 pounds). The average schoolie weighs 30 to 50 pounds, while the giant bluefins attain maximum weights estimated to be 1,500 pounds or more. The rod-and-reel record is 1,496 pounds.

FOOD: Bluefin tuna feed on whatever is available, including a wide variety of fish (including herring, sand lance, hake, and even dolphin), as well as squid and crustaceans.

Bluefin Tuna

FISHING METHODS: Trolling, chumming, and chunking

BAITS: Whole fish, cut baits, rigged baitfish, and artificial lures

■ Yellowfin Tuna (*Thunnus albacares*)

COMMON NAMES: Yellowfin tuna and allison tuna

DESCRIPTION: Considerably smaller than the bluefin, the yellowfin tuna is a top sport and commercial fish, particularly in the Pacific. In color, the yellowfin is steel blue or nearly black on the back and upper sides, silvery white on the lower parts. Characteristics that distinguish it from the bluefin are its much longer pectoral fins and the generous amount of the color yellow in most of the fins. The yellowfin is difficult to distinguish from some of the other tunas, but in large specimens the second dorsal fin and anal fin are much longer than those of any other tuna. The side markings of the yellowfin include a sometimes indistinct golden-yellow horizontal streak and white spots and vertical stripes on the lower sides.

RANGE: Yellowfins are found worldwide in tropical and subtropical waters. They are most numerous in the Pacific, where they are found widely off the coast of southern California and Baja California. They also range from the Gulf of Mexico north to New Jersey.

HABITAT: Yellowfin tuna are more southerly in general range than are bluefins. They are open-ocean fish, though there is some evidence that they do not make such long-range migrations as bluefins do.

SIZE: Yellowfins are thought to reach a maximum size of some 500 pounds. However, the rod-and-reel record is 405 pounds, and the average size is less than 100 pounds.

FOOD: See Bluefin Tuna.

FISHING METHODS: See Bluefin Tuna.

BAITS: Whole fish, cut baits, rigged baitfish, squid, and artificial lures

■ Bigeye Tuna (*Thunnus obesus*)

COMMON NAMES: Bigeye tuna, Pacific bigeye tuna, and Atlantic bigeye tuna

DESCRIPTION: Its eyes are not abnormally large, so it's difficult to determine how the bigeye tuna got its name. Its coloration is similar to that of its big brother, the bluefin, though its pectoral fins are longer. It is often hard to distinguish the bigeye from some of the other tunas. Its dorsal and anal fins are never greatly elongated (as in the large yellowfins), and the finlets running along the back and belly from the dorsal and anal fins to the tail are yellow with black margins. Though Atlantic and Pacific bigeyes are the same species, the International Game Fish Association separates them for record-keeping purposes.

RANGE: Bigeye tuna range throughout the world in tropical and subtropical waters.

HABITAT: Bigeyes are fish of the open oceans and deep water, as evidenced by the fact that many are caught by commercial longline fishermen.

SIZE: Bigeyes probably reach weights of 500 pounds and seem to grow somewhat bigger in the Pacific than in the Atlantic. The average size is about 100 pounds.

FOOD: See Bluefin Tuna.

FISHING METHODS: See Bluefin Tuna.

BAITS: Whole fish, cut baits, rigged baitfish, and artificial lures

Yellowfin Tuna

Bigeye Tuna

Blackfin Tuna

■ Blackfin Tuna *(Thunnus atlanticus)*

DESCRIPTION: Far more restricted in range than any of the other popular tunas, the blackfin is also one of the smallest members of the family. It is darker in color than the other tunas and has fewer gill rakers. The finlets behind the dorsal and anal fins are totally dark—not marked with yellow like most of the other tunas.

RANGE: Blackfin tuna are found only in the western Atlantic Ocean, ranging from Cape Cod south to Brazil.

HABITAT: Blackfins are open-ocean, deep-water fish, like almost all the other members of the tuna family.

SIZE: The blackfin's top weight is probably not much more than 40 pounds or so. Most average 10 to 15 pounds. The world-record, rod-caught blackfin—weighing 49 pounds, 6 ounces—is an exceptionally big tuna for this species.

FOOD: The blackfin's diet is about the same as that of the other tunas, except that its prey is properly smaller.

FISHING METHODS: Trolling, chumming, and jigging

BAITS: Cut baits, live pilchards, cigar minnows, rigged ballyhoo, and artificial lures

■ Albacore *(Thunnus alalunga)*

COMMON NAMES: Albacore and longfin tuna

DESCRIPTION: The albacore is what you are likely to get when you buy a can of all-white-meat tuna. It is one of the tunas, and thus a member of the mackerel family. The albacore's most outstanding physical trait is its abnormally long pectoral (side) fins, which extend from behind the gills well past the second dorsal fin, ending about even with the third dorsal finlet. The coloring is an iridescent steel blue above, shading to silvery white on the belly. The fins are generally blue and bright yellow.

RANGE: Albacore are found in tropical, subtropical, and temperate waters in most parts of the world. In U.S. and adjacent waters, they are primarily a Pacific species, being plentiful from southern British Columbia to southern California and Baja. In the Atlantic, quite a few are caught off Florida, and they are occasionally found as far north as Massachusetts.

HABITAT: Albacore almost never come close to shore. They haunt deep, open waters and often feed near or on the surface. When on top, they can be seen smashing wildly into schools of frenzied baitfish.

SIZE: Albacore of up to 90 pounds have been taken in nets, and the record rod-caught fish was 88 pounds, 2 ounces. The average weight is 5 to 25 pounds.

FOOD: Albacore feed on a wide variety of fish, as well as squid and crustaceans.

FISHING METHODS: Trolling and chumming

BAITS: Whole or cut baits, squid, and artificial lures

■ Oceanic Bonito *(Euthynnus pelamis* or *Katsuwonus pelamis)*

COMMON NAMES: Oceanic bonito, bonito, skipjack, skipjack tuna, oceanic skipjack, and striped tuna

DESCRIPTION: The oceanic bonito is the most important member of the bonito group (which also includes the common, or Atlantic, bonito and the striped bonito, among others) and is the only bonito classified as a game fish by the International Game Fish Association. The oceanic bonito is striking blue above and silvery below,

Albacore

Oceanic Bonito

with some shadings of yellow and red. It is unique in having four or more well-defined dark stripes running from the area of the pectoral fin to the tail along the lower part of the body.

RANGE: Oceanic bonito are found in tropical and sub-tropical waters throughout the world. In U.S. and adjacent waters, they are most common off the southern coasts.

HABITAT: All the bonitos are fish of offshore waters, though they come relatively close to shore if that is where their favorite food is. They are school fish and generally feed on or near the surface.

SIZE: The average weight of the oceanic bonito is probably 10 to 18 pounds. The maximum is about 40 pounds.

FOOD: All the bonitos feed on a wide variety of fish, plus squid and crustaceans.

FISHING METHODS: Trolling and chumming

BAITS: Cut baits, jigs, and artificial lures

King Mackerel
(Scomberomorus cavalla)

COMMON NAMES: King mackerel, kingfish, cavalla, and cero

DESCRIPTION: Fast, strong, and good to eat is the king mackerel, the largest member of the Spanish-mackerel family in U.S. waters. Its streamlined body—colored in iridescent bluish green above and shading to platinum below—seems built for speed, which the fish exhibits both in the water and above in soaring leaps. The king's meandering lateral line and its lack of other side markings set it apart from most other fish. The lack of black in the rear part of the first dorsal fin distinguishes the king mackerel from other Spanish mackerels.

RANGE: Generally found from Brazil north to North Carolina and occasionally up to Cape Cod, the king mackerel is most numerous in the Gulf of Mexico and southern Atlantic Ocean.

HABITAT: King mackerel range in schools and usually stick to open water, though they sometimes hover near the outer reaches of bays, feeding on baitfish. March is the peak of the king-mackerel season for Florida anglers, while in the Gulf the fishing runs from spring into September.

SIZE: The average rod-caught king mackerel weighs 5 to 15 pounds, but the species apparently reaches a length of 5 feet and a weight of 100 pounds.

FOOD: King mackerel feed mostly on smaller fish.

FISHING METHODS: Trolling and kite fishing with live bait

BAITS: Most live baitfish, pilchards, cigar minnows, ballyhoo, and artificial lures

Wahoo (Acanthocybium solandri)

COMMON NAMES: Wahoo, queenfish, peto, and ocean barracuda

DESCRIPTION: It is probably good that wahoo are neither as numerous as striped bass nor as large as bluefin tuna, for they are one of the wildest things with fins. They smash a trolled lure or bait with incredible force, make blitzing runs, and hurl themselves far out of the water (reports have it that wahoo have leaped over a fishing boat lengthwise!). The wahoo resembles no other fish, though it is shaped generally like the king mackerel. Its iridescent colors include blue or blue green above, shading through coppery tints to silver below. The sides have narrow, wavy, dark, vertical bars. Older fish may lack the side markings.

RANGE: Wahoo range throughout the world in tropical

Wahoo

and subtropical waters. In the Atlantic, they stray as far north as the Carolinas, but they are most often caught off the Florida Keys, Mexico, and the West Indies.

HABITAT: Unlike most other mackerel-like fish, wahoos are loners—that is, they do not range in schools. They live in deep water, often staying near the edges of deep drop-offs or along reefs.

SIZE: The average wahoo caught by anglers weighs 10 to 25 pounds, but the species is said to hit 150 pounds.

FOOD: Wahoos eat various fish, including flying fish, mackerel, mullet, and squid.

FISHING METHODS: Trolling

BAITS: Rigged baitfish, live baits, and artificial lures

▪ Cobia *(Rachycentron canadum)*

COMMON NAMES: Cobia, crabeater, ling, coalfish, black salmon, lemonfish, black bonito, cabio, and cobio

DESCRIPTION: The cobia is something of a mystery. Little is known of its wanderings or life history, and the species has no close relatives. In color, the cobia is dark brown on the back and lighter brown on the sides and belly. A wide, black, lateral band extends from its snout to the base of its tail. Less distinct dark bands are found above and below the lateral. The first dorsal fin is actually a series of quite short, stiff, wide spines that look nothing at all like a standard dorsal.

RANGE: The cobia is found in many of the world's tropical and warm, temperate waters. It occurs in the western Atlantic from Massachusetts to Argentina, but its greatest abundance is from Chesapeake Bay southeast to Bermuda and in the Gulf of Mexico.

HABITAT: Young cobia are often caught in inlets and bays, but older fish seem to prefer shallower areas of

Cobia

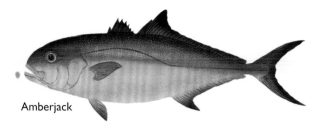

Amberjack

the open sea. Cobias are almost invariably found around some kind of cover—over rocks, around pilings or bottom debris, and particularly under floating objects such as buoys, weeds, cruising rays, and flotsam.

SIZE: Cobia reach top weights of more than 100 pounds. The average size is 5 to 10 pounds in some areas, though in other areas, notably the Florida Keys and Gulf of Mexico waters, 25- to 50-pounders are not uncommon.

FOOD: Cobias feed largely on crabs, though they also eat shrimp and small fish of all kinds.

FISHING METHODS: Trolling and sight casting (typically found feeding under cruising rays)

BAITS: Live baits, especially grunts, cut baits, and jigs

▪ Amberjack *(Seriola dumerili)*

COMMON NAMES: Amberjack, greater amberjack, and horse-eye bonito

DESCRIPTION: Amberjacks are related to pompanos and jacks, and more distantly to tunas and mackerels. The amberjack is a stocky, heavy-bodied fish with a deeply forked tail, the lobes of which are quite slender. Its body colors are blue green or blue on the back, shading to silvery on the underparts. The fins have some yellow in them. A well-defined dark band runs upward from the snout to a point behind the eye. Mostly a solitary wanderer, the amberjack sometimes gathers in small groups in preferred feeding areas.

RANGE: Though occasionally found as far north as New England, the amberjack is primarily a fish of southern Atlantic waters from the Carolinas south to Florida and nearby islands. In the Pacific, it is abundant from southern Mexico southward.

HABITAT: Reefs are the favorite habitat of amberjacks,

though these fish often cruise for food at moderate depths—approximately 20 to 40 feet.

SIZE: The average rod-caught amberjack probably weighs 12 to 20 pounds, though ambers of up to 50 pounds are far from rare. The maximum size is about 150 pounds.

FOOD: Amberjacks prey on many smaller fish, as well as on crabs, shrimp, and crustaceans.

FISHING METHODS: Bottom fishing

BAITS: Whole fish and cut baits

■ Pacific Yellowtail (*Seriola dorsalis*)

COMMON NAMES: Pacific yellowtail, yellowtail, and California yellowtail

DESCRIPTION: A member of the amberjack family, the Pacific yellowtail is probably the most popular sport fish on the Pacific coast. It is not, however, of great commercial value. The yellowtail has a horizontal swath, ranging in color from brassy to rather bright yellow, running from its eye to its tail. Above the stripe, the color is blue green to green; below it, the color is silvery. The fins are dusky yellow, except the caudal fin (tail), which is bright yellow. The yellowtail is a tremendously powerful fighter.

RANGE: Yellowtails have been caught from Mazatlan, Mexico, through the waters of Baja California, and north to the southern Washington coast. The world-record yellowtail was taken off the coast of New Zealand, but it is not known for sure whether it was of the same species as the Pacific yellowtail.

HABITAT: Yellowtails are fish of the mid-depths for the most part and are migratory. A preferred hangout is a kelp bed, and rocks often harbor yellowtails. Concentrations of yellowtails are around the Coronado Islands, Catalina Island, and off San Clemente, California.

SIZE: Yellowtails reach weights of more than 100 pounds, but the average size is 8 to 25 pounds.

FOOD: Like many other voracious marine species, the yellowtail usually feeds on whatever is available. It seems to prefer sardines, anchovies, mackerel, squid, and crabs.

FISHING METHODS: Casting live baits and trolling artificial lures

BAITS: Live sardines, anchovies, and artificial lures

■ Jack Crevalle (*Caranx hippos*)

COMMON NAMES: Jack crevalle, jack, cavally, cavalla, common jack, horse crevalle, and toro

DESCRIPTION: Probably the best-known member of a very large family, the jack crevalle is considered a fine game fish by some anglers but a pest by others. The crevalle is short, husky, and slab sided. It is yellow green on the back and the upper sides, yellow and silvery on the lower areas. There is a dark mark on the rear edge of the gill cover, and the breast is without scales except for a scaled patch just forward of the ventral fins.

RANGE: The jack crevalle is found from Uruguay to Nova Scotia in the western Atlantic, and from Peru to Baja California in the eastern Pacific. It is most numerous from Florida to Texas.

HABITAT: The crevalle seems to prefer shallow flats, though large, solitary specimens are often taken in deep offshore waters. It is a schooling species.

SIZE: Jack crevalles of more than 70 pounds have been caught, and 45-pounders are not uncommon in Florida waters. The average size is probably 2 to 8 pounds.

FOOD: Smaller fish are the main course of the jack crevalle, but shrimp and other invertebrates are also occasionally on the menu.

FISHING METHODS: Casting, live lining, chumming, and bottom fishing

BAITS: Live baits, cut baits, shrimp, and artificial lures

Jack Crevalle

■ Rainbow Runner
(Elagatis bipinnulatus)

COMMON NAMES: Rainbow runner, rainbow yellowtail, runner, skipjack, and shoemaker

DESCRIPTION: The rainbow runner, an excellent game fish, is a member of the jack family, but it doesn't look like most of the others. It is streamlined, not deep bodied and chunky, and its coloration is striking. The back is a vivid blue or green blue, while the lower areas and the tail are yellow. Along the upper sides is a broad dark-blue stripe, and below that are other, less prominent blue stripes. The fins are greenish yellow. Finlets at the rear end of the dorsal and anal fins distinguish the rainbow runner from the amberjack, which it somewhat resembles.

RANGE: Occurring in tropical waters worldwide, the rainbow runner is found in the Atlantic from Colombia to Massachusetts; in the Pacific, it has been recorded from Peru and the Galapagos Islands to Baja California.

HABITAT: The wanderings of this fish, which are nowhere numerous, are little known. Trollers catch rainbow runners off the east coast of Florida and in the Gulf of Mexico.

SIZE: The maximum size is about 30 pounds. Most caught rainbow runners are about 15 inches in length.

FOOD: Rainbow runners feed on smaller fish.

FISHING METHODS: Trolling

BAITS: Small baitfish and artificial lures

■ Permit *(Trachinotus falcatus or Trachinotus kennedyi)*

COMMON NAMES: Permit, great pompano, round pompano, and palometa

DESCRIPTION: The shy and wary permit, a much-prized game fish, is the largest of the pompanos. Blocky and very deep bodied (sometimes nearly half as deep as total body length), the permit's coloration varies greatly, especially in the young. Adults are generally bluish or gray on the back, with the rest of the body being silvery.

Permit

Very large ones may be almost entirely silvery with a green-blue tinge. Permit are far more numerous than many anglers think, but while they are often seen, they are much less often hooked and boated, for they put up a fight that is much more powerful than that of a bonefish. It usually takes at least a half hour to tire a big permit.

RANGE: In the Atlantic, permit are found from Brazil to Massachusetts, in the West Indies, and in Bermuda. A Pacific variety is found from Ecuador to southern California. It is most abundant off southern Florida.

HABITAT: Permit are found from the surf out to deep water. They tend to stay in channels and deep holes, but they often come onto shallow tidal flats to feed, at which time their tails and backs can be seen above the surface.

SIZE: Permit reach weights of 50 pounds, but those caught by anglers probably average 15 to 25 pounds.

FOOD: Mainly bottom-feeders, permit prefer crabs and other invertebrates, plus small fish.

FISHING METHODS: Bottom fishing, casting, live lining, and chumming (a favorite species for fly fishermen)

BAITS: Crabs, baitfish, shrimp, jigs, clams, bucktails, streamer flies, and artificial lures

■ Bluefish *(Pomatomus saltatrix)*

COMMON NAMES: Bluefish, chopper, tailor, snapper, and jumbo

DESCRIPTION: Savage, cannibalistic, delicious, abundant, willing—all these adjectives fit the bluefish, the only member of the family *Pomatomidae*. In coloration,

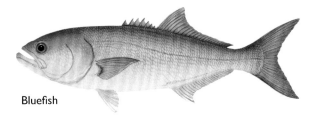

Bluefish

the bluefish is a rather dark blue on the back, shading through blue gray and gray silver to silvery on the belly. A fisherman getting his first look at a pack of blues attacking a horde of baitfish finds the sight hard to believe. The water boils white and then turns red and brown with the blood of the frenzied baitfish and the regurgitated stomach contents of the savage blues. Once hooked, the bluefish makes the angler fervently thankful that these fish don't reach the size of tuna, for blues are among the most powerful fighters in the sea.

RANGE: Blues are found in the western Atlantic from Massachusetts to Argentina, off the northwest coast of Africa, the Azores, Portugal, and Spain, and in the Mediterranean and Black Seas. They are also found in the eastern Indian Ocean, the Malay Peninsula, Australia, and New Zealand.

HABITAT: Though primarily a deep-water species, particularly the large ones, bluefish often come right into the surf and sometimes go quite a distance up brackish-water rivers. Blues are rather erratic wanderers, though their general migration routes are fairly constant. They usually travel in large schools. In winter, they are most numerous in Florida. As the waters warm, they head north to such bluefishing hotspots as the Carolinas, New Jersey, and New England. Tidal rips are top spots to look for blues.

SIZE: Bluefish average 2 to 5 pounds, though 15- to 20-pounders are not uncommon, and there was a 45-pounder taken off the coast of North Africa.

FOOD: Bluefish will eat anything they can handle—and

some things they can't, as many fishermen who have been bitten by a just-boated blue will attest. Menhaden is a bluefish's blue-plate special, and other preferred foods are mullet, squid, and eels.

FISHING METHODS: Live lining, chumming, and trolling

BAITS: Cut baits, bunkers, mullet, eels, jigs, and spoons

■ Dolphin *(Coryphaena hippurus)*

COMMON NAMES: Dolphin, bull dolphin, dorado, and mahimahi

DESCRIPTION: The dolphin (a cold-blooded species that should not be confused with the warm-blooded dolphin, which is a mammal and a member of the porpoise family) is spectacular in both coloration and fighting ability. Purple and blue on the dorsal surface, and iridescent green and yellow on the sides and lower body, the dolphin's merging colors are enhanced by scattered blue dots. The head is extremely blunt, being almost vertical in large specimens (called bulls, though they may be either male or female). The dorsal fin extends from the head nearly to the tail. The dolphin is an explosive battler and an acrobatic leaper.

RANGE: Dolphins range widely in tropical and subtropical seas. In the western Atlantic, they are found in relative abundance from North Carolina (particularly in or near the Gulf Stream) south into the Gulf of Mexico as far west as Texas. In the Pacific, they range as far north as Oregon, but they are most numerous off the coast of southern California.

HABITAT: Dolphins are usually school fish, though large ones are often loners. They are fish of the open oceans, but they lie under and cavort near various patches or bits of flotsam—floating grass, pieces of driftwood, and the like.

SIZE: The largest dolphin on record weighed 87 pounds. However, most rod-caught dolphins are 5 to 15 pounds.

FOOD: The food of dolphins includes a wide variety of smaller fish, squid, and crustaceans. In many parts of the dolphin's range, the flying fish forms a large portion of its diet, and the dolphin can often be seen soaring far out of the water in pursuit of a flying fish.

Dolphin

Why Dolphin Are the Perfect Game Fish

- Dolphin are everywhere, ranging from Massachusetts to Florida and the Bahamas throughout the Gulf of Mexico and the Caribbean down to Brazil. A highly migratory species, dolphin have been known to travel as far as 800 miles in 10 days.

- Dolphin are probably the fastest-growing game fish, growing nearly three inches a week and weighing as much as 40 pounds. Cows (females) grow to about 40 pounds, but the bulls regularly weigh in at 60 pounds. The world record, caught in Costa Rica in 1976, weighed 87 pounds. See accompanying chart for average length-to-weight ratios.

- Dolphin are prolific. They become sexually mature when they reach 14 inches in length. Females are in a constant state of egg production and spawn multiple times in a year. A single dolphin can produce about 555,000 eggs per spawn. Unfortunately, the annual mortality rate for juvenile dolphin runs about 98 percent. The dolphin is an important forage species and an easy target for all billfish and sharks. If that's not bad enough, if dolphin get hungry enough, they will eat one another.

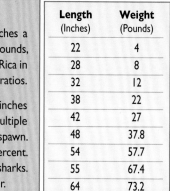

Length (Inches)	Weight (Pounds)
22	4
28	8
32	12
38	22
42	27
48	37.8
54	57.7
55	67.4
64	73.2

- Dolphin, generally listed as mahimahi on restaurant menus, is a superb food fish. Easy to fillet and prepare, the meat is flaky and moist. It can be broiled, grilled, fried, smoked, or steamed. Its unique flavor even makes it a good choice for ceviche.

FISHING METHODS: Trolling and sight casting

BAITS: Mullet, ballyhoo, squid, cut baits, and artificial lures

■ Tarpon *(Megalops atlantica)*

COMMON NAMES: Tarpon, silver king, and sabalo

DESCRIPTION: The tarpon, considered the king of game fish by the majority of those who have caught it, is a leaper to end all leapers. Tarpon jumps of 8 feet above the surface and 20 feet long have been measured. Tarpon are related to herring and shad, and, oddly enough, to smelt and salmon. Usually blue or greenish black on the back, the tarpon's sides and underparts are sparkling silver. The scales are very large, and there is a bony plate between the branches of the bottom jaw. The dorsal fin has no spines, but its last (rear) ray is abnormally extended and whiplike. The pectoral fins are quite low on the body. The tarpon's spectacular fighting tactics and hard, bony mouth make it difficult to subdue—one fish boated out of 20 strikes is about average success for a

tarpon fisherman. The tarpon's only shortcoming is that it isn't much on the table. Most rod-caught tarpon are released.

RANGE: Tarpon are found on both sides of the Atlantic in tropical and subtropical waters. In the western Atlantic, they stray as far north as Nova Scotia and range well south in the Gulf of Mexico. Main concentrations seem to be off southern Florida, Texas, and eastern Mexico.

HABITAT: Except in winter, when they apparently retreat to deeper water, tarpon are schooling fish of shallow waters. They frequent such places as mangrove flats, shoals, brackish bayous, cuts, inlets, and the lower reaches of coastal rivers. Sometimes they travel many miles upriver into fresh water. They are seldom far from the shore in summer.

Tarpon

SIZE: Though the rod-and-reel record is 286 pounds, 9 ounces, tarpon reportedly attain weights in excess of 300 pounds. The average size of an adult tarpon is probably 30 to 100 pounds. Tarpon of more than 100 pounds are subdued each year on fly rods!

FOOD: Tarpon feed on a variety of marine life, including pinfish, mullet, needlefish, and other small fish, plus crabs and shrimp.

FISHING METHODS: Sight casting and fly fishing

BAITS: Whole baitfish, mullet, crabs, shrimp, and artificial lures

■ Bonefish (*Albula vulpes*)

COMMON NAMES: Bonefish, ratfish, and banana

DESCRIPTION: What the tarpon is to leaping, the bonefish is to running. No one using sporting tackle can stop the blazing initial run of a hooked bonefish, which may tear 150 yards or more of line from a reel. The bonefish's body, built for speed, is shaped like a torpedo. The colors are bronze or blue green on the back, shading through bright silver on the sides to white on the belly. The sides occasionally have some dark mottling. The bonefish is sometimes confused with the ladyfish, but telling them apart requires only a look at the mouth. The bonefish's upper jaw—a snout, really—is far longer than the lower, giving the fish a sucker-like look. The ladyfish has jaws of about equal length. Bonefish are related to tarpon.

RANGE: Bonefish are found in all tropical marine waters, being caught in such widely separated places as South Africa, Brazil, and Hawaii, where the biggest ones are found. By far the largest concentrations of bonefish in North America are found around the Florida Keys and in the Bahamas.

HABITAT: Bonefish are a shallow-water species. They move onto very shallow tidal flats, sometimes in water only 6 inches deep, with the high tide to feed and then drop back into deeper water as the tide ebbs. On the flats is where fishermen—particularly fly fishermen—seek this ultrawary quarry.

SIZE: Bonefish probably reach a maximum weight of about 20 pounds or a bit more, but one of more than

Bonefish

8 pounds is worth bragging about. The average size is about 4 to 6 pounds.

FOOD: Bonefish are primarily bottom-feeders, preying on crabs (particularly the hermit crab), shrimp, squid, sand fleas, and other crustaceans and mollusks.

FISHING METHODS: Casting and sight casting (a favorite species for fly fishermen)

BAITS: Shrimp, crabs, artificial lures, and flies

■ Striped Bass (*Morone saxatilis*)

COMMON NAMES: Striped bass, striper, linesides, rock, rockfish, squidhound, and greenhead

DESCRIPTION: The striped bass is one of the most popular coastal game fish. It fights well, and it "eats well." It is not likely to be mistaken for any other game fish in its range, primarily because of its general shape, side stripes (there are seven or eight horizontal dark stripes on each side), and the separation between the front and rear dorsal fin. The coloration is dark green to almost black on the back, silver on the sides, and white on the underparts. The striper is anadromous, living in the sea but ascending rivers to spawn.

RANGE: On the Atlantic coast, the striped bass is found from the Gulf of St. Lawrence south to the St. Johns River in Florida and in the Gulf of Mexico from western Florida to Louisiana. Introduced on the Pacific coast in the 1880s, the striper is found there from the Columbia River south to Los Angeles, California. The center of the striper's range in the Atlantic is Massachusetts to South Carolina; in the Pacific, it is in the San Francisco Bay area. Efforts to establish the striped bass in fresh water have been successful in such spots as the Santee-Cooper impoundment in South Carolina, Kerr Reservoir in North Carolina, some stretches of the Colorado River, and elsewhere.

Striped Bass

HABITAT: Striped bass are almost exclusively coastal fish, seldom ranging more than a few miles offshore. Among the striper's favorite haunts are tidal rips, reefs, rocky headlands, jetties, bays, inlets, channels, canals, and reedy flats in tidal marshes.

SIZE: Most striped bass caught by anglers probably fall between 3 and 15 pounds, but many fish of 40 to 60 pounds are caught each year, most of them by trollers in the Cape Cod to Delaware range. The rod-and-reel record is an 81-pound, 14-ounce fish caught in Long Island Sound, Connecticut, but there are reliable records of a 125-pounder having been caught off North Carolina in 1891.

FOOD: The striper is a voracious feeder that preys on a wide variety of fish and invertebrates. The list includes herring, mullet, menhaden, anchovies, flounders, shad, silver hake, eels, lobsters, crabs, shrimp, sea worms, squid, clams, and mussels.

FISHING METHODS: Casting, trolling, sight casting, and chumming

BAITS: Live and cut menhaden, eels, crabs, sandworms, bloodworms, and artificial lures

■ Snook *(Centropomus undecimalis)*

COMMON NAMES: Snook and robalo

DESCRIPTION: A fine fighter and excellent table fare, the snook is a much-sought prize of southern waters. In color, the snook is brown, green, or brownish gold on the dorsal surface (back), shading to greenish silver on the sides, and becoming lighter on the belly. Distinctive traits include a depressed upper jaw and a jutting lower jaw, a somewhat humped back, and, probably most distinctive of all, a prominent dark lateral line that usually extends to and into the tail. The snook strikes a fisherman's offering with a startling smash, but it is an unpredictable feeder.

RANGE: Snook are found throughout tropical waters on the Atlantic and Pacific coasts, though they have been known to stray as far north as Delaware. They are plentiful along the Florida coasts and along the Gulf Coast in the United States and Mexico.

HABITAT: Snook are shallow-water fish that frequent such spots as sandy shores, mangrove banks, tidal bayous, canals, flats, bays, bridges, and pilings, and sometimes go upstream into fresh water. In cold weather, they lie in deep holes.

SIZE: Snook probably average 2 to 5 pounds, but 10-pounders are not rare, and the top weight is more than 50 pounds.

FOOD: The voracious snook feeds on many varieties of fish, particularly mullet, but also eats crabs, shrimp, and crustaceans.

FISHING METHODS: Casting, live lining, and trolling

BAITS: Live shrimp, mullet, pinfish, crabs, artificial lures, and flies

■ Great Barracuda *(Sphyraena barracuda)*

COMMON NAMES: Great barracuda, barracuda, and cuda

DESCRIPTION: This toothy warrior is the subject of misunderstanding by both anglers and swimmers. Proven records of barracuda attacks on swimmers are relatively rare, though this fish, apparently out of curiosity, often approaches quite close to swimmers. Many fishermen write the cuda off as a poor fighter, but it usually puts on a powerful, acrobatic battle when hooked on sporting tackle. Shaped much like the freshwater pikes, the great barracuda is bluish gray or greenish gray on the back, silvery on the sides, and whitish on the belly.

Snook

Great Barracuda

Dark, irregularly shaped blotches mark the sides, particularly toward the rear. The teeth are large and pointed. The cuda is a poor food fish and, in fact, may be poisonous.

RANGE: The great barracuda occurs in the American Atlantic from Brazil as far north as the Carolinas, though it occasionally strays north to Massachusetts. Centers of abundance are in Florida waters and in the West Indies.

HABITAT: Though barracuda are found in depths ranging from a couple of feet to 200 feet, they are mainly a shallow-water species. Preferred hangouts are reefs, flats, and around mangrove islands. The largest are usually found near offshore reefs.

SIZE: Known to reach weights of more than 100 pounds and lengths of 6 feet, the great barracuda probably averages 5 to 25 pounds. However, 50-pounders are not uncommon.

FOOD: Voracious in appetite, the barracuda feeds on a wide variety of smaller fish, preying largely on whatever is most numerous in any given area. A favorite prey is mullet, though it will eat everything from puffers to small tuna.

FISHING METHODS: Casting and trolling

BAITS: Almost any live baits and artificial lures

Channel Bass *(Sciaenops ocellata)*

COMMON NAMES: Channel bass, red drum, and redfish

DESCRIPTION: The name channel bass is actually a misnomer, for this species isn't a bass at all but rather a member of the croaker family. An important East and Gulf Coast game fish, the channel bass is copper or bronze in overall body coloration. It can be distinguished from the black drum, which it resembles, by its lack of chin barbels and the presence, at the base of the

upper part of the tail, of at least one large, black spot. Food value of the channel bass varies with size. Small ones—often called puppy drum or rat reds—are fine eating, but large specimens have coarse flesh and are only fair eating.

RANGE: Channel bass are found along the Atlantic and Gulf coasts from Massachusetts to Texas.

HABITAT: These coastal fish are found off sandy beaches for the most part, moving shoreward as the tide rises to feed in holes, behind sandbars, and on flats. They are also found in such spots as the lee of mangrove islands, sloughs, channels, and bayous.

SIZE: Channel bass reach weights of well more than 80 pounds, though those of 50 pounds or more are relatively rare.

FOOD: Channel bass are bottom-feeders, eating mainly crustaceans, mollusks, and sea worms, though they sometimes prey on smaller fish, particularly mullet and mossbunker.

FISHING METHODS: Casting and trolling

BAITS: Live baits, crabs, clams, cut mullet, and artificial lures

Weakfish *(Cynoscion regalis)*

COMMON NAMES: Weakfish, common weakfish, gray weakfish, squeteague, yellowfin, and tiderunner

DESCRIPTION: The weakfish gets its name not from its fighting qualities, which are excellent, but rather from its quite delicate mouth, which is easily torn by a hook. This popular, streamlined game fish is olive, green, or green blue on the back and silver or white on the belly. The sides are quite colorful, having tinges of purple, lavender, blue, and green, with a golden sheen. The back and upper sides contain numerous spots of various dark colors. The lower edge of the tail is sometimes yellow, as are the ventral, pectoral, and anal fins. The weakfish is excellent table fare.

RANGE: The weakfish occurs along the Atlantic coast of the United States from Massachusetts south to the east coast of Florida. Populations of the fish center around

Weakfish

the Chesapeake and Delaware Bays, New Jersey, and Long Island.

HABITAT: Basically a school fish (though large ones are often lone wolves), weakfish are a coastal species, being found in the surf and in inlets, bays, channels, and saltwater creeks. They prefer shallow areas with a sandy bottom. They feed mostly near the surface, but they may go deep if that is where the food is located.

SIZE: The average size of a weakfish seems to be declining. Today, most rod-caught fish are 1 to 4 pounds. Those early fall "tiderunners" of past decades, fish of up to a dozen pounds, are seldom seen nowadays. The biggest rod-caught weakfish was 19½ pounds.

FOOD: Weakfish eat sea worms, shrimp, squid, sand lance, crabs, and such small fish as silversides, killies, and butterfish.

FISHING METHODS: Casting, chumming, and jigging

BAITS: Shrimp, spearing, mullet, clams, crabs, and killies

■ Spotted Weakfish
(*Cynoscion nebulosus*)

COMMON NAMES: Spotted weakfish, spotted sea trout, speckled trout, trout, and speck

DESCRIPTION: This species is a southern variety of the common weakfish (see Weakfish), which it resembles. As its name might suggest, its markings (many large, dark, round spots found on the sides and back and extending onto the dorsal fin and tail) are far more prominent than those of the common weakfish. In general, body coloration of the spotted weakfish is dark gray on the back and upper sides, shading to silver below. Like the common weakfish, the spotted variety has a projecting lower jaw and two large canine teeth at the tip of the upper jaw. It is a top food fish.

RANGE: The spotted weakfish occurs throughout the Gulf of Mexico, in Florida waters, and north to Virginia, though it is found as a stray as far north as New York. It is most abundant in the Gulf of Mexico and in Florida.

HABITAT: See Weakfish.

SIZE: The average size of a spotted weakfish is somewhat smaller than that of a common weakfish. Most rod-caught spotted weaks fall in the 1- to 3-pound range. The maximum size is about 15 pounds.

FOOD: In many areas, spotted weakfish feed almost exclusively on shrimp. They may also eat various smaller fish, particularly mullet, menhaden, and silversides, as well as crabs and sea worms.

FISHING METHODS: See Weakfish.

BAITS: Cut baits, shrimp, worms, clams, killies, and artificial lures

■ California White Sea Bass
(*Cynoscion nobilis*)

COMMON NAMES: California white sea bass, sea bass, white sea bass, croaker, and white corvina

DESCRIPTION: Not a true sea bass, the California white sea bass is a relative of the weakfish of the Atlantic. It is a rather streamlined fish with front and rear dorsal fins that are connected. The body colors are gray to blue on the back, silvery on the sides, and white on the belly. The tail is yellow. The belly is somewhat indented from pelvic fins to vent. There is a dark area at the base of the pectoral fins.

RANGE: The California white sea bass has an extreme range of Alaska to Chile, but it is not often found north

Spotted Weakfish

of San Francisco. The population center seems to be from Santa Barbara, California, south into Mexico.

HABITAT: The white sea bass seldom strays far offshore and is most often found in or near beds of kelp. Night fishing is often very productive.

SIZE: The white sea bass averages about 15 to possibly 25 pounds, though specimens of more than 40 pounds are not uncommon. The maximum weight is a bit more than 80 pounds.

FOOD: White sea bass feed on a variety of small fish, as well as squid, crabs, shrimp, and other mollusks and crustaceans.

FISHING METHODS: Bottom fishing

BAITS: Baitfish, cut baits, crabs, shrimp, and clams

■ California Black Sea Bass
(Stereolepis gigas)

COMMON NAMES: California black sea bass, giant black sea bass, and giant sea bass

DESCRIPTION: This large, blocky fish is a Pacific version of the eastern sea bass. It is black or brownish black in general coloration, lighter on the underparts. Because of its size and color, the California black sea bass cannot be confused with any other species in its somewhat limited range.

RANGE: The California black sea bass is most numerous off Baja California and southern California, though it also ranges north to central California.

HABITAT: The California black sea bass is strictly a bottom-feeder, being found in deep water, usually over rocks and around reefs.

SIZE: The rod-and-reel record California black sea bass weighed 563 pounds, 8 ounces, which is probably about the maximum size for the species. The average size is 100 to 200 pounds.

FOOD: California black sea bass feed on a variety of fish, including sheepshead, and on crabs and other mollusks.

FISHING METHODS: Bottom fishing

BAITS: Baitfish, cut baits, crabs, clams, and shrimp

■ Black Drum (Pogonias cromis)

COMMON NAMES: Black drum, drum, and sea drum

DESCRIPTION: A member of the croaker family, the black drum is not as popular a game fish as the red drum. It is most easily distinguished from the red drum (channel bass) by the lack of a prominent dark spot near the base of the tail. The overall color of the black drum ranges from gray to almost silvery, usually with a coppery sheen. Young specimens usually have broad, vertical bands of a dark color. The body shape is short and deep, the back is arched, and the undersurface is somewhat flat. There are barbels on the chin.

RANGE: Black drums are an Atlantic species found from southern New England to Argentina, though they are rare north of New York. Centers of abundance include North Carolina, Florida, Louisiana, and Texas.

HABITAT: Usually found in schools, black drum prefer inshore sandy areas such as bays, lagoons, channels, and ocean surfs, and are also often found near wharves and bridges.

SIZE: The black drum is known to reach a maximum weight of nearly 150 pounds. However, the average size is 20 to 30 pounds.

FOOD: Black drum are bottom-feeders, preferring clams, mussels, crabs, shrimp, and other mollusks.

FISHING METHODS: Bottom fishing

BAITS: Clams, cut baits, and crabs

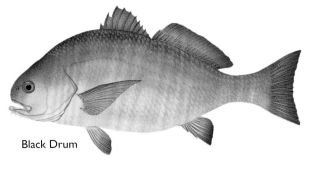

Black Drum

■ Goliath Grouper *(Epinephelus itajara* or *Promicrops itajara)*

COMMON NAMES: Goliath grouper, giant sea bass, spotted jewfish, jewfish, spotted grouper, and guasa

DESCRIPTION: Probably the largest of the groupers, the goliath grouper is not the gamest of fighters, but its weight alone makes up for that shortcoming. The overall color of the goliath grouper ranges from black to grayish brown, and the back and sides are mottled. The upper sides contain dark spots. The tail is convex along the rear margin. The flesh of the goliath grouper is quite tasty. During World War II, it was sold as "imported salt cod."

RANGE: The precise range of the goliath grouper seems uncertain. However, it is found in warmer waters of both the Atlantic and the Pacific and is most abundant in Florida waters and off the coast of Texas.

HABITAT: Despite its large size, the goliath grouper is most often found in relatively shallow water along the coast. It is at home under ledges and in reefs, in rocky holes, around bridges, and in deep channels.

SIZE: Though the rod-and-reel record is a 680-pounder, goliath groupers reach weights of at least 750 pounds. The average is probably 100 to 250 pounds.

FOOD: Goliath groupers feed on a great variety of small reef fish, including sheepshead, and also feed on crabs and squid.

FISHING METHODS: Bottom fishing

BAITS: Live baits, grunts, and almost any fish found on the reefs

■ Blackfish *(Tautoga onitis)*

COMMON NAMES: Blackfish, tautog, and oysterfish

DESCRIPTION: The blackfish is a member of the wrasse family, most of which are very brightly colored. The blackfish, however, is a drab gray or gray brown with irregular black mottling. Its body shape is relatively long and quite plump. The snout is blunt, the lips are thick, and the jaws hold powerful crushing teeth. The edge of the tail is straight. The dorsal fin is quite long and spiny. The blackfish's flesh is very tasty, but for some reason it is not much used. The blackfish is an accomplished bait stealer.

RANGE: The blackfish is an Atlantic species found from Nova Scotia to South Carolina. It is most numerous from Cape Cod to Delaware Bay.

HABITAT: Blackfish are a coastal bottom-feeding species, preferring such lies as mussel beds, rocky areas both inshore and offshore, the outer edges of jetties and piers, and old wrecks. They are seldom found in water deeper than 60 feet.

SIZE: The average rod-caught blackfish weighs about 3 pounds, but 6- to 8-pounders are far from unusual, and the species can reach a maximum weight of about 25 pounds.

FOOD: Blackfish are bottom-feeders that eat such items as barnacles, mussels, crabs, snails, sea worms, shrimp, and even lobsters.

FISHING METHODS: Bottom fishing

BAITS: Crabs, shrimp, cut baits, and clams

■ Sea Bass *(Centropristes striatus)*

COMMON NAMES: Sea bass, black sea bass, blackfish, humpback, and black will

DESCRIPTION: The sea bass, though small, is one of the most popular game fish in its somewhat restricted range. It has a rather stout body shape, with a high back and a moderately pointed snout. The apex of each gill cover holds a sharp spine. The overall color is gray to brownish gray to blue black, lighter on the fish's underparts. The sides are sometimes mottled and at other times appear to have light, horizontal stripes formed by rows of spots. The dorsal fin also has rows of spots. The most distinctive trait of the sea bass is the elongated ray on the upper edge of the tail—it sticks out far to the rear of the rest of the tail. Sea bass are fine eating.

RANGE: Sea bass are found from Maine to northern Florida, but they are most common from Cape Hatteras to Cape Cod.

HABITAT: Sea bass are bottom-dwellers of coastal areas. Their preferred depths seem to be 20 to 50 feet, though large sea bass are often found at depths of up to 100 feet, especially in winter. Sea bass like such spots as mussel beds, rocky areas, wrecks, pilings, bridges, offshore reefs and ledges, and rocky heads.

SIZE: Sea bass hit about 8 pounds maximum. The average weight is 1 to 3 pounds.

FOOD: Sea bass feed on smaller fish, but they prefer clams, mussels, crabs, shrimp, sea worms, and squid.

FISHING METHODS: Bottom fishing

BAITS: Cut baits, clams, crabs, shrimp, killies, and sea-worms

Atlantic Codfish (*Gadus morhua*)

COMMON NAMES: Atlantic codfish, codfish, and cod

DESCRIPTION: This pot-bellied heavyweight of the northern Atlantic is the cause of many a runny nose among commercial and sportfishermen in the cold-weather months. The thick-bodied Atlantic cod seems to have two color phases: red and gray. In the red phase, the fish may vary from orange to reddish brown. The gray phase ranges from black to greenish to brownish gray. The underparts are lighter, and the sides have many dark spots. The pale lateral line distinguishes the Atlantic cod from the haddock. The cod differs from the look-alike pollock in its longer chin barbel and the fact that its upper jaw projects past the lower (the opposite is true of the pollock). The cod's dorsal fin is in three spineless sections, and the anal fin, also spineless, has two sections—an unusual fin makeup.

RANGE: In the western Atlantic, the cod is found from Greenland south to North Carolina. In the eastern Atlantic, it ranges throughout the Baltic Sea, from northern Scandinavia east to some parts of Russia, and south to the Bay of Biscay.

HABITAT: Atlantic cod are schooling fish for the most part, bottom-feeders, and lovers of cold water. Though the young may be found in shallow water, cod generally prefer depths of 60 feet or more and are sometimes found down to 1,500 feet. Sportfishermen usually catch cod at the 50- to 300-foot levels. Cod migrate north and south to some extent, but most movement is from relatively shallow water, where they are likely to be found in winter, to the deeps, where they go in summer. Cod seem to prefer areas with a rocky or broken bottom and such places as wrecks.

SIZE: The average Atlantic cod taken by sportfishermen probably falls into the 6- to 12-pound category, but the rod-and-reel record is more than 80 pounds, and the species is known to exceed 200 pounds. Cod of up to 60 pounds are not unusual in the New Jersey to southern New England area.

FOOD: Atlantic cod feed on a variety of bottom life, including various small fish (notably herring), crabs, clams, squid, mussels, snails, sea worms, and lobsters.

FISHING METHODS: Bottom fishing

BAITS: Cut baits, clams, squid, bunkers, and herring

Pollock (*Pollachius virens*)

COMMON NAMES: Pollock, Boston bluefish, green cod, and coalfish

DESCRIPTION: The pollock, in effect, lives under the shadow of its famous relative, the Atlantic cod. A better fighter than the cod (probably because it is generally taken from shallower water), the pollock has a shorter chin barbel than its relative, and its lower jaw projects beyond the upper jaw (the cod's upper jaw projects farther than the lower jaw). The pollock is not spotted, as is the cod, and its tail is more severely forked. A pollock's colors range from dark-olive green to brownish on the upper parts, yellowish to gray on the lower sides, to silvery on the belly. Like the cod, the pollock's flesh is excellent eating.

RANGE: Pollock range in the western Atlantic from the Gulf of St. Lawrence to Chesapeake Bay and in the eastern Atlantic from Iceland south to the Bay of Biscay.

HABITAT: In general, pollock are found in somewhat shallower water than are cod, and they are often caught at intermediate depths. Occasionally, usually during May at such points as Cape Cod's Race Point Rip, pollock come into shallow water near shore and can be taken on or near the surface.

SIZE: Most pollock caught by sport anglers weigh 4 to 12 pounds. However, the species has a maximum weight of 45 pounds.

FOOD: Pollock feed on a variety of fish—including herring and small cod—and on shrimp and some crustaceans and mollusks, as well as sea worms.

FISHING METHODS: Bottom fishing

BAITS: Live baits, cut baits, herring, clams, and seaworms

■ Summer Flounder
(Paralichthys dentatus)

COMMON NAMES: Summer flounder, fluke, and flatfish

DESCRIPTION: The summer flounder is one of about 500 members of the flatfish family, a curious group. They begin life in an upright position and have an eye on each side of the head. As they grow, however, the body begins to tilt, in some species to the right, in others to the left, and the eye on the downward-facing surface begins to travel to the upward-facing surface. Finally, the transformation is complete, and the fish spends the rest of its life on its side, with both eyes on the same side of the head (above and just to the rear of the point of the jaw). The summer flounder is white on the side that comes in contact with the ocean floor. The color of the upper surface depends on the physical makeup of the ocean floor, but is usually olive, brown, or gray, with prominent dark spots and some mottling. The body is flat and quite deep. The dorsal and anal fins are extremely long.

RANGE: The summer flounder occurs in the United States from Maine to South Carolina.

HABITAT: The summer flounder lives on the bottom of the ocean floor, often buried in sand or mud. In summer, it is found in shallow water, sometimes in depths of only a few feet, while in winter, it moves offshore into as much as 50 fathoms of water. It frequents bays and harbors, the mouths of estuaries, and is also often found around various bottom obstructions such as wrecked ships.

SIZE: Most summer flounders caught by sportfishermen weigh 1 to 4 pounds, but the maximum size is probably close to 30 pounds.

FOOD: Summer flounders eat a wide variety of small fish, as well as sea worms, crabs, clams, squid, and shrimp.

FISHING METHODS: Bottom fishing, drifting, and jigging (bucktails tipped with bait)

BAITS: Live baitfish, cut baits, squid, and spearing

■ Winter Flounder
(Psuedopleuronectes americanus)

COMMON NAMES: Winter flounder, flatfish, blueback, blackback, black flounder, and mud dab

DESCRIPTION: One of the smaller members of the vast flatfish family, the winter flounder differs from the summer flounder in its smaller size and weight and in the fact that it is "right-eyed" (that is, it has both eyes and the skin pigmentation on the right side of its head) while the summer flounder is "left-eyed." The winter flounder is white on the underside (the side on which it lies on the ocean floor), while on the other side the colors range from reddish brown to slate gray, usually with some dark spots. The mouth is small, and the lateral line is relatively straight. The winter flounder is widely sought for food by both commercial and sportfishermen.

RANGE: The winter flounder has an extreme range of Labrador south to Georgia, but it is most common from the Gulf of St. Lawrence to Chesapeake Bay.

HABITAT: The winter flounder is found mostly in shallow water—as shallow as 1 foot, in fact—but is occasionally found at depths of up to 400 feet. It lies on the bottom, preferring sand or mud, but accepting clay, gravel, or even a hard bottom. In the fall, this species tends to move toward the shallows, while in spring the movement is toward deeper water.

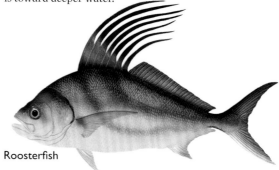

Roosterfish

SIZE: Winter flounders average from ½ to 1½ pounds in weight and 8 to 15 inches in length. The maximum size is about 8 pounds, and such heavyweights are often called snowshoes.

FOOD: Winter flounders eat such items as sea worms, crabs, shrimp, and minute crustaceans, as well as small fish and fish larvae.

FISHING METHODS: Bottom fishing and chumming

BAITS: Seaworms, clams, mussels, and squid

■ Roosterfish *(Nematistius pectoralis)*

COMMON NAMES: Roosterfish, papagallo, gallo, and pez de gallo

DESCRIPTION: The roosterfish—a relative of the jacks and pompanos, which it resembles at least in body shape—gets its name from the seven extremely long (far longer than the greatest body depth) spines of the forward dorsal fin, which vaguely resemble a rooster's comb. Its body colors are green to gray blue on the upper areas, white to gold below. Two black stripes curve downward and then rearward from the forward dorsal fin, which itself has a white, horizontal stripe. The roosterfish is a furious fighter and a fine table fish.

RANGE: Roosterfish are a Pacific species occurring from Peru as far north as southern California. They are particularly abundant in the Gulf of California.

HABITAT: Little is known of the movements and life history of the roosterfish. However, fishermen often catch them in sandy inshore bays and by trolling in open water. The fish are sometimes seen swimming on the surface, their dorsals erect and waving above the surface.

SIZE: The average size of a roosterfish is estimated at around 5 to 20 pounds. The maximum size is probably about 130 pounds.

FOOD: The dietary preferences of the roosterfish aren't known in detail, but these fish certainly feed on almost any small fish that is available. They strike artificial lures and plugs willingly.

FISHING METHODS: Casting and sight casting

BAITS: Live baits, cut baits, and artificial lures

■ Porgy *(Stenotomus chrysops)*

COMMON NAMES: Porgy, northern porgy, and scup

DESCRIPTION: The porgy (often called scup in some areas of its range) is what might be called a saltwater panfish. It has a somewhat ovate, high-backed body with a small mouth and strong teeth. The basic body color ranges from silvery to brown, and there are usually three or four dark, vertical bars on the sides. The dorsal fin is quite spiny. The porgy's flesh is highly palatable, and it is caught by both sport and commercial anglers, though in some areas rod fishermen consider the porgy a nuisance.

RANGE: The porgy (northern porgy) is found from Nova Scotia south to the Atlantic coast of Florida. In summer and fall, it is quite abundant off the coasts of New England, New York, and New Jersey.

HABITAT: Porgies seem to prefer some bottom debris, such as mussel beds. They live on or near the bottom in the middle depths of the continental shelf.

SIZE: Porgies average ½ to 2 pounds. The maximum size is about 4 pounds, and such individuals are often called humpbacks.

FOOD: Porgies feed mainly on small crustaceans, worms, mollusks, and occasionally on vegetable matter.

FISHING METHODS: Bottom fishing

BAITS: Cut baits, clams, squid, and crabs

■ Spanish Mackerel *(Scomberomorus maculatus)*

DESCRIPTION: This beautiful, streamlined fish—though of modest size as mackerels go—is a magnificent fighter, making sizzling runs and soaring leaps. Its body shape is rather compressed, and its colors range from iridescent steel blue or occasionally greenish on the dorsal surface to silvery blue below. The side markings are mustard or bronze spots, and are quite large. The dorsal fin is in two sections, and there are dorsal and anal finlets. Its side

Spanish Mackerel

spots, lack of stripes, and absence of scales on the pectoral fins distinguish the Spanish mackerel from the king mackerel and the cero.

RANGE: Spanish mackerel occur from Cape Cod south to Brazil, but they are never numerous in the northern part of their range. They are most plentiful from the Carolinas into the Gulf of Mexico.

HABITAT: This warm-water species is usually found in open waters, cruising near the surface and slashing into schools of baitfish. They do, however, make occasional forays into the surf and into bays and channels in search of food sources.

SIZE: Spanish mackerel average 1½ to 4 pounds, but they can reach a maximum weight of about 20 pounds. A 10-pounder is a very good one.

FOOD: Spanish mackerel feed primarily on a wide variety of small baitfish and on shrimp. A favorite bait in some areas, particularly Florida waters, is a very small baitfish called a glass minnow.

FISHING METHODS: Casting, chumming, and jigging

BAITS: Live baits, cut baits, shrimp, and artificial lures

■ Sheepshead
(*Archosargus probatocephalus*)

COMMON NAMES: Sheepshead and convict fish

DESCRIPTION: Similar in shape and appearance to the porgy, the sheepshead is a high-backed, blunt-headed species whose bait-stealing abilities have frustrated countless fishermen. Its small mouth has a formidable set of rock-hard, close-coupled teeth that are capable of demolishing a crab and biting through a light-wire hook. The basic color is silvery, though the dorsal surface's color is closer to gray. The sides have five to seven

dark, vertical bands, and the spines of the dorsal fin are large and coarse. Sheepshead fight well and are excellent on the table.

RANGE: The sheepshead is found from Nova Scotia south to the northeastern Gulf of Mexico. It is far more numerous in the southern part of its range, particularly in Florida waters.

HABITAT: The sheepshead is a gregarious species that moves with the tides to wherever the food is plentiful. It is an inshore fish, taking up residence in bays and channels and around bridges, piers, pilings, and the like.

SIZE: The sheepshead averages about 1 to 5 pounds, but it may attain weights in excess of 20 pounds.

FOOD: Its teeth are a dead giveaway to the sheephead's dietary preferences, which include crabs, mollusks, barnacles, and the like, as well as shrimp.

FISHING METHODS: Bottom fishing and chumming

BAITS: Crabs, clams, shrimp, mussels, sand bugs, and jigs

■ African Pompano (*Alectis crinitus*)

COMMON NAMES: African pompano, threadfish, Cuban jack, and flechudo

DESCRIPTION: The head profile in adult fish is slanted and almost vertical and the eyes are large. The body is flat with silver sides with an almost iridescent sheen. The forward rays of the dorsal and anal fins are long.

RANGE: The African pompano's range is from Brazil to Massachusetts. It is commonly caught in Florida waters.

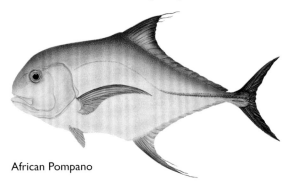

African Pompano

HABITAT: Young African pompano like shallow reefs. As the young Africans mature and become adults, they seek deeper reefs and wrecks.

SIZE: Adults can grow to lengths of 3 feet, and weights of 30 to 35 pounds are common. They are tough fighters, especially on light tackle. The record fish in Florida weighed 50 pounds, 8 ounces.

FOOD: Not a true pompano, the African feeds on small baitfish and can be caught by chumming over reefs. Drifting or trolling a rigged bait is the most common technique.

FISHING METHODS: Bottom fishing, chumming, drifting, and trolling

BAITS: Whole fish, cut baits, live baits, and squid

■ Pompano *(Trachinotus carolinus)*

COMMON NAMES: Pompano, common pompano, and sunfish

DESCRIPTION: This high-strung, slab-sided character is the most abundant and most important member of the pompano family, which includes such fish as the much-prized permit. It has a small mouth, blunt head, and a relatively shallow body (its body depth decreases proportionally with growth). Dorsal-surface colors range from gray, silver, or blue to blue green, and the sides and underparts are silvery. The ventral surfaces are flecked with yellow. The dorsal fin is bluish, and most of the other fins are yellowish. The pompano is an epicurean's delight.

RANGE: The pompano is found from Brazil north to Massachusetts, and also in the West Indies and in Bermuda waters. It is particularly numerous in Florida and the Gulf of Mexico.

HABITAT: Pompano are inshore school fish, feeding on the bottom in shallow water in the surf, in channels and inlets and bays, and around bridges. They occasionally range well up into rivers with the tide.

SIZE: Pompano average about 2 pounds in weight, and the maximum size is thought to be about 8 pounds.

FOOD: Pompano feed mostly on bivalve mollusks and

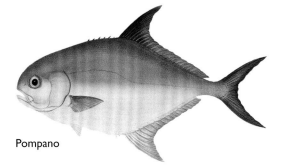

Pompano

on small crustaceans, notably a small beetle-like crustacean called the sand flea.

FISHING METHODS: Bottom fishing, casting, and jigging

BAITS: Shrimp, sand bugs, cut fish, clams, jigs, and bucktails

■ California Corbina *(Menticirrhus undulatus)*

COMMON NAMES: California corbina, corbina, corvina, whiting, and sea trout

DESCRIPTION: The wary and unpredictable corbina, a member of the whiting group, is among the most popular fish caught in inshore waters of the Pacific. The basic color is some shade of blue gray, and identifying characteristics include a blunt snout; a short, high, forward dorsal fin and a long, lower rear dorsal fin; and small barbels at the tip of the lower jaw. The corbina is a strong underwater fighter and an excellent food fish.

RANGE: The corbina is found from the Gulf of California north to Point Conception.

HABITAT: Primarily a target of surf fishermen, the corbina is an inshore species found mostly along sandy beaches and in shallow bays, moving into the surf line on the incoming tide.

SIZE: Corbina reach a maximum weight of about 8 pounds. The average size is 2 to 3 pounds.

FOOD: Crabs of various kinds are the favorite food of the corbina, but it also feeds on clams and sea worms.

FISHING METHODS: Bottom fishing and surf fishing

BAITS: Clams, squid, shrimp, and cut baits

■ Atlantic Croaker
(Micropogon undulatus)

COMMON NAMES: Atlantic croaker, croaker, hardhead, and golden croaker

DESCRIPTION: The most common and most prized of the eastern U.S. members of the huge croaker family, the Atlantic croaker is a strong fighter and makes for delicious eating. The croaker family gets its name from the sound it makes—audible for quite a distance—by repeated contractions of its swim bladder and a unique "drumming muscle." The Atlantic croaker has a small, tapered body; a short, high, forward dorsal fin and a long, lower rear dorsal fin; and small barbels on the chin. The colors are brassy gold and silver, and the upper parts of the body contain numerous dark spots that sometimes form slanting bars.

RANGE: The Atlantic croaker is found from Massachusetts south to Florida and west to Texas and eastern Mexico. In recent years, however, its numbers have declined in the northern part of the range. The center of abundance seems to be from the Carolinas to Florida and in the northern Gulf of Mexico.

HABITAT: Atlantic croakers are seldom found far from estuaries, preferring sandy shallows, shallow shell beds, sloughs, lagoons, and weedy flats. However, cold weather often sends the fish into deeper water.

SIZE: Atlantic croakers average ½ to about 2½ pounds and attain a maximum size of about 5 pounds.

FOOD: Predominantly bottom-feeders, Atlantic croakers feed on clams, crabs, sea worms, shrimp, snails, mussels, and sand fleas.

FISHING METHODS: Bottom fishing and chumming

BAITS: Shrimp, crabs, seaworms, clams, and cut baits

■ Red Snapper *(Lutjanus blackfordi)*

DESCRIPTION: Most widely known for its eating qualities, the red snapper is among the best known of the more than 200 species of snappers found in the world's warm seas. The red snapper's color pattern (rose red overall, though paler red on the underparts, with red fins

Red Snapper

and eyes, and a black spot on each side), long pectoral fin, and more numerous anal-fin rays distinguish this species from other snappers.

RANGE: The red snapper occurs from the Middle Atlantic and Gulf Coast of the United States southward throughout the tropical American Atlantic.

HABITAT: The red snapper's preference for deep waters—it is sometimes found as deep as 100 fathoms and seems most prevalent at 20 to 60 fathoms—detracts from its importance as a sport fish. It usually is found a few feet above a hard bottom.

SIZE: Most red snappers caught commercially run from 5 to about 30 pounds. The maximum size seems to be about 35 pounds.

FOOD: Red snappers eat baitfish and various deep-water mollusks and crustaceans.

FISHING METHODS: Bottom fishing, drifting, and chumming

BAITS: Squid, cut baits, crabs, and live baits

■ Yellowtail Snapper
(Ocyurus chrysurus)

COMMON NAMES: Yellowtail snapper, flag, and tail

DESCRIPTION: This fish is easily identified by the yellow stripe that runs the entire length of the body from the eye to the forked tail. It has a bluish tint above the yellow stripe and a silver underbelly. The colors become mottled as the yellowtail grows in size. Yellowtail are excellent eating and one of the best of the reef species.

RANGE: Yellowtail snappers range from Florida to the Bahamas and the Caribbean.

HABITAT: The yellowtail snapper is a popular school fish that lives on the coral reefs of southern Florida and the Florida Keys.

SIZE: The average weight is about 1 to 4 pounds. Yellowtails that weigh more than 5 pounds are called "flags." The top weight is about 8 pounds.

FOOD: Yellowtail snappers eat mainly small baitfish and shrimp.

FISHING METHODS: Bottom fishing, chumming, and drifting baits (Yellowtail snappers are fussy eaters. Under clear water conditions, light leaders and 10-pound-test line are a must. A small jig baited with shrimp and drifted into a chum slick is the most productive technique.)

BAITS: Small baitfish, cut baits, shrimp, and small jigs

■ Northern Whiting
(Menticirrhus saxatilis)

COMMON NAMES: Northern whiting, whiting, northern kingfish, and kingfish

DESCRIPTION: The northern whiting is one of four whitings (all members of the large croaker family) that inhabit the Atlantic and Gulf coasts of the United States. The basic color is silver gray or silver brown, and the upper part of the body contains rather indistinct dark, vertical bands. The mouth is small, and there is a single chin barbel. The northern whiting is the only one of the four U.S. whitings in which the third and largest spine of the forward dorsal fin, when laid flat, reaches well past the beginning of the long and soft rear dorsal fin. The northern whiting is an excellent food fish.

RANGE: The northern whiting is found on the Atlantic coast of the United States from Maine to Florida.

HABITAT: Northern whiting are usually found over a sandy bottom in the surf, shallow sloughs and bays, and, as the water temperature cools, in depths as great as 100 feet or more.

SIZE: Averaging about 1 pound, the northern whiting reaches a maximum size of about 3 pounds and 18 inches in length.

FOOD: The northern whiting feeds mainly on small baitfish, sea worms, and small crustaceans.

FISHING METHODS: Bottom fishing, drifting, and surf fishing

BAITS: Baitfish, seaworms, crabs, and clams

■ Hogfish (Lachnolaimus maximus)

COMMON NAMES: Hogfish, hog snapper, hog wrasse, captain, perro perro, and pargo gallo

DESCRIPTION: The hogfish is unmistakable. It has a long snout with a purple band extending from its snout to its dorsal fin. The color is reddish, and the most noticeable features are the three long rays of the dorsal fin. Hogfish rank very high in taste and are one of the best of the reef species. They are sometimes called the captain's fish because this is one species captains prefer to keep for themselves.

RANGE: Hogfish can range from North Carolina to Bermuda, the Caribbean, and Florida, especially the reefs of the Florida Keys.

HABITAT: Hogfish are basically a reef fish. They are typically caught by fishermen bottom fishing or chumming for snappers on patches of coral.

SIZE: Average hogfish run 1 to 6 pounds. Hogfish can grow to more than 20 pounds, but such fish are unusual. Some reports claim hogfish can reach 45 pounds.

FOOD: Hogfish eat mainly baitfish, shrimp, and crustaceans.

FISHING METHODS: Bottom fishing, chumming, and drifting baits (usually a bycatch of chumming coral reefs for snappers)

BAITS: Baitfish, cut baits, shrimp, and jigs

COOKING
TECHNIQUES

Section Eight
COOKING TECHNIQUES

FROM HOOK TO TABLE

There are certain species of fish that should be released unharmed after a good fight. Billfish, bonefish, and tarpon, for example, should be released to protect and ensure a healthy population of these great fighters. Fortunately, there are many other healthy species of fish that can be caught, cooked, and fed to millions of fishermen without hurting the species. Dolphin, for example, grow 3 inches a week and up to 40 pounds a year. A single dolphin produces 555,000 eggs several times a year. There are also many other species that can be harvested for the kitchen, including snappers, crappies, and some groupers. (Before taking any fish home, always consult local and state regulations on seasons, restricted species, size requirements, and limits.)

What happens to these species from hook to table, however, can make the difference between a delicious fish dinner and a culinary nightmare. In this chapter, I offer good advice on the proper field care and dressing of fish, as well as how to properly fillet, smoke, and freeze a fish.

Next comes the choice of a good recipe for your fish. Some recipes are based on a particular species. Trying to make dolphin ceviche out of a king mackerel, for example, would be a disaster. Follow the species recommendations as closely as you can, but if a recipe says "fish fillets," you are safe to use a fresh fillet from almost any other species. And don't be afraid to use fish that have been properly frozen and thawed.

The key word here is "fresh." Fish should smell fresh and not fishy. If it's a whole fish, the eyes should be clear and not cloudy and sunken. The flesh should be firm. Press your finger into the flesh; the flesh should spring back. Fresh fish will almost always produce a memorable dining experience.

FIELD CARE AND DRESSING OF FISH

If you sit down at the dinner table and bite into a poor-tasting bass or walleye fillet from a fish you caught, there's a good chance that the second-rate taste is your own fault. In all probability, the fish was not handled properly from the moment it came out of the water. Fish spoil rapidly unless they are kept alive or quickly killed and put on ice.

Here are the necessary steps involved in getting a fresh-caught fish from the water to the table so that it will retain its original flavor.

First, the decision to keep a fish dead or alive depends on conditions. For example, if you're out on a lake and have no ice in your boat, you'll want to keep all fish alive until it's time to head home. Under no circumstances should you toss fish into the bottom of the boat, let them lie there in the sun, and then gather them up at the end

With safety-pin-type stringers, run the clip through the thin membrane behind the lower lip. This lets the fish swim freely and won't injure the fish should you decide to release it.

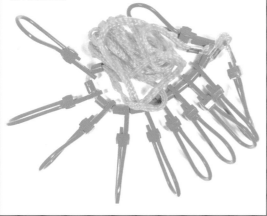

of the day. If you try that stunt, the fillets will reach your table with the consistency of mush and a flavor to match. Instead, put your fish on a stringer as quickly as possible and put them back into the water, where they can begin to recover from the shock of being caught.

Use the safety-pin-type stringer and run the wire up through the thin, almost-transparent membrane just behind the fish's lower lip. This will enable the fish to swim freely, and the fish will recover from this minor injury should you decide to release it at the end of the day.

Do **not** shove the stringer under the gill cover and out of the mouth. This damages the gills and kills fish fast. Also, avoid cord stringers, where all fish are bunched in a clump at the end of the cord. This is perhaps acceptable on short trips for small panfish, which are generally caught in big numbers and quickly cleaned, but if you're after bigger fish and want to keep them alive and fresh—either for the table or release at the end of the day—use the safety-pin stringer. It does its job well.

If you're rowing or trolling slowly, you can probably keep the stringer in the water. If you have a big boat and motor, however, it's a good idea to take the stringer into the boat for those fast runs to other hot spots. If the run is fairly long, wet down the fish occasionally, but don't tow a fish in the water at high speed—you'll drown it.

If you're several miles from camp, use the following technique to get fish back alive. When returning to camp with a stringer of fish, stop your boat every half

mile or so and ease the fish over the side. Let the fish swim around for five minutes or so before hauling them back into the boat and continuing the trip to camp. This way, you should have no trouble reaching camp with lively walleyes to be put in your shoreline live box. Keeping fish alive is especially important on extended trips to remote areas, where ice in sufficient quantities isn't generally available.

On the subject of lengthy fishing trips to remote areas where ice is not available, you can still keep fish alive for a week or more. Your best bet is to use a home-made collapsible fish box, which can be weighted with a rock in a foot of water onshore or floated in deep water. Either way, the fish will stay alive until the end of the trip. Keeping fish alive for lengthy periods in remote areas is impossible without such a box. Keeping fish on a stringer at dockside will **not** work for long periods. With some wood and wire mesh, a fish box is easy to build. This assumes, of course, that a fish has been unhooked and is placed in the fish box in good condition. If it has been deeply hooked and appears to be dying slowly, however, it's best to kill the fish immediately, gut it, and keep it on ice.

Killing a fish quickly is simple. Holding the fish upright, impale it between the eyes with the point of your knife or rap it on the head with a heavy stick. The

A wicker creel still does its job well. Lined with wet ferns, grass, or newspapers, it will keep fish reasonably cool on the hottest days. Canvas creels are also readily available and simple to use. Occasionally dipping the entire creel in a stream, wetting it thoroughly, will keep the fish inside in good shape during a daylong trip. If you're a surf fisherman, you can also bury your fish in damp sand. This will keep your fish cool and out of the sun.

How to Field Dress a Fish

Step 1 • With the fish belly up, make a cut from the anal opening to the gills.

Step 2 • Make two cuts at the gills, one below and one above the gills where they form a V.

Step 3 • Next, stick a finger into the gullet as shown and begin to pull downward. The gills and entrails should come out easily.

Step 4 • With the entrails out, run your thumbnail along the backbone to break and clean the blood sac. Wash the fish. Once is enough—the less water coming into direct contact with the meat, the firmer the flesh will be when you eat it.

important factor is killing it quickly, since the more slowly it dies the more rapidly the flesh will deteriorate.

If you're a stream fisherman, it's wise to carry your catch in a canvas or wicker creel. The canvas creel works fine, so long as it is occasionally immersed in water. The traditional wicker creel will work just as well, but it should be lined with ferns, leaves, or wet newspaper.

If you're a surf fisherman, you can bury your catch in the damp sand. Just remember to mark the spot. A burlap sack occasionally doused in the surf also makes a practical fish bag. The important factor is to keep the fish cool and out of the sun.

Regardless of the various ways to keep fish cool, they should first be cleaned properly. With a bit of prac-

tice and a sharp knife, the job can be done in less than a minute.

Take a sharp knife and insert it in the anal opening on the underside of the fish. Slit the skin forward from there to the point of the V-shaped area where the forward part of the belly is attached to the gills. Put your finger into the gills and around that V-shaped area, and pull sharply to the rear. You will thus remove the gills and all or most of the entrails. Then, with the fish upside down, put your thumb into the body cavity at the anal opening, and press your thumbnail against the backbone. Keeping your nail tight against the bone, run your thumb forward to the head, thereby removing the dark blood from the sac along the backbone.

Electric Fillet Knives—When You Have More Than One Fish

If you're fishing for species where there is no bag limit and you're fishing for the freezer or you just want a fillet knife that's fast, you should shop for an electric fillet knife.

Those early electric fillet knives were too heavy and came with a 6-foot power cord. They worked fine, as long as you were within 6 feet of a power outlet. Today, electric fillet knives have seen big improvements. There are now cordless models with rechargeable batteries and models that can be plugged into your automobile's cigarette lighter or clamped to your boat's batteries. You can also buy electric fillet knives with interchangeable blades of different lengths and serrated stainless-steel blades.

Filleting a fish with an electric knife doesn't require drastic changes in technique. Lay the fish on its side, cut down just behind the pectoral fin until you hit bone, and then turn the blade sideways and run it flat against the backbone to the tail, but don't cut the fillet from the fish. Next, run the electric knife between the skin and flesh until the fillet is skinned.

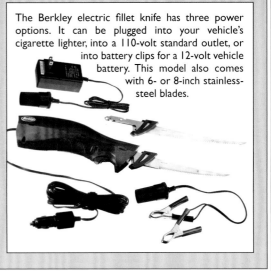

The Berkley electric fillet knife has three power options. It can be plugged into your vehicle's cigarette lighter, into a 110-volt standard outlet, or into battery clips for a 12-volt vehicle battery. This model also comes with 6- or 8-inch stainless-steel blades.

One more tip: More good fish meat is probably ruined during the drive home than during any other point in the trip from the water to the plate. Take the time to ice the fish properly for the trip home. Don't pack the fish in direct contact with the ice. The ice is sure to melt, and the fish, lying in the water, might well deteriorate, becoming soft and mushy. It's far better to put the fish in plastic bags, seal the bags so that they are watertight, and then pack the bags in ice. The fish will stay cool—and dry—until you get home.

When you get the fish home, scale or skin them. If they are freshwater fish, wash them thoroughly, inside and out, in cool tap water. If they are saltwater fish,

prepare a heavy brine solution, and brush them thoroughly (a pastry-type brush works well) with the brine until they are clean.

Separate the fish into lots, each of which will make a meal for yourself or your family, and wrap each lot in freezer paper or plastic wrap. Then, package them in sealable plastic bags, sealing as tightly as possible to prevent freezer burn. Freeze the fish as quickly as possible.

Some fishermen prefer not to field dress their fish, but to fillet and skin them. This method, which appears difficult but is actually quite simple, is described in the next section.

HOW TO FILLET FISH

Filleting a fish is easy and doesn't have to be a messy chore. The two methods described here have a number of advantages. First, gutting the fish is not necessary since entrails are left intact and never touched with a knife. Second, scaling the fish is also eliminated because the fillet is skinned and the skin is discarded, scales and all. Finally, and most important, the

fillets are bone free, which is especially important when serving fish to children.

Filleting is also a good idea for fishermen on extended trips, where sizable quantities of fish are to be packed out or transported home. The head, entrails, fins, and skin are left behind and only the clean and meaty fillets are brought home.

How to Fillet a Fish

Step 1 • Using a sharp knife, make two initial cuts, one behind the gill plate (as shown) and another at the base of the tail down to the backbone or spine. The cut at the base of the tail is optional. Some fishermen prefer to extend the final fillet cut through the tail.

Step 2 • Next, make a cut on one side of the dorsal fin lengthwise from the first two initial cuts, starting behind the head and cutting down to the base of the tail. As you extend the cut, carefully begin to separate the fillet from the backbone.

Step 3 • Your slice downward will begin to separate the fillet from the backbone. A good fillet knife should have a 7- or 8-inch blade with some flex. A stainless-steel blade may be easier to maintain and will not rust, but carbon-steel fillet knives are easier to sharpen and will take an edge faster.

Step 4 • As you continue to separate the fillet, make sure you avoid the stomach and organs. Note that on this fillet there are no broken organs, digestive juices, or blood to taint the fillet.

Step 5 • Now, carefully begin to cut the fillet free from the fish. Keeping the blade as flat as possible will avoid damaging the fillets.

Step 6 • The final cut will free the clean fillet from the fish. If you prefer to skin your fillets, place them flesh side up, flat on the table. Work your knife blade between the skin and the meat, holding the skin down with your fingers. With a sawing motion, holding the blade flat and down against the skin, cut the meat free of the skin. The fillet and skin will separate easily.

Step 7 • This is how the fillet should look when cut from one side of the fish. Next, turn the fish over and remove the fillet from the other side of the fish exactly the same way. The next step (not shown here) is to remove the pinbones, which are in the forward third of the fillet. You can feel them easily with your fingers. Using needle-nose pliers, pull them out of the fillet. With a slight wiggle, they should slide out easily.

Step 8 • This is the final product—two clean salmon fillets. With the exception of flatfish, this technique will work on all other species with similar body types, such as striped bass, grouper, largemouth bass, and walleyes.

A word of caution: Check fish and game laws where you plan to fish. Some states and countries require that the skin be left on the fillets so the species can be identified at border crossings. Also, in some coastal states, fish with size limits cannot legally be filleted at sea.

There are two techniques to use when filleting a fish. The first, which requires an initial cut along both sides of the dorsal fin and a cut down to the backbone before slicing off the fillet, will salvage a bit more meat from the back of the fish. It is, however, more time consuming.

How to Fillet a Flounder

Step 1 • Filleting a summer flounder or fluke is a simple process. An 8- to 10-inch fillet knife with a flexible blade works best. The same technique can also be used on winter flounder, a much smaller flatfish. First, lay the flounder on a large cutting board.

Step 2 • Next, cut around the head and down along the lateral line to the tail, and then across the tail as shown. Make sure the cuts are down to the backbone. Some fillet knives have a serrated tip, which makes it easier to start that initial cut through the skin and scales.

Step 3 • Using your fillet knife, begin to cut between the flesh and the rib bones, starting at the base of the head and working toward the tail. It's important to keep the knife blade as flat as possible against the bones.

Step 4 • Use long, smooth strokes to separate the fillet from the bones. Gently hold back the fillet as you make the cut to make sure the blade is against the bones.

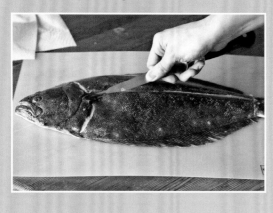

If you're filleting one or two big fish, use this technique.

If you are filleting a bunch of fish, however, take the shortcut technique, which is quick, easy, and clean. This method will work on any bass-shaped fish or walleye. Lay the fish flat and make a diagonal cut from behind the head to just behind the entrail sac, which holds the stomach. Next, turn the blade of the knife toward the tail and, holding the blade flat along the backbone, slice down to the tail until the fillet is cut clean off the fish. The little bit of waste along the top of the back is negligible.

Step 5 • Continue to use long, smooth strokes while cutting until the fillet is free from the body. Avoid using short strokes, which will make your fillet look as if it has been chopped off.

Step 6 • The end result is a clean fillet. Each fillet will have a ribbon fin along the outside edge. Peel or cut it away from the fillet and save it for your next flounder trip. The ribbon fin makes an excellent bait.

Step 7 • The next step is to remove the skin. Hold the fillet skin down as shown, and, using a sawing motion with the blade flat against the skin, separate the skin from the fillet. You can use your finger to hold the fillet, but the tines of a fork may hold it more firmly to the cutting board.

Step 8 • Turn the flounder over, belly side up, and make the identical cuts to remove the fillets. Each flounder will produce four clean fillets ready for your favorite recipe.

The Tastiest Fish

I live on the New Jersey shore, where the striped bass is king. But I don't like eating stripers because they are one of the blandest fish I've ever eaten. Unless you cover a striper fillet with some fancy sauce or dressing, it will have nearly zero taste. You don't agree? Maybe you have different taste buds. I love to catch stripers; I just don't like to eat them. In the Northeast, I'll swap a striper any day for a fluke or sea bass.

I'm also convinced that where you eat your fish makes a difference. A fried grouper sandwich in the Florida Keys will always taste better than the same sandwich in New York. So, with that geographic disclaimer, just what is the tastiest fish? Let's get started by listing what I believe are the top 10 tastiest fish in salt water. Some of these species can't be found in all parts of the country, but I'm still going to try to rate the species regardless of where they are found.

1 • Hogfish — This species is sometimes called the captain's fish because some charter captains will take it home for dinner.

2 • Yellowtail Snapper —There are more than 100 species of snappers all over the world, but the yellowtail gets the highest rating, followed by the red snapper, mutton snapper, and then mangrove snapper. Admittedly, all snappers taste great.

3 • Summer Flounder (Fluke) — My Northeast favorite, the summer flounder is great breaded and fried golden brown with a touch of lemon juice.

4 • Grouper — Like the snapper, there are many species of groupers and they all taste good. The 5- to 15-pounders are preferred for the dinner table. Stay away from the heavyweight groupers. Fish biologists claim these older fish may have consumed too many smaller fish that feed on toxin-producing algae. There is always the risk of ciguatera poisoning. Ciguatera toxin is harmless to fish, but poisonous to people.

5 • Salmon (Wild) — Only wild salmon get a top rating. Farm-raised salmon are sometimes tasteless.

6 • Tripletail — Maybe because they hide under crab pots and are hard to catch, tripletail are excellent eating. Or maybe it's because they look so much like freshwater black crappies, which are superb eating.

7 • Dolphin — Encrusted with coconut, fried, and flambéed with Grand Marnier, you would be hard put to find a better fish dinner than dolphin.

8 • Yellowfin and Bluefin Tuna — The best way to eat tuna is sushi, or coated with black pepper, seared 10 seconds on each side, and served with lots of wasabi.

9 • Cobia — Beer-battered and deep-fried chunks are delicious, but cobia is also a favorite on the grill. Look for cobia feeding under huge rays in clear water.

10 • Sea Bass — Sea bass fillets, fried or baked, always produce great-tasting flakey fish dinners. Unfortunately, sea bass are small, averaging only 1 to 3 pounds, but they make up for their pint size in taste.

Runners-up are cod, wahoo, striped bass, halibut, snook, weakfish, mako shark, and swordfish. Of this group, cod and wahoo are the best. Wahoo may look a bit like a king mackerel, but that's where the similarity ends. Wahoo meat is white and tastes great.

Here are a few fish that will never make my list of tasty fish: amberjack, king mackerel (unless smoked), grunts, bluefish (unless they are small 2- to 4-pounders), bonito, pickerel, or pike.

For freshwater fishermen, I have a short list and I can only come up with five species that I rate high for the table. Here they are in order of taste:

1 • Walleye	**4 • Trout**
2 • Black Crappie	**5 • Yellow Perch**
3 • Catfish	

I suspect that at least half of the fishermen who read this will not agree with my choices. I will also admit that fish preparation may be a critical factor, but I will still stick to my guns. These species are my top choices.

Fish Fillet Knives

Hold a knife in your hand. Do you like the way it looks and feels? If you do, you can probably do any cutting job with it, including filleting everything from a walleye to a 500-pound bluefin tuna. If you don't like the way a knife fits in your hand, you will never learn to use it effectively and it can literally be dangerous to use.

It's important to separate fish knives from hunting knives. I cherish my hunting knives and some of them may become family heirlooms. A hunting knife that may be used once a year to field dress a buck can cost hundreds of dollars. Fish knives are different. They rarely cost more than $15 to $35. Fillet knives are also work tools and designed for hard usage and abuse from the elements, especially salt water. I have even used sandpaper to remove rust from a knife left too long on a boat. It's not that difficult to put a good edge back on a fillet knife, even if it has a stainless-steel blade.

Choosing blade steel is actually a simple choice. I prefer stainless steel for fish knives. Carbon steel may be easy to sharpen, but, unfortunately, it will rust and require more care than stainless steel. If you prefer a knife that's easy to sharpen, but tougher to maintain, then buy a fillet knife with a carbon-steel blade. It's easy to put a razor edge on carbon steel with a whetstone. A good whetstone will last a lifetime with some care. Never use it dry. After you sharpen your knife, apply more oil to it and wipe it clean. Oil floats steel particles above the surface, so they do not clog the stone. Use a Washita stone, preferably mounted and clamped to your work surface so it does not move. It is very important that you maintain a 45-degree angle between the back of the blade and the stone as you draw the blade across the stone, as if you were taking a slice off the top.

On the other hand, if you want a fish knife that is nearly maintenance free, buy a knife with a stainless-steel blade. You can put a sharp edge on stainless steel with a whetstone, but if you're worried about maintaining that all-important 45-degree angle on the edge, an electric knife sharpener or a sharpening kit will ensure the correct angle and make the job easier.

The blade on a fillet knife should always have a slightly upturned tip. This design keeps the blade tip from accidentally tearing skin or flesh during filleting. If you can find one, buy a fillet knife with a serrated tip, which will make that initial cut into the fish skin easy. Blade length can vary, depending on the species of fish you usually fillet. A 4-inch blade makes an excellent trout knife, but an 8- to 10-inch blade is better for bigger fish and saltwater species.

Avoid fish knives with smooth, slick handles. Fish slime will make them dangerous to use. Fish knives should have rough, nonslip rubber or plastic handles. Many fillet knives on the market today have checkered polypropylene handles that are sanitary and easy to keep clean.

Most fishermen tend to be careless with fish knives because they are inexpensive and will invariably be lost long before they wear out. But that's not reason enough for letting a knife get rusty and dull. All knives should be kept sharp, clean, and coated with oil when not in use. Never store a knife in a sheath, especially a leather sheath, which will spot and corrode a blade from the acid in the leather. Remember, if a knife looks good and feels good in your hand, you probably picked the right knife.

This Dexter-Russell 8-inch fillet knife is a good size for nearly all fish species. The handle is slip-resistant polypropylene. Travel with the knife in a sheath, but never store it long-term in a sheath. Keep knives sharp, oiled, and stored with the blade wrapped in wax paper.

SMOKING YOUR FISH

Smoking your catch is simple, and you can easily turn out great-tasting smoked fish of a variety of species, from salmon to tuna. You can make your own smoker, but it may be more practical to buy a manufactured model. The method described here is "hot" smoking, which produces smoked fish that should be eaten within several days.

Before any fish is smoked, it must be brined. The brine solution will put salt in your fish to increase preservation, leech out blood, and intensify the smoke fla-

Smoker

Best Woods for Smoking

Alder: This is the sportsman's favorite. It is a good flavor for all fish and seafood.

Cherry: This type of wood is distinctive and delicious. It is excellent for all dark meats and game. Combine it with other woods for new flavors.

Apple: This is the sweetest and mildest of all flavors. It has a subtle, velvety flavor.

Hickory: The commercial favorite, hickory is famous for flavoring hams and bacons.

Mesquite: A Western favorite, mesquite has a hearty, clean, smoky flavor. It is especially good for meat and poultry.

voring. Commercial brine solutions are available, or you can mix your own.

Fish fillets are the easiest to smoke. Make sure all the bones are removed, cut the fillets into sections, and rinse them off with water. You can make a basic do-it-yourself brine solution with 1 gallon of water, 4 cups of salt, 2 cups of brown sugar, 2 tablespoons of crushed black pepper, and 2 tablespoons of crushed bay leaves. Next, soak the fillets in the brine for four to six hours in your refrigerator. If the fillets are thick, keep them in the brine for up to 10 hours. Use a glass, stainless-steel, or plastic bowl. Do **not** use aluminum, which will affect the flavor.

After brining, pat the fillets dry and let them air-cool for 30 minutes or so. When a glaze forms on the surface, the fillets are ready to smoke. Use good-flavored wood and keep your smoker at about 160°F to 180°F. Your smoked fish should be ready in six to eight hours.

HOW TO FREEZE FISH

The biggest problem in freezing fish is preventing "freezer burn." That's when all of the moisture has been drawn out of the flesh and you are left with dried-out fillets. It is more likely to occur in "frost-free" freezers because they are designed to pull moisture from the air inside the freezer.

One way to guard against freezer burn is to freeze your fish in a block of ice. When your fish is completely encased in ice, no air can get at it. Freezing fish in this manner ensures maximum storage life for your fish. You can keep fish frozen in ice for up to two years without much flavor loss. The only disadvantage of container

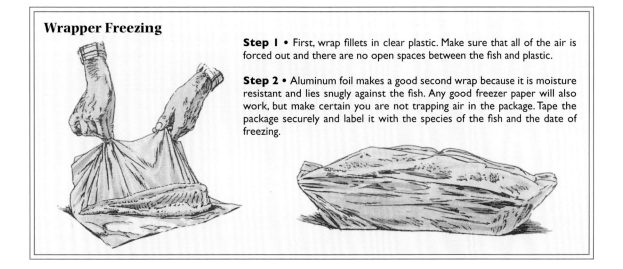

Wrapper Freezing

Step 1 • First, wrap fillets in clear plastic. Make sure that all of the air is forced out and there are no open spaces between the fish and plastic.

Step 2 • Aluminum foil makes a good second wrap because it is moisture resistant and lies snugly against the fish. Any good freezer paper will also work, but make certain you are not trapping air in the package. Tape the package securely and label it with the species of the fish and the date of freezing.

freezing is that it's bulky, awkward, and takes up more freezer space than wrapped packages. If freezer space is at a premium, double-wrap your fish tightly in plastic wrap and tightly wrap again in aluminum foil, which will maintain quality and flavor up to six months.

Unfortunately, trapped oxygen, which is virtually impossible to eliminate completely with traditional packaging, will promote bacteria that will spoil the quality of the fish and this will show up in odor and color. The best solution is vacuum packaging. Vacuum-packaging machines have proven their worth to sports-

men, who can now safely freeze and preserve fish for longer periods of time than with traditional methods. Vacuum-packaging machines work on a simple principle. They literally suck all the oxygen out of a package before it is placed in a freezer. Freezer burn is virtually eliminated because the fish no longer comes in contact with cold, dry air. In an oxygen-free environment, such as vacuum packaging produces, the bacterium that causes spoilage does not multiply fast and loss of food quality is slowed down drastically. The major advantage, of course, is the length of time vacuum-packaged fish can be safely frozen in your freezer. Vacuum-packed fish, depending on the fish species, can be safely stored in a freezer for up to two years.

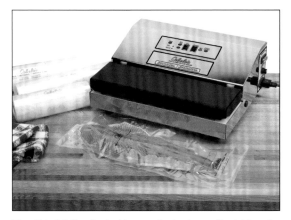

The Cabela's Pro Series Vacuum Sealer is an affordable solution to freezing quantities of fish. This machine will prevent freezer burn and extend freezer life. It will keep fish fresh for up to two years.

The Foodsaver Game Saver Deluxe is designed to vacuum seal food for long-term storage. Vacuum sealers literally suck all the oxygen out of a package before it is placed in a freezer. Freezer burn is eliminated because fish no longer come in contact with cold, dry air.

SURVIVAL

Section Nine
SURVIVAL

Survival is the art of making efficient use of any available resource that can help sustain an individual. Few survival situations are identical, but it is important to prepare for any possibility. If a person is able to think clearly and objectively about an emergency situation—because he has prepared for it—he is far more likely to survive than someone who panics and is unable to take full advantage of the resources that may be at hand.

PLANNING AHEAD

It is ironic that many survival situations often strike the ill prepared. A boater who is wearing nothing but shorts and a T-shirt invariably is the one caught in an unexpected late-spring squall, and boats never seem to sink when there are enough life jackets to go around.

Planning and preparing for emergencies is about more than checking life jackets though. Preparation requires investing time to be physically and mentally fit, thoughtful planning, and an intelligent selection of resources that will be available when you need them.

Mental preparation starts with the belief that it can happen to you. Nobody buckles their PFDs with the intention of getting into a boating accident. Likewise, it is foolhardy to head offshore without enough gear to help you get through a day when Mother Nature throws you a curveball.

The will to survive is influenced by skill, faith, and

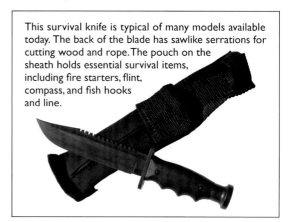

This survival knife is typical of many models available today. The back of the blade has sawlike serrations for cutting wood and rope. The pouch on the sheath holds essential survival items, including fire starters, flint, compass, and fish hooks and line.

courage. The more practice, the more skill. The more skill, the greater the faith. The greater the faith, the more confident you are, and the more enjoyable your outdoor experience can be.

PREPARING A SURVIVAL KIT

Preparation is the key to surviving any situation. Far more is involved than simply buying a prepackaged survival kit. It is unlikely that any single prepackaged kit will meet your specific needs, but you should think about those needs in the context of the environment that you will be in.

Select the items for your survival kit based on their versatility, multifunctionality, and practicality. Improvising is an important process in bringing all of these needs together. For example, surgical tubing, selected as a tourniquet for a first-aid kit, can also be used to make an emergency fishing lure.

◾ Boating Survival Kit

The following items are recommended for a complete boating survival kit. These items have been selected for their versatility for all survival-related emergencies. No kit, however, can be entirely right for every situation. These items form the basic foundation on which you should build after taking into account your activity and the environment. While the list may seem long, consider that many of these items are small and light. The boating survival kit includes:

- Fully charged cell phone
- GPS (global positioning system)
- Navigation chart
- 1-gallon water bag or container (collapsible or folded)
- Water-purification tablets
- 3,600-calorie, nonperishable food ration
- Hard candy
- Large, fixed-blade knife
- Pocket knife with locking blade
- Windproof and waterproof matches (strike-anywhere versions are best)
- Waterproof match case
- Lighter
- Flashlight with spare batteries
- Three 12-hour, high-intensity Cyalume snap lights

- Signal mirror
- Whistle
- Aerial flares
- Orange smoke signals
- Compass
- Compact strobe light
- First-aid kit (should include prescription medicines and large compresses, and should be adequate for the environment)
- Space blanket
- Wool gloves
- Wool hat
- Dry socks
- Emergency poncho or rain jacket
- 50 feet of cord or rope
- Multitool (Leatherman, etc.)
- Sharpening stone
- Fishing kit
- Surgical tubing
- Gas can
- Spool of 20-gauge wire
- Ground tarp
- Jumper cables
- Tool kit
- Tow rope
- Shovel
- Duct tape

SUSTENANCE

Sustenance is the need for food and water, which supplies your energy, increases your metabolism, regulates your temperature, and allows your mind to work rationally. Most healthy adults can miss a few meals without significant distress. However, even the healthiest adults can go no longer than a few days without water before they become delirious and lose vital body functions. While ready-to-eat, low-water rations make excellent additions to many survival kits, far too much emphasis is placed on food and not nearly enough on water, water storage, and water purification.

◾ Making Potable Water

Rainwater collected in clean containers or in plants is generally safe for drinking. However, you must purify water from lakes, ponds, swamps, springs, or streams, especially those near human habitation. When at all possible, you must disinfect all water by using iodine or chlorine or by boiling. You can purify water by:

- Using water-purification tablets.

- Pouring five drops of 2 percent tincture of iodine in a canteen full of clean water, and 10 drops in a canteen of cloudy or cold water. (Let the canteen stand for 30 minutes before drinking.)

- Boiling water for one minute at sea level, adding one minute for each additional 1,000 feet above sea level, or boiling for 10 minutes no matter where you are.

- Using a commercial water-purification device.

POTABLE DRINKING-WATER SYSTEM DEVICES: Having to purify water is a bother. The only reason to carry any drinking-water purifier at all is to protect your health

How to Signal for Help

Most fishermen, hikers, and campers never really get hopelessly lost, but if you ever find yourself in that unfortunate situation, you'd better learn how to use signals to help your rescuers locate you more quickly. This means sight and sound signals.

If you're a waterfowl hunter stranded on a beach, the standard three-shot signal is effective, but don't waste your ammunition during daylight hours when shots are commonplace. Wait until dark, when your friends may be searching for you and your three-shot signal will be more likely to attract attention . . . even if it's from a game warden. You should also be carrying a loud, piercing dog whistle. The sound will carry farther and last longer than your voice.

Build big fires! Your fire and smoke will signal help as well as keep you warm. Remember that the international distress signal is three fires about 50 feet apart in the shape of a triangle. Keep the fires smoky during the day and burning brightly at night. The most effective signal is black smoke because it can't be mistaken for a campfire. You can get black smoke by burning rubber or some synthetics. In an emergency, you can burn your gun's recoil pad or your rubber boot heels. If you can't make black smoke, you will have to settle for dense white smoke by piling leaves, grass, or moss on the fire.

If you're in an open area, learn the ground-to-air signals set by the International Civil Aviation Organization (ICAO). These signals are understood worldwide and every sportsman should know them. You can also tramp out SOS in snow, sand, or dirt. Another good daytime distress device is a signal mirror. There's no excuse for not carrying a 2-by-3-inch mirror in your shirt pocket. Search-and-rescue pilots claim they have spotted mirror flashes as far away as 25 miles.

The whole business of signaling simply means that you should do all in your power to let people know you're in trouble and exactly where you are. Remember to remove all distress signals as soon as you are located and rescued.

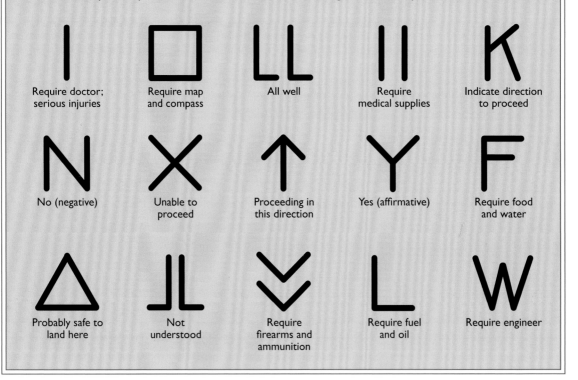

against microbiological and chemical contaminants. Water-related health threats can occur any time you are in contact with water: drinking water directly, using water as a food or beverage ingredient, using water for washing or brushing your teeth, or using water to clean cookware.

Primary exposure to drinking-water contaminants occurs at the following times:

- When collecting raw water for purification. To avoid this threat, use a separate container for your raw water supply whenever possible. Be selective when possible. Choose a source least likely to be badly polluted.

- During purification. Be careful to prevent dirty water from dripping or flowing into purified water.

Remember, the primary microorganisms of concern in most areas are tough, hardy cystic parasites that resist heat and cold (even freezing temperatures), drought, chlorine, iodine, and just about everything else. And while bacteria are relatively fragile and have very short life cycles, often less than a day, cysts can exist for months. All microorganisms of chief concern are invisibly small and cannot be seen, smelled, or detected in any quick and easy manner. Accordingly, you must rely on knowledge of your area and on common sense.

It is widely known today that *Giardia* or *Cryptosporidium* have been found in water supplies essentially in every country in the world. Therefore, you should always protect against parasitic cysts and insist on 100 percent reduction. Where one cyst can infect, a 99.9 percent reduction may not be good enough, especially when there is no known treatment for some cysts.

There have been essentially no waterborne typhoid, cholera, or Hepatitis A epidemics in the United States for

Solar Still for Safe Water

No matter how fresh and clean water may appear to be in that mountain stream or creek, you can never be sure that it isn't contaminated with chemicals and bacteria that make it unsafe for drinking. It is common sense to always carry a container of water with your gear, especially in warm climates where dehydration is a danger. In a survival situation, a sportsman can get safe drinking water by building a solar still, which will usually provide at least a pint of water every 24 hours. Here's how to use the sun to get safe drinking water:

Step 1 • Dig a hole in the ground about 2 feet deep and 3 feet across.

Step 2 • Place a clean bucket or pan at the bottom of the hole.

Step 3 • Set a plastic sheet over the hole and hold it in place by piling stones or dirt around the edges.

Step 4 • Place a small stone in the center of the plastic sheet so that the water formed by condensation on the sheet's sides is funneled down into the catch container.

The sun causes condensation to form on the sides of the plastic sheet. As the water collects at the bottom of the sheet, it drips into the bucket. As an extra precaution, boil the water for 10 minutes or add a commercial water-treatment tablet.

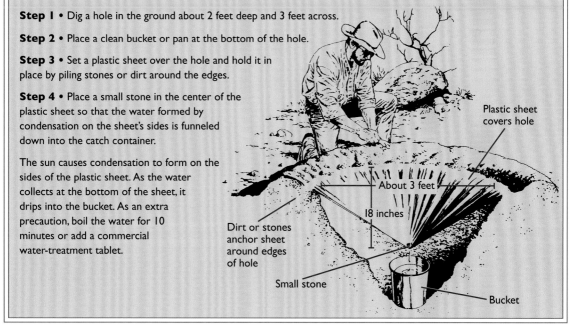

Plastic sheet covers hole

About 3 feet

18 inches

Dirt or stones anchor sheet around edges of hole

Small stone

Bucket

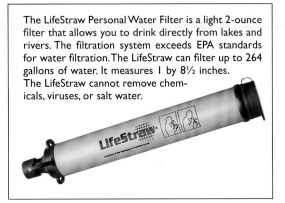

The LifeStraw Personal Water Filter is a light 2-ounce filter that allows you to drink directly from lakes and rivers. The filtration system exceeds EPA standards for water filtration. The LifeStraw can filter up to 264 gallons of water. It measures 1 by 8½ inches. The LifeStraw cannot remove chemicals, viruses, or salt water.

the last 50 years, so the likelihood of their occurrence from a U.S. wilderness water source is very low.

Pesticides, herbicides, and other chemicals can be present anywhere downwind or downstream from major agricultural and industrial areas even hundreds of miles away. These contaminants concentrate in streams, rivers, and lakes.

Asbestos fibers can be found in very high numbers of more than a million fibers per liter in most western and some eastern wilderness waters. Even though trace amounts of these chemicals won't make you ill today, no one wants to drink asbestos fibers if they can easily be avoided.

Micron ratings must be absolute to be meaningful, and precise measurements are essentially impossible to make. Micron ratings pertain only to the physical removal or straining of particles, so absolute micron ratings are only one means of evaluation for removal effectiveness. Removal of pesticides, herbicides, tastes, odors, and most colors and solvents require other purification (separation) mechanisms. Many units, even those with very low micron ratings, have little or no ability to remove anything other than particles.

According to federal regulations, all water-purification devices are defined as being either pesticide or device products. Pesticide products rely on chemically poisoning organisms (pests), while devices rely on physically removing them.

It's easy to tell whether a product is categorized as a pesticide or a device. All products must carry an Environmental Protection Agency (EPA) establishment number. Pesticide products, however, must carry two EPA numbers, one for the manufacturing establishment and one for the pesticide being used. So, decide if you want to use a device or a pesticide for your water-purification needs, and be sure to check the label to choose the right type. In certain applications, it may be desirable to use a pesticide to purify water, but complete removal of the pesticide is very desirable after enough kill time is allowed. It is important to note that iodine resins are not effective against cysts.

All products being marketed today that carry an EPA establishment number are deemed to meet all current, pertinent EPA and other federal regulations. Otherwise, they would not be permitted on the market.

SURVIVING THE COLD

There is no way to beat the cold, but you can learn how to survive in it. High-tech manufacturing now offers clothing that is insulated, waterproof, and windproof, but even with all of these advantages, there will always be someone who will get into trouble. Hypothermia is the cold-weather killer, and it is caused by exposure to wind, rain, snow, or wet clothing. (For treatment of hypothermia, see Section Ten: First Aid for Boaters.) Allow your body's core temperature to drop below the normal 98.6°F, and you will start to shiver and stamp your feet to keep warm. If these early signs are ignored, the next symptoms will be slurred speech, memory lapses, fumbling hands, and drowsiness. If not treated quickly, hypothermia can kill its victim when body temperature drops below 78°F, and this can happen within 90 minutes after shivering begins.

If you detect these symptoms in yourself or a friend, start treatment immediately. Get to shelter and warmth as soon as possible. Get out of wet clothing and apply heat to the head, neck, chest, and groin. Use body heat from another person. Give the victim warm liquids, chocolate, or any food with a high sugar content. Never give a victim alcohol. It will impair judgment, dilate blood vessels, and prevent shivering, which is the body's way of producing needed heat.

Cooling Power of Wind Expressed as Equivalent Chill Temperature

Wind Speed		Temperature (°F)																				
Calm	Calm	40	35	30	25	20	15	10	5	0	-5	-10	-15	-20	-25	-30	-35	-40	-45	-50	-55	-60
Knots	MPH	Equivalent Chill Temperature (°F)																				
3–6	5	35	30	25	20	15	10	5	0	-5	-10	-15	-20	-25	-30	-35	-40	-45	-50	-55	-65	-70
7–10	10	30	20	15	10	5	0	-10	-15	-20	-25	-35	-40	-45	-50	-60	-65	-70	-75	-80	-90	-95
11–15	15	25	15	10	0	-5	-10	-20	-25	-30	-40	-45	-50	-60	-65	-70	-80	-85	-90	-100	-105	-110
16–19	20	20	10	5	0	-10	-15	-25	-30	-35	-45	-50	-60	-65	-75	-80	-85	-95	-100	-110	-115	-120
20–23	25	15	10	0	-5	-15	-20	-30	-35	-45	-50	-60	-65	-75	-80	-90	-95	-105	-110	-120	-125	-135
24–28	30	10	5	0	-10	-20	-25	-30	-40	-50	-55	-65	-70	-80	-85	-95	-100	-110	-115	-125	-130	-140
29–32	35	10	5	-5	-10	-20	-30	-35	-40	-50	-60	-65	-75	-80	-90	-100	-105	-115	-120	-130	-135	-145
33–36	40	10	0	-5	-15	-20	-30	-35	-45	-55	-60	-70	-75	-85	-95	-100	-110	-115	-125	-130	-140	-150

Little Danger — Increasing Danger (flesh may freeze within one minute) — Great Danger (flesh may freeze within 30 seconds)

Danger of Freezing Exposed Flesh for Properly Clothed Persons

Note: Winds above 40 miles per hour have few additional effects.

You can also survive the cold by staying in shape and getting a good night's sleep before going out on the water. Carry candy, mixed nuts, raisins, and any other high-energy food. Stay as dry as possible and avoid overheating. Most important, dress properly. This means several layers of clothing and rain gear. And wear a wool hat with ear protection. An uncovered head can lose up to 50 percent of the body's heat.

SURVIVING THE HEAT AND SUN

To survive heat, you must know about and be prepared for the environmental conditions you will face. You must determine the equipment you will need, the tactics you will use, and how the environment will impact them and you.

A key factor in survival is understanding the relationship between physical activity, air temperature, and water consumption. The body requires a certain amount of water for a certain level of activity at a certain temperature. For example, a man fighting a big fish in the sun at 110°F requires 5 gallons of water a day. Lack of the required amount of water causes a rapid decline in a person's ability to make decisions and to perform tasks efficiently.

Your body's normal temperature is 98.6°F. Your body gets rid of excess heat by sweating. The warmer your body becomes, whether caused by work, exercise, or air temperature, the more you sweat. The more you sweat, the more moisture you lose. Sweating is the principle cause of water loss. If a man stops sweating during periods of high air temperature and heavy work or exercise, he will have a heat stroke. This is an emergency that requires immediate medical attention.

Understanding how the air temperature and your physical activity affect your water requirements allows you to take measures to get the most from your water supply. These measures are:

- Find shade. Get out of the sun. Go in the cabin or stay under canvas. Place something between you and the hot sun. Limit your movements. Always wear a hat.

- Conserve your sweat. Wear all of your clothes, including a T-shirt. Roll the sleeves down, cover your head, and protect your neck with a scarf or similar item. This

Protect Your Eyes

The sun is hard on eyes, especially if you spend a lot of time on the water in the summer. In fact, the effect of glare on the water can be 25 times brighter than if you stayed indoors. To protect your eyes, you need good sunglasses and the right type.

Sunglasses are one of those pieces of equipment that you shouldn't scrimp on. If you try to make do with a cheap pair, you're asking for eye strain, fatigue, and maybe a bad headache. For everyday use, most sunglasses should be able to absorb 60 percent or more of the sun's rays. If you're a hard-core fisherman or boater, look for sunglasses with darker lenses that absorb at least 80 percent of the sun's rays. Industry standards require that sunglasses designed for water sports absorb up to 95 percent of the sun's ultraviolet rays.

How can you tell if sunglasses are dark enough to provide the degree of protection that you need? Quality sunglasses will have tags indicating the degree of UV protection, but if the manufacturer does not disclose the rating on the tag, it might be difficult to determine. There is, however, a simple in-store test for lens darkness. Pick sunglasses off the rack, put them on, and look into a mirror. If the lenses are dark enough for general outdoor use, you will have some difficulty seeing your eyes in the reflection. This test doesn't work for photochromic lenses, which darken in reaction to the amount of light striking them.

Photochromic or all-weather sunglasses are good choices if you wear prescription glasses or if you want only one pair for both indoor and outdoor use. In cloudy weather, the lenses range from light to medium density and are usually amber or brown in color. In this state, negative blue filters screen out the scattered blue light that creates haze. The result is improved contrast and sharper details. When the sun breaks out, the lenses change to a deeper gray or brown for glare protection.

As for color, most vision experts agree that green, gray, or brown lenses work best to shield the eyes. Under extreme glare conditions, mirror lenses are most effective. If you're a fisherman, go with polarizing lenses, which are made by sandwiching polarizing film between two pieces of glass or plastic. This helps eliminate or greatly reduce reflections on the surface of the water. Taking it another step, choose sunglasses with side shields or mini lenses  that further block the sun's rays. It's also smart to attach a cord to the frame of the glasses so you don't lose them in the heat of a battle with a big fish or while you're running down the lake. If the earpieces aren't predrilled at the factory for such an attachment, it's easy enough to do it at home.

Regardless of the style of sunglasses you choose, it's important that they provide good protection against the sun's ultraviolet rays, which can be irritating and dangerous to vision. Ultraviolet rays can cause short- and long-term harmful effects, such as photokeratitis, cataracts, and various types of cancer.

Finally, if your sunglasses steam up in hot, humid weather or blotch in the rain, try rubbing the lenses with one of those new antifogging concoctions that are available at most sporting-goods stores. They're great for sunglasses.

will protect your body from hot-blowing winds and the direct rays of the sun. Your clothing will absorb your sweat, keeping it against your skin so that you gain its full cooling effect. By staying in the shade, not talking, keeping your mouth closed, and breathing through your nose, your water requirement for survival drops dramatically.

- If water is scarce, do not eat any food. Food requires water for digestion. Eating food will use water that you need for cooling.

Thirst is not a reliable guide for your need for water. A person who uses thirst as a guide will only drink two-thirds of his daily requirement. To prevent this "voluntary" dehydration, use this guide:

- At temperatures below 100°F, drink 1 pint of water every hour.

- At temperatures above 100°F, drink 1 quart of water every hour.

Drinking water at regular intervals helps your body to remain cool, decreasing sweating. Even when your water supply is low, sipping water constantly will keep your body cooler and reduce water loss through sweating. Conserve your sweat by reducing activity during the heat of the day. Do not ration your water. If you attempt to ration your water, you stand a good chance of becoming a heat casualty.

■ Intense Sunlight and Heat

Intense sunlight and heat can always be a potential problem on the water. Air temperature can rise as high as 140°F during the day. Heat gain results from direct sunlight, hot-blowing winds, and reflective heat (the sun's rays bouncing off the water).

Intense sunlight and heat also increase the body's need for water. To conserve your body sweat and energy, you need shade to reduce your exposure to the heat of the day.

Sunburn results from overexposing your skin to the sun's rays. Keep your body completely clothed, including gloves on your hands and a scarf around your neck. Use sunscreen liberally on any exposed areas of skin. Sun poisoning equals nausea and dehydration. In addition, burns may become infected, causing more problems. Remember the following:

- There is as much danger of sunburn on cloudy days as on sunny days.

- Most sunscreens do not give complete protection against excessive exposure.

- The glare on water causes eyestrain and inflammation. Wear sunglasses.

- The combination of wind and salt spray can cause your lips and other exposed skin to chap. Use lip balm and skin ointments to prevent this problem.

DEALING WITH DANGEROUS WATER

When you are in a survival situation in any area except the desert, you are likely to encounter a water obstacle. It may be in the form of a river, stream, lake, bog, quicksand, quagmire, or muskeg. Whatever it is, you need to know how to cross it safely.

■ Rivers and Streams

A river or stream may be narrow or wide, shallow or deep, slow moving or fast moving. It may be snow-fed or ice-fed. Your first step is to find a place where the river is basically safe for crossing. (For more information on how to wade a river, see Section Five: Fishing Basics for Boaters.) Look for a high place from which you can get a

good view of the river. If there is no high place, climb a tree. Check the river carefully for the following areas:

- A level stretch where the river breaks into a number of channels. Two or three narrow channels are usually easier to cross than a wide river.

- Obstacles on the opposite side of the river that might hinder your travel. Try to select the spot from which travel will be safest and easiest.

- A ledge of rocks that crosses the river. This often indicates dangerous rapids or canyons.

- A deep or rapid waterfall or a deep channel. Never attempt to ford a stream directly above or even close to such spots.

- Rocky places. Avoid such places; you can be seriously injured from falling on rocks. An occasional rock that breaks the current, however, may assist you.

- A shallow bank or sandbar. If possible, select a point upstream from a bank or sandbar so that the current will carry you to it if you lose your footing.

- A course across the river that leads downstream. This will help you cross the current at about a 45-degree angle.

■ Rapids

Crossing a deep, swift river or rapids is not as dangerous as it looks. If you are swimming across, swim with the current—never fight it—and try to keep your body horizontal to the water. This will reduce the danger of being pulled under.

In fast, shallow rapids, go on your back, feetfirst; fin your hands alongside your hips to add buoyancy and to fend off submerged rocks. Keep your feet up to avoid getting them bruised or caught by rocks.

In deep rapids, go on your belly, headfirst; angle toward the shore whenever you can. Breathe between wave troughs. Be careful of backwater eddies and converging currents, as they often contain dangerous swirls. Avoid bubbly water under falls; it has little buoyancy. If you are going to ford a swift, treacherous stream, remove your pants and underpants so that the water will have less grip on your legs. Keep your shoes on to protect your feet and ankles from rocks and to give you firmer footing.

Tie your pants and important items securely to the top of your pack. This way, if you have to release your pack, all your items will be together. It is easier to find one large pack than to find several small items.

Carry your pack well up on your shoulders so you can release it quickly if you are swept off your feet. Not being able to get a pack off quickly enough can drag even the strongest of swimmers under.

Find a strong pole about 5 inches in diameter and 7 to 8 feet long to help you ford the stream. Grasp the pole and plant it firmly on your upstream side to break the current. Plant your feet firmly with each step, and move the pole forward a little downstream from its previous position, but still upstream from you. With your next step, place your foot below the pole. Keep the pole well slanted so that the force of the current keeps the pole against your shoulder.

If there are other people with you, cross the stream together. Make sure that everyone has prepared their

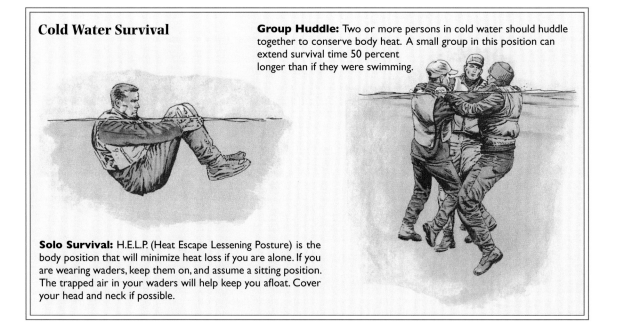

Cold Water Survival

Group Huddle: Two or more persons in cold water should huddle together to conserve body heat. A small group in this position can extend survival time 50 percent longer than if they were swimming.

Solo Survival: H.E.L.P. (Heat Escape Lessening Posture) is the body position that will minimize heat loss if you are alone. If you are wearing waders, keep them on, and assume a sitting position. The trapped air in your waders will help keep you afloat. Cover your head and neck if possible.

pack and clothing as described above. Have the heaviest person get on the downstream end of the pole and the lightest person on the upstream end. This way, the upstream person will break the current, and the people below can move with comparative ease in the eddy formed by the upstream person. If the upstream person is temporarily swept off his feet, the others can hold steady while he regains his footing.

As in all fording, cross the downstream current at a 45-degree angle. Currents too strong for one person to stand against can usually be crossed safely in this manner.

Do not be concerned about the weight of your pack, as the weight will help rather than hinder you in fording the stream. Just make sure you can release the pack quickly if necessary.

■ Surviving in Cold Water

Spring and fall are traditional times for trout fishing and waterfowl hunting, and this means greater chances of accidentally finding yourself in cold water. If you are suddenly the victim of a capsizing, you can survive a cold-water dunking if you follow a few survival rules.

First, don't panic. Clothing will trap body heat, so don't remove your clothes. If you are wearing a life jacket, restrict your body movements and draw your knees up to your body, a position that will reduce heat loss.

Don't try to swim or tread water. That will just pump out warm water between your body and clothing. Instead, get into a protective posture and wait for rescue. See the accompanying illustrations for the body positions that will minimize heat loss and increase your chances of survival.

How to Stay on Your Feet

On one of our salmon fishing trips to Alaska, we beached our boat and started to hike some rough terrain to fish the upper reaches of a stream loaded with sockeye salmon. I was trying to reach those salmon with my buddy Chris Batin, who is an Alaska guide.

I learned a lesson on that trip. Chris was using hiking or trekking poles. He used two of them on rough ground, and I learned fast that four legs are better than two. These are not the tree limbs that we used to chop off and use as staffs to poke around in the woods when we were kids. These are well-designed hiking poles that have become valuable safety gear for sportsmen—especially those who enjoy shoreline camping with their boats, or fishermen who enjoy floating rivers and streams, where they may frequently have to beach their boats to fish. Our boat got us within reach of salmon, but it took a tough hike to get to those sockeyes.

The HikeLite XL Four-Season Hiking Poles will reduce your hiking energy by 21 percent and put less stress on your knees and ankles.

I now keep a couple of those poles in my boat. The poles also come in handy to check depth when wading ashore from your boat or as a wading staff for flats and shallow-water fishing. You can also use them to snag a dock line. It's generally agreed that hiking poles also reduce your hiking energy by about 21 percent and put less stress on your knees and ankles.

There are a variety of hiking poles available today. One manufacturer builds three-piece carbon-fiber telescopic poles that are easy to store on a boat. Some models have a collapsible range that extends from 20 inches to about 62 inches. It's a good idea to have a hiking pole handy. It could prevent you from falling down and busting a bone.

Weighing only a pound, these three-piece telescoping poles also come with snow baskets.

FIRST AID FOR BOATERS

FIRST AID FOR BOATERS

EMERGENCY MEDICAL TREATMENT

When boaters head for the water they will always be confronted with a special bunch of hazards. Rocking boats, seasickness, slippery rocks, or sharp fishhooks may turn their day into an accident or a trip to the emergency room. This chapter on first aid for boaters is designed to help everyone avoid some of those inherent dangers, as well as suggest treatments for accidents and illnesses that would otherwise ruin a day of cruising or fishing. It is important to remember, however, to seek medical attention as quickly as possible for serious injuries and attacks.

This chapter will give detailed step-by-step procedures for every first-aid situation the boater is likely to encounter. It should be remembered, however, that these procedures, though vitally important, aren't the only forms of first aid. The victim's mental distress also needs treatment. A reassuring word, a smile, and your obvious willingness and ability to help—all will have an encouraging effect.

The knowledgeable first-aider also knows what not to do and thereby avoids compounding the problem by making errors that could be serious.

The procedures and instructions that follow reflect recommendations of the American Red Cross, the American Medical Association, the U.S. Department of Agriculture, and, of course, respected physicians.

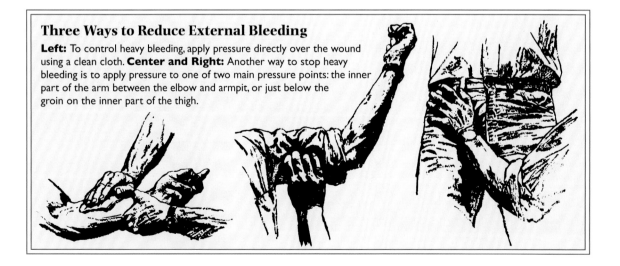

Three Ways to Reduce External Bleeding

Left: To control heavy bleeding, apply pressure directly over the wound using a clean cloth. **Center and Right:** Another way to stop heavy bleeding is to apply pressure to one of two main pressure points: the inner part of the arm between the elbow and armpit, or just below the groin on the inner part of the thigh.

◼ Bleeding

EXTERNAL BLEEDING: If a large blood vessel is severed, death from loss of blood can occur in three to five minutes, so it is vital to stop the bleeding at once. Always do so, if possible, by applying pressure directly over the wound.

Use a clean cloth—a handkerchief, an item of clothing, or whatever else is near at hand. Use your bare hand if nothing else is available, and then, once the bleeding is under control, apply a cloth. Put on additional layers of cloth, and when the covering is substantial, bandage snugly with strips of cloth cut from a bedsheet, neckties, or similar materials. Don't remove the bandage. If it becomes saturated with blood, put on more layers of cloth, and perhaps tighten the dressing directly over the wound.

If you are sure that no bones are broken, try to raise the bleeding area higher than the rest of the body.

If extremely quick action is needed, or if the above method fails to stop the flow of blood, you may be able to diminish the flow by pressing your fingers or the heel of your hand at one of two pressure points. One of these is located on the inner half of the arm midway between the elbow and armpit; pressure applied here will reduce bleeding in the lower area of the arm. Pressure on the other point, located just below the groin on the front, inner half of the thigh, will reduce bleeding on the extremity below that point.

INTERNAL BLEEDING: Often caused by a severe fall or a violent blow, bleeding within the body can be difficult to diagnose, though it may be revealed by bleeding from the nose or mouth when no injury can be detected in those organs. Other symptoms may include restlessness, nausea, anxiety, a weak and rapid pulse, thirst, paleness, and general weakness.

The first treatment procedure is to use pillows, boat cushions, folded clothes, or something similar to raise the victim's head and shoulders if he is having difficulty breathing. Otherwise, place him flat on his back.

Keep him as immobile as possible, and try to have him control the movements caused by vomiting. Turn his head to the side for vomiting.

Do not give the victim stimulants, even if the bleeding seems to stop.

If the victim loses consciousness, turn him on his side, with his head and chest lower than his hips.

Medical care is a must. Get the victim to a doctor or hospital as soon as possible.

Applying a Tourniquet

Since a tourniquet can cause the loss of the affected limb, it should be applied only when no other means will reduce blood flow enough to prevent the victim from bleeding to death. **Left:** Wrap strong, wide cloth around the limb above the wound, and tie a simple overhand knot. **Center:** Place a short stick on the knot, tie another overhand knot over the stick, and twist the stick to stem bleeding. **Right:** Bind the stick with the ends of the tourniquet, but be sure to loosen it every 15 minutes.

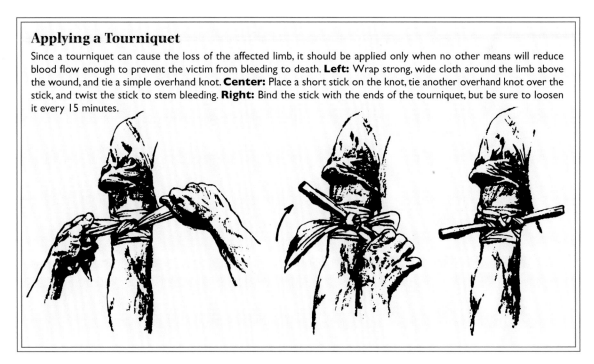

NOSEBLEED: Nosebleeds often occur for no reason, while at other times they are caused by an injury. Most of them are more annoying than serious. It occasionally happens, though, that the bleeding is heavy and prolonged and this can be dangerous.

The person should remain quiet, preferably in a sitting position with his head thrown back or lying down with his head and shoulders raised.

Pinch the victim's nostrils together, keeping the pressure on for five to 10 minutes. If the bleeding doesn't stop, pack gauze lightly into the bleeding nostril and then pinch.

Sometimes the application of cold, wet towels to the face will help.

USE OF A TOURNIQUET: According to the American Red Cross, the use of a tourniquet to stop bleeding in an extremity is "justifiable only rarely." Because its use involves a high risk of losing a limb, a tourniquet should be applied only if the bleeding seems sure to cause death.

Use only a wide, strong piece of cloth—never a narrow strip of material such as rope or wire. Wrap the cloth around the upper part of the limb above the wound, and tie a simple overhand knot (half a square knot). Place a short stick on the knot, and tie another simple overhand knot (that is, complete the square knot) over the stick. Twist the stick just enough to stop the bleeding. Loosen the binding (untwist the stick) for a few seconds every 15 minutes. (See illustrations on previous page.)

Once the bleeding has been controlled, keep the victim quiet and warm. If he is conscious and can swallow easily, give him some water or maybe some weak tea—no alcoholic drinks. If he is not conscious, or if abdominal or other internal injuries are suspected, do not give him any fluid.

■ Artificial Respiration

Artificial respiration, now commonly called resuscitation, is the technique of causing air to flow into and out of the lungs of a person whose normal breathing has stopped. Causes of stoppage of normal breathing include inhalation of water, smoke, or gas, electric shock, choking, or drug overdose. In most instances, death will result within six minutes unless artificial respiration is administered.

The treatment may also be needed if breathing does not stop completely but becomes slow and shallow and the victim's lips, tongue, and fingernails turn blue. If you're in doubt, give artificial respiration—it is seldom harmful and can save a life.

Before beginning the artificial-respiration methods described below, check the victim's mouth and throat opening for obstructions; remove any foreign objects or loose dentures.

MOUTH TO MOUTH: Place the victim on his back. Put one hand under the victim's neck. At the same time, place the other hand on his forehead and tilt the head back.

Using the hand that was under the neck, pull the victim's chin up, thereby ensuring a free air passage. Take a deep breath, place your mouth over the victim's mouth, trying to make the seal as airtight as possible, and pinch the victim's nostrils closed. Blow into the victim's mouth until you see his chest rise.

Lift your head from the victim, and take another deep breath while his chest falls, causing him to exhale. Repeat the process. For the first few minutes, do so as

Mouth-to-Mouth Resuscitation

Remember the ABCs: airway, breathing, and circulation, in that order.

Airway. If there are no head, neck, or back injuries, gently tilt the victim's head and raise the chin. This will lift the tongue and ensure a clear air passage. Check for breathing by placing your ear over the victim's mouth and feeling for any exhalation.

Breathing. If the person is not breathing, pinch his nose, take a deep breath, and place your mouth over his. Breathe into his lungs two times slowly—one and a half to two seconds each time. If the victim's chest does not rise, re-tilt the head and repeat the cycle at a rate of 15 times per minute, until the victim can breathe on his own.

Circulation. Check for a pulse. Keeping the victim's head tilted, place your index and middle fingers on the victim's Adam's apple, and then slide your fingers down to the next "ridge" on the neck. This is where you'll find the carotid artery. Press firmly to determine if there's a pulse. If there isn't, proceed with chest compressions.

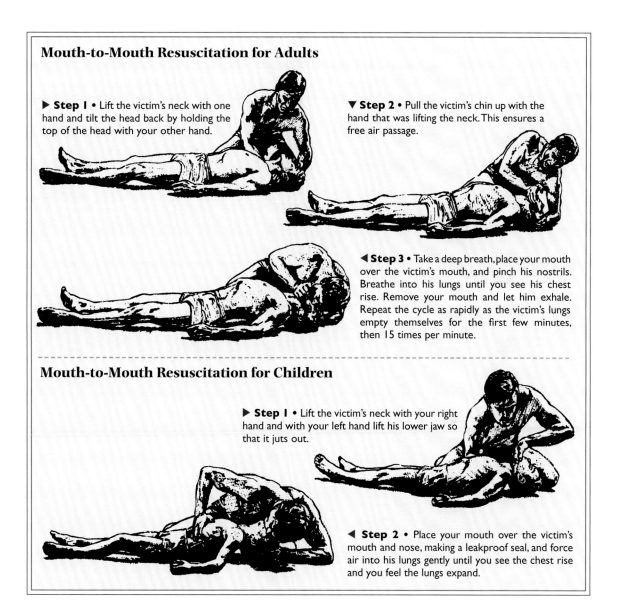

Mouth-to-Mouth Resuscitation for Adults

▶ **Step 1** • Lift the victim's neck with one hand and tilt the head back by holding the top of the head with your other hand.

▼ **Step 2** • Pull the victim's chin up with the hand that was lifting the neck. This ensures a free air passage.

◀ **Step 3** • Take a deep breath, place your mouth over the victim's mouth, and pinch his nostrils. Breathe into his lungs until you see his chest rise. Remove your mouth and let him exhale. Repeat the cycle as rapidly as the victim's lungs empty themselves for the first few minutes, then 15 times per minute.

Mouth-to-Mouth Resuscitation for Children

▶ **Step 1** • Lift the victim's neck with your right hand and with your left hand lift his lower jaw so that it juts out.

◀ **Step 2** • Place your mouth over the victim's mouth and nose, making a leakproof seal, and force air into his lungs gently until you see the chest rise and you feel the lungs expand.

rapidly as the victim's lungs are emptied. After that, do it about 15 times per minute.

If the victim is an infant or small child, use the same procedure, but place your mouth over both the mouth and nose, and force air into his lungs gently.

HEART STOPPAGE (CPR): If artificial respiration produces no response in an injured person, it may mean that his heart has stopped beating. You can make a fairly certain diagnosis by checking his pulse at the wrist and holding your ear to the victim's chest. If you feel no pulse and hear no heartbeat, you will have to use external heart massage (Cardiopulmonary Resuscitation, or CPR) in addition to artificial respiration.

Here are the warning signs of a heart attack:

- Pressure; feeling of "fullness"; squeezing or pain in the center of the chest lasting more than two minutes

Chest Compressions

For heart stoppage, employ extended chest compressions (CPR) using the weight of the upper part of your body.

- Pain radiating to shoulders, neck, jaw, arms, or back; tingling sensation down left arm
- Dizziness, weakness, sweating, or nausea; pale complexion and shortness of breath

If the victim's heart and breathing have stopped, begin CPR. The technique involves mouth-to-mouth resuscitation, which delivers air to the lungs, and chest compressions, which help circulate the blood.

CHEST COMPRESSIONS: Positioning yourself perpendicular to the victim, place the heel of one hand on the lower third of the victim's sternum (breastbone). Place your other hand on top of the first one. Press down firmly with both hands about 1½ to 2 inches and then lift both hands to let the chest expand. Repeat at a rate of 80 to 100 compressions per minute. The mouth-to-mouth breathing should continue at a rate of two steady lung inflations after every 15 chest compressions.

▓ Choking

More than one person has died from choking on a fish bone, an inadvertently swallowed hard object, a piece of food that went down the "wrong pipe," and the like. Anything that lodges in the throat or air passages must be removed as soon as possible. Here's how to do it.

If the victim is conscious, give him four back blows between the shoulder blades. If the victim is lying down, roll him on his side, facing you with his chest against your knee. If the victim is sitting or standing, you should

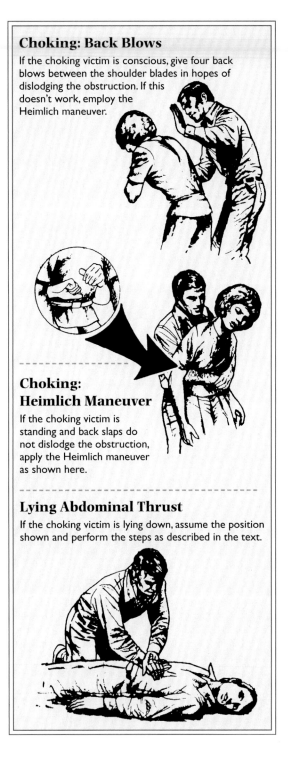

Choking: Back Blows

If the choking victim is conscious, give four back blows between the shoulder blades in hopes of dislodging the obstruction. If this doesn't work, employ the Heimlich maneuver.

Choking: Heimlich Maneuver

If the choking victim is standing and back slaps do not dislodge the obstruction, apply the Heimlich maneuver as shown here.

Lying Abdominal Thrust

If the choking victim is lying down, assume the position shown and perform the steps as described in the text.

be behind and to one side of him. If the victim is an infant, place him on your forearm, head down. Make sharp blows with the heel of your hand on the spine, directly between his shoulder blades.

If this doesn't remove the object, and the victim is standing or sitting, employ the Heimlich maneuver:

1. Stand behind the victim and wrap your arms around his waist.

2. Place the thumb side of your fist against the victim's upper abdomen, just below the rib cage.

3. Grasp your fist with your other hand and press into the victim's abdomen with two or three quick upward thrusts.

If the victim is in a lying position, do this:

1. Place him on his back and kneel close to his side.

2. Place your hands, one on top of the other, with the heel of the bottom hand in the middle of his abdomen, just below the rib cage.

3. Rock forward so that your shoulders are directly over the victim's abdomen and press toward the victim's diaphragm with a quick forward thrust.

4. Don't press to either side.

If the victim is unconscious, tilt his head back and attempt to give him artificial respiration. If this fails, give the victim four back blows in rapid succession. If the object has still not been forced out of the air passage, then stand behind the victim, put both of your fists into his abdomen, and give eight upward thrusts.

Finally, if none of these methods work, you should insert your index finger deep into the victim's throat, using a hooking action to try to dislodge the object.

FOR A SMALL CHILD: Put one arm around the youngster's waist from behind, and lift him up so that his head and upper torso are leaning toward the ground. With your free hand, give him several sharp taps between the shoulder blades. When the object has been dislodged, clear his throat with your fingers, and pull the tongue forward.

FOR AN INFANT: Hold him up by the ankles, head hanging straight down. Open his mouth, pull his tongue forward, and the object will likely fall out. If not, give him a tap or two on the back.

BITES AND POISONOUS PLANTS

▣ Snakebites

It is doubtful whether any other first-aid situation is more feared and less understood than snakebites, and there is little agreement, even among leading authorities, about their treatment.

Chances are most boaters and fishermen will never encounter venomous snakes, but it is possible. When cruising the backwaters of the Southeast, you may well encounter snakes. About 6,500 people are bitten by venomous snakes in the United States each year. Of those, only about 350 are boaters, hunters, or fishermen. And the death rate is very low, an average of 15 persons annually in the entire country. Most of those bites occur south of an imaginary line drawn from North Carolina to Southern California. More than half occur in Texas, North Carolina, Florida, Georgia, Louisiana, and Arkansas.

There are four kinds of venomous snakes in the United States. Three are of the pit-viper variety: rattlesnakes, copperheads, and cottonmouth moccasins. The fourth, the coral snake, is a member of the cobra family. The pit vipers are so named because they have a small, deep depression between the eyes and the nostrils. The coral snake has broad red and black bands separated by narrow yellow bands, giving rise to the saying, "Red on yellow, kill a fellow."

The bite of a venomous snake—except for the coral snake, which chews rather than bites—is in the form of fang punctures of the skin. If you are bitten by a snake that leaves two U-shaped rows of tooth marks on your skin, relax—it is almost certainly a nonvenomous snake. The bite of a nonvenomous snake produces little pain or swelling.

Symptoms of the bite of a venomous snake include immediate pain, swelling and discoloration in the area of the wound, general weakness, nausea and vomiting, a weak and rapid pulse, dimming of vision, faintness, and eventually unconsciousness.

Most medical authorities now agree that the preferred treatment for a snakebite is antivenin administered as quickly as possible after the bite. If a

North American Venomous Snakes

Cottonmouth • Eastern cottonmouths as well as Florida and western cottonmouths are frequently confused with non-venomous water snakes. Cottonmouths have dark blotches on an olive body and broad, flat heads.

Coral Snake • This snake is dangerously venomous, but its small mouth prevents it from biting most parts of the body. It has red and black rings wider than the interspaced yellow rings. The habitat is open woods in the East and loose soil and rocks in the West.

Timber Rattler and Canebrake Rattler • In the South, there is a dark streak from the canebrake's eye to mouth, and dark chevrons and a rusty stripe along the midline. In the North, the timber rattler has a yellowish body and dark phase in parts of its range. The habitat for the canebrake is lowland brush and stream borders. The timber rattler prefers rocky wooded hills.

Eastern Diamondback • The body has dark diamonds with light borders along a tan or light-brown background. The diamonds gradually change to bands in the tail. The habitat is lowland thickets, palmettos, and flatwoods.

Copperhead • This snake has large, chestnut-brown cross bands on a pale pinkish or reddish-brown surface with a copper tinge on the head. The habitat in the North is wooded mountains and stone walls; in the South, it is lowland swamps and wood suburbs.

Western Diamondback • This snake has light brown to black diamond-shaped blotches along a light gray, tan, and sometimes pink background. It also has black and white bands of about equal width around the tail. The habitat includes woods, rocky hills, deserts, and farmland.

snakebite victim is within a two-hour drive of a medical facility, get the person there as fast and calmly as possible. Keep the bite location immobile, even if you have to splint it. Also keep the bitten body part below the level of the heart. A snakebite victim may walk up to a half hour before symptoms start. If the distance is longer to transportation, the victim should be carried. If you are alone, you should still be able to walk for several hours before symptoms start.

Bites often occur many miles from a marina or launch site, however, so the victim cannot always get antivenin quickly enough. Survival in such cases depends upon the first-aid steps taken by the victim and his companions. And here is where the disagreement among medical authorities is most prevalent.

Proper treatment for a snakebite continues to confuse sportsmen, but the most reliable medical opinions today agree that the old treatments did more damage than good. There are still snakebite kits on the market, but the best advice is don't use them. The use of a scalpel and making incisions is no longer recommended and may cause further injury. Suction devices used without incisions are of questionable value. Some tests indicate that such suction devices may only remove about 1 to 2 percent of the venom.

Here's the currently recommended treatment for a snakebite. Call 911 or get to a hospital where you can get antivenin as quickly as possible. Properly treated with antivenin, snakebites are rarely fatal. If you can't get to a hospital within 30 minutes, immobilize the bite and, if possible, keep it lower than the heart. Wrap a bandage 2 to 4 inches above the bite. The bandage should not cut off blood flow from a vein or artery. Make the bandage loose enough so that a finger can slip under it. Do not put ice on the bite. Avoid exertion and excitement. Sit down and try to calm yourself. Panic could bring on shock. Do not eat or drink alcohol. Do not remove any dressings until you reach a hospital. If possible, kill the snake and take the head for identification later. Use caution: the head of a snake can still bite through reflex action up to one hour after it is killed. Get to a hospital or doctor as soon as possible with a minimum of exertion.

Coping with Bugs

The outdoors is a great place, but bugs can turn a pleasant day into a nightmare. You can fight back! There are five bugs that will give you the most trouble: mosquitoes, black flies, no-see-ums, deerflies, and ticks. Mosquitoes,

the worst of the bunch, are most active at dawn and dusk. Mosquitoes are attracted to dark colors, so wear light-colored clothing. Black flies draw blood. Male black flies use blood for food, and the female needs blood to complete her breeding cycle. Common throughout Canada and the northern United States, black flies bite as soon as they land and they zero in on the face, hairline, wrists, and ankles. The peak period is spring and early summer. Aside from using a repellent, you should wear a hat, tuck pants into socks, tape cuffs around ankles, and wear long sleeves. No-see-ums are so small you can't see them, but they hurt when they bite. You'll find no-see-ums along lakes, beaches, and marshes. The deerfly is another painful biter and will attack the face, legs, arms, and neck. Once again, wear light-colored clothing. The tick, because of the threat of Lyme disease, is the most dangerous pest. Wear light-colored clothing, tuck pants into socks, avoid wooded areas and high grass, and use a tick repellent. The most effective repellent against these bugs contains DEET.

Bee Stings

Stinging insects are seldom more than an annoyance, even if they hit the target on your hide. Some people, however, are highly allergic to the stings of certain insects. If you or a member of your party has had a severe reaction to a bee sting in the past and is stung, take the following steps:

1. Use a tight, constricting band above the sting if it is on the arm or leg. Loosen the band for a few seconds every 15 minutes.

2. Apply an icepack or cold cloths to the sting area.

3. Get the victim to a doctor as soon as possible.

For the average bee-sting victim, these procedures will suffice:

1. Make a paste of baking soda and cold cream (if it is available), and apply it to the sting area.

2. Apply cold cloths to help ease the pain.

3. If there is itching, use calamine lotion.

Chigger and Tick Bites

The irritation produced by chiggers, which are the larval stage of a mite, results from fluid the tiny insects inject. Chiggers do not burrow under the skin, as is often suggested.

How to Battle the Bugs

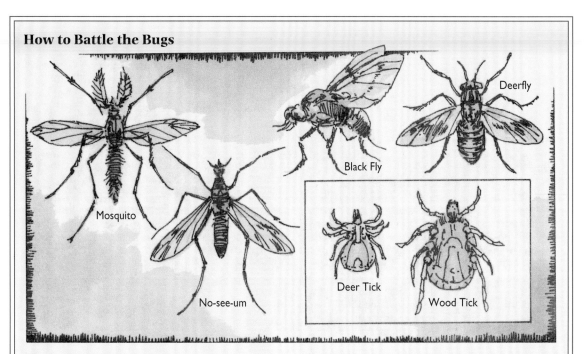

Mosquito

No-see-um

Black Fly

Deerfly

Deer Tick

Wood Tick

Mosquitoes home in on warmth, carbon dioxide, and the odor of human skin. Your best weapon is a repellant on your skin that will set up a barrier that will confuse the mosquito's sensors.

Black flies are inactive at night but a problem during the day. You will rarely feel the bite. The first thing you may notice is the blood. If you get bitten and begin to itch, coat bites with alcohol or witch hazel.

Deerflies are found anywhere in the northern woods, and both sexes can inflict painful bites. Use a headnet and tape cuffs, but be aware that deerflies can also bite through clothing.

No-see-ums are troublesome because it is difficult to protect yourself from them. They can fit through head-nets, screens, clothing—almost anything. A repellant helps, but the only sure cure is a stiff wind.

Deer ticks pose a Lyme disease threat. They are half the size of the common wood tick and are orangish brown with a black spot near the head. Symptoms of Lyme disease include a red, ring-shaped rash, fever, chills, headache, stiff joints, and fatigue. Learn how to identify ticks and remove them from your body with tweezers. Don't burn, twist, or crush a tick on your body.

Since chiggers do not usually attach themselves to the skin until an hour or more after they reach the body, bathing promptly after exposure, using a brush and soapy water, may eliminate them. Once the bites have been inflicted, the application of ice water may help. The itching and discomfort can be relieved by applying calamine lotion or a paste made of baking soda and a little water.

Ticks—flat, usually brown, and about ¼ inch long—attach themselves to the skin by making a tiny puncture, and they feed by sucking blood. They can thereby transmit the germs of several diseases,

including Rocky Mountain spotted fever and Lyme disease. A new strain, granulocytic ehrlichiosis, has flu-like symptoms nearly identical to Lyme disease. Protecting yourself from granulocytic ehrlichiosis is the same as with Lyme disease.

If you have been in a tick-infested area, be sure to examine your clothes and body for the insects, paying particular attention to hairy areas. Removing ticks promptly is insurance against the transmission of any germs they may be carrying since that process seldom begins until six hours or so after the insect attaches itself and begins to feed.

The Fisherman and Lyme Disease

A deer tick is a speck of a bug, but unnoticed on your body its bite can infect you with spirochete bacteria, which produces the crippling Lyme disease. Deer ticks are found on a wide variety of wild and domestic animals, but about 75 percent of deer ticks live on whitetail deer. This means that fishermen in deer country have a greater risk of contracting Lyme disease than most other sportsmen.

Fishermen hiking in the woods along streams and lakes should tuck in the bottoms of their pant legs. If you prefer to wear your pants outside your boots, so that your pants shed rain outside your boots rather than inside, use masking tape to close off your cuffs. Before you go into the woods, spray yourself with a good tick repellent. There are several on the market that will do the job well, especially if they contain the ingredient DEET.

After a day of fishing, check your body for ticks. The bite of a deer tick is painless, so you may never know you've been bitten unless you look for a tick or signs of a bite. Look wherever you have hair. Check your scalp, and the back of your neck and head. Two favorite spots of ticks are your armpits and groin. It's important to check everywhere.

If you find a tick, don't panic. Grab the tick as close to the skin as possible and pull outward slowly and steadily with firm force. Don't twist or jerk the tick out, which may break off parts of the tick in your skin. Squeezing it is also risky because you may release bacteria into your body.

It takes at least several hours for a deer tick to release its bacteria into your bloodstream, so it's critical to remove the tick as quickly as possible. When the tick is out, wash and disinfect the bite area thoroughly. If you see signs of redness or a rash, call a doctor immediately.

Use tweezers to remove a tick, but don't yank—that may cause the tick's head or mouth parts to break off and remain in the flesh. Pull it gently, taking care not to crush the body, which may be full of germs. If it can't be pulled off gently, cover the entire tick with heavy oil, which closes off its breathing pores and may make it disengage itself.

■ Spider and Scorpion Bites

Scorpions are most common in the southwestern United States and are found in such spots as cool and damp buildings, debris, and under loose banks. Most species of scorpions in the United States are nonvenomous; few of their stings are dangerous.

The biting spiders in the United States include the black widow, brown widow, and tarantula. The brown widow—its abdomen has a dull-orange hourglass marking against a brown body—is harmless in almost all cases. The tarantula is a large (up to 3 inches long, not including the legs) and hairy spider, but despite its awesome appearance its bite is almost always harmless, though it may cause allergic reactions in sensitive people. The black widow—the female's body is about ½ inch long, shiny black, usually with a red hourglass marking

on the underside of the abdomen—has a venomous bite, but its victims almost always recover.

The symptoms of these bites may include some swelling and redness, immediate pain that may—especially with a black-widow bite—become quite severe and spread throughout the body, much sweating, nausea, and difficulty in breathing and speaking.

First-aid procedures are as follows:

1. Keep the victim warm and calm, lying down.
2. Apply a wide, constricting band above the bite, loosening it every 15 minutes.
3. Apply wrapped-up ice or cold compresses to the area of the bite.
4. Get medical help as quickly as possible.

■ Poison Ivy, Poison Oak, and Poison Sumac

You cannot escape from poison ivy, poison oak, and poison sumac. There are virtually no areas in the United States in which at least one of these plants does not exist. Poison ivy is found throughout the country, with the possible exception of California and Nevada. Poison

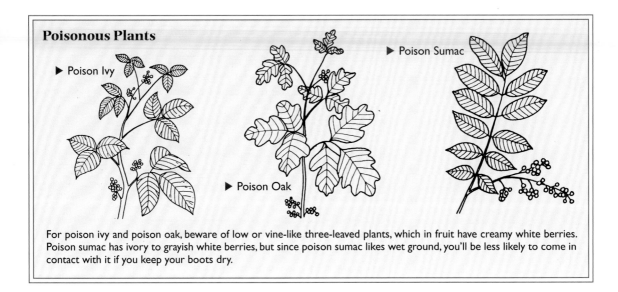

Poisonous Plants

▶ Poison Ivy

▶ Poison Oak

▶ Poison Sumac

For poison ivy and poison oak, beware of low or vine-like three-leaved plants, which in fruit have creamy white berries. Poison sumac has ivory to grayish white berries, but since poison sumac likes wet ground, you'll be less likely to come in contact with it if you keep your boots dry.

oak occurs in the southeastern states, and a western variety exists in the West Coast states. Poison sumac grows in most of the states in the eastern third of the country.

If you're lucky, you may be among the 50 percent of the population that is not sensitive to these poisonous plants. If you are not lucky, however, and you've already had a few run-ins with poison ivy, oak, or sumac, you better know how to identify these plants and learn where they grow. Poison ivy grows along streams, lakes, and on sunny hillsides. It can also grow as a shrub, a small tree, or a vine.

If you want to avoid poison ivy and poison oak, beware of low or vine-like three-leaved plants, which in fruit have creamy white berries. Poison sumac has ivory to grayish white berries. Poison sumac likes wet ground, so you are less likely to come in contact with it if you keep your boots dry.

Urushiol is the sticky, colorless oil that comes from the leaves and stems of poison ivy that, when it gets on your skin, causes the irritation. Urushiol in poison ivy is nearly the same in poison oak and poison sumac. If you're sensitive to one, you're sensitive to all of them.

If you don't wash the poison sap off your skin quickly, you will develop a rash within a couple of days. The rash will eventually produce swollen patches with blisters that will break and ooze.

Healing will take about two weeks, no matter what you do, but here is some advice to ease the intense itching and promote healing. The best medicine against poison ivy is cortisone, if given within the first 24 hours. Oral

prednisone will also help. If you are sensitive to poison ivy, take a supply of cortisone along on your trips.

Here are other remedies that will at least relieve some of the symptoms:

1. Cool compresses with Burow's solution will ease itching and speed up the drying process. Apply them for 15 minutes three or four times a day.

2. Calamine lotion will also relieve the itching.

3. Oatmeal baths are helpful. Add a cup of Aveeno oatmeal to the tub and soak in it for 15 minutes two or three times a day.

4. Aloe vera will aid in skin healing. Apply the lotion twice a day.

5. Oral antihistamines will help eliminate the itching, but antihistamine lotions don't help. Don't use anesthetic sprays or lotions, which may actually sensitize the skin and irritate the rash.

6. If you're very sensitive to poison ivy, try Ivy Shield, an organic clay barrier that will give 95 percent protection to the skin.

7. If you come in contact with poison ivy, shower with soap and water immediately.

The best protection is learning how to identify these plants and avoid them. The shiny leaves grow in groups of three, so try to remember the saying, "Leaves of three, beware of me."

SUNBURN

Not everyone is aware of the genuine health hazard from the solar system. The National Cancer Institute estimates 600,000 malignancies a year are a direct result of careless exposure to the sun. Of that number, close to 7,000 people will die from malignant melanoma, the most deadly skin cancer.

The sun is the bad guy, causing at least 90 percent of all skin cancers. Fortunately, the sun warns its victims with early symptoms. Those symptoms include those fashionable tans you see around town and usually ignore.

The sun produces two different types of ultraviolet rays, both harmful to the skin. Beta rays (UVB) can cause skin cancer. Alpha rays (UVA) can cause both skin cancer and premature wrinkling of the skin. The easiest and most effective way of protecting yourself from these rays is through the use of a good sunscreen that is rated with an SPF (sun protection factor) of at least 15.

There are sunscreens with ratings of SPF 35 and higher, but in most cases, a rating of SPF 15 is all that is necessary for daily use. With an SPF 15, a person can stay in the sun 15 times longer than without any protection at all. Some doctors claim that regular use of an SPF 15 for the first 18 years of life may reduce the risk of skin cancer by 78 percent. For this reason, it's extremely important for parents to remember to keep small children out of direct sunlight, especially between 10:00 a.m. and 3:00 p.m., when the sun is the strongest and can do the most damage to the skin. Choose a waterproof sunscreen. Apply it liberally an hour or two before you go out in the sun, and reapply it every two or three hours, especially after swimming and sweating. Some newer sunscreens are formulated to last all day, even after swimming.

Your skin type is also an important factor. If you're a Type I or II, which means fair skin, blond hair, and blue eyes, you will need more skin protection and a doctor should check you for skin cancer at least once a year. At the other extreme is Type V or VI, which includes people of Middle Eastern and African descent, who will burn only after heavy exposure.

If you spend a lot of time in the sun, you should know about the types of skin cancers and how to detect them early. There are three kinds of skin cancers: basal cell carcinoma, squamous cell carcinoma, and malignant melanoma.

Basal cell carcinoma is the most common skin cancer (about 80 percent) and is seldom deadly. It usually appears on the neck, head, face, and hands. It may be as small as a pinpoint or as large as an inch. It may also crust and bleed.

Squamous-cell carcinoma is the second-most common and looks like a raised pink wart. If left untreated, it can spread to other parts of the body.

Malignant melanoma is the least common, but it is the most deadly skin cancer. It usually appears quickly on the upper back or legs. It can be brown, black, or multicolored. Malignant melanoma grows fast and spreads to other organs.

If you spend a lot of time in the sun, check your skin regularly. Look at the back of your hands and your face. Look for scaly, rough patches of skin. Are there any white spots or red nodules with scales? If you see anything that looks suspicious, see your doctor. Most of the time, skin cancers are easily and successfully removed.

SURVIVING HEAT AND COLD

■ Sunstroke

Sunstroke is extremely dangerous. Aged people are the most susceptible. The usual symptoms are headache, dry skin, and rapid pulse. Dizziness and nausea may occur, and in severe cases the victim may lapse into unconsciousness. The body temperature soars, sometimes as high as 109°F.

Medical help, as soon as possible, is a must. Until it arrives, do the following:

1. Undress the victim, and sponge the body freely with cool water, or apply cold cloths, the objective being to reduce body temperature to a tolerable level of 103°F or below. If you have no thermometer, check the victim's pulse; a pulse rate of 110 or below usually means a tolerable body temperature.

2. When the body temperature lowers to 103°F, stop the sponging or cool-cloth treatment for about 10

Dogs and Summer Heat

I was running some errands last summer when I saw a young boy pedaling his bike down the road with his Brittany spaniel in tow. The temperature was in the 90s, but that didn't slow the boy down. The dog, however, was having trouble keeping up. My heart went out to the dog. I also often see dogs on boats with little protection from hot sun.

The summer heat is tough on all pets, but especially dogs. Though they can't tell you when they have had enough, they will give you some signals that something is wrong. Pay attention or you can kill your dog.

We humans are lucky. When it gets hot, we can take our shirts off and wipe our brows. Dogs are not so lucky. Dogs have to cool themselves by evaporation, and they do this by panting. When temperature and humidity rise, however, this evaporation process slows down and body temperature rises. When this happens, high body temperatures can harm the circulatory and respiratory systems, and the dog suffers. In some cases, high body temperatures can kill a dog.

Couple heat and humidity with hard exercise and a very definite danger of heat stress exists. Learn to recognize the signals that your dog may be in trouble.

First, not all dogs are created equal in how they handle the heat. Puppies, older dogs, overweight animals, and pets that you just recently moved to a warmer climate are more susceptible to heat problems than young dogs in peak condition.

Next, don't be alarmed if your dog loses his appetite during the summer months. According to a major dog food company, dogs need about 7.5 percent fewer calories with each 10-degree rise in temperature. When you walk or exercise your dog, constantly look for heat problems. Symptoms could vary, including heavy panting, dark red gums, a staring or anxious expression, a failure to respond to commands, high fever, excessive salivation, or vomiting.

If you recognize any of the signs, get the dog into the shade. Flush the dog's mouth with cool, not cold, water. Don't allow him to drink too much. Wet the bare skin areas of his underbelly and flanks. As with the tongue, it's here that blood flows close to the surface for cooling before returning to the body core.

Summer heat, however, doesn't mean you can't train or exercise your dog. How much of a workout can your dog handle? Short-haired breeds can cool down and run a lot longer than dogs with heavy coats. A heavy-coated dog, such as a setter, can run hard for about 30 minutes. The short-haired breeds can run for about an hour. Obviously, temperature and lots of other variables are involved. Use your judgment. If you suspect a heat problem, stop the training session immediately.

Traveling with a dog in summer also takes some special consideration. Even if it's cool outside, the temperature in a car can rise to a dangerous level quickly. If you must leave your dog in a car, park it in the shade and leave the windows slightly lowered. In summer weather, never leave your dog in a parked car for more than 30 minutes.

---

minutes. If the temperature again starts to rise, resume the sponging.

3. If the victim is conscious and can swallow, give him as much as he can drink of a saltwater solution (1 teaspoon of salt to 1 quart of water).

4. Later, cover according to the victim's comfort.

■ Hypothermia

Hypothermia is one of the major causes of death among outdoor people, and it will strike anyone who is not prepared to handle extreme weather conditions. Hypothermia is caused by exposure to high winds, rain, snow, or wet clothing. A person's normal core (inner body) temperature is 98.6°F. When the body begins to lose heat, early stages of hypothermia will be apparent. The person will start to shiver and stamp his feet.

If these early signs of hypothermia are ignored, the next stage of symptoms will be uncontrollable spells of shivering, fumbling hands, and drowsiness. If not treated quickly, hypothermia will likely kill its victim when the body temperature drops below 78°F and this can happen within 90 minutes after shivering begins.

Hypothermia's Effects on the Body

When extreme cold causes the body to lose its interior heat, these symptoms occur as your temperature drops:

99 to 96 degrees • Shivering becomes intense; ability to perform simple tasks is slowed

95 to 91 degrees • Skin tone pales; shivering turns violent and speech is impaired

90 to 86 degrees • Muscular rigidity replaces shivering; thinking is dulled considerably

85 to 81 degrees • Victim becomes irrational and may drift into a stupor; pulse is slow

80 to 78 degrees • Unconsciousness occurs; reflexes cease to function

Below 78 degrees • Condition may be irreversible; death is likely at this point

If you're outdoors and detect any of these symptoms in yourself or a friend, start treatment immediately. First, get to shelter and warmth as soon as possible. If no shelter is available, build a fire. Get out of wet clothing and apply heat to the victim's head, neck, chest, and groin. Use chemical heat packs if you have them. If not, use body heat from another person. If you have a sleeping bag, the victim should be placed in it with another person.

As the victim begins to recover, give him warm liquids, chocolate, or any other high-sugar-content foods. Never give a hypothermia patient alcohol. It will only impair judgment, dilate blood vessels, and impair shivering (the body's way of producing heat).

If you're in a boat and capsize into cold water, don't take off your clothing; it will help trap heat. If you are wearing a life jacket, draw your knees up to your body, which will reduce heat loss. If there are several people in the water, huddle together so you can conserve heat. Survival in cold water depends on the water temperature. If the water temperature is 32.5°F, survival time may be under 15 minutes. If the water is more than 80°F, survival time is indefinite.

Preventing hypothermia is a lot easier than treating it. First, stay in shape and get a good night's sleep before going outdoors. Always carry candy, mixed nuts, or some other high-energy food. Stay as dry as possible and avoid getting overheated. Wet clothing will lose 90 percent of its insulating qualities and will rob the body of heat.

Dress properly. This means wearing several layers of clothing to form an insulating barrier against the cold. Always carry rain gear and use it when the first drops fall. Wear a wool hat with some kind of ear protection. Several manufacturers make wool knit caps with a Gore-Tex lining, which will keep your head and ears dry in a downpour. It's a fact that an uncovered head can lose up to 50 percent of the body's heat.

You should also carry a survival kit with a change of clothing, waterproof matches, and candy bars or other high-energy snacks.

■ Frostbite

Frostbite is the freezing of an area of the body, usually the nose, ears, cheeks, fingers, or toes.

Just before the actual onset of frostbite, the skin may appear slightly flushed. Then, as frostbite develops, the skin becomes white or grayish yellow. Blisters may develop later. In the early stages the victim may feel pain, which later subsides. The affected area feels intensely cold and numb, but the victim is often unaware of the problem until someone tells him or he notices the pale, glossy skin. First-aid treatment is as follows:

1. Enclose the frostbitten area with warm hands or warm cloth, using firm pressure. Do not rub with your hands or with snow. If the affected area is on the fingers or hands, have the victim put his hands into his armpits.

2. Cover the area with woolen cloth.

3. Get the victim indoors or into a warm shelter as soon as possible. Immerse the frostbitten area in warm— not hot—water. If that is not possible, wrap the area in warm blankets. Do not use hot-water bottles or heat lamps, and do not place the affected area near fire or a hot stove.

4. When the frostbitten part has been warmed, encourage the victim to move it.

5. Give the victim something warm to drink.

6. If the victim must travel, apply a sterile dressing that widely overlaps the affected area, and be sure

that enough clothing covers the affected area to keep it warm.

7. Medical attention is usually necessary.

■ Sun and Eyes

Boaters and fishermen are probably already aware of the punishing effects of the sun's glare on your eyes. In fact, the effect of glare on the surface of the water can be 25 times brighter than the light level indoors. For most activities, sunglasses should be able to absorb about 60 percent of the sun's rays. For fishing or boating, however, sunglasses should be darker, absorbing up to 95 percent of the sun's rays. Bausch & Lomb suggests this simple in-store test for lens darkness: Look in a mirror with the sunglasses on. If the lenses are dark enough, you will have some difficulty seeing your eyes. This test does not work for photochromic sunglasses because they would be at their light stage indoors. If you are a fisherman, you should select sunglasses with polarizing lenses, which are usually made by sandwiching polarizing film between layers of dark glass or plastic. They eliminate reflections on the surface of the water and allow fishermen to see beneath the surface. Sunglasses

Effects of Sun Rays

Ultraviolet (UV) rays, hidden in the sun's rays, can be irritating and dangerous, causing both short- and long-term harmful effects on the eyes. Industry standards require that sunglasses designed for water sports should absorb up to 95 percent of UV rays. Make sure that the sunglasses you select are ones that afford UV protection.

Ultraviolet Rays

Visible Spectrum

Ultraviolet Rays

Lens

come in a variety of lens colors, but most eye-care professionals recommend green, gray, or brown for outside activities.

SPRAINS

Sprains are injuries to the soft tissues that surround joints. Ligaments, tendons, and blood vessels are stretched and sometimes torn. Ankles, wrists, fingers, and knees are the areas most often affected.

Symptoms include pain when the area is moved, swelling, and tenderness to the touch. Sometimes a large area of skin becomes discolored because small blood vessels are ruptured.

It is often difficult to tell whether the injury is a sprain or a fracture. If in doubt, treat as a fracture. Otherwise, take the following steps:

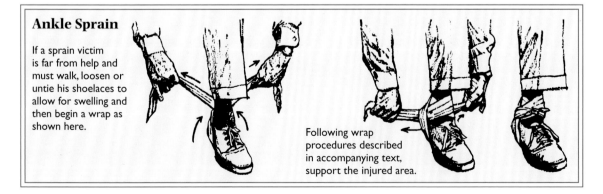

Ankle Sprain

If a sprain victim is far from help and must walk, loosen or untie his shoelaces to allow for swelling and then begin a wrap as shown here.

Following wrap procedures described in accompanying text, support the injured area.

I. Elevate the injured joint, using pillows or something similar. A sprained ankle should be raised about 12 inches higher than the torso. For a wrist or elbow sprain, put the arm into a sling.

2. Apply an ice pack or cold cloths to reduce swelling and pain. Continue the cold treatment for a half hour.

3. Always have a sprain X-rayed. There may indeed be a fracture or a bone chip.

If the victim of a sprained ankle is far from help and must walk, make the following preparations:

I. Untie the shoelaces to allow for swelling, but do not take off the shoe.

2. Place the middle of a long bandage (a folded triangular bandage is best) under the shoe just forward of the heel.

3. Bring the ends of the bandage up and back, crossing them above (at the back of) the heel.

4. Bring the ends forward around the ankle, and cross them over the instep.

5. Bring the ends downward toward the heel, and slip each end beneath the wrap that comes up from each side of the heel.

6. Bring the ends of the bandage around the ankle again and pull on the ends to produce the desired tension.

7. Tie a square knot in front.

OTHER INJURIES

■ Eyes Injuries or Foreign Body in Eye

For first-aid purposes, eye injuries fall into three categories: injury to eyelids and soft tissue above the eye, injury to the surface of the eyeball, or injury that extends into the tissue beneath the eyeball surface.

In Category 1, treatment involves putting on a sterile dressing and bandaging it in place. If the injury is in the form of a bruise (the familiar "black eye"), the immediate application of cold cloths or an ice pack should halt any bleeding and prevent some swelling. Later, apply warm, wet towels to reduce discoloration.

Injuries in Category 2 usually occur when a foreign body lodges on the surface of the eyeball. To remove the object, pull the upper eyelid down over the lower one, and hold it there for a moment, instructing the victim to look upward. Tears will flow naturally and may wash out the object.

If that doesn't work, put two fingers of your hand on the skin just below the victim's lower eyelid, and force the skin gently downward, thereby exposing the inner area of the lower lid. Inspect the area closely, and if the object is visible, lift it out carefully, using a corner of a clean handkerchief or a small wad of moistened sterile cotton wrapped around the end of a toothpick.

If the foreign object can't be seen, it can sometimes be flushed out. Boil some water, add table salt (¼ teaspoon to an average glassful), and let the salt water cool to about body temperature. With the victim lying down, tilt his head toward the injured side,

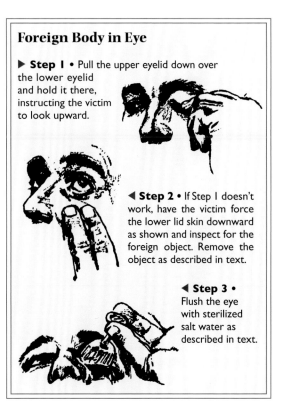

Foreign Body in Eye

▶ **Step I** • Pull the upper eyelid down over the lower eyelid and hold it there, instructing the victim to look upward.

◀ **Step 2** • If Step I doesn't work, have the victim force the lower lid skin downward as shown and inspect for the foreign object. Remove the object as described in text.

◀ **Step 3** • Flush the eye with sterilized salt water as described in text.

hold his eyelids open with your fingers, and pour the liquid into the inner corner of his eye so that it runs across the eyeball and drains on the opposite side.

Eye injuries in Category 3 are extremely serious. Never attempt to remove an object that has penetrated the eyeball, no matter how shallow. Apply a sterile compress or clean cloth, cover it with a loose bandage, and get the victim to a doctor at once.

Cuts, Abrasions, and Bruises

Minor mishaps frequently involve one of these three injuries. With abrasions (the rubbing or scraping off of skin) and small cuts, the emphasis should be on preventing infection.

Immediately clean the cut or abrasion and the surrounding area with soap and warm water. Don't breathe on the wound or let fingers or soiled cloth contact it.

If there is bleeding, put a sterile pad over the wound and hold it there firmly until the bleeding stops. Then apply an antiseptic, if available, and apply a fresh sterile pad, bandaging it in place loosely.

A bruise results when small blood vessels under the skin are broken, causing discoloration of the skin and swelling, which is often painful.

First aid may be unnecessary if the bruise is minor. If it is more severe, apply an ice pack or cold cloths to reduce the swelling and relieve the pain. Bruises on an extremity can be made less painful if the limb is elevated.

Puncture Wounds

A puncture wound results when a sharp object—knife, needle, fishhook, or the like—penetrates the skin and the tissue underneath. The first-aider's primary objectives here, and with all other wounds, are to prevent infection and control bleeding.

Puncture wounds are often unusual in that they may be quite deep but the bleeding, because of the small opening in the skin, may be relatively light. The lighter the bleeding, generally, the lesser the chance that germs embedded by the penetrating object will be washed out. This means that the danger of infection is greater in puncture wounds than in other wounds. The danger of tetanus (lockjaw) infection is also greater in puncture wounds. First-aid procedures are as follows:

1. If the bleeding is limited, try to increase the flow by applying gentle pressure to the areas surrounding the wound. Do not squeeze hard, or you may cause further tissue damage.

2. Do not probe inside the wound. If a large splinter or a piece of glass or metal protrudes from it, try to remove it, but do so with extreme caution. If the sliver cannot be withdrawn with very gentle pressure, leave it where it is, or you may cause further damage and severe bleeding.

3. Wash the wound with soap and water.

4. Apply a sterile pad, and bandage it in place.

5. Get the victim to a doctor for treatment, including a tetanus shot if necessary.

Fishhook Removal

A doctor's care—and a tetanus shot, if needed—are recommended for anyone who has had a fishhook

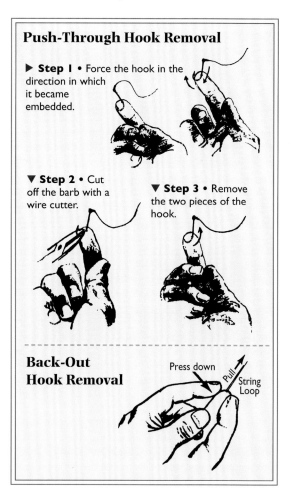

Push-Through Hook Removal

▶ **Step 1** • Force the hook in the direction in which it became embedded.

▼ **Step 2** • Cut off the barb with a wire cutter.

▼ **Step 3** • Remove the two pieces of the hook.

Back-Out Hook Removal

Press down

Pull

String Loop

How Not to Get Seasick

I haven't been seasick in the last 25 years or so. The night before a trip, I stay away from alcohol and get a good night's sleep. The following morning, I sip a cup of black coffee before I get on the boat. If I still feel good by 10:00 a.m., I'll start to eat . . . but never before. Will this simple formula work for you? To be quite honest, I don't know.

Finding a cure for seasickness is often a matter of trial and error. Everyone has a different approach. Some fishermen are convinced that a full stomach before a fishing trip is the best way to avoid seasickness, and that may work for some people. It doesn't work for me. I can, however, tell you what doesn't work for anyone—stay out late, overindulge, get on a boat tired and hungover, and I can guarantee that you will get sick in even a small chop.

In the simplest terms, seasickness is the inability of your body to adjust to motion. Your body has a built-in gyroscope to keep you on an even keel, much the way a gyroscope keeps a rocket upright as it travels in space. This system works on solid ground, but on a rocking boat or a bumpy airplane, the mechanism sometimes fails and you get seasick.

This means, of course, that when you start feeling seasick, you should try to reduce movement as soon as possible. If you are on a boat, sit in the center and at the stern, where movement will be minimized. It also helps to keep your eye on a stationary object, such as a bridge or tower on the shoreline. You are trying to send a message to your brain that you are not really rocking and have no reason to be seasick. It sometimes works.

Fight the urge to go into the cabin. There is nothing stationary in a cabin; you have no fixed object, and you will likely get sicker. In fact, if you get seasick and head for the cabin, you will probably be there the rest of the day.

Over the years I've heard of dozens of concoctions to cure seasickness. Some may be effective for some people, but most wacky formulas don't work. A doctor once suggested cold stewed tomatoes and saltines, a formula that originated aboard an oil tanker. I suggested it to a friend and he still got sick. It could, however, work for you.

Fortunately, modern medicine has made great strides in helping people cope with an illness that will make you feel like you're dying. These seasickness drugs fall into two categories: antihistamines and scopolamine. These drugs are designed to inhibit the flow of nerve impulses from the vestibular system to the brain. Which drug will work for you? You may have to try them all until you find the one that works best for you.

Antivert and Bonine are nonprescription antihistamines that you take every 24 hours. They will make you drowsy. Marezine is another antihistamine, but it is taken every four to six hours.

Dramamine is the old standby. If the weather forecast calls for rough seas, I will take a Dramamine tablet the night before and another one hour before I get on a boat. It works for me. An antihistamine that is taken every four hours, Dramamine is a nonprescription drug and it will make you drowsy unless you get the "less drowsy" formula.

Transderm Scop is perhaps the most effective drug in fighting and preventing seasickness. It's a patch you put on the skin behind the ear that slowly releases scopolamine into your system for days. The side effects can sometimes be severe, however, and should be discussed with your doctor.

There's a lot you can do to protect yourself from getting seasick, but first, accept the fact that everyone will eventually get seasick. When someone brags that he doesn't get seasick, don't believe him. His time at the rail has not yet arrived! There is also no reason to be apologetic or embarrassed about getting seasick. Finally, never poke fun at someone who is seasick, especially a youngster. You may get paid back on your next trip!

embedded past the barb in the flesh. In many cases, however, medical help is not within easy reach. The severity of the injury and the size of the hook determine what action the first-aider should take.

If the hook has penetrated only up as far as the barb or slightly past it—and if it is not in a critical spot such as the eye—you should be able to pull or jerk it out. Then clean the wound, and treat it as you would any other superficial wound. If the hook has penetrated well past the barb and is not in a critical area, there are two recommended methods of removal:

1. Force the hook in the direction in which it became embedded so that the point and barb exit through the skin. Try to make the angle of exit as shallow as possible. This can be quite painful, so the victim should anchor the affected part as solidly as possible before beginning the process. Using wire cutters or a similar tool, cut the hook in two at a point on the shank just before the bend. Remove the two pieces.

2. Have the victim anchor the affected part solidly. Take a 12- to 18-inch piece of strong string (30-pound-test fishing line is ideal), and run one end around the bend of the hook as if you were threading a needle. Bring the two ends together, and tie them in a sturdy

knot. With the thumb and forefinger, push down (toward the affected part) on the shank of the hook at the point where the bend begins. This disengages the barb from the tissue. Maintaining that pressure, grasp the line firmly at the knotted end, and give a strong yank. The finger pressure on the shank should reduce flesh damage to a minimum as the barb comes out the same way it went in. Do not use this method if the hook is large.

If bleeding is minimal after either of these procedures, squeeze the wound gently to encourage blood flow, which has a cleansing effect. Put on a sterile dressing, and get medical help.

If the hook is a large one and is deeply embedded, or if it is in a critical area, do not try to remove it. Cover the wound, hook and all, with a sterile dressing, and get the victim to a doctor.

ILLNESS

■ Appendicitis

The principle symptom is pain in the lower right part of the abdomen and sometimes over the entire abdominal region. Nausea and vomiting may be present, as may a mild fever. Constipation often occurs and is sometimes thought to be the cause of the victim's discomfort. Do not give a laxative if appendicitis is suspected—it will increase the danger that the appendix will rupture.

1. Have the patient lie down, and keep him comfortable.

2. Do not give him any food or water.

3. An ice pack placed over the appendix area may relieve pain. Do not apply heat to the appendix area.

4. Get medical help as soon as possible.

■ Diarrhea

Diarrhea is a common malady among outdoorsmen. Its causes are often associated with change: during an extended cruise or fishing trip, for example, the sportsman's eating and drinking habits are often much different than what they are at home. Attacks of diarrhea usually subside once the body adapts to those changes.

Paregoric is helpful in combating diarrhea, as are many of the products designed for that purpose and sold in drugstores. If you or your companions are particularly prone to attacks of diarrhea, see a doctor and ask him to prescribe a drug, preferably in tablet form, that will combat the problem during trips afield.

■ Toothache

First-aid procedures are as follows:

1. Inspect the sufferer's mouth under the strongest light available.

2. If no cavity is visible, place an ice pack or cold compress against the jaw on the painful side. If that doesn't provide relief, try a hot-water bottle or hot compress.

3. If a cavity can be seen, use a piece of sterile cotton wrapped on the end of a toothpick to clean the cavity as thoroughly as possible.

4. Oil of cloves, if available, can give relief. Pack it gently into the cavity with a toothpick. Do not let the oil touch the tongue or the inside of the mouth—the stuff burns.

FIRST-AID KIT

Improvisation is an ability that most outdoors people seem to develop naturally. But an improvised dressing for a wound, for example, is a poor second-best for a prepackaged, sterile dressing. Any first-aider can function more effectively if he has the proper equipment. A first-aid kit—whether it is bought in a pharmacy or is put together by the individual—should meet the following requirements:

- Its contents should be complete enough for the purposes for which it will be used.
- The contents should be arranged so that any component desired can be located quickly and without removing the other components.
- Each component should be wrapped so that any unused portion can be repacked and thereby prevented from leaking or becoming soiled.
- How and where the kit will be used are the main factors to consider when assembling a first-aid kit. The two kits described below should fill the needs of most outdoor situations.

■ POCKET KIT

Suitable for one-day, overnight, or short-term trips in areas not far from medical help.

- 1-by-1-inch packaged sterile bandages (2)
- 2-by-2-inch packaged sterile bandages (2)
- 2-by-2-inch packaged sterile gauze pads (2)
- Roll of adhesive tape
- Band-Aids (10)
- Ammonia inhalant (1)
- Tube of antiseptic cream
- Small tin of aspirin (or 12 aspirins wrapped in foil)

■ ALL-PURPOSE OUTDOORS FIRST-AID KIT

Suitable for general outings.

- 4-inch Ace bandages (2)
- 2-inch Ace bandages (2)*
- 2-by-2-inch sterile gauze pads (1 package)*
- 5-by-9-inch combine dressing (3)
- Triangular bandage (1)
- Sterile eye pads (2)
- ½-inch adhesive tape (5 yards)
- Assorted Band-Aids (1 package)*
- Betadine liquid antiseptic
- Yellow mercuric oxide ointment (for eyes)*

- Bacitracin (ointment)
- Tylenol (aspirin substitute)
- Dramamine (for motion sickness)
- Sunscreen
- Insect repellent
- Single-edge razor blade
- Tweezers (flat tip)
- Small scissors
- Eye patch
- Needle
- Matches in waterproof container
- Needle-nose pliers with cutting edge
- First-aid manual

Add these items if you are going into a remote area for an extended period of time:

- Tylenol with codeine (painkiller)**
- Tetracycline (antibiotic)**
- Lomotil, 2.5 milligrams (for cramps, diarrhea)**
- Antihistamine tablets
- Phillips Milk of Magnesia (antacid, laxative)

* Items, in fewer quantities, are recommended for a small first-aid kit for day trips. ** Requires a prescription.

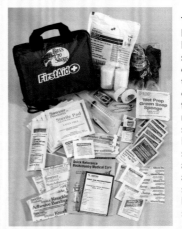

The Bass Pro Family First-Aid Kit is tailored specifically for outdoor activities and includes everything most families would need for a six-day trip. If you're not sure how to assemble a first-aid kit, a professionally packaged kit is a safe and sensible choice.

Index

Acknowledgments

The author would like to thank the following people, companies, organizations, and agencies for their permission, cooperation, and assistance in compiling information and photographs for this book:

Andy Anderson • Joe Arterburn, Cabela's • Scott Atkinson, USA Water Ski • Amy Bahr, West Marine • Tom Beard • Candace Cockrell, Triton Boats • Dean Corbisier, Suzuki • Chris Corey, L.L. Bean • Kevin Coullahan, West Marine • James Daley, Orvis • Laura Davidson, A Beautiful Plate • Dan Dejkunchorn, Sea Eagle • Brittney Dileo, BOTE Board • Margo Donohue, West Marine • Daniel D. Dye II, Florida Backyard Snakes • Greg Eck, Yanmar America Corporation • Jim Edlund, Traditions Media • Steve Fleming, Mercury Marine • Kelly Flory, Martin Flory Group • Pete Frederiksen, Viking Yachts • Gary Giudice, Ron Giudice, and Tonya Giudice, Blue Heron Communications • Rus Graham, Rushton Gregory • Christina Harris, World Cat • William W. Hartley, Hartley Industries • Isaiah James, Windsor Nature Discovery • Andrea Jansen, Mercury Marine • Charlie Johnson, Maverick Boat Company • Jeff Kauzlaric, Furuno USA • Karen Kinser, Wright & McGill/Eagle Claw • Dave Kotlan, Seven Marine/DRK Creative • Jim Martinson, Sheldon's • Stephen Matt, G3 Boats • Mac McKeever, L.L. Bean • J. Richard McLaughlin • Tom Mielke, Mercury Marine • Stacy Miller, World Cat • Katie Mitchell, Bass Pro • Kellie Mowery, Cabela's • Terri Nuechterlein, HydraSports • Peter Orlando, EdgeWater Boats • Martin Peters, Yamaha • Cason Pilliod, Kalkomey • Tom Richardson • Al Ristori • Tom Rosenbauer, Orvis • David Scott, Martin Flory Group • Dusan Smetana • Elizabeth Smith • Tanza Smith, Bass Pro • Sarah Stern, Sabre Yachts • Mitch Strobl, Kalkomey • Josh Ward, Ranger and Stratos Boats • Heidi Weber, Yamaha • Bobby Wheaton, Yamaha • Leslie Zlotnick, Yamaha

■ ■ ■

Photography Credits

Courtesy of Action Craft/Martin Flory: p. 31 (bottom).

© Andrew Allport/Dreamstime.com: p. 210 (top right and bottom).

© Andy Anderson: pp. 2–3, 9, and back cover.

Courtesy of Bass Pro: pp. 16 (top left), 17 (top right), 31 (top), 36, 40 (top left and top right), 45 (middle), 72 (both), 76 (middle and right), 78 (all), 79 (top), 80 (both), 82, 91, 123 (all), 126 (all except top right), 130 (all), 131, 133 (top and bottom left), 135, 137 (all), 150 (all), 151 (all), 152 (all), 153 (all), 154 (top left and middle), 155 (all except top left, second from top left, and top right), 156, 157 (all except second from bottom right), 160 (middle right, bottom left, and bottom right), 165 (top), 206, 207, 283, 289, 298, 325, and front cover (all except second from top left, middle, and bottom).

Courtesy of Berkley: p. 160 (top and middle left).

Courtesy of Boston Whaler: pp. 20 (middle) and 33 (top left).

Courtesy of Bote Board: pp. 45 (top) and 46.

Courtesy of Cabela's: pp. 81, 154 (top right), 157 (second from bottom right), and 291 (both).

© Rafal Czajka/Dreamstime.com: p. 213.

© Laura Davidson/www.abeautifulplate.com: pp. 286–287 (all).

© Daniel D. Dye II: p. 312 (all).

Courtesy of Eagle Claw: pp. 138, 146 (all), 154 (bottom left), 155 (top right), 180 (both), and 281 (top).

Courtesy of Evinrude/Rushton Gregory: p. 70 (bottom).

Courtesy of Furuno: p. 79 (bottom).

Courtesy of G3 Boats: pp. 16 (all except top left), 20 (top), 24, 30, 31 (second from bottom), 32, 35, 92, and front cover (second from top left).

© Gydyt0jas/Dreamstime.com: p. 210 (top left).
© William W. Hartley: p. 133 (bottom right).
© Robert Holland/EdgeWater Boats: p. 114.
© Tech. Sgt. John Hughel/Air National Guard: pp. 292–293.
Courtesy of Humminbird/Traditions Media: p. 76 (left).
Courtesy of HydraSports: p. 33 (bottom).
© Bob Krist Photo/Florida Keys News Bureau: p. 97.
Courtesy of Lehr Propane-Powered Outboards: p. 70 (top left).
Courtesy of L.L. Bean: pp. 40 (middle left, middle right, and bottom), 45 (bottom), 281 (bottom), 303, and front cover (bottom).
Courtesy of Maverick: p. 17 (top left).
© J. Richard McLaughlin: p. 294.
Courtesy of Mepps: pp. 154 (bottom right) and 155 (top left and second from top left).
Courtesy of Mercury: pp. 70 (middle and top right) and 74 (top right).
Courtesy of Ocean Kayak: p. 39.
Courtesy of Ocean Master/Martin Flory: p. 33 (middle).
Courtesy of Old Town/Traditions Media: p. 41 (both).
Courtesy of Orvis: p. 165 (all except top).
Courtesy of Pflueger: p. 126 (top right).
© Sigurbjorn Ragnarsson/Dreamstime.com: p. 209.
Courtesy of Ranger: p. 31 (second from top).
© Tom Rosenbauer: p. 145.
Courtesy of Sabre Yachts: p. 12 and front cover (middle).
Courtesy of Sea Eagle: p. 27.
Courtesy of Seven Marine: p. 71 (top right).
© Shutterstock.com/18042011: pp. 304–305.
© Shutterstock.com/withGod: p. 300.
© Dusan Smetana: pp. 28–29, 115, 120–121, 218–219, 248–249, and 278–279.
© Vin Sparano: pp. 119, 139 (both), 141 (both), 158 (both), 282 (all), 284–285 (all), and 336.
Courtesy of Suzuki: p. 71 (bottom).
© Tanya2015n/Dreamstime.com: p. 211 (bottom).
© Tonybrindley/Dreamstime.com: p. 212.
Courtesy of Triton: p. 49.
Courtesy of USA Water Ski: pp. 51–65 (all).
Courtesy of Viking: pp. 17 (bottom left) and 34.
Courtesy of West Marine: pp. 10–11, 66–67, and 98–99.
Courtesy of World Cat: pp. 20 (bottom) and 33 (top right).

Courtesy of Yamaha: pp. 48 (both), 71 (top left), and 75 (both).
Courtesy of Yanmar: p. 74 (top left).
Courtesy of Yellowfin: p. 17 (bottom right).
© Lisa F. Young/Dreamstime.com: p. 211 (top).
© Michael Zysman/Dreamstime.com: p. 208.

ILLUSTRATION CREDITS AND OTHER NOTES

Unless otherwise noted here, all black-and-white line art was picked up from the fourth edition of Vin Sparano's *Complete Outdoors Encyclopedia*.

© Tom Beard: pp. 110, 111 (both), and 112 (all).
© James Daley: pp. 12, 18 (both), 30, 68, 100, 122, 220, 250, 280, 294, and 306.
Courtesy of Kalkomey.com: pp. 13 (all), 14 (all), 44 (all), 47 (both), 68, 69 (top left, middle, top right), 74, 81 (all), 105 (all), and 106 (all).
Courtesy of the United States Coast Guard: p. 117.
Courtesy of USA Water Ski: p. 49 (all).
Courtesy of Windsor Nature Discovery: pp. 220–234 (all), 236–246 (all), 250–269 (all), 272, and 274–276 (all).

• Illustrations and information on boat hulls, cruisers and runabouts, sailboats, jet skis, marine motors, anchors, personal flotation devices, and buoys were provided courtesy of Kalkomey Enterprises (see page numbers listed above). For more information, visit the company's website at www.boat-ed.com.

• Photos and information on water skiing, wakeboarding, ski aids for the young beginner, and tubing in the Water Sports section (pp. 49–65) were provided courtesy of USA Water Ski. For more information, visit www.usawaterski.org.

• Information and illustrations in the Small-Boat Navigation section (pp. 110–112) were provided courtesy of Lieutenant Commander Tom Beard, USCG (Retired).

• 10 Tips for Proper Catch and Release (pp. 206–207) was written by Tom Richardson and used with his permission.

• Fishing by the Birds (pp. 208–213) was written by Al Ristori and used with his permission.

■ ■ ■

About the Author

Vin T. Sparano has been an outdoor editor and writer for more than 50 years. He earned his B.S. degree in journalism in 1960 from New York University. Sparano is editor emeritus of *Outdoor Life* magazine, having served as editor in chief from 1990 to 1995 and previously as executive editor for more than 10 years.

In addition to his long career with *Outdoor Life*, Sparano was a syndicated features writer for *USA Today* and Gannett newspapers. He has written and edited more than 20 books—including Universe's *Complete Outdoors Encyclopedia*, the full-color fifth edition of his classic encyclopedia originally published in 1976, *Complete Guide to Fresh and Saltwater Fishing*, and *Complete Guide to Camping and Wilderness Survival*—and has produced electronic software focusing on fishing techniques and hot spots through the use of navigational charts and satellite photos. Sparano has also produced five anthologies covering the classic stories in outdoor literature: *Tales of Woods and Waters, Greatest Hunting Stories Ever Told, Classic Hunting Tales, Game Birds and Gun Dogs*, and *Hunting Dangerous Game*.

Sparano and his wife, Betty, live in Waretown, New Jersey, where he is a familiar sight fishing from his boat, *Betty Boop*. During the fall, his focus is on the great striped bass fishery off Barnegat Inlet. In the winter months, Sparano travels to Florida, where he fishes the famous Islamorada Flats for tarpon and bonefish, as well as the offshore waters for sailfish, tuna, and other bluewater game fish.

A certified NRA rifle, pistol, shotgun, and hunting safety instructor, Sparano has been a member of the Outdoor Writers Association of America, fulfilling a term on its board of directors, and is also a heritage member of the Professional Outdoor Media Association. Sparano was a recipient of a Lifetime Achievement Award from both the New York Metropolitan Outdoor Press Association and the Fisherman's Conservation Association.

In 1996, Sparano was awarded the United States Department of the Interior Conservation Award by Secretary of the Interior Bruce Babbitt for his extraordinary contributions to conservation and outdoor journalism. In 2013, he was enshrined in the Fresh Water Fishing Hall of Fame. In 2015, he won the POMA Pinnacle Award and Foreword Book of the Year Gold Award (Sports) for the fifth edition of *Complete Outdoors Encyclopedia*. Sparano is also listed in *Who's Who in America*.

■ ■ ■